Early Soviet Writers

VYACHESLAV ZAVALISHIN

EARLY SOVIET WRITERS

PUBLISHED FOR THE
RESEARCH PROGRAM ON THE U.S.S.R.

Essay Index Reprint Series

BOOKS FOR LIBRARIES PRESS
FREEPORT, NEW YORK

Copyright © 1958 by the East European Fund, Inc.

Reprinted 1970 by arrangement with Praeger Publishers, Inc.

STANDARD BOOK NUMBER:
8369-1740-5

LIBRARY OF CONGRESS CATALOG CARD NUMBER:
75-117864

PRINTED IN THE UNITED STATES OF AMERICA

Acknowledgments

The author wishes to express his gratitude to the Research Program on the U.S.S.R. and to Professor Philip E. Mosely, its director, for the assistance which made possible the preparation and publication of this book. The generous encouragement and support received during the course of the work from Dr. Alexander Dallin and Mr. Robert Slusser, associate directors of the Research Program, are acknowledged with sincere thanks. The criticisms of the manuscript by Professor Ernest J. Simmons, chairman of the Department of Slavic Languages of Columbia University; by Dr. William B. Edgerton, also of this department; and by Mrs. Vera Alexandrova, formerly of the Chekhov Publishing House, proved of genuine value in writing the book. Miss Valentine Snow and Mrs. Nicholas Vakar translated the original Russian text. Their scrupulous handling of a manuscript which often demanded—and received—far more than the customary efforts of a translator is fully and gratefully appreciated. Because of the basic reorganization of the material after translation, it is all but impossible to designate their separate contributions in respect to the text. A special debt is owed to Miss Snow, however, for her rendering of the verse quoted. All translations of verse are hers except for those otherwise credited below. Mrs. Olga Nekrasova and Mrs. Wassilij Alexeev were very helpful in the process of documentation.

The author's deepest gratitude goes to Miss Louise E. Luke, assistant director of the Research Program on the U.S.S.R., whose resourceful editing has been of vital benefit to the book. The author, of course, takes full responsibility for statements of fact and interpretation. Thanks are due to Mr. Boris Nicolaevsky for his kindness in making available various rare archival materials, and to Mr. Avrahm Yarmolinsky, former chief of the Slavonic Division of the New York Public Library, for his many courtesies. Finally, for permission to use the copyrighted material included in this book acknowledgment is made to the following publishers and others: passages from Babette Deutsch's translations of Aleksandr Blok's "The Twelve" and "The Scythians," Anna Akhmatova's "Courage," and Sergei Yesenin's "The Jordan Dove" and "A Moony Thin Desolation," from *A Treasury of Russian Verse* (1949), edited by Avrahm Yarmolinsky, by permission of Mr. Yarmolinsky and of The Macmillan Company; passages from George Z. Patrick's translations of Nikolai Klyuyev's "Red Song" and untitled lines beginning "Not with the moans" and "We have revolted," and Pyotr Oreshin's "Crimson Temple" and "Kvass," from Mr. Patrick's *Popular Poetry in Soviet Russia,* by permission of The University of California Press; and lines from George Reavey's translation of Sergei Yesenin's "Tavern Moscow," from *Soviet Literature: An Anthology,* edited and translated by Mr. Reavey and Marc Slonim and copyrighted in 1934 by Covici, Friede, Inc., by permission of Crown Publishers, Inc.

Contents

INTRODUCTION ... 1

I. Major Prerevolutionary Writers on the Bridge Between Two Cultures

1. THE SYMBOLISTS ... 5
   Blok, Voloshin, Belyi, Bryusov, Emigrés and Irreconcilables

2. THE ACMEISTS ... 41
   Gumilyov, Anna Akhmatova, Mandel'shtam, Others

3. GORKI AND THE REALISTS ... 61
   Gorki, Veresayev, Artsybashev

II. Poets in the Ascendant

4. THE FUTURISTS ... 68
   Khlebnikov, Mayakovski, Other Cubo-Futurists, The Ego-Futurists, The Old "Centrifuge"

5. PEASANT POETS ... 90
   Klyuyev, Klychkov, Oreshin, Yesenin, Minor Peasant Poets

6. THE IMAGINISTS ... 133
   Shershenevich, Marienhof, Others

7. DEM'YAN BEDNYI ... 138

III. The Proletcult and the Smithy

8. BOGDANOV AND THE PROLETARIAN CULTURE
   ORGANIZATIONS   141
9. PROLETCULT POETS   145
   Gastev, Cosmism or Planetarity, Kirillov,
   Gerasimov
10. THE SMITHY (KUZNITSKA) AND ITS POETS   157
    Aleksandrovski, Kazin
11. PROSE WRITERS OF THE PROLETCULT
    AND SMITHY SCHOOLS   172
    Bessal'ko; Sivachov; Bibik, Dorokhov and
    Skachko; Lyashko; Nizovoi

IV. The Pathfinders in Fiction

12. STYLISTS AND STYLIZERS   179
    Zamyatin, Shklovski, Babel', Pil'nyak
13. THE DOCUMENTARY APPROACH   202
    Furmanov, Budantsev, Arosev
14. THE POLITICAL POSTER   211
    Serafimovich, Larisa Reisner
15. REVOLUTIONARY NATURALISM   215
    Tarasov-Rodionov, Yakovlev, Neverov

V. Rival Camps of the NEP Period

16. THE SERAPION BROTHERS   224
    Lunts, Ivanov
17. L.E.F. (LEFT FRONT OF THE ARTS)   229
    Aseyev, Tret'yakov, Others
18. OCTOBER AND THE ON-GUARDISTS   233
    Libedinski, Bezymenski, The "Zhutkins" and
    Other Komsomol Poets
19. *PEREVAL*   240
    Voronski, Vesyolyi, Platonov, Key Members of
    Pereval and Standpatters, Vikhryov, Yevdokimov,
    Peasant Writers, Malyshkin

Contents ix

20. THE CONSTRUCTIVISTS 260
    Sel'vinski, Vera Inber

VI. Prose During the Uneasy Truce (1925-1929)

21. THE NEW REALISTS 269
    Slonimski, Romanov, Lidiya Seifulina, Sobol',
    Slyozkin, Gladkov
22. THE END OF PROSE ROMANTICISM 298
    Olesha, Leonov, Lavrenyov, Grin
23. NATURALISM BIDDING FOR TROUBLE 318
    Gumilevski, Malashkin, Kozakov, Grabar'
    Nikiforov
24. SATIRISTS AND HUMORISTS 329
    Bulgakov, Erdman, Zoshchenko, Il'f and Petrov,
    Vetov, Pod"yachev, Volkov

POSTSCRIPT 348

NOTES 349

INDEX 387

Introduction

With a few happy exceptions, Soviet Russian literature of the last two decades repels the Western reader by its provincialism, lack of originality and spiritual impoverishment, and makes him wonder whether this is indeed all that is left of a great tradition, the tradition of Lev Tolstoi and Fyodor Dostoyevski. That Russian literature has lost its character and Russian writers their individuality since the revolution is self-evident.

The primary purpose of this book is to trace the course of the decline by following, at close range, the development of individual writers, with the emphasis on their written word rather than on biographical data.

Under the Bolshevik cultural policy—a planned and systematic attempt to stifle that which Aleksandr Blok called "the freedom of creation, the inner freedom"—some writers readily renounced their creative individuality, others under duress. The most talented often protested and rebelled. Boris Pasternak, for example, declared that the dictatorship of the proletariat need not be a dictatorship of the mediocre. Among the onetime rebels were Vladimir Mayakovski, Artyom Vesyolyi and even Mikhail Sholokhov, who resigned himself but is still not wholly tamed. In the case of Andrei Platonov, on the other hand, the "inner freedom" was reduced to compassion; his work is one sustained plea for compassion. Aleksandr Grin, in a supreme revolt of the imagination against the Communist order of things, preserved his individuality by escaping, in his fantastic tales, to a romantic continent of his own creation. Others fell silent or were silenced. Still others joined the dictators in their intellectual inquisition. This book is by and large a portrait gallery of early postrevolutionary writers in their search for a way out of the dilemma of Soviet artists.

The reader is bound to ask whether, if Soviet writers have lost their individuality, there is any good reason for detailed individual studies of such writers, particularly minor ones, whether it is worthwhile to consider the minutiae of a literature that has patently degenerated and gone to seed. The fact is that the general character of Soviet literature has been shaped at least as much by little known or disregarded writings as by the celebrated works of those relatively few writers who have won recognition in the West. Because of the strictures of censorship, certain productions of even the most prominent writers and the entire output of others have been suppressed and are half forgotten in their own land. Outside the Soviet Union, where critics and literary historians are dependent to considerable extent on the publications of their Soviet counterparts and on materials released for foreign consumption, much of interest has remained almost unknown. Only by rescuing the castaways from oblivion, however, can we see postrevolutionary literature whole and comprehend the effect of Soviet totalitarianism upon it. The author of this book, writing from the vantage point of one who lived all his early life in the U.S.S.R. and watched Soviet literary history in the making, has attempted to restore some obliterated parts of the record.

The best of postrevolutionary Russian literature is a crusade for truth, against increasingly heavy odds on the side of the Bolshevik cultural policy. Frequently writers were far more interested in what they were writing about than in how they wrote and sacrificed form to their material. At first the revolution turned writers into stenographers, taking dictation from events themselves, which were ready-molded to art and which, upon being faithfully reproduced, quite naturally took on the forms of tragedy. The great upheaval offered to witnesses with no particular gifts an advantage over major writers of other times. The main requirement was the ability to observe. This early documentary practice, which often produced a truthful and objective, if bald, recording of life, persisted well beyond the Civil War period. Furmanov's *Chapayev* (1923) and

Introduction

Rebellion (1925) and Aleksandr Yakovlev's *October* (1923), for instance, are little more than skillful stenographic transcripts; and a writer like Georgi Nikiforov, who continued as late as the mid-1930's—when he paid for his audacity—to write in the same vein of accurate description of reality, no matter how depressing and painful that reality might be, has nothing but his candor, sincerity and truthfulness to recommend him. Despite their deficiencies as artists, it was not of such writers that N. I. Bukharin said, "If all documentary material about our revolution were to vanish one fine day and nothing but literature were left, the idea it would give of our times would be incorrect."

Other mediocre or now obscure writers of the early period succeeded in portraying national types characteristic during and shortly after the revolution, as did Mikhail Sivachov in his forgotten novel *Yellow Devil,* and on this score deserve to rank, in any impartial account, with the Communist-applauded Fyodor Gladkov.

Thus, throughout the course of Soviet literature writers and works apparently of little importance, when taken together, contribute to an overall impression of Russian life since 1917 and of the effect of the revolution and the new regime on the minds of men.

In order that Soviet writers and their writings may eventually be "taken together," however, they must first be considered individually. There is no other way of tracing with any certainty the long-drawn-out and painful process of the development of post-revolutionary Russian literature. This book contains some of the requisite materials for such a history; it is not a history itself.

In the course of assembling these preliminary materials, the conviction has formed that the eventual history of Soviet literature under its specific conditions will inevitably be written in terms of its writers' need for "freedom of creation, the inner freedom." This conviction has dictated the unconventional arrangement of the materials. So far as possible, the body of each writer's work is considered as a whole in which different phases may often be discerned in accordance with his enjoyment or relinquishment of creative freedom or struggle for it. The period in his career when he appeared to write most freely is then used as the criterion for a loose chronological grouping of his work with that of others who also expressed themselves with least inhibition at approximately the same time. Admittedly, such a classification rests upon subjective judgments. So be it! Is there a possibility of, or virtue in, ruling out the subjective factor? To the fullest extent that space permits, passages on which the underlying value judgments rest are quoted.

The structural scheme chosen means that many writers will not be found at the chronological stage to which those acquainted with Soviet literature are accustomed to relate them. Gorki, for instance, who was most loudly acclaimed at a much later period, will be encountered, briefly, in the early pages, among writers of the old regime; and Fyodor Panfyorov, although he began to write soon after the revolution and rose to prominence during the 1920's, reached his full stature, however puny, only after World War II (in the personal opinion prevailing here) and will not be considered.

The present volume deals only with those Soviet writers who before 1929 experienced the highest degree of "freedom of creation" which they were to know.

The arrangement followed has precluded systematic exposition of the organizational history of Soviet literature, of governmental and Party measures taken to dye and channel literature. In view of the fact that these questions have been extensively treated elsewhere and are more familiar to Western readers, they have been slighted with good conscience in favor of presenting little known writers.

Vyacheslav Zavalishin

April, 1957
New York City

1

Major Prerevolutionary Writers on the Bridge Between Two Cultures

1. The Symbolists

The dominance of the Symbolist school in Russian literature had come to an end even before the First World War, its mystical "otherworldliness" challenged by two new rivals of the prewar years, Acmeism and Futurism. Even within the Symbolist group, its greatest poet, Aleksandr Blok, had turned in revulsion against the metaphysical excesses of his fellow writers.

ALEKSANDR BLOK (1880-1921)

Blok welcomed the revolution with faith in an impending miracle. Early in 1918 he published the two poems "The Twelve" and "The Scythians."

In the first, rebellion is shaking Petrograd. Through the streets, black with night and white with snow, stride twelve Red Army men, who are one with the savage wind.

> Black, narrow rifle straps,
> Cigarettes, crumpled caps.
>
> A convict's stripes would fit their backs,
> Fires, fires mark their tracks. . . .[1]

The "has-beens" of the old world abroad in the streets Blok describes with mischievous and biting irony. A man of the bourgeoisie, nose in collar, stands motionless at the crossing,

> While, tail between his legs, beside him
> Shivers a cringing, mangy cur.

Suddenly a sleigh cuts across the path of the Twelve. In the sleigh are Vanka, a soldier, and his Katya. One of the Twelve catches sight of the girl.

> "You used to go a pretty pace,
> Wearing linen trimmed with lace;
> You used to whore with the gold-braid crew—
> Whore then, and get along with you!
> Eh, eh, whore all you wish—
> You make my heart leap like a fish!

> "Say, recall that officer,
> Katya—how I knifed the cur?
> Don't tell me your memory's vague,
> Just refresh your wits, you plague.
> Eh, eh, refresh me, too,
> Come and let me sleep with you."

The Red Army men move to settle accounts with Vanka, who was once "one of them."

> "Andrukha, stop them, hold the horse!"
> "Run back, Petrukha! Cut their course!" ...

> The sleigh and Vanka are out of sight.
> "Now cock the gun again, wheel right!"

> Crrack! "You'd better watch your game:
> . . .   Stealing another fellow's dame!"

> "The rat is gone. But I know who
> Tomorrow will be quits with you."

> And where is Katya? "Dead. She's dead!
> The pretty slut shot through the head!"

> "Happy, Katya? Don't you crow?
> You carrion, lie there in the snow...."

Horror and remorse take possession of Petrukha.

Major Prerevolutionary Writers

And again the twelve go marching,
Shoulders back and guns in place,
Only he, the poor assassin,
Marching, does not show his face.

. . . .

"Comrade, what on earth has got you?
Why is it you act so dumb?"
"Spill it, Pyotr, is it Katya
Makes you look so God-dam' glum?"

"Well, comrades, you know the story.
Katya was my girl by rights.
Yes, I loved her. God, our roaring
Black and drunken summer nights!

"Her bright eyes—they drove me to it—
How they dared you, black as coal!
And her shoulder, well I knew it
With its poppy-colored mole....
I, mad fool, I had to do it,
Went and killed her ... damn my soul...."

There is someone among the Twelve who directs their actions, an Invisible One deliberately kept in the shadows, whose task is to wipe out both remorse and the wish to atone. Petrukha's comrade says to him:

"... Pyotr, you're a dunderhead—
Did your Saviour and His kin
Save you from committing sin?
Pyotr, you are talking rot!

"Whose fault is it Katya's dead?
You're a murderer—understand?
There is blood upon your hand!"
March to the revolution's pace:
We've a grim enemy to face!

The Invisible One achieves his purpose:

Pyotr moves at a slower pace
And he shows a careless face.

. . . .

Lock your doors and windows tight!
There are looters out tonight!
Burst the cellars—wine is free!
Tonight the rabble's on the spree!

The Twelve move forward into battle, to storm the gates of the old world.

> "We will get you and your comrades too!
> Best surrender while you're breathing still."
> "Comrade . . . it will be the worse for you.
> Come out! or we'll shoot to kill."

By forcing the man with the gun, the crumpled cap and the cigarette between his teeth to do his bidding, the Invisible One transmutes anger and rage into revolutionary will, which is the *leitmotiv* of the poem:

> Hey, comrade,
> Look sharp!
> . . . .
> March to the revolution's pace:
> We've a grim enemy to face!
>
> On and on the steady beat
> Of the workers' marching feet!

In the strange and sudden ending, the way of the rebels leads on through blizzard and wind, through and beyond hatred and blood:

> . . . Forward as a haughty host they tread.
> A starved mongrel shambles in the rear.
> Bearing high the banner, bloody red,
>   That He holds in hands no bullets sear—
>   Hidden as the flying snow veils veer,
> Lightly walking on the wind, as though
> He Himself were diamonded snow,
>   With mist-white roses garlanded:
> Jesus Christ is marching at their head.

The core of "The Twelve" is Petrukha's killing of Katya, through jealousy or accident—a personal tragedy which occurs one night in the streets of revolutionary Petrograd. But the whole may be known through its parts. Blok makes Katya's blood and Petrukha's mad despair a symbol of the bloodshed and mad desperation of the Russian Revolution.

Blok's poetry marks the twilight—beautiful and spell-binding as the twilight is—of syllabic (*sillabotonicheskii*) versification in

Russian meter. He himself, however, was one of the first and most striking of the many postrevolutionary experimenters in verse forms. He wrote in one of his notebooks: "The artist is absorbed in a search for forms capable of withstanding the pressure of the access of creative energy."[2]

"The Twelve" is an experiment in synthesis. It is built on dissonance, syncopation, counterpoint, and abrupt changes from syllabic to purely accentual (*tonicheskii*) meters. The alternation is never random or arbitrary, but planned and internally justified, a means of portraying the crumbling of the old world and the passionate, stormy surge toward the new. The new is described mostly in accentual verse, the old in the conventional syllabic. The conflict between the rhythm produces the effect of a storm; the short and rapid stanzas move with the force of a gale.

Blok used bits of folk-dance rhythms, *chastushki*[3] and "pathetic" ballads. Petrukha's confession, for instance, is written in the style of a hurdy-gurdy "pathetic" ballad. Ivan Bunin, who violently disliked "The Twelve," reproached Blok for having undertaken a stylization of folk motifs without knowing folk speech; a St. Petersburg workingman would never have heard of a "poppy-colored mole," for example. It is Bunin who was mistaken. Blok, with his extraordinarily sensitive ear, had accurately recorded a peculiarity in the speech of the St. Petersburg outskirts whose residents were very fond of cheap novels and frequently borrowed "high-flown" turns of phrase from their reading. Using *chastushki* and vulgar ballads—in which one sometimes hears, through all their bad taste, strong passion and an altogether genuine grief—Blok made a beautiful thing out of material from which other poets might have turned away fastidiously.

"The Twelve" is broken up into twelve episodes, in nearly every one of which there is a rallying cry or a marching tune.

"As I worked on 'The Twelve' and for several days afterwards I kept hearing—I mean literally, with my ears—a great noise around me, a steady noise (probably the noise of the old world crumbling),"[4] Blok wrote later.

Long before the Revolution of 1917 Blok had felt the shocks

preceding the catastrophe with the sensitivity of a seismograph recording a temblor. In 1908 he borrowed Gogol's symbol of the galloping *troika* to foreshadow the fate of the Russia of his day:

> Do you hear the breathless rush of the *troika?* Do you see it diving in and out of the snowdrifts on the dead and desolate plain? The richly decorated *troika* is bearing Russia at headlong speed to an unknown destination, into the deep-blue abyss of time. Do you see her starry eyes, pleadingly gazing upon you? "Love me, love my beauty! . . ."
>
> Who will find his way along the secret path of wisdom to intercept the flying *troika,* who with a gentle word will stop the foam-flecked steeds?[5]

Russia was rushing toward the abyss, and there were no men in the land able to stay her course. The Romanovs and the nobility were too senile to withstand the catastrophe:

> In the valleys and by the side of the road, half-hidden by greenery or by snowdrifts, the manor houses of the gentry are decaying, rotting, crumbling into dust with their marble, their cupids, their ivory and gilt, their high fences around century-old parks of linden trees, and sculptured icons six rows high in private churches . . . and there is no one left to die any more, and nothing to resurrect. This way of life is going, and is replaced by shapelessness. . . .[6]

The Russian intelligentsia, divided from the people, was too weak to fight for survival. Blok loved and hated this decaying Russia and warned of its imminent destruction:

> This shuddering away from living
> And this insatiable desire,
> This hating Russia, yet forgiving,
> This black and earth-bound blood afire
> Are heralds, in our veins upwelling,
> Heedless of man-made boundaries,
> Of thrust and change beyond foretelling,
> Of unimagined mutinies.[7]

His tale "Neither Dream nor Waking," 1921, based on much earlier fragments and partly autobiographical, to a certain extent parallels "The Twelve." The story opens on a landowner's estate. "We were sitting under the linden trees and drinking tea." Men were mowing a field nearby. One of the mowers began to sing. "The strong silver tenor rose effortlessly and instantly filled the gully, the grove and the garden." [8] The peasants' and landowners' whole way of life, deep-rooted in the soil, is shaken by the stormy song. A spellbound merchant takes to drink and sets hay barns on fire. A mischief-maker, a political agitator on a bicycle, appears in neighboring villages and sows the seeds of wrath everywhere. The peasants' huts are sagging, but, the habit of work replaced by a thirst for rebellion, they make no repairs. Their work-worn hands reach not for the plow, but for the club and the ax. The song goes to their hearts and raises from the depths of their subconscious the age-old yearning for another, a better life, for a peasant kingdom. The hero of the tale, in the anger awakened by the song, seizes an ax and starts to hack at a lilac bush. "The flower clusters are thin and bluish in color, but the trunk is so thick that the ax won't go in." [9] Infuriated, he falls to chopping down a grove beyond the lilac bushes.

In his dream the hero of the tale hears an uneasy rustling of leaves. The forest is swaying in a gale. Peasants emerge from the forest, mobs of peasants, mobs without end. Their eyes, under their bushy eyebrows, gleam with a frenzied rage. Some are carrying pitchforks, and other heavy swords. On the hill next to the forest a horseman, surrounded by horsed knights, stretches out his arm, in a gesture of resolution and command, to subordinate the wild fury of the peasants to his will.

There is a similarity between the gesture and the action of the Invisible One who commands the Twelve, while the Twelve themselves play the part assigned to the knights in "Neither Dream nor Waking."

Blok saw the potential Russian Revolution as a chaotic, popular, peasants' revolution, as a stroke of the ax in an attempt to break through from decaying Russia into the peasant kingdom.

In one of his notebooks there is a quatrain (written in April 1907) similar in spirit to the scene in the story in which the armed peasants appear:

> With pitchforks we will bring them low,
> And in the noose we'll swing them high
> Until their blood spurts on the snow,
> And we will curse them as they die.[10]

Yet the Twelve are not peasants, but hotheads from the industrial outskirts of St. Petersburg, *Lumpenproletariat* rather than proletariat, neither workers nor peasants. In the Bolshevik revolution this tattered-cap contingent replaces the knights who, in Blok's prefiguration, were to take control of the frenzied and infuriated peasant mobs. The Invisible One of "The Twelve" personifies Bolshevism or, rather, the implacable iron will of the Bolsheviks.

The seizure of power by the Bolsheviks was an attack by a political party on chaos—a combat between a small but perfectly organized political party and the popular revolution, the hopes and aspirations of all Russia—and the attack was carried out through those Bunin called "the dregs of the proletariat, the penniless rabble in the saloons, the bums—all those whom Lenin captivated by his unqualified permission to rob the robbers."[11] " 'The Twelve' portrays reality with great talent, almost with genius. . . . In it is extolled that which we old socialists fear most of all,"[12] O. Kameneva, the wife of L. B. Kamenev, acknowledged.

The bold and desperate struggle of the Bolsheviks with the unleashed elements captured Blok's imagination. It was the audacity, the recklessness—of a daredevil who throws himself forward and seizes a maddened stallion by the mane, knowing that he must either saddle the stallion or be trampled down—that Blok admired, and not the program of Bolshevism. His admiration of the Invisible One for mastering the twelve Red Army men gives no grounds for identifying Blok with the Communists. He realized that the Bolsheviks were staking their game on the shady side of the revolution:

> The yellowish-brown clouds of smoke are creeping up to the villages. Broad strips of shrubbery and grass burst into flame, but God sends no rain and there is no harvest, and what there is is burning. And such yellowish-brown clouds of smoke, which conceal flames and smouldering ashes, are drifting through the souls of millions of men: hostility, savagery, the heritage of the Tatars, anger, humiliation, op-

pression, mistrust, vengeance burst into flame here and there; Russian Bolshevism is rampant, and still there is no rain, and God sends none.[13]

Both the Invisible One and his fighters are driven by the fever to transform the globe and faith that they can beat a way to a new world through fire and smoke and blood, that the new world can be built on the smouldering ruins, that the stronger the passion for destruction in the Russian peasant and artisan, the more beautiful and majestic will be the new world which will arise on the ashes of the old. To Russia, the revolution meant self-destruction, self-burning. In this faith in the cleansing power of fire Lenin and the Russian people were at one.

Blok, too, at one time believed that fire may heal and cleanse: "Patriotism is so much dirt, religion is so much dirt, everything that settles down like dust and dogma is so much dirt."[14] In January 1918, in "The Intelligentsia and the Revolution," he wrote:

The task of the artist, the duty of the artist, is to penetrate the conception, to listen to the music thundering in the wind-torn air. Change it all. See to it that everything becomes new, that our lying, dirty, tedious, discordant life becomes a just, clean, gay and beautiful life....[15]

With your whole body, with your whole heart, with all you are— listen to the REVOLUTION![16]

And in his diary:

This is the task of Russian culture: to direct this fire to that which should be burned; to transform the rioting of Stenka Razin and Yemel'yan Pugachov into a harmonious wave of music; to set limits to destruction which will not weaken the force of the fire but will guide it in the right direction. To organize the impetuous will, the lazy smoldering which conceals latent violence, to send it into the darkest and vilest corners of the soul and there to fan it into flame —sky-high—to burn the sly, lazy, servile flesh.[17]

Although the Bolsheviks and the rebellious Russian people shared the belief that Russia could be transformed through fire and blood, their visions of the result were entirely different. To the Bolsheviks, the social aims of Karl Marx were the new religion destined to refute and replace Christianity, but to the Russian folk the longed-for world was one ruled by Jesus Christ.

Blok was concerned not with programmatic Bolshevism but with that yearning for a new world for the sake of which Russian peasants were willing to burn themselves alive. ("Self-burning as a religious act," wrote N. A. Berdyayev, "is a national Russian phenomenon, practically unknown in other countries.")[18]

The old dissenters who sought to reach Christ by burning themselves alive had once captured the poet's imagination,[19] and he had long been interested in the relationship between religion and the revolution.

After Blok's death a copy of a poem by Vsevolod Krestovski (1840-1895) in which Blok had underlined passages in red pencil was found, and Mme. Blok said that the poem had attracted Blok's attention when he was working on "The Twelve." In Krestovski's poem, "Paris, July 1848" (written in 1860), when the strongholds of the defenders are falling, One in white and shining garments rises above the slain, above the flames and smoke and the blood-red banner, and stands on the barricade.

> With a crown of thorns on his brow
> And the anguish of death in his eyes.
> He spread out his hands before him
> His nail-pierced hands. . . .
> A branch of peace for the entire world
> He held among the fallen fighters,
> And blood dripped from a new wound
> In his right side.[20]

Blok's decision to use the figure of Christ in "The Twelve" cost him much doubt and anxious thought and makes the ending of the poem strange and difficult to understand. It is a mistake to assume that Blok blessed the revolution in the name of Christ, and equally a mistake to identify the Invisible One either with Christ or with the poet himself. Blok wrote in one of his notebooks after publication of the poem that he himself was ready to "hate that effeminate phantom"[21] (Jesus Christ):

The question is not whether they [the Red Army men] are worthy of Him; the dreadful thing is that he is once more with them, and that there is still no other. But must there be the Other?[22]

The "Other," the Invisible One, is only sensed in "The Twelve." We come to be aware of his presence, to guess who and where he is only by the consequences of the actions he provokes. The Red Army man Petrukha is horrified by the murder he has committed. Weighed down by consciousness of his sin, he murmurs, "God rest the soul of thy servant, Katerina." When he speaks the word "Saviour," one of his comrades jeers at his belief in a gilded iconostas; thus the Invisible One erases remorse from Petrukha's soul. The purpose of the Invisible One is to eradicate from the feelings and thoughts of the insurgent Red Army men every vestige of the Orthodox Church, every reminder of holiness, to release the triumphant beast and throw it into combat against the old world. He is the Antichrist. "The Twelve" is a tale of the struggle between Christ and the Antichrist for the soul of Russia.

Although in the poem the insurgents obey the Invisible One, Blok believed that the longing of the Russian people for the kingdom of God upon earth would sooner or later remake the country and permit it to shed its suffering and grief. In his later notes on the poem he reiterated that he had glimpsed Christ in the whirling snow of St. Petersburg and that, by putting Him at the head of the Red Army men, he merely stated a fact.

Even after he reconsidered his early view of the revolution and recognized the Russian passion for self-destruction and self-burning as a vicious and criminal passion, Blok did not lose his faith in a religious rebirth, but merely transferred that rebirth to a distant future: ". . . All will yet be well. Russia will be great. But how long we have to wait, and how hard it is to wait." [23]

The ending of "The Twelve," which puzzled and outraged Blok's friends and readers at the time of its publication, stemmed from his extraordinary farsightedness—part and parcel of the "principle of two kinds of time" he had evolved. A poet who has attained spiritual independence becomes the master of time and space. A true poet may exist simultaneously in the past, the present and the future. There are, as it were, two continua: the one chronological, measured by calendars, the other nonchronological and verging on music.

Blok sometimes felt that he was living in the fourth dimension. Stanislavski used to hold it against the poet that he switched too abruptly from calendar time to musical time, losing all sense of proportion, and decided that Blok's play "The Song of Fate" (1907) could not be produced by the Moscow Art Theater because the audience would be baffled by such slipping off into another dimension. Herman, hero of the play, a man of the twentieth century, says in a monologue:

> Take it that I am mad, if you like. Yes, I may well be on the threshold of madness . . . or of second sight. I am surrounded by all that ever was, all that ever will be. These days I seem to be living in all times, feeling on my body the torments of my country. I remember the fearsome day of the Battle of Kulikovo [in which the Russians defeated the Tatars in 1380]. The prince and his guard took up a position on the hill. The earth rang with the creaking of the Tatars' carts; the screaming of the eagles foretold disaster. Then the ominous night closed in and the river Nepryadva was clad in mist like a bride in a bridal veil. The prince and his captain went down to the bottom of the hill and laid their ears to the ground. Swans and geese were splashing furiously. A widow was weeping. A mother clung sobbing to her son's stirrup. Only the Russian camp lay silent under the fitful flashes of heat lightning. But the wind scattered the mist, a gray autumn morning came, even as now, and, even as now, I remember there was a smell of burning; and the prince's shining banner moved down the hill. . . . The armies clashed and fought and slashed and stabbed all day long . . . while the fresh force had to lie in ambush all day and could only watch and weep and long to rush into battle And the captain kept warning: "It is too early, the hour has not yet come." Lord, I know, as well as any warrior in that ambush, how it is when the heart clamors for work and it is too early, still too early. . . . That is why I don't sleep nights—with all my heart I wait for one who will come and say: "The hour has struck. It is time!" [24]

Conversely, the ending of "The Twelve" may be explained by the hypertrophied vision which is to be found throughout Blok's work; the poet transposed the coming of Christ to his own day from a distant future in which Russia's faith in the power of fire would, like his own, give way to repentance and in which Russia would attain to the new world not through self-burning but through awareness of her sins and a desire to cleanse herself of darkness and evil.

In one of his last poems dealing with Pushkin, Blok indicated that, by concluding "The Twelve" with the figure of Christ, he was giving his blessing not to the present but to the future:

> But we looked...
> To the ages yet to come,
> Looked away from the delusion
> Of the transient days of pain,
> To the issue, the conclusion,
> On the future's misty plain.[25]

Blok's poem "The Scythians," written immediately after "The Twelve" (also in January 1918), is in a somewhat archaic, ponderous meter, which bears evidence of fatigue and of a relaxation of that nervous tension with which Blok worked on "The Twelve"; nevertheless its passionately felt idea and its impressionism speak directly to the emotions and the intuition.

The poem is a summons to the West to join revolutionary Russia in making peace:

> Come unto us from the black ways of war,
> Come to our peaceful arms and rest.
> Comrades, before it is too late,
> Sheathe the old sword; may brotherhood be blest.
> If not, we have not anything to lose.[26]

It is also a warning:

> ... Yea, we are Scythians,
> Yea, Asians, a slant-eyed, greedy brood.
>
> ... Like slaves obeying and abhorred,
> We were the shield between the breeds
> Of Europe and the raging Mongol horde.
> . . . .
> Yea, Russia is a Sphinx. Exulting, grieving,
> And sweating blood, she cannot sate
> Her eyes that gaze and gaze and gaze
> At you with stone-lipped love for you, and hate.
> . . . .

It is our wont to seize wild colts at play:
They rear and impotently shake
Wild manes—we crush their mighty croups.
And shrewish women slaves we tame—or break.
. . . .
Know that we will no longer be your shield
. . . .
We will not move when the ferocious Hun
Despoils the corpse and leaves it bare,
Burns towns, herds cattle in the church,
And smell of white flesh roasting fills the air.

For the last time, old world, we bid you rouse,
For the last time the barbarous lyre sounds
That calls you to our bright fraternal feast
Where labor beckons and where peace abounds.

The critic Lundberg found that the descent of "The Scythians" was to be traced from Pushkin's poem "To Those Who Slander Russia,"[27] written in defense of Russian action in putting down the Polish insurrection of 1831. It has also been pointed out that "The Scythians" shows the influence of Vladimir Solov'yov's alarm at the "Yellow Peril" (Blok used a couplet from Solov'yov as epigraph to "The Scythians": "Pan-Mongolism—a slogan quite bizarre,/But none the less like music to my ear"),[28] of Ivanov-Razumnik's mystical insistence on the messianic role of Russia in revolution, and of Dostoyevski's theme of the Russian genius for comprehending and assimilating the cultures of all nations. In addition, attention should be drawn to Berdyayev's pamphlet *The Soul of Russia* (1915),[29] which was known to Blok and the basic ideas of which have left clear traces in "The Scythians."

Finally, by an ironic twist, Blok's views on the relationship between East and West are identical with those developed by his father, A. L. Blok, a noted professor of law, in the book *Politics Among the Sciences*,[30] written toward the end of the nineteenth century. In the long unfinished narrative poem "Retaliation" (1910-1919) the son had confessed that intellectually and temperamentally he had not shared the convictions of his father.

In his *Politics Among the Sciences* the poet's father argued that the Western world had always treated Russia shabbily, responding to friendliness with perfidy and deceit and to sincerity with hypocrisy and falsehood, and had mockingly condescended to the East's passionate love of culture. He foresaw that the Russian aristocracy would sooner or later be removed from power and replaced by a peasant kingdom, the new rulers of which would immediately proceed to transplant technological civilization to the steppes of Eastern Europe. Thus stirred to pride and independence, Russia would inevitably defy the world. With fire and sword she would revenge herself in full for the humiliations and sorrow inflicted by the West. Russians too could shed all principles, they too knew "virulent mockery and evil shorn of all hypocrisy, which make us proudly conscious of our barbarian superiority." [31]

Blok the poet came with horror to the conclusion that his father, Blok the sociologist, might well be right. He wrote in his diary:

If you will not wash off the shame of your wartime patriotism at least by a "democratic peace," if you wreck our revolution, then you are not Aryans any more. And we will open wide the gates to the East. We looked at you with Aryan eyes so long as you had faces. Your snouts we will sweep with our slant-eyed, cunning, rapid glance; we will turn into Asiatics and the East will pour over you.

Your hides will be stretched on Chinese tambourines. A man who has covered himself with shame and snared himself in his own lies is no longer an Aryan.

You say we are barbarians? Very well. We will show you what barbarians are like. And our cruel answer, our terrible answer, will alone be worthy of man.[32]

But in "The Scythians" he speaks from a passionate desire to reconcile the East and the West. The West must be warned, must be made to understand that, if only out of an instinct of self-preservation, it must prevent Russia from embarking on world crime. If the West is without good will and impervious to kind words, it may perhaps be moved by fear.

Blok never ceased to believe that, sooner or later, the West would give proof of that good will which would end Russia's militant messianism, and he could not resign himself to the idea that it might be shown only after terrible cataclysms.

After "The Twelve" and "The Scythians" Blok's rejoicing in

the revolution gave way to disillusionment and remorse. He tried to pull himself together and to keep on working, but his creative powers were failing. He wrote a few poems, a historical drama, a number of articles (including "The Collapse of Humanism" [*Krusheniye gumanizma*]), made translations, and began a prose piece, "Confession of a Pagan." He was one of the first writers to serve in Soviet institutions. As a member of the editorial board of the World Literature Publishing House established by Gorki, he edited the works of Heine. He was chairman of the repertory section of the government Theater Division and, as an associate in the directorship of the Bol'shoi Theater, wrote the introductory speeches which actors delivered to the new audience of workers and Red Army men before the curtain rose. "We should not hide from life, never expect things to be made easier for us personally, but look events straight in the eye, as hard as we can,"[33] he wrote.

But the large public was not yet ready for such cultural efforts; they were of interest only to the survivors of the old intelligentsia. As he contemplated the disintegration of Russian culture, the poet changed his attitude toward tradition and came to believe that viable traditions should be sorted out from the superannuated and preserved so that the past might rejoin the future through a transformation of the present. On December 30, 1918, he had written in a letter to Mayakovski:

I hate the Winter Palace and the museums no less than you do. But destruction is as old as construction and every bit as traditional. When destroying what is hateful to us, we are just as bored and inclined to yawn as when we watched it being built. The tooth of history has much more venom in it than you think. . . . To break with tradition has become traditional. There is a great curse upon us—we cannot do without sleeping or without eating. Some will build, others will destroy, since there is "a time for everything under the sun," but all will be slaves, until we find a third method, equally unlike construction and destruction.[34]

He had once condemned the church—the Russian Orthodox as well as the Roman Catholic—to extinction:

> These solemn chants of nasal choirs,
> Church roses with their smell of death,
> Sick yearnings rising to the spires
> Shall vanish in the future's breath.[35]

The church is dead and the place of worship has become an extension of the street. . . .[36]

If there were a real priesthood in Russia, and not merely a class of morally dense people who are priests by profession, it would long ago have taken into account the fact that Christ is on the side of the Red Army men.[37]

As K. S. Mochul'ski has noted, these are the opinions not of an atheist but of a Christian who recognized that the church had lost the spirit of Christ. Later, however, Blok's tone toward the church became gentler and less mistrustful:

> We Russians are always thinking of the church. Few are altogether indifferent to it; some hate it greatly, others love it—in both feelings there is an admixture of pain. . . .
> And I too used to go to church. True, I would choose a time when the church was empty. . . . In an empty church I was sometimes able to find that which I looked for in vain in the outside world. . . .
> I have not been to confession for a very long time, and I need to confess.[38]

In the speech which he made in February 1921 on the anniversary of Pushkin's death, and in the year of his own death, Blok said:

> It was not at all the bullet of d'Anthès that killed . . . Pushkin. . . . He was killed by lack of air. His culture was dying about him. . . .
> There is no happiness in the world, but there is peace and freedom. Peace and freedom. They are essential to the poet for the release of harmony. But peace and freedom are also taken away. Not the outward peace, but that of creating. Not the childish freedom, not the freedom to be a liberal, but the freedom of creation, the inner freedom. And the poet dies because there is nothing for him to breathe. Life has lost its meaning.[39]

Blok too felt that he could not breathe; the culture which had enabled him to find himself was dead and his dreams had died with it. Like Pushkin in the reign of Nicholas I, when civic liberty was in chains, Blok too was a casualty, of an era when not even man's inner freedom—the freedom of spiritual experience, thought and imagination—remained inviolate. The final words of Blok's poem to Pushkin dated February 5, 1921, are:

> ... in gathering dusk,
> Driven home by darkness now,
> To him from the Senate Square
> So respectfully I bow.[40]

Weary, sick and embittered in a world from which the "spirit of music" had fled, Aleksandr Blok died in August 1921.

MAKSIMILIAN VOLOSHIN (1877-1932)

Voloshin (whose full name was Kiriyenko-Voloshin) lived and traveled in Western Europe for many years before the revolution. In Paris he studied painting and began to write poetry. After his return to Russia not long before the February revolution of 1917, he lived at Koktebel' in the Crimea, a "spiritual émigré" under the Soviet regime. Until the mid-1920's Voloshin's work continued to appear, although rarely, in Soviet reviews and anthologies, but during the last few years of his life he was denied publication.

"Voloshin," it is stated categorically in the Soviet *Literary Encyclopedia* in regard to the first period of his writing, "is a typical disciple of the French Parnassian poets . . . and Impressionist painters."[41] The French Parnassian poets unquestionably affected Voloshin's work, but only to the extent of giving a higher polish to the Byzantine mystical religious element in his poetry, with its chill, ornate and somewhat somber majesty. In his article "Archaism in Russian Painting" (1909), in which he indicates his special attraction to the Byzantine, he writes:

The archaic is the last and most secret dream of the art of our day, which so closely scrutinizes all periods of history, seeking in them that which is rare, odd, and obscurely akin to it. Artists and poets revolve world history before their gaze like a many-faceted mirror, in order to see a fragment of themselves in every facet.[42]

In the article he discusses the Byzantine tradition—particularly marked in Constantine Manasses—of identifying plants, animals and man through a common mood or experience: "Rocks become plants, plants become animals, animals become men, and men turn into demons."[43] The tradition is followed in Voloshin's own poetic images.

There is an obvious similarity between Constantine Manasses' comparison of a cliff jutting out over the sea to a pride of "gold-springing" lions and Voloshin's comparison of rocks to tawny lions. Less obvious is the deep-lying, intuitive process by which Voloshin evolves his Byzantine-inspired images. For example, the Byzantines, like the ancient Greeks, were fond of equating human joy or sorrow with the sound of a musical instrument. In his own poems Voloshin was often a far more successful master of the device than were other Russian poets translating from the original language, such as Innokenti Annenski, who translated the tragedies of Euripides.

When Voloshin speaks of pain as "a 'cello softly played," the figure is an original variation on the Byzantine style. The best of Voloshin's prerevolutionary verse is colored by Byzantium, as are these stanzas from "Noon" and "Constellations," published in 1909:

Stirring grasses ring thin in the pulsing heat,
The hills like tawny lions crouch on the desert's edge.
Unto the copper clouds rises the bitter-sweet
Scent of wormwood and sedge.
. . . .
Grasses of ancient graves, we have sprung from the stones and the dust,
From darkness and night to the sun, the god of rebirth.
We spread in the glare of noon, trembling with fear and lust,
The dead secrets of Earth.[44]

("Noon")

    Odysseus traced your pattern in the sky,
    Your wavering gleam in centuries long past.
    Night sowed your golden seeds haphazardly
    Where trembling waters caught and held them fast.[45]

("Constellations")

Voloshin's poetry also displays the influence of the Belgian poet Emile Verhaeren, of whom he wrote that, although Verhaeren's poetry was too journalistic, "his over-lengthy passages are interspersed at every turn with such brilliant flashes of genius that everything else is consumed in their flame. . . ."[46] In 1919 Voloshin published a small book on the subject of Verhaeren containing translations into Russian of eighteen of his poems.[47]

The war and the revolution brought about a radical change in Voloshin's verse. The Byzantine motifs were replaced by the headlong sweep of bold and untrammeled Cossack folk songs on the Russian steppes:

> None but St. Nicholas and St. George,
> Guardians of man and maid,
> Know in what cove or what gorge
> The bones of Cossacks are laid.
>
> . . . .
>
> Our freedom's cup no man can drain,
> None can take us in hand—
> Broad is our Savage Plain,[48]
> Boundless our Scythian land.[49]

In this poem, "Savage Plain," Voloshin the painter matched his verse colors to those of Roerich's painting, for which he had a lifelong admiration:

> Our land was torn and dismembered
> By Tatars and princelings in strife,
> But in forests and by the river,
> Moscow came strangely to life.
> The Kremlin, in fairy-tale glory,
> Rose in vestments of bright brocade,
> White-walled and golden-headed,
> Over smoke-stained huts in the glade.
> And the church that Fioravanti
> In a magic vision had seen
> Stood mirrored in azure water
> That lay framed in brilliant green.[50]

In "Dmetrius Imperator" he borrowed motifs, archaic words and turns of phrase from the religious chants of the Old Believers.

Many years before his final return to Russia in 1917—in fact after the revolution of 1905—Voloshin had undertaken a spiritual pilgrimage to the Holy Russia of long ago. In 1919, with *Demons Deaf and Dumb*, he began publication of the series of poems that span Russian history from the introduction of Christianity into Kievan Russia to the Civil War. In his delvings into the past his main themes are the philosophy of Russian history and the philosophy of religion, and the mentors of his mystical thought are the artist Nesterov, the religious philosopher Fyodorov, author of *The Philosophy of the Common Cause*, and Dostoyevski.

Of Nesterov's paintings Voloshin wrote:

Nesterov has felt the mystical strength of the people, welling up from the very depths of the children's eyes; he has captured its reflection in the pale northern landscape, in the touching tiny white leaves of birches in the spring, and he discovers it whenever, with his prophetic brush, he paints rivers under an evening sky, and grave girls' faces, and spring woods. . . . [51]

Nesterov's art shows both a gentle, quietist resignation and a deep and anguished grief. In his historical poems Voloshin endeavored to trace this grief to its roots and emerged urging the Russian people from civil war to reconciliation and quietism.

Fyodorov feared and dreaded the future, for its seeds lay in the present, which itself rested on a blasphemous destruction of the past. He saw salvation and fulfillment for mankind only in the "common cause" of ending death by resurrection of the dead. Voloshin, too, saw an indissoluble connection between the present and the past and in it found the key to the enigma of the Russian love of religion, to that mystic force, with its trappings of custom and ritual, which has shaped the spiritual and moral aspects of the national character.

The First World War Voloshin interpreted in terms of Dostoyevski's philosophy. In "The Prophecy" [*Prorochestvo*] he evokes Raskolnikov's dream and treats the war and the specter of Russian rebellion as the realization of Dostoyevski's prophecy.

For Voloshin belief in Christ is so closely interwoven in the Russian people with love for the hearth and ancestral graves that, if the latter are taken away, faith, too, will wither at the root. Without God and love for the past, Russia is inevitably transformed into a breeding ground of cosmic evil.

Dmitri the Pretender (Voloshin's "Dmetrius Imperator") saw Russia as a primitive rock, grown over by the moss of the past, which must be hewn into shape and given a rational form, through the adoption of Western culture. He was the first to draw his sword against the historic past of the Russian state. But, while engaged in his duel with the past, he unwittingly thrust his sword through the time-darkened image of the Russian Christ and shook the people's faith in God. Once that faith was shaken, the persecution of the past aroused the latent thirst for blood and let it run in the Russian steppes:

> Such a famine none could have foretold.
> Wood and excrement went into bread,
> Pasty made with human flesh was sold,
> Men ate the frozen earth and fell down dead.
> And city mobs on state barns filled with grain
> Converged, cursing Godunov and his reign,
> Milling about and freezing in the snow.
> Then did the earth itself tremble and cleave
> In answer to their anguished pleas—and lo!
> I rose triumphant from a martyr's grave.
> . . . .
> With feverish visions of a better day
> Troubling Russia, leading her astray,
> In disaster bravely did I reign—
> And in three centuries I'll come again.[52]

In the narrative poem "Archpriest Avvakum," which is also in the volume *Demons Deaf and Dumb,* Patriarch Nikon (1605-1681) unconsciously and intuitively continues the accursed work of Dmitri the Pretender, and Avvakum (d. 1682) is represented as a misunderstood martyr, hounded to death for his attempts to save Russia from disaster. Nikon was a religious reformer whose intention was to reform the Orthodox Church, eliminating both the provincial deviations which had crept in and the atavistic holdovers from the days of paganism; but in revising archaic practices and altering religious ritual, Nikon came into a head-on conflict with Russia's love for the traditions of her past, and, instead of strengthening orthodox belief, he destroyed it. Voloshin's Avvakum is not a man who clings blindly to the relics of the past but a realist who sees clearly that drastic attempts to bury a living past threaten the Russian idea of Christ and with it the faith of the people:

> Winter has come.
> My heart is chilled.
> My knees tremble.[53]
> . . . .
> For Nikon's spirit is the Antichrist's.[54]

In Stenka Razin's insurrection (1670-1671) and in Pugachov's uprising (1773-1775) Voloshin saw a logical historical development, an inevitable result of the defeat of the cause to which Avvakum had sacrificed his life. In "Stenka's Judgment," Razin says:
> I would shout to the nearest sentry:
> "Get me Uss, Sheludyak and the Pig—
> Let them shake down the landed gentry,
> Make the lords and the priests dance a jig!"[55]
> . . . .
> Sword in hand, we'll bring in a new order.
> Like three saints, we will rise from the dead—
> Otrep'yev* from over the border,
> Pugachov, and myself at their head.[56]

Nikon's religious reform paved the way for the reform of Peter the Great, whom Voloshin calls "the first Bolshevik." Thrusting the country centuries ahead into her distant future in violation of ancient ways and customs, he embodied a will in history which acts, faceless and mute, regardless of human wills.

From Russia's past Voloshin then turned to the Bolshevik Revolution:
> What is changed? The title and the name?
> Howling gales are everywhere the same.
> Autocratic are the Commissars,
> And revolt was brewing in the Tsars.

---

* Dmitri the Pretender.

> ... To smoke out Russia from her poultry-shed
> And to fling her centuries ahead,
> Contrary to Nature's very laws,
> Is still the maddest dream that ever was.[57]
>
> . . . .
> No, not Moscow, Astrakhan or Yaik
> Ever knew a bitterer day than this.[58]

The volume which contains these lines—*Poems of the Terror*—for obvious political considerations was not published in Soviet Russia, but in Berlin in 1923. In its surrealist sketches Voloshin depicts with horror the hatred and bloodspilling of the Civil War. These lines are from "Terror":

> To the gully's edge they were pushed in the dark,
> Unshriven, unblest.
> For half a minute the machine guns barked.
> Bayonets did the rest.[59]

Another poem bears the title "Slaughter":

> "Don't bawl. They deserved a dog's death."
> But she will not go, she stands there weeping,
> And says, looking the soldier straight in the eye:
> "Think you I weep for those who are dead?
> I weep for those who have long to live."[60]

In "Red Spring," dated April 1920, Voloshin, unlike Blok, deplored that Christ could have turned his face away from Russia:

> Nature herself exhibited a face
> Ravaged by rage and horror. And the souls
> Of those who met their death by violence
> Blew in the wind along the dusty roads,
> Maddened the living with the venom'd drug
> Of unspent passions, life unsatiated,
> Breeding revenge, and panic, and disease.
> Lent in that year came in the dead of winter,
> The May and Easter both were red with blood;
> But on that spring Christ rose not from the dead.[61]

Again unlike Blok, Voloshin was a stranger to both camps. Blok erred along with the mob which was possessed by the spirit of destruction. Voloshin deprecated that spirit and appealed for reconciliation and forgiveness:

> And I—I stand between the two
> Alone, amid the flame and smoke,
> And God's great mercy I invoke
> On both of you, on both of you.[62]
>
> ("Civil War," 1920)

The somber, rhetorical and at times even funereal quality of Voloshin's poetry is relieved by his faith in man and in the submerged instinct which would eventually, through a religious renascence, free the human personality from slavery:

> Batter us and knife us in the breast,
> Light the fires of warfare and unrest—
> Through centuries, defying every wind,
> Across the frozen wastes of ice we go,
> Stumbling ... and we will perish in the snow,
> Or else our desecrated temple find.[63]

He offered himself, if need be, as a sacrificial victim:

> Providence in its eternal might
> Loosed the ancient chaos from its chains,
> And from Russia's blackened, charred remains
> I do say to It: "You judged aright!"
> All of matter, all of life, must be
> Tempered to a diamond hardness—so,
> If the fiery furnace for its glow
> Needs more fuel, mighty God, take me![64]

Voloshin believed that, sooner or later, through the revelation of Christ, man would escape from enslavement by the machine into true freedom and learn to make nature subservient to his spiritual power:

> World systems are but models of men's souls,
> The mirrored madness of the bright reflection
> Of two opposing chasms, each in each.
> There is no way out of the maze of knowledge,
> And questing man will never rise above
> That which he holds in passionate belief.
> . . . .

> Then be creator and creation both!
> Oh, known thyself eternal and divine,
> And make a world to fit thy soul's full measure![65]

ANDREI BELYI
(pseudonym of Boris Nikolayevich Bugayev, 1880-1934)

Although Andrei Belyi remained in Russia after the Revolution except for a brief period in the early 1920's when he lived in Berlin, he was constitutionally incapable of adapting his unique and insistently experimental art to the service of the regime. The most original of the Russian Symbolist poets, he wrote little poetry after 1917. Only the small volume of verse *The First Meeting* (1921),[66] a nostalgic and delightful evocation of the life of the Moscow intelligentsia during the period of his youth, may be compared with his prerevolutionary poetry. Even his fiction, despite the intellectual power and brilliance of several of the later novels, displays a gradual decline in artistic mastery. From the point of view of form, imagery and composition, all his postrevolutionary novels are inferior to *St. Petersburg* (1913-1916), and are only parts of larger designs—two series of epic proportions—which were never completed. Nonetheless Belyi remained a very great writer and left a deep imprint on Soviet prose, officially decried though his influence was.

He was a many-faceted writer, who experimented in reminting in literary form the coin of other arts. In *The Crisis in Art* (1918), Berdyayev endeavored to trace the relationship between Belyi's innovations and "modernist" art at the beginning of the twentieth century, which in Berdyayev's view constituted

> a recognition of the impotence of man's creative impulse, of the great gap between artistic purpose and artistic achievement. Our time is one of both unprecedented ventures in art and unprecedented weakness of execution.[67]

Belyi is assigned a place of distinction among the artists who sought to evolve new synthetized forms—for instance, Churlyanis experimenting with musical painting and Skryabin with pictorial music.

Berdyayev regarded Belyi's prose as literary cubism and compared Belyi with Pablo Picasso.

Belyi has an artistic conception of the world which is his and his alone: a sense of cosmic fragmentation and dissolution, a decrystallization of all material things, a disintegration and disappearance of all firmly fixed boundaries separating one object from another.
His characters themselves become dissolved and diffused; the sharp limits which divide one man from another and from all the objects in his physical environment are blurred and fade away. . . . In the end, Andrei Belyi's style always passes into something resembling a whirlwind. It is a cosmic hurricane expressed in terms of speech. The impression of a rising hurricane, produced by the combinations of words and sounds, reflects a mounting cosmic tension which is bound to end in catastrophe.[68]

For his treatment of human existence as an eternal struggle between the conscious and the subconscious—reason being a weak and shaky dam which cannot long withstand the pressure of raging elements—Belyi fused in his prose an entirely new alloy from the classical heritage and the devices of synthetized art. He accomplishes a syncretism of moods derived from Apollon Grigor'yev's *My Literary and Spiritual Wanderings* (1864) and Gogol's rhythmic recitative, which on occasion renders the melancholy beauty of Russia's open spaces through the music of words, and gives these moods an intensely dynamic cast.

When Belyi describes the conscious, his prose moves with the speed of an express train, and when his purpose is to reveal the subconscious, the concatenations of words form the spouts of invisible whirlwinds. His prose may well be termed suprematic, in the sense in which the cubist painter K. S. Malevich defined suprematism:

. . . The cosmic flame exists in a disembodied state, and it is only when it is trapped in the skull of thought that it is cooled by the realization of its incommensurability, and thought, itself representing a certain degree of stimulation, being fired by this flame, reaches out further and further, thrusts itself forward into infinity, creating all the worlds of the universe in its path.[69]

This is Malevich's cosmic suprematism, "life in the spirit." Mechanical suprematism is revealed in painting as "life in the machine." Geometry is a static representation of visible objects, while technology is an enemy of the static, suspending an engine to every stationary object. The world tends to disintegrate into a multitude of component atoms; motion is the means of holding it together.

As soon as we turn our intelligent instruments on the objects of the material world they scatter; the sharper the intelligence, the deeper, wider, further is the scattering.[70]

It is not enough to portray the outward semblance of an object. The artist must "reproduce the spirit of stimulation, the spirit of creation, which is alive in man."[71]

The following passage is an example of Belyi's mechanical suprematism:

The black little train, like a straight snake uncoiled, swung past in a glissade; shattered in size and sound, cleanly breaking up into cubes of cars; now someone invisible before the onrushing steam and dust rang a rail, and like a rail vanished, and pursuing someone invisible the cars flickered by without a stop.[72]

When you read Belyi's prose, you have the impression that the writer is speeding over the vast free expanse of Russia in an airplane. The speed blurs the outlines of the material world and they flow together in a superimposition of cubes, triangles, ellipses, parallelograms and circles which rush past and are united by their cyclonic motion. Now the airplane reduces its speed and lands. Brakes are applied, and reality, divorced from motion, once again falls apart into a collection of the static, and therefore separate, objects, which the eye is accustomed to seeing. All that remains is the feeling that these objects have not yet fully calmed down, have not caught their breath after their rapid run, and are still permeated by a certain excitement.

Mechanical suprematism, however, is but a frail bridge erected by reason over the subconscious, the latter being the subject of cosmic suprematism. In S. A. Alekseyev-Askol'dov's description of Belyi's cosmic suprematism,

[Belyi gives us] "symphonic pictures of Being," seen from some newly-gained height. The most important feature of these symphonies is that their basic melodies are the melodies not only of this empirical life of ours, but of a different, otherwordly life, which the author senses and perceives through a sort of second sight. . . .[73]

Imagine that you are looking at an ordinary tree with a two-dimensional eye capable of seeing in only one plane. You will perceive unrelated flat sections of different parts of the tree; at some points you will discern little circles which are twigs and branches, at others lines formed by blossoms and leaves. Much of it will strike you as unnecessary, nonsensical, meaningless.

It is only when the mind grasps all these cross sections in their stereoscopic unity that what appeared meaningless and haphazard falls into place and assumes the shape of a recognizable tree. Such basically different views—the stereoscopic and the two-dimensional—may also be taken of life in history and in art.[74]

In his mystical dynamism Belyi attempts to wed the word to the motion of light, to free himself from the tyranny of time and space:

In the wild madness of the glance, madness there was none, but firmness: to demand an accounting: on the basis of what law had arisen such a whirligig of worlds in which the kindest and the most intelligent had their eyes burned with hot irons; it seemed that the enterprise of the creation was about to go bankrupt, that the line of the earth's fall was a zigzag over a yawning abyss, that this head, not of our planetary system at all (in ours it looks different), would break away from the neck and, splitting the roof with its swollen lips, would force its way out of the earth's and the sun's gravitational field.

To raise a tremendous shout so that the wheel of the Zodiac would shed its petals like a faded wreath—in front of this perplexed little huddle, trembling with fear, whose eye lenses had a tickling sensation which produced the mirage of a blood-stained body—in front of the perplexed little huddle he stood, screaming with grinning mouth: "The Last Judgment!"[75]

Cosmic suprematism found its way into Andrei Belyi's prose through Churlyanis' painting and Skryabin's pictorial music. To compare Belyi with Picasso, as Berdyayev did, or with James Joyce, as did V. Stenich, may serve a purpose in that it helps to bring Belyi's art within the general scope of European culture, but while the Russian Symbolist has certain points of contact with the great experimental artists of the West, he was deeply indebted to the daring attempts of Russian artists to create a synthetic form of art. Belyi wanted his words to sing and to glow with color. At the same time he differed fundamentally from an artist like Churlyanis, who, straining in imagination to penetrate other worlds, blindly believed the otherworldly to be real. Belyi's mystical vision was often corroded by skepticism, and at such times he turned upon his own dream with bitter, sick mockery.

For obvious reasons his work was not within the grasp of ordinary readers, and even the sophisticated often failed to appreciate it or found it intolerable. Nonetheless, despite the incompatibility of his philosophical, political and aesthetic views with those of the Bolsheviks, he at first "accepted" the revolution and put himself at its service. He gave lectures on the theory of poetry and prose at the Moscow Proletcult (Proletarian Culture and Educational Organization) and advised young proletarian poets about their work. He edited the "left-wing" Symbolist journal *Zapiski mechtatelei* [Dreamers' Journal], which was published from 1918 to 1922 and which contained much of the outstanding writing of the period—of Belyi himself, Blok, Zamyatin, Remizov, Gershenzon and Vyacheslav Ivanov. Even at this time, however, he could not conceal his uneasiness and disillusionment. An artist who worked on a heroic scale, he complained that his attention was constantly being diverted by trifles: "I have ruined so many *St. Petersburgs* [he revised the novel for a postrevolutionary edition], and so much is being ruined in St. Petersburg!" "Leave me free to choose my own subjects. . . ." "They set me at trifles, which they commend to my attention as interesting work. . . ."[76]

Cast into a society in which individuality counted for nothing, he felt his inner world impoverished, and noted in his "Diary of a Writer" for 1921: "To explore one's ego fully means clearly and consciously to experience the destruction of all that which kept the ego alive. . . ." [77]

Whether deliberate or not, the core of all Belyi's novels published after the revolution is not the fate of Russia as a whole but the unhappy position of the Russian intelligentsia in the new period.

The world of reality is frightening, terrible, and in it man is beset by loneliness and dread. We live among constant wrecks, in the power of devouring passions and antediluvian worlds,[78]

says A. K. Voronski with reference to Belyi's novel *Kotik Letayev*.

Kotik Letayev, published in 1917-1918[79] although in large part written several years earlier, was intended as the beginning of a series of novels; only the first two, however, were completed (the second is *The Baptized Chinese* or, as originally entitled, *The Crime of Nikolai Letayev*).[80]

Kotik Letayev is the story of a child's developing consciousness of his world, with a strong autobiographical tinge. It begins with prenatal experiences of nightmare and moves through an infancy of delirium and horrors:

> Imagine a human skull. Enormous, enormous, enormous. Large out of all proportion, larger than any cathedral, imagine. . . . Its nostrilled whiteness rises in the shape of a cathedral cut from a mountain. . . . A mighty cathedral with a white dome peers at you out of the dark. . . .[81]

Kotik is the sickly and gifted son of a university professor, and the household in which he grows up is a frail spiritual island that will never be able to resist the coming hurricane. Childish fear is magnified into a foreboding of something obscure, evil and frightening, something which will ruin the whole of life:

> In this strange event all the darkly flowing images have become solid for the first time and are cut by the deceptive light of looming darkness. The mazes are illuminated; in the midst of yellow sunlit honeycombs I recognize myself: there is the circle; round about it are benches. On them are dark images of women, like images of the night; they are the nurses, and next to them, in the light, are children, clinging to their dark skirts. . . .[82]

Kotik lives in a world of tragic antagonism between the intelligentsia and the people, in which the raging Asiatic element has come to the fore. In his future everything for which he has been reared will have turned to dust.

> My consciousness will be a man then, my consciousness is like a baby still: I shall be born a second time; the ice of conceptions, words and meanings will break, will be grown through with meaning.
> These meanings are nothing to me now, and all former meanings

are senseless; they rustle and flutter about the dry wood of the cross, where I hang within myself.
I crucify myself![83]

The theme of the *déclassement* of the Russian intelligentsia is presented with even greater power in *A Moscow Crank* and *Moscow in Jeopardy* (1926), the first two parts of the uncompleted epic novel *Moscow*. No other work of postrevolutionary Russian literature can compare with these two books in intellectual depth, intuitive premonition of Russia's future, understanding of Russian psychology, or vastness of conception.

The action of *Moscow* takes place before and during the First World War. In opposition to the Marxian interpretation of history in terms of class struggle, Belyi treats history as a struggle between races and nations first, and between classes second. The Germans are represented by the scoundrel Mandro and the maniac Donner, who have "pierced the globe with the blade of war," [84] and the Russians by the Bolshevik Kiyerko. Kiyerko is endowed with great breadth of vision and with a feeling of kinship for the soil.

In both Mandro and Kiyerko there is much that is bestial. Professor Korobkin, whose spiritual wrestings are the main subject of the book, reflects:

The dark prehistoric period has not yet been conquered by culture and reigns in the subconscious. Culture is a thin coating—scratch a bit, and it will come off, leaving a hole, through which, swinging their axes, men wearing skins of antediluvian beasts will, by God, jump right out.[85]

In the struggle between beasts Kiyerko finally overcomes Donner and Mandro; there is a streak of good humor in him which comes from his sense of unity with space, whereas the Germans, in spite of all their other advantages, are undone by the atrophy of their sense of space.

After these two books Belyi wrote little fiction. His last novel was the sequel *Masks* (1932), a much weaker effort.

Belyi lived into the period of Soviet literature when his vein of experimental art was no longer tolerated. Some writers renounced experimentation and learned to leave their personality out of their fiction, turning to the conservative, the archaic or to the primitive. Belyi could not. Toward the end of his career he wrote his memoirs, critical essays and theoretical treatises.

The three volumes of his memoirs *(At the Turn of the Century,* 1929, *The Beginning of the Century,* 1932, and *Between Two Revolutions,* 1933) constitute a splendid, if capricious, history of Russian Symbolism. His earlier reminiscences of Aleksandr Blok were reworked for incorporation in these memoirs. Belyi's book *Gogol's Mastery,* 1934, is one of the best of the stylistic analyses of Gogol.

VALERI BRYUSOV (1873-1924)

Of the Symbolists, Bryusov was perhaps the most successful in adapting himself to the new order. He was an unemotional, calculating analyst, a master architect and mathematician of Russian poetry. He accepted the Bolshevik government without reservations, but not for ideological considerations.

Bryusov joined the Communist Party in 1919, was elected to the Moscow City Soviet, held an important position in the People's Commissariat of Education under Lunacharski, conscientiously attended innumerable meetings, lectured at the First Moscow State University and the Higher Institute of Arts and Letters, which he himself organized in 1921, and gave courses at a Proletcult studio. He was a strict, honest and highly capable teacher, wholly devoted to his pedagogical task which he approached in all sincerity, without a trace of irony. His influence on postrevolutionary Russian literature was a salutary one in that in some measure it counteracted the crudity and provincialism of the younger "proletarian" writers. In general, during the last years of his life Bryusov became a teacher and critic rather than creative writer.

If his own poetry after the revolution is negligible, it is only the end product of a steady decline in power which had begun many years before. The several collections of verse which he published—including *In Such Times,* 1921, *Vistas,* 1922, and *Mea,* 1924—consist mainly of the dull civic exercises of a superannuated poet laureate and a cold, dispassionate and documentary record of the destruction wreaked by the revolution.

THE EMIGRES AND IRRECONCILABLES

Vyacheslav Ivanov (1866-1949), high priest of Symbolism for years before the First World War, who had hymned revolution as a mystic presage of renascence, found in the actual events of 1917 and the following years none of the exultation stirred by the revolution of 1905. In poems and articles published in Belyi's *Zapiski mechtatelei*,[86] in *Winter Sonnets* (1920),[87] and in *Correspondence from Two Corners* (1921)[88]—an exchange of letters between Ivanov and the philosopher Gershenzon—he voiced the dismay and grief of the intelligentsia at the wholesale destruction, and defended the culture of the past as fertilizer for a new growth. In 1924 he left the country, in the wake of others of the former Symbolist coterie, including Dimitri Merezhkovski and Zinaida Gippius.

Fyodor Sologub (1863-1927) turned his back to the new regime, and lived apart, in hardship and misfortune. He produced a considerable amount of work, but little of it was published in Russia.

One Symbolist poet, V. A. Zorgenfrei, formerly a sedulous imitator of Blok, greatly increased in stature during the postrevolutionary period. He won a place in Russian literature by his compassionate record of the suffering and sorrows of Petrograd. "On the Neva" was written in 1920:

> Raising a cross above his crown,
> A marble angel gazes down
> On palaces forgotten,
> On broken beams and rotten.
> It's bitter cold; a harsh wind blows;
> Beneath the ice the river flows.
> Upon the ice the bonfires burn.
> Patrols march by in grim concern.
>
> Telephone wires hum overhead:
> Hail Petrograd, the Tsar is dead!
> Inside the palace, its only host,
> Slowly walks a royal ghost....
> While in the street, beside the brands,
> The shade of the last Peter stands

> And wrings its hands in consternation,
> In shuddering repudiation.
>
> . . . .
>
> Citizen hails citizen on the icy street:
> "Tell me, citizen, what have you had to eat?
> Did you break your fast, citizen, today?"
> "I slept badly, citizen, I regret to say—
> For some petrol I gave my soul away. . . ."
> A gale comes tearing from the sound,
> Hastily whirling snow around
> To dim the light and bank the posts
> And stop communion with the ghosts.[89]

Zorgenfrei continued to write poetry which was full of hopelessness and despair and was never published. In 1938 he was arrested on suspicion of anti-Soviet activities.

Two of the greatest Russian writers of the period of Symbolism, Aleksei Remizov (1877-   ) and Vasili Rozanov (1856-1919) —friends of the Symbolist movement rather than Symbolists themselves—soon found life in Russia insupportable after the revolution. Rozanov died in miserable circumstances in 1919, and two years later Remizov, his close friend, emigrated. Before the end, however, both had their eloquent say about the revolutionary scene.

Remizov's "Lament for the Ruin of Russia" was published in 1918 in Petrograd;[90] the remainder of his chronicle of the Revolution and Civil War was published abroad.[91] The "Lament" was dismissed in the Soviet *Literary Encyclopedia* as a full disclosure of the author's reactionary temper. Nonetheless Remizov the stylist has set his stamp on much of the best Soviet writing.

From 1917 to his death Rozanov lived at Sergiyev Posad, not far from Moscow, with Father Belyayev, an Orthodox priest. There from time to time he issued, in pamphlet form, *The Apocalypse of Our Times,* which bears a distant resemblance to Dostoyevski's *Diary of a Writer* and at the same time brims with the kind of biting and rueful irony characteristic of Mikhail Zoshchenko's stories.

Clanging and creaking, the iron curtain comes down on Russian History.
"The performance is over."
The audience rises.

"Time to get our fur coats and to go home."
It then turned out that they had neither coats nor homes left.[92]

Sometimes the irony covers up pangs of hunger:

> Rolls, fresh rolls ...
> Oh for a little bread ...
> Oh for a little meat ... .[93]

"Rejoice, oh Russian literature—and here rye flour has gone up to 350 rubles a pood." [94]

In tracing the roots of the revolution, Rozanov lays part of the blame on the inertia and conservatism of Russian industrialists, who had failed to keep up with the tempo of the times and to make full use of the opportunities offered by technical development. He strikes out at Russian literature too for succumbing to the conservative spirit under the tsarist regime. But the primary cause was the cachexia of Christianity:

In European society [including the Russian], there formed great voids, which had been previously occupied by Christianity; into these voids, everything fell: thrones, classes, rank, labor, wealth. Everything was shaken, everyone was shaken. Everything was perishing, everyone was perishing. All these things collapsed into the emptiness of the soul which had lost its immemorial content. . . .[95]

". . . Only priests have failed to realize that the Church has been destroyed even more terribly than the state. . . ."[96] "Well, death has come; this must have been its appointed time. . . ."[97]

Socialism, an attempt to bring paradise down to earth and to make up for the failure of Christianity to arrange human life better, had, without knowing it, inherited the void left by Christianity. The result was emptiness to the second power: "And so we see that before the revolutionary has worn out his new boots, he sinks into the grave."[98]

Otherwise ready to make his peace with Marx, the old man was infuriated by Marx's theory of class struggle and foresaw that the new rulers of Russia would pay dearly for adhering to it in the future when Russia and Germany would again be at each other's throats.

2. The Acmeists

In discussing postrevolutionary Russian literature it is no longer appropriate to speak of Acmeism (or Adamism, as it is less frequently called) as a distinct school. It had developed its artistic canons and flourished as a coherent group in the period before the First World War. After the revolution it was less an active movement than an effect already well diffused throughout Russian literature, although the three outstanding exponents of Acmeism—Gumilyov, Anna Akhmatova and Mandel'shtam—were then just reaching the peak of their talent.

Gumilyov and Gorodetski had first enunciated the principles known as Acmeism, in a reaction against the excessive abstraction and mysticism of the Symbolists. "The main function of literature," wrote Gumilyov, "has been seriously threatened by the Symbolist mystics, for they have made it into formulas for their own esoteric brushes with the unknowable."[1] The Acmeists endeavored to return literature from cold celestial space to earth, to the sounds and colors and forms of "this world," the world of weight and time, "our earthly planet." In Gorodetski's words:

For the Acmeists a rose has again become good in itself, by virtue of its petals, its fragrance and color, and not because of its imagined similarities to mystical love or anything else.[2]

Thus the primary distinction between Acmeism and Symbolism is that the former strove for moderation in describing mystical experiences and in attempting to correlate the material and the metaphysical. The Acmeists also emphasized "the will principle in poetry" and concentrated on techniques which would give the line a strong, muscular, energetic movement without sacrificing the musical quality. They advocated a return to the clarity and virile classicism of Pushkin.

NIKOLAI GUMILYOV (1886-1921)

After Gumilyov's execution in Soviet Russia in 1921, Georgi Ivanov, one of his followers, paid him the following tribute:

> Why is it that he traveled to Africa, went to war as a volunteer, took part in a conspiracy, and demonstratively, with a sweeping gesture, made a sign of the cross in front of every church he passed in Soviet Petrograd, and told the examining official to his face that he was a monarchist, instead of attempting to exonerate and save himself?
> His close friends know that there was nothing of the warrior or the adventurer in Gumilyov. In Africa he was hot and bored, as a soldier he was painfully miserable, and he had very little faith in the conspiracy for which he perished. His attitude to all these matters was that of a typical Chekhov intellectual. He really loved and was interested in only one thing in the world—poetry. But he was firmly convinced that only that man has the right to call himself a poet who will endeavor to be first in any human undertaking and who, more deeply aware than others of human weakness, selfishness, mediocrity and fear of death, will strive afresh each day to overcome the old Adam in himself.
> And so this naturally timid, gentle, sickly, bookish man commanded himself to become a big game hunter, a soldier—and as such he was twice awarded the Order of St. George—and a conspirator who risked his life to re-establish the monarchy. What he did with his life, he also did with his poetry. A dreamy, melancholy lyricist, he stifled his lyrical strain and changed the pitch of his not overly strong but remarkably clear voice in an endeavor to return to poetry its former majesty and direct effect on men's souls, to be a ringing dagger, and to set men's hearts afire. . . . He sacrificed himself to his ideal of unflinching strength of will, high human integrity and conquest of the fear of death.[3]

Originally a disciple of Bryusov, to whom the architectonics of verse was an end in itself, Gumilyov strove for virtuosity merely as a means of expressing thought and "the will principle." He studied at the Sorbonne and translated Théophile Gautier, but his early poetry—*The Way of the Conquistadors* (1905) and *Romantic Flowers* (1908)—is reminiscent rather of Edgar Allan Poe and Rider Haggard.

Pearls (1910) is an excursion of a romantic dreamer into the epoch of the discovery and conquest of new territories, in which

Major Prerevolutionary Writers

the exotic past comes suddenly alive with a flapping of ships' sails, cracking of pistols and muskets, and whistling of arrows.

The Quiver (1916), which contains Gumilyov's war poems (he had enlisted in a cavalry regiment in 1914), voices his belief in the righteousness of Russia's cause and in the duty of every Russian to fight in her defense.

> I shout, and my voice is savage,
> Like brass on brass—and free;
> A vessel of living thought,
> I cannot cease to be.
> Like thunderous hammer blows,
> Like tides that never rest,
> The golden heart of Russia
> Is beating in my breast.[4]

In battle the poet is sustained by a deep religious feeling:

> Our cause is great and blessed,
> In pride our banner flies,
> And shining winged seraphim
> Behind each warrior rises.[5]
>
> . . . .
>
> Here a white-faced soldier kisses
> His fallen comrade on the lips,
> There a priest in tattered robes
> Chants a psalm, beatified.[6]
>
> . . . .
>
> Give him strength, oh Lord, on earth below,
> Give him victory in war's alarms
> Who can say unto the conquered foe:
> "Let me clasp you in a brother's arms!"[7]

Gumilyov has been accused of giving expression to tsarist Russia's imperialist aspirations in his narrative poem *Mik* (1918) and in *The Tent* (1921), both of which were based on his travels in Africa before World War I (his last trip, in 1913, had been made as chief of an expedition organized by the Academy of Sciences).

The Soviet writer A. Volkov, in his *Poetry of Russian Imperialism* (1935), treated Gumilyov as a disciple of Kipling, that "bulldog of His Britannic Majesty," and asserted that Gumilyov undertook his journey to Africa with a view to impressing the colonial experience of British imperialists into the service of their Russian counterparts. To be sure, Gumilyov at one time looked upon Abyssinia as a logical area for the extension of Russian rule. He was incapable of remaining a passive observer of the collapse of the Russian state, and had mourned the downfall of the monarchy even before its occurrence:

> Burdensome, burdensome, shameful—
> To live, having lost our king.[8]
> ("Agamemnon's Warrior")

> Years of disaster followed
> The end of the kingly race,
> As freedom, that will-o'-the-wisp,
> Led us a merry chase.[9]
> (*Gondla*)

In the belief that the stability of the British throne was in part the result of Great Britain's colonial policy, Gumilyov desired to see that policy in operation in Africa. The observations which he expressed symbolically in *Mik*, however, are far from bearing out the opinions on racial superiority ascribed to him.

Just as Lermontov had admired the conquered Caucasian mountain tribes for their courage, heroism and sense of honor, Gumilyov admires the same qualities in the Africans. And in *Mik*, although the young French boy, symbol of "white supremacy," is at first made king of the beasts of the forest, it is the native slave boy Mik, son of a defeated Abyssinian chieftain, who finally returns to civilization as a triumphant prince, having given himself to the forest forces which Louis had deserted and which had finally killed him.

Gumilyov found that Russian imperialism was more merciful and humane than British, but that Great Britain too was progressing toward friendly treatment of the conquered. He also saw Great Britain beginning to overcome a defect which threatened the Russian state as well—the sharp cleavage between the government and the intellectuals on the one hand and the people on the other. The antiquated Russian monarchy, he concluded, could maintain itself only in a union with the Russia of the peasants.

Gumilyov's political views were set forth not in the conventional medium of political articles, but in his poems, and before the revolution little attention was paid to that side of him; in 1921, however, he was shot for counterrevolutionary activities.

In time, the flowering of Gumilyov's talent coincided with the revolution, and the volume entitled *Pillar of Fire* (1921) contains some of the best poems he ever wrote. Their common denominator is hatred of the revolution, which coerced people into surrender of the individual will principle and turned them into a mob blindly obeying the organizers.

The mood is surrealist:

> Look, there's a vegetable store,
> Its sign in letters dripping red;
> Those are not pumpkins on the floor—
> Each object is a human head.
> The blank-faced executioner
> Chopped off my head as well, you know.
> It lay with all the others there
> In staring-eyed and grinning show.[10]

The presentiment of death, which gave a bitter tang to his early *Romantic Flowers* but which disappeared from Gumilyov's poetry for a long time, is strong in *Pillar of Fire*, as in his other poems of the revolution.

In "The Worker" the poet foretold his own death at the hands of those schooled to destruction by the new leaders:

> He stands before his flaming forge,
> An aging man of middle height.
> His eyes have a submissive look
> From blinking at the reddish light.
> His comrades are asleep in bed.
> He wakes alone, he will not rest,
> Intent on fashioning the lead
> That will fly homing to my breast.[11]

In a collection of poems published posthumously, in Petrograd, *To the Blue Star* (1923), Gumilyov once more returned to his delicate lyricism.

His prose has not received the recognition it deserves. It has had an undoubted influence on Soviet literature, in particular on the work of Tikhonov and Grin in his later period. Gumilyov's last stories were published after his execution in the book entitled *Shade from a Palm*, 1922.

Despite his hostility to the new regime, Gumilyov served as associate in Gorki's publishing firm World Literature, for which he made several brilliant translations, notably of Coleridge's *Rime of the Ancient Mariner* and of the Babylonian legend of Gilgamesh (from a French translation). He also issued some of his own work and several collective volumes under the imprint of the Poets' Guild [*Tsekh poetov*], the name adopted by the Acmeist group in 1912. For a time he taught younger writers although, unlike Blok, who wanted to bring the semi-literates in Red Army helmets into the stream of Russian culture, Gumilyov desired to protect that culture from the onslaught of the Bolsheviks. The disagreements between the two poets after the Revolution arose largely from their difference of opinion on that score.

ANNA AKHMATOVA
(pseudonym of Anna Andreyevna Gorenko, 1888-   )

Anna Akhmatova's teacher was Innokenti Annenski, a poet and scholar whom she has remembered with gratitude all her life. In 1945 she wrote of him:

> And he whom as my master I revere
> Passed like a shadow, and no shadow left;
> Absorbed the poison, all the opiates drained,
> Hoped for immortal glory, but in vain.
> He was a sign, a forecast of the future,
> He pitied all, he filled us all with longing—
> And died for want of air....[12]

Married to Gumilyov at the time of the establishment of the Poets' Guild, she was one of the original members, and her first volume of verse, *Evening*, 1912, was published under its imprint, with a preface by the poet Mikhail Kuzmin, to whose praise and practice of "beautiful clarity" the Acmeists were heavily indebted

Major Prerevolutionary Writers

for their theories. Vyacheslav Ivanov said to her of "Song of Our Last Meeting" in this volume, "Anna Andreyevna, I congratulate you and welcome you. That poem is an event in Russian letters." [13]

With the publication of her second book, *Rosary*, 1914, she took her place as one of the most exquisite and widely read lyric poets of the time.

After the revolution the near-idolatry in which Anna Akhmatova was held among the intelligentsia only increased with the appearance of each new volume in the brief series which continued for a few years: *White Birds Flying* (1917), *Plantain* (1921), *Anno Domini MCMXXI* (1921), and *By the Sea* (1921).

Her poems with their sharp, spare images almost always tell a story, compress a profoundly moving tragedy into a few brief stanzas. The recurrent theme of her lyrics is confession of love and the pain of unrequited love. Blok accepts the antagonism between spiritual love and physical passion as a curse hanging over man. Akhmatova's poetry is illumined by her need to merge love and passion. Like Pushkin, whom she deeply admires, she is able to recreate sensual delight without a trace of lewdness or cynicism. She seeks tenderness ("There's no mistaking tenderness, / It is a quiet thing"), but it is physical desire which falls to her share:

> In vain with show of loving care
> You wrap me in my furs—
> How well I know that stubborn,
> That hungry look of yours! [14]

Again and again she protests as in these lines of 1921:

> I swear to you by Holy Paradise
> And by the icon shining on its rack
> And by the flaming madness of our nights
> That you shall never, never have me back. [15]

Her refuge is the quiet life of the country, the past, the peasants, folklore.

> The river gently wanders on its way,
> Upon the knoll a rambling house is spread,
> And there we live as in good Catherine's day,
> Waiting for crops and having masses said. [16]

In her poems of the village, Akhmatova ceases to be a Russian gentlewoman and shares the emotional experiences of the humble peasant. Often the mood is inspired by the songs and lamentations of folklore.

A poet who draws on folklore has the choice of two methods, that of "stylization" and that of counterpoint. Stylization—that is, outright imitation, pastiche—is the easier method of the two, and Akhmatova has resorted to it upon occasion, but her contrapuntal verse, in which she adds her own voice to the folklore style, is more profound and handled with greater virtuosity than her stylized poems. Contrapuntal treatment enables her most effectively to tap the artistic heritage of the people, with all the beauty of its songs, legends, and tales.

As she came to know the sufferings of her country more intimately, social themes with a religious coloration of popular belief began to recur in her work with increasing frequency. In a poem entitled "July 1914" she wrote:

> The day of doom is nearing. Soon
> New graves will hem us in.
> There will be famine, plague, typhoon,
> Eclipses daily seen.
>
> And yet the enemy shall not
> Our land in slavery hold.
> The Holy Virgin o'er our lot
> Shall spread her cloth of gold.[17]

In an untitled poem dated 1919 she made one of her first, and extremely rare, political comments:

> While in the West the sun is shining still
> And in its rays gleams many a roof and dome,
> Here Death chalks crosses on our doors at will
> And calls the ravens, and the ravens come.[18]

Paradoxically the lyrical poems of Akhmatova and of Mayakovski —when Mayakovski takes off the leather jacket of a public speaker —have much in common, as the critic Kornei Chukovski pointed out in 1920.[19] Akhmatova herself, in the poem entitled "Mayakovski in 1913," two stanzas from which follow, spoke of the dramatic dualism of Mayakovski—on the one hand, the propagandist and Futurist poet and, on the other, the tender lyricist:

> I did not know you in your later glory.
> My memory is of your stormy start.
> Yet it seems fitting now to tell the story
> Of those lost years—such centuries apart. . . .
> . . . .
> The things you merely brushed against were never
> Again the same to the beholder's eye;
> What you undid remained undone forever;
> You sentenced right and left without a sigh.[20]

After 1921 there was a long hiatus in the publication of Akhmatova's poetry until 1940, when a collection entitled *From Six Books* was brought out. The volume comprised selections from the earlier volumes as well as new poems written between 1921 and 1938 but never published. There has been much speculation concerning the influence at work behind the scenes which brought this book into the light of day after Akhmatova's long silence. It was rumored that Svetlana Dzhugashvili, Stalin's daughter, had a hand in the affair; in other quarters the explanation ran that Yuri Tynyanov, Alisa Koonen, an actress of the Kamernyi Theater, and Vsevolod Vishnevski interceded in Akhmatova's behalf. During her eighteen-year eclipse as poet Akhmatova had succeeded in publishing two studies of Pushkin (one in 1933, another in 1936) and a few translations (including Rubens' letters in 1933).

During the Second World War the pages of Soviet journals and newspapers were still open to Anna Akhmatova. Her poem "Courage," published in 1942, is a passionate appeal not only for defense of Russia against the enemy but also for salvation of the Russian tongue, the national literary language, which journalistic and propaganda abuse and the burning out of their folklore from the peasants' memories have bled white:

> To die of a bullet is nothing to dread,
> To find you are roofless is easy to bear;
> And all is endured, O great language we love:
> It is you, Russian tongue, we must save, and we swear
> We will give you unstained to the sons of our sons.[21]

Other wartime poems by Akhmatova, from which the following lines are taken, appeared in the journal *Znamya* in 1945:

> And you, my friends, the eager and the brave,
> I'll mourn you not, though a charmed life I bear,
> Nor stand, a weeping willow, o'er your grave,
> But shout your names for all the world to hear.
> But what are names? I shut the register.
> Down on our knees! A lurid light pours down.
> The men of Leningrad in serried ranks appear,
> The living with the dead, for both are Glory's own.[22]

In a resolution of the Central Committee of the All-Union Communist Party, issued on August 14, 1946, Akhmatova was described as "a typical exponent of the empty ... poetry alien to our people":

Her verses, shot through with a spirit of pessimism and depression, expressing the tastes of the old *salon* poetry jelled in postures of bourgeois aristocratic aestheticism and decadence—"art for art's sake" ... are a detriment in the matter of bringing up our young people and cannot be tolerated in Soviet literature.[23]

She bowed to the inevitable. In 1950 a few labored verses, from a cycle of poems entitled "Hail Peace!" appeared in the popular magazine *Ogonyok*. These lines speak for themselves:

> Where Stalin is, there's freedom,
> Peace and earth's majesty.[24]

OSIP MANDEL'SHTAM (1891- ?)

Fidelity to the principles of Acmeism, which he set forth in one of the manifestoes of the school,[25] marked the poetry of Osip Mandel'shtam throughout his career. In 1929, during the period of Akhmatova's silence, a Soviet critic referred to Mandel'shtam as the "last representative of Acmeism in Soviet Russia."[26] Thoroughly schooled in classical and European art, he wrote poetry for the few. Among his nineteenth-century predecessors he particularly admired Batyushkov, Zhukovski and Boratynski (of the *Poslednii poet* [Last Poet] period). One of Mandel'shtam's last published poems, in 1932, was a curious tribute to Batyushkov:

> Like a roué with a magic cane,
> Tender Batyushkov lives with me.
> He strides in poplars out beyond the bridge,
> Smells a rose and sings of Daphne.
> Never for a moment believing in a separation,
> I think I bowed to him.
> His cold hand in its light-colored glove
> I press with feverish envy.
> He smiled. I said, "Thanks,"
> And found no words in my embarrassment;
> No one has such curves of sound,
> And never such speech of waves . . .
> Our torment and our wealth,
> A stutterer, he brought with him
> A noise of verses and a bell of brotherhood,
> And a harmonious shower of tears.[27] *

In his first book, *Stone* (1913), Mandel'shtam displayed his predilection for the past and his gift for conjuring it up like a mirage through the surface of the present.

His treatment of the world is similar to that of Gumilyov and Akhmatova in its concreteness and solidity except that he often veils the outlines of objects with a mist or dusk which—not without its own substance—lends the real a mysterious quality. In the poem entitled "The Shell" he writes:

> It may be that you need me not,
> Night; from the deep of the world,
> Like a shell without pearls,
> I have been cast on your shore.
> . . . .
> You will lie down on the sand beside it,
> Clothe it in your vestment;
> You will link with it inextricably
> The vast bell of the swells;
> And the walls of the fragile shell—
> Like the house of an uninhabited heart—
> You will fill with the whispering of the foam,
> With fog, wind and rain.[28]

---

* The translator has not undertaken a rhymed translation of Mandel'shtam's poetry because of the difficulty of the material.

In his *St. Petersburg Winters,* Georgi Ivanov recalls that when listening to Mandel'shtam read his poems, he experienced "a sort of shiver, a fear, an excitement, as though in the presence of the supernatural. Never at any other time have I witnessed such an unparallelled manifestation of the very essence of poetry as in that reading, and in that man."[29]

His world is full of pain, and even everyday objects radiate grief and fear:

> Inexpressible sorrow
> Opened two enormous eyes;
> The flower vase awakened
> And spilled its crystal.[30]

One of his deepest sorrows stemmed from the falling apart of the triad of beliefs around which the Russian Orthodox Church has historically centered: God is love, God is the Church, God is ritual.

> What shall I do with the wounded bird?
> The firmament is silent, is dead.
> From the belfry veiled in mist
> Someone has removed the bells.[31]

Mandel'shtam loved the Middle Ages as a time when the trinity of belief was still inalterable in the mind of man:

> Fair is the temple bathing in the sea,
> And its forty windows are a triumph of light,[32]

he writes of the Cathedral of St. Sophia, and of Notre Dame:

> The more often I thought: out of an evil weight
> I too shall some day create beauty.[33]

Of men who have not yet lost faith in God but who reject the Church and its ritual, he says in "The Lutheran":

> And so I thought: no need to speechify,
> We are not prophets, not even precursors,
> We do not love paradise, we are not afraid of hell,
> And in the dull light of noon we burn like candles.[34]

Mandel'shtam's impressions of the First World War and the Russian Revolution are recorded in *Tristia* (1922) and in *Poems* (1928), a collection containing his poetry written from 1921 to 1925 as well as almost all his earlier work.

After the Revolution he became a spiritual *émigré* staring with horror at the fragments of the shattered past in a country of death:

> Blood the builder gushes forth
> From all earthly things.[35]

In "Twilight of Freedom," written during the Civil War, he says:

> Let us celebrate the fateful burden
> Which the leader of the people assumes with tears.
> . . . .
> Whoever has a heart must hear, O Time,
> Your ship foundering and sinking.[36]

In Mandel'shtam's eyes, the war and the revolution had meant an end of compassion and love.

> Let them say: love is wingèd,
> Death is one hundred times more wingèd still.
> The soul is still possessed by struggle,
> But our lips fly to death.[37]

And again, in 1920:

> A man dies, the warmed sand cools,
> And yesterday's sun is borne past on a black stretcher.[38]

Another frequent theme in *Tristia* is fear for a culture which is balanced on the brink of an abyss. Mandel'shtam communicates this fear to his very landscapes:

> And the spiky cathedrals of the mad cliffs
> Hang in the air, in which are wool and silence.[39]

Like Voloshin, Mandel'shtam turned to Russian history to discover in the calamities of the distant past the pattern of sufferings by which the country, in the throes of another upheaval, would be plagued. But whereas Voloshin was mainly concerned with the philosophy of history, Mandel'shtam was interested in the effect of the historical process on man's inner world.

To him history is a succession of periodically recurring cycles; everything changes, everything is in flux, yet everything repeats and falls back into place.

> Oh meager foundation of our lives!
> The language of joy is all too poor.
> Everything was once, everything will be repeated,
> And only the moment of recognition is sweet.[40]

As for his own time:

> The buds will swell again,
> The flow of greenery will spill,
> But your spine has been broken,
> My beautiful, pitiful century![41]

It was an era which annihilated the human personality:

> Time files me down, like a coin,
> And I am no longer adequate unto myself.[42]

At times the black pessimism of Mandel'shtam's poetry is dispelled by a sudden outburst of bright, refreshing gaiety and health, in his last poems as well as in his first volume of 1913. The following lines appeared in the periodical *Novyi mir* [New World] in 1932:

> Where bathhouses, paperweaveries,
> And the broadest of green gardens lie,
> On the Moscow River there is a lightspeakery,
> With ripples of rest, culture and water.
> . . . .
> The River Oka has sprained an eyelid,
> That is why there is a breeze on the Moscow River.
> Sister Klyaz'ma* has a bent eyelash,
> That is why a duck is swimming on the Yauza River.[43]

---

* Another river.

These sudden flashes of playful happiness are infrequent and usually occur when Mandel'shtam turns to nature, forgetting man and human history, to study the "nervous system" of the green world. "The tempo of modern times, their velocity, is measured not by the subway or the skyscraper, but by the gay little blades of grass which force their way through city pavements,"[44] he wrote.

From the mid-1920's Mandel'shtam's new published work consisted mainly of prose. *The Sound of the Time* (1925) is a small volume of autobiographical sketches, later incorporated in *The Egyptian Stamp*, which was published in 1928.

His prose is as imaginative and distinctive as his poetry. A character in the sketch "The Royal Mantle of the Law" says:

Then he revealed to me the somnambulistic region in which he lived. The most important feature of this region was the abyss which had formed where Russia had been. The Black Sea now reached all the way up to the Neva. Its waves, of the thickness of tar, licked the marble slabs of St. Isaac's Cathedral and broke into black foam on the steps of the Senate. Along this waste of space, somewhere between Kursk and Sevastopol', like a lifebuoy, floats the royal mantle of the law.[45]

The best of these pieces—really a poem in prose—is "The Egyptian Stamp," in the volume of the same name. It is a mercilessly honest and intensely compassionate story of an intellectual, Parnok, who has been hounded and debased by the Communist system; but pathetic, ill-adjusted and impractical as he is, he has inner reserves of nobility and capacity for self-sacrifice. He represents those among the intelligentsia who chose to maintain their moral standards at the price of social degradation. In his portrayal Mandel'shtam achieves a remarkable synthesis of crystal-clear, clairvoyant lyricism and grotesque, morbid comedy.

It is frightening to think that our life is a tale without a plot or a hero, made up of emptiness and glass, of the hot babble of retreats only, of St. Petersburg influenza delirium,[46]

observes the narrator, who at times seems to be a counterpart of Parnok, although he says, "Lord! Don't make me like Parnok! Give me the strength to be different from him!"[47]

Postrevolutionary Russia as described by Mandel'shtam in this story appears to be suffering from brain fever. Inanimate objects seem to be running a temperature; they are all pleasurably excited and seriously ill. "A bird's bloodshot eye sees the world in its own way."[48]

Mandel'shtam's personal life was unhappy. Soviet literary critics persecuted him. After 1933 his work ceased to appear in print, and it is known that he spent some time in a concentration camp. According to one report, he died shortly after his release; according to another he perished in the Jewish ghetto of one of the small Russian towns occupied by the Germans during the war.

Mandel'shtam has passed along the outer edge of Russian literature, like a shadow or a phantom, but he has exerted a tremendous influence on the development of Russian culture. The work of Pasternak is directly descended from Mandel'shtam's.

OTHERS

Sergei Mitrofanovich Gorodetski (1884 -   ) made a brave beginning as a Symbolist poet. In 1912 he repudiated Symbolism and joined Gumilyov in establishing the Acmeist school. Not long after the Revolution he joined the Communist Party. When Gumilyov was executed, Gorodetski quickly disavowed any connection with the Acmeists.

He had already petered out as a poet. His two volumes of verse, *The Sickle*, 1921, and *Scrapped World* [*Mirolom*], 1923, resemble a hurriedly gotten up exhibition of scenes in garish colors intended to idealize the life of Soviet workers and peasants. His prose collection *Scarlet Cyclone*, 1918, is no better. It is hard to believe that the author is the same Gorodetski who wrote the poems in his volume *Spring Corn* [*Yar'*] of 1907 and the remarkable philosophic fairytale "Jungle of Anger."

Now and then in the 1920's when the poet forsook propaganda, he still sounded like his former self, as in lines from a poem dedicated to Blok:

> There was the usual Russian road
> Whose bumps and ruts before you spread,

> The driver urging on his nag,
> The thin wires singing overhead.
>
> . . . .
>
> But do you know the seeds you sowed
> In us are germinating fast,
> And that a new and freer song
> Will ring on Russia's plains at last?[49]

Mikhail Kuzmin (1875-1935?), whose "Clarism," the pursuit of "beautiful clarity," was the forerunner of Acmeism and who was associated with Gumilyov's Poets' Guild in its early days, continued to write and publish for a few years after the revolution. There was no pronounced change except that the earlier intellectual sybarite—a feast in the face of death was the gist of his prerevolutionary work—showed himself sobered and more deeply interested in religion.

In "Vagrant's Evening," Kuzmin is concerned with the fate of those pauperized by the revolution:

> The tiny beads of the rain
> Slide down their dangling threads;
> My coat whips like a sail
> As spindle-legged I tread . . .
> Is a merrily blazing stove
> A mirage in this dreadful town?
> What's happened, what's happened, Lord,
> That there's not a place to lie down?
>
> . . . .
>
> Fain would I shut my eyes
> On a world grown sad and thin.
> Will there never be light again,
> Nor a house that will take me in?[50]

In the same poem:

> The mind's white vapors heal.
> I am ready to go once more
> When the Te Deum's notes
> Plaintive above me soar.[51]

In 1929, after a silence of years, Kuzmin brought out his last volume of verse entitled *The Trout Breaks the Ice*.

Vladimir Narbut (1888- ?) and Mikhail Zenkevich represented the left wing of the Acmeist movement. Narbut joined the Communist Party in the Ukraine during the Civil War, then went to Moscow, where he was in charge of the publishing house *Zemlya i fabrika* (Land and Factory). In the early 1920's he published several small books of verse, including *In Pillars of Fire*, 1920, and *The Soviet Land*, 1921. Two recurrent themes run through these poems—the necessity of learning to speak the language of the present and concern for the intellectuals who chose to serve the revolution. Lines from "October" read:

> The gusts of wind are a song of fear
> Beating against the window pane.
> October, how can your way be clear
> When the sky is awash with a crimson rain?
> . . . .
> Lice in our overcoats, and yet
> Faith in the heart. . . . The wagons sway.
> Whether by shot or bayonet,
> Death's sure to take us on the way.[52]

Narbut's forebodings were justified in his personal life. In 1928 the poet was expelled from the Communist Party and prohibited from occupying an executive position in Soviet publishing houses.

After a prolonged silence Narbut again appeared in print with a few poems in periodicals.[53] At this period he resorted to a bald physiological approach. No doubt as a result of the dreadful famine with which the Ukraine was stricken in the thirties and by means of which the Party deliberately condemned the recalcitrant to starvation or semi-starvation, Narbut, born in the Ukraine, was obsessed by one image, that of the hungry man who greedily, ferociously, and rather repulsively satisfies his hunger.

It is rumored that Narbut was arrested in 1937 or 1938.

Mikhail Zenkevich (1888-), one of the original Acmeist group, has found it possible to maintain a place for himself, however modest, in Soviet literature without doing violence to his talent, also modest. If he has not won official favor, he has apparently at least enjoyed forbearance.

Zenkevich accepted the revolution as inevitable:

> I can bear anything I must,
> And for this thing alone I pray:
> That my wolf's appetite for life
> May forever howl away.[54]

Without idealizing the revolution Zenkevich wrote two truthful and original poems about it, *Ploughland of Tanks*, 1921,[55] and "Wake for Chapayev," 1925.[56] In the first, he looks upon the catastrophe of war as having ploughed the field for the harvest of the future. To ancient Russia, work on the land and fighting had been merely different forms of the labor exacted of the men, but after several centuries of a settled and peaceful existence this concept was forgotten. In "Wake for Chapayev" Zenkevich develops the same idea, arguing that the Russian peasant rejoiced in the Civil War as a revival of the bloodthirsty bellicose traditions which had lain dormant in his soul for centuries but which were too deep-rooted to have lost their potency.

New poems by Zenkevich continued to appear occasionally during the twenties and thirties, still in his former Acmeist manner. The relish for the physical texture of things, sensation, the physiological, elemental forces, filth and violence, murder and death—which in his earliest work had made the prehistoric life of man all but palpable—remained.

In "Steer in the Slaughter House," for instance, Zenkevich treats capital punishment and the laws sanctioning it as deriving directly from the bestial in human nature:

> The balking beast was dragged in at rope's end,
> And bloody hands pushed at its heaving flanks.
> The iron rack looked like the guillotine,
> And the black floor like a black scaffold's planks.[57]

And the pessimism that Zenkevich had once displayed in representing man as pathetically weak and helpless against the forces of nature extended to daily life, disorganized under the Bolshevik regime until it had become a systematic torture. In "Dawn on Myasnitskaya Street" he writes:

> Is it my fault that the cook was charred,
> Like a crashed pilot, by an exploding stove,

> That the mice at the molding are gnawing hard,
> And a seamstress killed herself on the floor above?
> They are nothing to me. But it hurts to hear
> This constant ringing inside my head,
> As though I held to my tortured ear
> A ghostly telephone, humming but dead.
> No use shouting "Hello!" I am quite alone.
> The wind and I have held converse before,
> And I hardly dare to expect the dawn
> To send an ambulance to my lonely door.[58]

Although Zenkevich continued to publish his own work (a volume of *Selected Poems* was brought out in 1933, and another book in 1937), he has evidently devoted much of his time to translating and editing since the late 1920's.

Except for a little book of verses in the nature of schoolboy exercises, Vsevolod Rozhdestvenski (1895-   ) first appeared in print after the revolution. The volumes published during the 1920's —*Summer,* 1921, *The Golden Spindle,* 1921, *The Big Bear,* 1926, and *Garden of Granite, 1929*—showed the strong influence of Aleksandr Grin as well as of his older fellow-Acmeists. With the book of lyrics written from 1929 to 1932, *Earth's Heart,* 1932, which touched upon "socialist construction" under the First Five-Year Plan, Rozhdestvenski began to ingratiate himself with the Bolsheviks. This collection and his subsequent work often give the impression that he is steering a safe course by confining himself to descriptions of nature. His volume *Selected Poems* was published in 1936, and *Window on a Garden* in 1939. In them, as before, he painted landscapes with deep feeling and considerable felicity:

> Rest from your travels, stranger, on this slope,
> Where far below you sways the azure brine.
> There Theodosia lies—an empty cup,
> With a faint fragrance still of Attic wine.[59]

Rozhdestvenski's verse is very musical, but it not infrequently descends to the level of a popular love song.

He has also written many stories for children. Like Zenkevich, Rozhdestvenski established a reputation as a translator.

Other Acmeists who left Russia after the revolution and whose work mainly belongs to émigré literature include Georgi Ivanov, Georgi Adamovich and Nikolai Otsup.

3. Gorki and the Realists

MAXIM GORKI
(pseudonym of Aleksei M. Peshkov, 1868-1936)

Gorki, apotheosized by Soviet critics as the founding father of proletarian and Soviet literature, in point of fact belongs wholly to the prerevolutionary period of Russian literature, in spirit if not chronologically, and his later writings and efforts in behalf of other writers are too well known to require more than enumeration.

Gorki's immediate attitude toward the Bolshevik role in 1917 was one of hostility. He decried the debasement of culture and the countenancing or encouragement of bestiality ("Men-beasts have broken loose from the chain of culture, have torn its fine vestments")[1] and bluntly accused the revolutionary leaders of "reckless demagogy":[2]

Lenin, Trotsky and their followers have already succumbed to the corrupting poison of power, as witness their shameful attitude toward freedom of speech and of the individual and the sum total of the rights democracy fought for.[3]

"The great joy of freedom must not be besmirched by crimes against the individual, or we will be murdering freedom with our hands."[4]

Nonetheless his sympathies were with the revolutionary cause, and he appealed to the intelligentsia to join forces with the government against the counterrevolutionary forces. He himself made valiant efforts to rescue Russian literature by alleviating the situation of writers. He organized a publishing project, state supported, which provided great numbers of writers and scholars with the means of survival in translating and editorial work. He interceded in behalf of those who had incurred official displeasure, and assisted promising young writers and their organizations.

In 1921, however, Gorki left Russia, ostensibly because of tuberculosis. When he returned permanently in 1929 he was received with official honors and great fanfare. Thereafter, as a creative writer, Gorki lived on his reputation.

He continued to work on *The Life of Klim Samgin*, publication of which had begun in the Soviet Union before his return. It is a very long and very tiresome novel of four volumes, the last remaining unfinished.[5] It was intended as a chronicle of the development of Russian society, particularly the intelligentsia, from the end of the 1870's to 1917. Lines from one of Gorki's own poems might well have served as epigraph:

> Little thoughts and stolen ones at that,
> Words that are the fashion of the day—
> Soft they crawl along the edge of life,
> Futile little people, dull and gray.[6]

Two of the new plays which Gorki wrote after his return, *Yegor Bulychov and Others* (1933) and *Dostigayev and Others* (1934), deal with the merchant class on the eve of the Revolution. Bulychov is a more moderate Foma Gordeyev (the hero of Gorki's best novel of the same name), who has devoted himself to moneymaking and suppressed his inner rebellion and who, dying as the revolution begins, realizes that he has wasted his life "on the wrong street."[7] *Dostigayev and Others* may be regarded loosely as a sequel. The third play of the trilogy, *Somov and Others*, was not published until 1941, five years after the author's death.

Although as a rule Gorki was brilliantly successful in portraying the decline of the merchant class, as in *Foma Gordeyev*, and although *Yegor Bulychov and Others* still bears traces of the old power, the most striking feature of these new plays—as well as of all his major work after his return to the U.S.S.R.—is that Gorki is turned wholly to the past. He shunned a representation of the Soviet scene, in repetition of his practice during the immediate postrevolutionary period when in his only major nonjournalistic publication, *Reminiscences of Lev Tolstoi* (1919),[8] he drew on materials of earlier years.

As before, he was active as a publicist and editor. In 1929 he founded the review *Nashi dostizheniya* [Our Achievements], which existed for several years and then quietly folded up. He edited the literary almanacs named *God XVII* [The Seventeenth Year], *God XVIII* [The Eighteenth Year], and so forth. In the 1930's Gorki encouraged a number of writers to work up the history of various plants and factories,[9] and edited jointly with Averbakh and Firin a compilation of articles about the Belomor-Baltic Canal (1934),[10] and with K. Gorbunov and S. Luzgin a collection of articles on the Bolshevo community of juvenile delinquents (1936).[11] He was also a prolific writer of newspaper articles and literary criticism, which, in contrast to his vivid and objective journalism in the early years of the revolution, suffer from the writer's developing intellectual arteriosclerosis. Even so, a debt of gratitude is due Gorki in his role of archpresbyter of postrevolutionary literature.

Of the other major prerevolutionary realist writers associated with Gorki in the group known at the turn of the century as the *Znaniye* school (from the name of the publishing house *Znaniye* [Knowledge] under Gorki's control), none made any contribution to Soviet literature. Ivan Bunin and Aleksandr Kuprin left Russia very soon after the revolution. Leonid Andreyev had lived in Finland for years before 1917, and died there in 1919. The lesser writers Ivan Shmelyov, Yevgeni Chirikov and Sergei Gusev-Orenburgski emigrated as opportunity offered. Of those who remained, only Aleksandr Serafimovich achieved prominence under the Soviet regime. His work will be discussed elsewhere.

V. V. VERESAYEV
(pseudonym of Vikenti V. Smidovich, 1867-1945)

An early member of the *Znaniye* group, Veresayev belongs to those of whom the critic Voronski said, "Many recognized writers discovered that the revolution was too much for them."[12] Long known as a fictional historian of the Russian intelligentsia, Veresayev continued his chronicle with the novel *In a Blind Alley* (1922), which deals with the ineffectiveness, depression and vacillation of the liberals after 1917. The scholar and democrat Sartanov and his daughter Katya, a fine and sincere girl, a Menshevik, are unable to acquiesce in the terrorism and violence which the Bolshevik Leonid, Sartanov's nephew, and the other daughter Vera justify as necessary for the cause.[13]

In *The Sisters,* written from 1928 to 1931, a similar clash occurs between two Communist sisters over the methods employed in the enforced collectivization of agriculture.[14]

One of Veresayev's last pieces of fiction—he wrote almost none after *The Sisters*—was the remarkable story "Isanka" of 1928, in which Veresayev conscientiously records a not uncommon phenomenon among Soviet young people of the time and of later years. Isanka, a university student from the old intellectual milieu and thus at best merely tolerated under the new regime, holds her head high and, without departing from her principles or currying favor, tries to help in cultivating the good aspects of Soviet life. Rejecting dialectical materialism, which, like all Soviet students, she is compelled to study, she intuitively evolves a pantheistic philosophy of her own. The character of Isanka is not invented; it is true to life and drawn in the round.

Walking along the seashore with Bor'ka Chertov—the clever and ingenious "son of a landowner" who has shipped as a seaman in the merchant marine in order to transform himself into a proletarian and gain admission to a Soviet university but has returned with a dislike of the West and a desire to serve Russia in all sincerity—Isanka sees a sea gull soaring up into the sky and a cascade of naive pantheistic associations tumbles through her mind:

> That sea gull, just now, right there, behind that cliff, sprang into being out of all the dead things around us—the waves of the sea, the drift on the shore, the gleam of sunlight. It sprang into being alive and free, shook off inertia, and flew off as it liked, where it liked—to the left, up, down, across the wind and the waves. As though millions of years of evolution were fused into a single instant. I jumped up, waved my arms—I felt that I too, I too am not stone, not a wave, that I am free, like that sea gull—so free, so unhampered, in its living flight! It was an amazing sensation—as though I were just born, in some very special way.[15]

Bor'ka is a good fellow, but a sailor's life has taught him a coarse and uncomplicated attitude toward women, and, captive to dialectical materialism, he misunderstands Isanka's meaning. In the end she yields to his passion.

> Bor'ka was struck by the new, exceptional beauty of her face. Her lips were resolutely pressed together, her huge eyes shone with a concentrated light that came from within.[16]

Isanka is a frank, proud girl unafraid of gossip, but she feels the lack of emotion, of real love, in her relations with Bor'ka and resolutely puts an end to them: "Borya! Darling! I haven't had any peace since yesterday! I am so ashamed! I don't really know of what! But I am ashamed, so ashamed!"[17] Bor'ka seeks solace in the arms of more complaisant girls but finds no happiness and finally comes, too late, to an understanding of Isanka's purifying pantheistic philosophy.

The sex life of Soviet youth during the time of the "free-love" fetish was described by many writers, but none surpassed Veresayev in accuracy of observation. And none brought out more clearly than he—with his physician's knowledge of the most intimate problems of the young—the morally clean and healthy instincts which often lay at the bottom of their resistance to attempts to foist dialectical materialism upon them.

After *The Sisters*, in which he had ventured to suggest that the promptings of common sense and human kindness were a more reliable guide to action than Party instructions even in carrying out Party policy, Veresayev abandoned fiction. He had many strings to his bow. Classical scholar and literary historian as well as novelist and physician, he resumed translating and the writing of biographical studies and his memoirs. To his four-volume work *Pushkin in Life*, 1926-1927, based on a painstaking compilation of accounts of Pushkin's contemporaries, Veresayev added *Gogol in Life*, 1933.

His best-known translations from the Greek are of Homer and of Hesiod's *Works and Days*.

Veresayev's memoirs published in the 1920's have the same ring of scrupulous veracity as has his fiction;[18] but in "Uninvented Tales of the Past," which appeared in 1940,[19] one feels that a frightened old man is falsifying in self-defense.

MIKHAIL ARTSYBASHEV (1878-1927)

The prerevolutionary writer Artsybashev gained in stature after 1917. His earlier novels dealing with sexual problems—including *Sanin* (1907), *The Woman Who Stood Between* and *Breaking Point* [*U poslednei cherty*, 1912]—had brought him great notoriety and as great reprobation. It is true that in these novels there is a racy, ostentatious sexiness which robs them of esthetic value. At the same time most critics, engrossed in accusing Artsybashev of vulgarity and pornography, have tended to deny his genuine talent and to overlook the fact that his sometimes offensive naturalistic descriptions are accompanied by keen psychological insight and sociological analysis.

The Russian Revolution sobered Artsybashev into a reappraisal of the doctrine of sexual license as the ultimate good, which had been expressed through Sanin. The short novel *The Dikii Family*, written during 1917-1918 but not published until 1923, when Artsybashev was an émigré, is graver and deeper than his earlier work, and is indeed one of the gems of postrevolutionary Russian literature. Despite the fact that Artsybashev's work was taboo in the U.S.S.R. and that *The Dikii Family* was published only abroad (it is now a bibliographic rarity), its influence has been apparent in Soviet writing. For example, the Grigori-Anis'ya-Stepan triangle in Sholokhov's *Silent Don* is most certainly a projection of Artsybashev's Klim-Zakhar-Glafira triangle.

The setting is that of peasant and merchant Russia—the common people for whose sake poets suffered and revolutionaries laid down their lives, in utter ignorance of what the people were really like. Klim Dikii, a harsh, thrifty money-grubber, is head of the patriarchal Dikii family. His wife Glafira, at the insistence of her parents, has married him not out of love but for his possessions, in accordance with the order of things sanctioned by centuries of custom. Glafira and Zakhar, Klim's brother, drawn together by a strong and healthy physical attraction, fall in love. When Klim discovers that Glafira is unfaithful to him, he thrashes her within an inch of her life, and the brothers set to with their fists in a cruel fight. Zakhar leaves the home of his fathers, where Klim is master. Everyone takes

Klim's side. They look on Glafira as a "whore," for whom killing is too good, and on Zakhar as a criminal who has defiled his brother's sacred property. Not long afterwards Klim is murdered, and Zakhar is suspected.

Dukhovetski, counsel for the defense, a Social Revolutionary and a man of integrity who is concerned for the welfare of the people, is convinced that Zakhar is innocent, but the court finds him guilty and sentences him to hard labor. Dukhovetski advises Zakhar's mother to appeal the case and is astounded by the old woman's refusal. In her eyes Zakhar is guilty no matter who killed Klim. He must pay for his misdeeds. And yet Dukhovetski senses that she loves Zakhar more than she had Klim. In the end Dukhovetski discovers that one of the jurors, a solid merchant with all the prejudices of his class, was aware even before the trial that Klim met his death at the hands of the youngest brother, Pet'ka, a moron who himself had an eye on Glafira. In the merchant's opinion too, however, Zakhar must be punished, as a lesson to others. He has violated the sacrament of marriage and—what is worse—has committed adultery with his brother's wife. As for the question who actually killed Klim—that is immaterial. Dukhovetski is also struck by the fact that both Zakhar and Glafira have resigned themselves to their fate. A flare-up of passion had made them human beings for a brief moment; but as soon as it was over, they once more submitted to the laws and customs of their patriarchal society.

This resignation destroys Dukhovetski's revolutionary illusions. The coming revolution, for which, as a party member, he has been working diligently,

suddenly appeared to him in another light, blurred and painful, as though tinged with blood. He looked down at the muddy road flowing past and thought: "No, we can't understand them! . . . We speak different languages! Revenge? Yes, they will take their revenge and shed streams of blood, and then they will once more endure . . . any punishment, any calamity, any disaster. . . ." [20]

For Dukhovetski the Russian people has become as a mob of savages, whose ideal is anarchic freedom, freedom to rob and rape, and who are at the same time subconsciously aware that they will have to pay for their bloody feast by decades of new suffering and a new slavery.

2

Poets in the Ascendant

4. *The Futurists*

The Russian writers who had caught fire from the sparks of Western European Futurism had a revolutionary program for literature in readiness for 1917. They joined the Italian Futurists in attempting to discard all the culture of the past and to devise revolutionary art forms in keeping with the new age of machinery and speed.

The most important of the several groups in Russia, the Cubo-Futurists, issued their literary manifesto in 1922. Under the title "A Slap in the Face of Public Taste," it called for "throwing Pushkin, Dostoyevski and Tolstoi overboard from the steamship of modernity."

Politically, however, the Russian Futurists were at odds with the authoritarian, militarist views of the spokesman of the Italian movement, Marinetti. In their destructive rebellion against the traditional, the majority of the Cubo-Futurists were in 1917 prepared to make common cause with Communism.

The outstanding writers of the Cubo-Futurist group in the early Soviet years were Khlebnikov, Mayakovski, Kemenski, Kruchonykh, and David Burlyuk.

VIKTOR KHLEBNIKOV (1885-1922)

Some literary critics regard Khlebnikov as a genius, others as a charlatan or megalomaniac, a case for psychiatric rather than literary study. In the opinion of Yuri Tynyanov, Khlebnikov originated "undersurface literature," a "deeper" poetry of fresh, uncommon vision,[1] and Roman Jakobson has credited him with a re-appraisal of values in Russian poetry.

Khlebnikov divided Russian words into two categories, the so-called functional words and the purified or "distilled" words. Words, in the course of time, undergo semantic changes. Eventually, their meaning calcifies, and they become more or less permanent symbols of certain things. These words form the large "functional" category in our vocabulary. On the other hand, a word is "distilled" and made "pure" when, through the work of "restoration or excavation," its original meaning is disclosed. Khlebnikov described the purified word as "the enemy of the literary petrification of language."[2]

Roman Jakobson wrote on this subject:

Only against a familiar background can the unfamiliar be perceived and its impact felt. . . .

Form enfolds and absorbs substance, becomes stereotyped, then lifeless. An influx of new material, of fresh elements from practical language, is needed to make the irrational poetic structures effective again and again—that is, enjoyable, startling, provocative.[3]

Imagine an old painting so covered with dirt and varnish that the image has almost disappeared. When these layers are removed, we see it in its original beauty. What Khlebnikov did with language was, in a sense, restoration work. But he was also a creative artist endowed with an extraordinary imagination, and a poet of great originality.

"Khlebnikov works on words like a mole, and he has bored underground passages into the future for a whole century ahead,"[4] said Osip Mandel'shtam.

In search of original and striking effects, he experimented endlessly with imagery, metaphor and simile, and prosodic systems, restoring old forms and producing new (Khlebnikov devised a whole system of neologisms), cocking an extremely sensitive ear toward folklore and ancient Russian poetry and often using them in combination with modern forms. He was one of the greatest masters of syncopated verse.

Experiments conducted on such an immense scale inevitably produced failures along with the outstanding successes. Until the latter have been properly sifted out, it will be impossible to evaluate Khlebnikov's contribution objectively. The task, brilliantly begun by Jakobson, is still unfinished.

Jakobson is fascinated by Khlebnikov's formal achievements and sees abstract word-patterning as the essence of Khlebnikov's poetry. "In many instances," he says, "we can see how words in Khlebnikov's poems lose first their referent, then their inner and finally even their outer form."[5]

However important and valuable Khlebnikov's experimentation with word, image and meter may be, it is only one aspect of the poet who vibrantly responded to the burning issues of his time. Khlebnikov moved from his laboratory to the human scene, and his postrevolutionary verse reflects the battle within himself between the friend and the foe of the Revolution. Eventually, he turned resolutely against the new order. Jakobson wrote in his essay "On the Generation That Squandered Its Poets" of

Gumilyov's ... execution, Blok's ... long spiritual and physical agony and his death, Khlebnikov's ... cruel privations and atrociously painful end, the premeditated suicides of Yesenin ... and Mayakovski. ... Thus, in the twenties of this century, at the ages of thirty to forty, perished the poets who inspired our generation, every one of them with a sense of hopelessness unbearably drawn-out and acute. Not only those who were killed or took their own lives but Blok and Khlebnikov on their sickbeds, too, were casualties.[6]

A Night in a Foxhole, expressing horror of death, is the first of Khlebnikov's "human" poems after the Revolution.[7] He had at first interpreted the revolution as the victory of peace over war, of life over death, but soon expressed a different attitude, as in the poem "Refusal" (1922):

> I find it more agreeable
> To contemplate the stars
> Than to sign a death warrant.
> I find it more agreeable
> To listen to the flowers
> Whisper "It is he!"
> When I walk through the gardens
> Than to stroke the rifles
> That are to kill those who wish
> To take my life.
> That is why I shall never—
> No, never—
> Become a ruler.[8]

In "Raid at Night," one of his best poems, there is hardly a trace of experimentation with form—it is clear, simple, completely intelligible, and obviously the work of a great master of verse. There is practically no description of the characters; the poem is almost entirely dialogue. A squad of "revolutionary good fellows" is hunting White game. In the first episode we see an old woman who suddenly loses her son, and the courageous man dying with dignity, and the churlish, power-drunk "good fellow" of a revolutionary in whom the killer has stirred.

> "Off to work—
> Do not shirk,
> Grab your guns!"
> . . . . .
> "Mother, hey, mother!
> Mother, you hear?
> Tell us outright—
> Are you hiding a White?
> The Soviet meets later tonight."
> "I am old, you see.
> Red or White
> Is the same to me.
> Bone is white,
> And my hair is white as can be.
> I am a mother."
> . . . . .
> "Old woman, look away.
> We will give the White bastard

A taste of the gun!"
"What! My son?"
"Take off your shirt, another man can use it,
You can go naked to your grave,
There are no ladies there.
Off with your pants,
And turn around . . ."
"Goodbye, Mamma,
Blow out the candle on my desk."
. . . .
"Goodbye, you fool. And thanks
For your bullet."
"Why, you . . . In the name of the people!"
Tra-ta-ta-ta . . .
Ta. . . .[9]

The idea occurs to the "good fellows" that they cannot kill with impunity:

"Come on, gang,
Hit the bottle!
Comrades,
What's our next meeting place?
A common grave?"[10]

Like Blok, Khlebnikov had succumbed to the elemental power of the Revolution. "Raid at Night" is "the morning after."

With his abysmal lack of practical sense, Khlebnikov busied himself periodically with quixotic schemes for the future of mankind—from 1916 until after the November revolution of 1917 he tried to organize a society of "presidents of the earth," which would include the leading minds in the fields of science, technology, literature, and fine arts, and which would constitute an ideal "State of the Era"; at the same time he knew perfectly well that he was incapable of carrying through any practical plan, and that in matters of politics he was as helpless as a child. In *Zangezi* (1922) he wrote:

I am a butterfly, caught in a room
Men call the world. I can do no more
Than leave the dust from my beating wings
On its cold windows, like a prisoner's scrawl.[11]

In the utopian poem "Ladomir" he decries coercion, terror and capital punishment:

> Then let the pages of existence
> Be black with pestilential tales.
> The breath of fate dispels resistance,
> Freedom herself falters and fails.
> It is for you, O great of soul,
> To muzzle pestilence and plague.[12]

The hatred modern man keeps up in his soul as his prehistoric forebears kept up a fire must eventually lead him back to a savage state.

> I can foresee an equine freedom
> And equal rights for cows and bulls.[13]

And elsewhere:

> Within the chain of city squares
> Let them be shot upon the spot!
> The bride of all the ages bears
> The brand of hatred like a blot.[14]

In his long poem *Siniye kovy*, the word *"kovy"* stands for *okovy* (fetters), and they are "blue" (*sinye*) because they are decked out with noble words.

> Off with you, to search
> For the vanished sun![15]
>
> . . . .
> You hills, valleys and plains,
> Do you really want blue chains?[16]

Khlebnikov defined his dispute with Bolshevism as "the right to say 'but.'"

> In the log-cabin of events
> I see a window squarely cut—
> Glass to the sense,
> The pensive "but." [17]

Khlebnikov's language in "Blue Fetters" is difficult, and here, as elsewhere, much in his polemics with Communism still awaits deciphering.

His meaning is unequivocal, however, in *Zangezi*, which was published a few days after his death:

> I sank my nails into my flesh,
> I clutched my head between my hands,
> And all the while the swallow sang
> Of happy and untroubled lands.[18]

Khlebnikov's prose writing also changed after the Revolution. Here, too, he abandoned experimentation and turned away from nonrepresentational word play.

At first glance, Khlebnikov's prose sketches seem to be a jumble of unrelated, random drawings. In them there is a kind of unsullied naïveté, as though they were written by a child genius through whose eyes the horrors of the Revolution become all the more terrible. In "October on the Neva," written at the end of 1917 and the beginning of 1918, and in several untitled pieces of approximately the same time, he catches the very heartbeat of Petrograd during and immediately after the revolution:

All this in the days when mad dreams had invaded the city, when the soil-tiller and the steppe horseman fought over the dead city dweller, and Pugachov's laughter sounded from beyond the vernal mouth of the Volga. . . . The name of Jesus Christ, the name of Mohammed and of Buddha quivered in the fire like the fleece of a lamb offered up by me in sacrifice to the year nineteen eighteen.[19]

"The Crimson Sword" describes Moscow at the time when "the stallion of civil war, lowering his yellow teeth, tore at and ate the grass of people."[20] The inhabitants fled "as from a city of pestilence."[21]

You suddenly fled from the city to the quiet estate, to the green orchard where cherry and apple trees bloomed. . . . But even the peace of turtle doves was disturbed by single shots. Into this secluded country-seat a stone had fallen, and . . . troubled its quiet waters.[22]

There someone says, "I am happy as a nightingale in a cat's paws."[23]

Poets in the Ascendant

VLADIMIR MAYAKOVSKI (1894-1930)

Mayakovski was a revolutionary before he became a poet. In 1909 he was arrested in connection with the discovery of an illegal printing press. Being under age, he was released but kept under police surveillance. His first poems were written in a prison cell.

In 1911, Mayakovski enrolled in a school of painting and sculpture. There he met David Burlyuk, who prompted him to concentrate on poetry. His first poems appeared in the Cubo-Futurist anthology *A Slap in the Face of Public Taste* [*Poshchochina obshchestvennomu vkusu*] of 1912, which contained the literary manifesto of the same name.

In form, Mayakovski's poems were something entirely new in Russian literature. He used free stress and syncopated verse, and some of his meters have an astounding impact. The distinctive feature of his rhythmics lies in his original use of the metrical pause. Paradoxical as it may seem, his rhythms often come close to those of Orthodox religious chants, and he even borrowed much of his vocabulary and imagery from church ritual:

> To all of you
> Who are uppermost,
> You, icon-protected from fear or malice,
> Ceremoniously
> I propose a toast,
> And a skull full of verse
> I raise like a chalice.[24]

Mayakovski's poetry is singularly enriched by these borrowings. Ancient Russia blends happily with the new forms introduced under the influence of Apollinaire and Verhaeren.

Suprematism appears in Mayakovski's poetry in a still more crystallized form than in Belyi's writing; that is, mechanical suprematism only, for Mayakovski's poetry has nothing in common with cosmic suprematism. Mayakovski did for poetry what Malevich had done for painting. Malevich used cubes, triangles and ellipsoids to render a world in motion. Mayakovski prints his verse in a staggered pattern that gives the same feeling of speed.

Kornei Chukovski said that the early Mayakovski was "a poet of catastrophes and convulsions."[25] Maxim Gorki commented on the tragic essence of his art. It is true that Mayakovski was the poet of the big city of the industrial age, and that in his youth he saw it as an inferno. Holes in the pavement reminded him of a syphilitic's nose. The street lights were constellations of pain and grief.

Mayakovski was no believer in humility. To him, a poet was a prophet and must break into poetry and life like a rebel, a mutineer. The secret of Mayakovski's popularity and influence lies, above all, in his passionate protest against the enslavement of man. It was his tragedy as an artist and as a thinker that he never resolved the dilemma—present since long before the revolution—between freedom of the individual and collectivism, between the Marxist idea which his reason accepted and Bakunin who appealed to his heart. The critic P. S. Kogan and Mayakovski disliked each other intensely, but Kogan, who described him as an "anarchic individualist uncongenial to our Revolution,"[26] understood him better, perhaps, than anyone else.

Despite the predominance of civic motifs in Mayakovski's poetry after 1917, he was above all a lyric poet, and, here, he has nothing of the innovator. His lyricism is subtle and tender and in the old tradition of Russian poetry. In signing the Futurist manifesto he had agreed with those who felt that it was time to "throw Pushkin, Dostoyevski and Tolstoi overboard," but on May 26, 1924, speaking at a forum on literature and the theater, Mayakovski said:

... Anatoli Vasil'yevich [Lunacharski] reproaches [me] for lack of reverence toward the ancients—yet only a month ago, during work, when Brik started to read *Yevgeni Onegin*, which I know by heart, I could not tear myself away and listened to the end, and for two days afterwards lived under the spell.... And no doubt we shall hundreds and thousands of times return to such works of art—even at the instant when death throws its noose around our necks—to learn this utterly conscientious creative technique assuring both infinite satisfaction and perfect formulation of a heart-inspired thought.[27]

Unrequited love is the main theme of Mayakovski's lyric poetry, and even his long prerevolutionary poems on civic themes such as *Spine Flute*, 1915, *Man*, 1917, and particularly *A Cloud in Pants*, 1915, are laced, incongruously and miraculously, with lyric motifs of tragic love.

Even before the revolution Mayakovski was a believer in Marx, and in the poem *Man* had smashed the image of Christ against city pavements. Now, however, he had to smash Bakunin's image as well as Christ's. A born anarchist, a protagonist of the freedom of the individual, he deliberately stifled his natural inclinations in order to serve the new regime.

After the revolution Mayakovski branched out in four directions: propaganda posters, political lampoons, plays, and movie scripts.

His propaganda work brought to the fore a heavy-handed, prosaic quality that had always been present in his poems but had scarcely been noticed because of their striking metaphors, their compelling mood and the underlying dramatic tension. In the special-purpose political pamphlets the verse is weak on occasion, and the prosaisms become conspicuous. However novel and provocative at the time were the topical poems he churned up without end in response to his interpretation of the "social command," they seem now, when the issues are dead, merely doggerel tricked out in ingenious mechanical devices. At the end Mayakovski himself was well aware that he had squandered his talent. In his last long poem *At the Top of My Voice*, left unfinished at the time of his suicide in 1930, he wrote:

> And I'm
>   fed to the teeth
>   with agit-prop,*
> And I'd rather
>   toss off
>   love songs to you—
> there's more money in it
>   and it's pleasanter.
> But I've
>   suppressed
>   myself,
>   setting my foot
> on the throat
>   of my own song.[28]

The best-known of Mayakovski's postrevolutionary poems are

---
* An abbreviation of *agitatsiya i propaganda* (agitation and propaganda)

Vladimir Il'ich Lenin (1924), *It's Good!* (1927) and *At the Top of My Voice*.

The first of these, written immediately after Lenin's death, is a kind of political poster painted in words, and Lenin appears in it as a godlike superman of the industrial era. It must be said, however, that Mayakovski merely blew up some of Lenin's real traits—out of all proportion, to be sure. The author's faith in the coming world revolution is obviously sincere, and the poem's purpose was to bolster that faith in the popular mind, which had long since begun to doubt.

>   Lenin's
>   even now
>   most alive of all the living.
>   Our knowledge,
>   power
>   and weapon.[29]

Sten'ka Razin wanted to set Russia on fire, but Russia alone is not enough for Lenin. He wants the whole world:

>   Yesterday four,
>   Perforce we lay low.
>   We're four hundred today,
>   and tomorrow
>   we rise.
>   Today's
>   four hundred
>   to thousands will grow.
>   We'll rouse the world's workers
>   to capture the prize.[30]

Mayakovski's militant faith, the messianic religion of Marx and Lenin, is directed against Christianity, and primarily against the Orthodox Church. The fisherman says in *Mystery-Bouffe*, the first of his plays after the revolution:

>   No more prophets for us—
>   We're all Nazarenes![31]

Poets in the Ascendant

In the blasphemies of *Mystery-Bouffe*, the first variant of which was written in 1918 and the second, greatly expanded, in 1921, the old gods, battered and reviled, are offered in sacrifice to the new gods of steel.

It's Good! is not ordinary propaganda. Lunacharski had grounds for saying that "Mayakovski's poem for the tenth anniversary of the October Revolution is a magnificent fanfare in honor of the great day. There is not a single false note in it, and workers' audiences applaud it."[32] Another time, Lunacharski said that the poem was "the October Revolution cast in bronze."[33]

Although the poem celebrates the achievements of the new regime, Mayakovski boldly disregards Party directives in it. His defeated Whites are honorable and selfless. Patriotism and chivalry can be found in both camps. General Wrangel, as Mayakovski paints him, commands respect:

> We were attacking
>   with shells and mortars,
> The last
>   White troops
>   were piling aboard.
> He came out
>   of his empty
>   Headquarters,
> Stiff
>   and dry
>   as an army report.
> With downcast
>   eye,
> At a smart
>   pace
> Wrangel
>   strode
> Away from the place.
> The city, abandoned,
> Looked bare
>   and severe.
> A long-boat,
>   manned,
> Lay
>   at the pier.

> Like one to the lees spent,
> Or coming to grief,
> Down on his knees went
> The Commander-in-Chief.
> Three times
>   he kissed
>   the ground,
> Three times
>   the city
>   he blessed with love.
> Bullets
>   were whistling
>   as he jumped down
> Into the boat.
>   "Your orders, sir?"
>   "Push off." [34]

Emigré literature can boast of no portrayal of the White hero less biased than the one drawn by the militant minstrel of Communism.

Mayakovski believed that Bolshevism, with its indomitable will and energy, was the force that could mechanize rural, sprawling Russia into an industrial Eden, and in poem after poem—the "Story of Kusnetskstroi and the People of Kusnetsk" (1929), the "March of the Shock-Worker Brigades" (1930), the "March of the Twenty-five Thousand" (1930), and many others—Mayakovski extols the efforts toward industrialization.

In his eyes it was the duty of a Soviet poet to participate in the remolding of life, to keep up his spirits when the tornado of revolution was over and to help in the work of rebuilding. After Yesenin's suicide Mayakovski wrote in the poem "To Sergei Yesenin," 1926:

> There is still
>   entirely
>   too much tripe,
> There is still
>   a lot for us to do.
> First
>   we must rebuild our way of life—
> Only then can we extol it, too. . . .
> Our planet
>   for merriment is very ill-equipped,

> We must wrest
>   delight
>   from the future's grasp.
> Let me tell you, friends,
>   dying is no trick,
> Making life worth living
>   is a harder task.[35]

In "Home" [*Domoi*] of the same year he called upon Gosplan to sweat over debating his next year's assignment, and upon Stalin to make reports, in the name of the Politburo, on the production of poetry as well as of pig iron. He wanted the pen put on a level with the bayonet.

At the beginning of the First Five-Year Plan in the late 1920's Mayakovski was still working in his poetry to keep alive the people's faith in Stalin. At the same time he was deviating more and more frequently from the Party line in his slashing political satires on the growing evils of the new system to which he could not reconcile himself.

He decried the subservient, humiliating role of the poet under the new order: "Here is my pen, comrades—do your own writing!" ("Conversation about Poetry with a Tax Inspector," 1926).[36] He decried the intrigues, informing, and the "criticism" singularly like slander which were becoming common among writers: "Comrades, let us stop sticking pins into one another" ("A Letter to the Proletarian Poets," 1926).[37] He decried nepotism and corruption ("Patronage" [*Protektsiya*], 1926, and "Bribe-Takers" [*Vzyatochniki*], 1926) and the increasing dreariness and boredom of the Red commemorative holidays.

Degeneration of the Bolshevik Party that might throw the country back to capitalism was to Mayakovski the greatest evil. He attacked the monstrous growth of the Soviet bureaucratic machine ("Lost in Conference" [*Prozasedavshiyesya*], 1922, and "Manufacturing Bureaucrats" [*Fabrika byurokratov*], 1926), opportunism and sycophancy among the Communist elite ("The Bootlicker" [*Podliza*], 1928, and "Manual for Beginners in Bootlicking" [*Obshcheye rukovodstvo dlya nachinayushchikh podkhalimov*], 1927), and deterioration in the character of leadership ("For a Refined Life"

[*Dayosh izyachnuyu zhizn'*], 1927; "Two Cultures," 1928; "Pompadour," 1928; "The Gossip," 1928; and the play *Bedbug*, 1928). Toward the end of his life Mayakovski worked on a poem entitled "It's Bad" [*Plokho*], an antithesis to his enthusiastic *It's Good*. The drafts, which, it may be assumed, constituted an indictment of Stalinism, have never been published.

To Mayakovski, the new "Red aristocracy" has abolished hereditary monarchy but, in the craving for personal profit and comfort, had reasserted the idea of absolutism which the revolution had been intended to destroy:

> Middle-class ways are a trickier snare
> For the Revolution than Wrangel and his brood.
> Hurry,
> Wring the neck of every canary,
> Before the canaries
> Wreck Communism for good![38]

As the years passed, Mayakovski realized, with horror, that his long fight had been useless. In 1928 he finished the play *Bedbug*, a satire on the average Bolshevik, which he had first written as a movie script, under the title "Forget About the Fireplace" [*Pozabud' pro kamin*]. The play was produced by Meierhold in February 1929, with the "Russian Chaplin," Igor' Il'inski, in the role of Pyotr Prisypkin. In form *The Bedbug* resembles Fonvizin's comedies, with an admixture of Aristophanes, vulgarized. There is also a noticeable influence of the circus performers Bim and Bom, Vitali Lazarenko, and Vladimir and Anatoli Durov. In the original version the "hero," then named Pierre Skripkin, was a Party member. The censor made Mayakovski change him into a trade-union member. *Bedbug* shows that the possession of a Party card provides the most insignificant person with power and a standard of living he could never have had otherwise.

Mayakovski's last comedy "The Bathhouse" [*Banya*], also staged by Meierhold in 1929, although weaker than *Bedbug*, is another fierce attack on bureaucracy and a warning to the new aristocracy that sooner or later it will be called to account for betraying the revolution and that the workers and peasants and intelligentsia will be compensated for all they have unjustly endured.

The movie scripts which Mayakovski wrote perhaps in lieu of prose fiction offered an eminently suitable vehicle for his dynamism. He wrote some fourteen scenarios, but only about one-third of them reached the screen. He was extraordinarily unlucky in his film ventures.

His most interesting screenplays are "Not Born to Make Money" [*Ne dlya deneg rodivshiisya*] and "History of a Gun" [*Istoriya odnovo nagana*]. In 1918 Mayakovski was commissioned to adapt Jack London's *Martin Eden* to the screen, but he was so carried away by his own ideas that little of Jack London remained in the retitled "Not Born to Make Money." From accounts of several persons who worked on production of the film or saw it on the screen—the scenario is not available—it may be assumed that the adaptation was affected by Mayakovski's views on immortality, developing to some extent under the influence of Nikolai Fyodorov. The hero, Ivan Nov, is a Russian poet, a modernist like Mayakovski himself, who joins the revolution because he is enthralled by its sweeping power and filled with a desire to make immortality descend from heaven to earth. Soon, however, he realizes that his ideas are only the delusions of a lonely and spiritually bankrupt mind, that the revolution and capitalism are equally alien to him, that life has neither meaning nor value.

Mayakovski's work is decidedly uneven. In his political propaganda verse after the revolution there was a decline in his mastery of form. On the other hand, he grew in stature as a lyric poet.

His poems *I Love*, 1922, and *About That* [*Pro Eto*], 1923, are both on the theme of rejected love. In the latter he writes:

> Put a heart in my breast!
>   Let my blood
>   course free.
> Long with this thought I strove:
> I have not had my due of life on earth,
> I have not
> Had my fill of love.[39]

The personal note merges with the political; the poet had sought escape from loneliness in the revolution, but the revolution had deceived him:

>   Resurrect me
>   if only
>   for being
>   a poet.
>   Awaiting you,
>   rejecting the humdrum.
>   Resurrect me
>   if only because you know it.
>   I want my just due
>   of the days to come.[40]

He reaches that supreme simplicity which lends dramatic power to the intimate lyrical experience:

>   The boy stared at the sunset as he trudged—
>   A yellow sunset in an ochre sky.
>   The very snow with yellow flecks was smudged.
>   The boy walked over it unseeingly,
>   Then
>   Took his
>   Stand,
>   A gun
>   In his
>   Hand.
>   For an hour the sunset watched the red
>   Border round the body of the boy
>   Widen relentlessly and spread.
>   For what reason?
>   With what purpose?
>   Why?
>   Pickpocket wind went through his coat
>   And brought to light a folded note,
>   And then in the park's ear declaimed:
>   "Goodbye ...
>   my own life ...
>   no one be blamed...." [41]

The artist Vasili Chekrygin, author of the "Resurrection of the Dead" series of paintings, had introduced Mayakovski to the philosophy of Fyodorov's *The Common Cause*, which N. A. Berdyayev epitomizes as follows:

> To N. Fyodorov, death is the supreme, the intolerable evil, the source of all evil, the only evil. He sees the ultimate triumph over death not in the birth of new life but in the resurrection . . . of the dead. The will to resurrect the dead testifies to Fyodorov's exceptionally lofty moral sense. Man must be a giver of life, he must make it eternal. That is the highest moral truth, whatever we may think of the "project" itself. . . . In Fyodorov's attitude toward death there was a great truth, but there was also a great error, a faulty understanding of the mystery of death. Fyodorov was a Christian by conviction, but he seems to have failed to comprehend the mystery of the Cross and of Calvary and to accept the redemptory meaning of death.[42]

In Fyodorov's imagination, advanced technology was the miraculous power that could regenerate and ennoble humanity and thus achieve victory over death through resurrection.

Like Chekrygin, Mayakovski took from Fyodorov his faith in the ultimate victory of eternal life and in the omnipotence of technology—and this explains his peculiar "urbanistic messianism," of which Roman Jakobson has given an extraordinarily penetrating analysis[43]—but he scorned the idea that the future must be built, by way of changing the present, on the resurrection of the past. The religious philosopher Fyodorov and the poet Yesenin had, by different roads, arrived at the same belief, that no happy future was possible until the present redeemed its heavy guilt toward the past. Mayakovski differs from them in that victory over death was, to him, the victory of the new life, born in the fire and storm of the revolution, over the decayed past. Berdyayev writes of Fyodorov that he

> thinks of the dead forebears, of death in times past, and finds therein a source of grief. . . . In the history of mankind there has been no one to equal Fyodorov's dolor over death, nor his ardent longing to restore life to all those who have died.[44]

Mayakovski thought that the human beings of the future would themselves become gods and create a life that would be free both of the ruins of the past and of the misery of the present. Despite

Mayakovski's abhorrence of the past and of the present, Fyodorov diverted him, briefly it is true, from the highway of militant Bolshevism to the pathway lighted by Fyodorov's two suns—faith in the victory of life over death and faith in the miracles that modern technology would eventually be able to work.

Is it true that Mayakovski was above all a lyric poet, that his tragedy was the same as Yesenin's—living and writing in an "unlyrical era"? Mayakovski's case was more complex. He started out worshiping the revolution and ended by passionately denouncing the evils of Bolshevism. Wittingly or unwittingly, he demonstrated that in the new era love was rejected and brutalized. His own unfulfilled love and the common calamity were too much for him, and on April 14, 1930, he committed suicide.

> I want my native land to understand
> My verse—but if it doesn't,
>   then
> I will have done no more than skirt my land
> Like a wind-driven, slanting rain.[45]

Mayakovski was canonized by Stalinist propaganda in the mid-1930's. Stalin himself called him the most talented poet of the Soviet period.

OTHER CUBO-FUTURISTS

Vasili Kemenski (1884-   ), one of the "old-guard" Cubo-Futurists, was well known before the revolution. His work bears some resemblance to that of Khlebnikov and Severyanin, but he made his own contribution to poetry in blending the new forms with popular epic songs. In the fragments of an epic poem about Sten'ka Razin, his best work, written in 1920-1921, Kamenski borrowed from the imagery of folk songs and caught their spirit and rhythm to a remarkable degree.

His anarchic individualism and erratic work methods barred him from becoming one of the foremost of the later modernist poets. The poem about Razin was left unfinished. His novel *Stepan Razin*, although it has a number of engrossing passages, is not well worked out and occasionally becomes gaudy and cheap. First published in 1916, it was twice reissued under the Soviet regime, in 1919 and 1928. Kamenski also wrote a play *Sten'ka Razin*, 1919, another interesting but careless piece of work. It too ran through three editions.

After this glorification of the stormy Pugachov-Razin spirit of the Revolution, revolutionary motifs faded from his work, and he spent much of his time editing Futurist publications. His later novels, particularly *Pushkin and D'Anthès*, 1928, were unfavorably received.

Aleksei Kruchonykh (1886-   ), who with Khlebnikov had originated trans-sense (*zaumnyi*) verse, carried on his prosodic experiments and development of Cubo-Futurist theory as long as such linguistic capers were countenanced.

In his *Sdvigologiya russkovo stikha: Traktat obizhal'nyi i pouchal'nyi*—a title which, in English, would be something like "Displaceology of Russian Verse: Offensatial and Instructual Treatise"— he wrote:

We are still children in the use of language, yet we take it upon ourselves . . . to solve all the problems of the universe and are ashamed to study art as a thing in itself.[46]

After the late 1920's art as a "thing in itself," divorced from politics, was no longer a legitimate concern of Soviet writers, and Kruchonykh dropped from prominence.

His postrevolutionary poems which are not "trans-sense" breathe utter despondency:

> Bones frozen to the marrow,
> I stride through picket fences of falling snow,
> Naked, barefoot,
> With tingling teeth.
> How c..c..cold! The cold is a knife
> Slashing at the screaming sky.
> The earth's cistern is cracked,
> The axis has been broken
> By the rising ice. . . .[47]

Among Khlebnikov's followers, the most gifted was Grigory Petnikov (1894-   ) who, like Kruchonykh, was considered something of an outsider among postrevolutionary Futurists. Neither of them joined forces with Communism. While the left-wingers in the Cubo-Futurist group worshiped industrialization, Petnikov resisted the deification of machines and the gearing of life to industrial tempos ("You hide yourself in speed . . .")[48] and became primarily a landscape painter, decidedly anti-urbanistic. In poems published in 1922 he writes:

> The air pours forth like a song
> The evening carelessly spilled . . .
> A tipsy freshness
> Comes from the blue pool
> And the fields are the eyes of God.[49]

Fyodor Bogorodski, too, stood somewhat apart from the other Futurists. He published one collection of poems in 1922, *Let's Have It: Poems of a Sort*,[50] which contains articles on his work by Kamenski and Khlebnikov, among others, and then he gave up writing and devoted himself to painting.

Poet protégés of Kruchonykh who also experimented in "displacing" and "deforming" word, syntax and rhyme included N. Khabias, N. Saksonskaya and Nataliya Benar.[51]

The prominent left-wing Futurists Aseyev, Kirsanov and Tret'yakov produced their best work at a later period and will be discussed in connection with the LEF.

THE EGO-FUTURISTS

Igor' Severyanin (pseudonym of I. V. Lotaryov; 1887-1942), a self-styled Futurist disdained by the Mayakovski-Khlebnikov group, had enjoyed a brief vogue before the revolution because of a certain vivacious but superficial charm appealing to many readers. He left Russia for Estonia during the Civil War and died there in 1942, during the German occupation. It has been reported that his late poems which remained in manuscript, particularly those written in tribute to victims of the Nazis, had far greater depth and power than might have been expected from him on the basis of his published work.

The remaining Ego-Futurists, including Tufanov, Smirenski, Olimpov (a son of Konstantin Fofanov), Vaginov, and Spasski, tried to remain aloof from politics, and this attempt was their undoing. The run-of-the-mill poet, or the poet limited to one minor theme, had to lend his services to the propaganda bureau or stop writing. Of the group, Konstantin Vaginov (1900-   ), author of the novel *Goat's Song*,[52] is the most talented. Sergei Spasski managed to keep his head above water somewhat longer than the other Ego-Futurists.

THE OLD "CENTRIFUGE"

Of all the prerevolutionary Futurist groups, the members of the Centrifuge, an association of "scholarly" Futurists, to which Pasternak at one time belonged, were least successful in adapting to the new propaganda demands upon writers. Sergei Bobrov (1889-   ), former leader of the group, continued to write during the 1920's. He has been underrated as a poet.

His tale *The Revolt of the Misanthropes* (1922), like Zamyatin's more famous *We*, is a vision of the Soviet future. Bobrov's hero, an intelligent and cynical turncoat, prophesies accurately: "We'll drag out a couple of hoary hypotheses. . . . These hypotheses will be repeated by millions of mouths. Then they shall become truths."[53] Much effort is needed to build a new world. Those who will not make the effort can be forced. With workmen it will be easy—they are used to discipline. The peasant is a different matter, he cannot be bent. Therefore famine is certain to accompany the age of building. "We will let them feed on warm water and on bread of husks and bark, weighed out in carats."[54]

"Thus the new times are born, in the din of toil, in eyes glazed and dying with fatigue.... Do you know how to cook soup out of a hatchet? We shall teach you this magic chemistry."[55]

The propaganda machine will take care of the masses. "The devil himself will envy the ease with which we shall fool you."[56]

The conquerors, too, whose "madness consisted chiefly in a desire to shed the blood of their brethren and to devastate fertile lands, in order to reign over graveyards,"[57] have an unenviable lot:

"Life, life everywhere, while I am disappearing, dying in unutterable anguish, in a chaos of blood, malice and cursing. Let the earth have life—we are tired of raging and killing." [58]

Later, Bobrov himself turned into a cynical opportunist.

5. Peasant Poets

For the first decade after the Bolshevik Revolution the nature of peasant literature was usually regarded as self-evident. It was only during preparations for sweeping collectivization of agriculture and "liquidation of the kulaks as a class" that desultory debate on the subject was exacerbated into a violent controversy.

The critic Vyacheslav Polonski stated at the plenum of the All-Russian Society of Peasant Writers in November 1929:

A peasant writer, in my opinion, is a writer whose art ... expresses a perception of life characteristic of a person who has grown up in the country and looks at the world from a peasant's, not a city dweller's, point of view, a perception determined by the conditions of agricultural rather than industrial production, an attitude toward the world reflecting the point of view of a person having to do not with factory buildings but with the soil, not with industry but with nature.[1]

Thus, in essence, Polonski maintained that for a Russian peasant his "occupational characteristics," stemming from his closeness to the soil, were more important than the "class differentiations" foisted upon him by propaganda, and suggested that literature should be approached from the same point of view; that is, there were no poor-peasant, average-peasant and kulak writers, but only "peasant writers" and "peasant literature."

The rejection of Polonski's argument was a foregone conclusion. The Party policy of whipping up class antagonisms in the village required, as a concomitant, the splitting of the ranks of peasant writers, the isolation of "kulak literature" from the body of "peasant literature." By decision of the plenum, peasant literature was defined as only that "literature which reflects the interests of the main peasant masses on the road to socialism." [2]

Until this time the outstanding peasant writers (in Polonski's sense), regardless of their material circumstances, displayed distinct solidarity. Not only did the literature of the peasant intelligentsia afford an extraordinary example of humanist teaching, striving to evolve a peasant ethics as well as peasant esthetics, but it expressed concerted opposition to the agricultural policies of the Bolshevik Party.

NIKOLAI KLYUYEV (1887 - 1937)

Until the early 1930's the culture of pre-Petrine Russia was miraculously preserved among the Old Believers on the White Sea coast and in the Olonets Lake region, frozen in their way of life as in a block of ice. Two Russian cultures existed side by side, the one fathered by Peter the Great and the one which dates back to Kievan *Rus'* and which was hidden away in the retreats of the Old Believers. At times the younger culture was enriched by its contact with the old. Nikolai Klyuyev's poetry is a case in point.

As a poet and as a man, Klyuyev was a mysterious personality. He liked to enlarge upon his family tree, and indulged in poetic fantasy on its roots and the "curly luxuriance" of its branches. The truth is that on the paternal side the tree had its roots in a Samoyed tent. Klyuyev's father's people were Christianized northern tribesmen. Klyuyev did not like to admit this fact. Yet he retained a profound attachment for the ancestral tent:

> Seals frolic in the setting sun,
> A tent is mirrored in the lake.
> Here browse my golden-antlered deer—
> The thoughts I think, the songs I make.[3]

In the foreword to a collection of his poems, *The Copper Whale*, Klyuyev reveals a weakness for Lapp folk tales: "I offer you these ringing sounds, splashes of the copper whale upon whom, according to the old Lapp folk tale, rests the song of the world."[4]

Klyuyev's origins partly explain the pose he affected. He always wore a high felt hat, of the kind worn by prosperous Russian peasants at the end of the eighteenth century and the beginning of the nineteenth, a *poddyovka* or an *armyak* (peasant coats), tarred Morocco or box calf boots, an embroidered Russian shirt reaching to his knees, and a silk cord with tassels for a belt. The Old Believers' style of dress was meant to divert attention from his Mongoloid features and figure. In the literary milieu to which he had come to belong it would not have done for everybody to know that the spiritual head of the Russian peasant intelligentsia and the leading peasant poet was of Eskimo stock.

On his mother's side, Klyuyev's family tree does spread "intricate luxuriant branches" in the culture of seventeenth-century *Rus'*. His mother was a professional weeper, a "bearer" of the laments or "wails" of ancient Russian poetry.

In Klyuyev's poetry the cultures of the two Russias achieved a harmonious balance.

His first book of verse, *Carillon of Pines,* was published in 1912. Three others appeared before the revolution. The contents of these four books were assembled with his later writings in the two volumes published in 1919 under the title *Pesnoslov* [Songbook].[5] The separate collection published earlier in the same year, *The Copper Whale,* contains only one poem that is not included in *Pesnoslov*. Five more books came out during the 1920's: *Lion's Bread,*[6] *The Fourth Rome,*[7] *Mother-Saturday,*[8] *Lenin* (largely drawn from *Pesnoslov* and *Lion's Bread*), and *Cabin and Field*.[9] Klyuyev's "Lament for Sergei Yesenin" was part of a book written in collaboration with P. N. Medvedev.[10] His other major poems are "The Land Beyond the Lakes,"[11] "The Village,"[12] 1927, and "Aftermath of Fire."

As a result of the publication of "The Village" in a Leningrad magazine, the managing editor was removed from his job and severely reprimanded by the Party. "Aftermath of Fire," which, except for Blok's "The Twelve," is the highest achievement of Russian postrevolutionary poetry, has never been printed in the Soviet Union. A manuscript was brought out of the country, however, by Professor Ettore Lo Gatto, and from it the text of the poem was published in a 1954 edition of the complete works of Klyuyev.[13]

This is how Klyuyev describes his literary beginnings:

> I came and found your houses mountainous,
> Steel whales afloat upon your waves—
> And so I sang of forests perilous,
> Of Northern pines and hermits' caves.[14]

Along with the folk laments and Old Believers' chants in Klyuyev's early work, Aleksandr Blok may occasionally be clearly heard. Somewhat later he also admitted his fondness for Nekrasov, of which he had once seemed to be somehow ashamed. His was not slavish imitation, but a mature and independent adoption of another poet's manner—the borrowings served his own art for new and original creation. Klyuyev admired Bunin, too, for his preciseness, clarity, and the realistic concreteness of his nature descriptions. With a kind of peasant practical sense, Klyuyev appreciated Bunin's technique of combining mood with factualness, and adapted it to the hushed beauty of his North Russian landscape. In his own original approach to nature Klyuyev feels no difference between a North Russian forest and a wooden chapel, between a water-meadow and the tablecloth in a peasant's home; God has put together His world, and the peasant his house, with the same conscientious, proprietary care.

> Today the forest holds carouse.
> The alders in their scarlet dress
> Welcome the stranger to their house.
> The clearing smells of cake, no less.
>   The anthill's like a sugar loaf,
>   That stump might be a jug of wine.[15]

The North Russian peasant is a great dreamer, but his dreams are of the past, not of the future. A muzhik living in a little hut in the woods, with spruce and pines for company, sings epics of princely Kiev or Muscovite *Rus'*, of gold-domed cathedrals, and exquisite pearls adorning the beauties of ancient Russia. The riches and splendor denied him in life fill his dreams. He is as dependent on his epics as he is on his fishing net or boat. The North Russian dream was Klyuyev's by birthright. He visualizes the village lifted out of the forest and set down in the midst of the golden dream:

> He who has faith in the incredible
> And loves the villages instinct with power
> Shall waking see his dream made palpable
> And golden India on the icons flower.[16]

In this poem, reality engenders dream. In another, the dream clothes itself in reality:

> The folk in our village are handsome and sunny.
> The girls are like swans and the lads are like honey,
> Their shirts are of linen embroidered in gold,
> Their language is measured, their glances are bold.[17]

To understand these lines, it is necessary to have seen Northern peasants on a church holiday, when, until recently, they wore the clothes preserved in family chests for a hundred years, or perhaps several hundred. *Sarafans** of the fifteenth and sixteenth centuries have frequently been found in the homes of peasants on the White Sea coast and around Olonets. On Easter Sunday Olonets peasants used to come to church in boyar and *strelets*† headgear. Klyuyev's poem is not a picture of Utopia, but simply a description of a North Russian village on a church holiday, paying a visit to seventeenth century Muscovite Rus'.

The war and the revolution marked a turning point in Klyuyev's poetry. Even earlier he had declared his solidarity with the Socialist Revolutionary Party. The revolutionary mood is reflected in his verse:

> Remember in the darkness,
> And so be comforted,
> That I went to the scaffold
> As to a bridal bed.[18]

Paradoxically, the civic motif in his revolutionary poems dissolves in the religious. The way to resurrection is through death. Consequently, the greater the suffering the more one should rejoice, because it leads to eternal life. Here the Old Believers, with their passion for self-destruction—for burning themselves alive together

---

* Women's national dress.

† Sixteenth and seventeenth century Moscow soldier.

with their log chapels—speak in Klyuyev. The power of his revolutionary poetry lies not in its revolutionary feeling, but in a kind of lyrical ecstasy of self-immolation.

The revolution had the same effect on Klyuyev as on other peasant writers, irrespective of their talent—the poet grew in stature overnight. In one leap, as it were, he achieved superb craftsmanship, from the need for self-affirmation and the hope that it might now be attained.

Immediately and without reservations, Klyuyev accepted the democratic, "peasants' " revolution as his own:

> Not with the moans of my fathers
> Shall my song resound;
> But with the force of thunder
> It shall fly over the earth.
> Not as an inarticulate slave
> Continually cursing his life,
> But as a free eagle
> Will I sing my song.[19]

The plundering of landlords' estates seemed to him necessary and legitimate. Lenin's slogan "Rob the robbers" appealed to him.

> The heart of the people, the storm of October
> Are wedded together—friends, let us rejoice,
> While leather-bound Turgenev mourns on the shelf
> Over ravaged estates in a paper-thin voice.[20]

Toward the revolutionaries in the cities Klyuyev took a cautious but on the whole approving attitude, pointing out that "we are all brothers" and yet reminding them that the muzhik put a price on giving them his support and would not welcome interference in the country. This practical self-defense trend is curiously interwoven with religious feeling:

> We have revolted more mightily than thunder
> To see the sky sparkle like diamonds,
> To grasp the praise of the angels,
> To receive communion from the cup of our Saviour.[21]

Klyuyev wanted to believe that the revolution heralded the coming of Belovod'ye, the land of freedom and plenty, a paradise on earth, in the legend treasured by the Old Believers:

> Over Russia there passed a fiery pheasant,
> Kindling vehement wrath in the heart....
> Virgin-Mother—our little earth Thou art—
> Bear Thou the free bread for the peasant!
> The rumors of old and the dreams came true,
> Svyatogor* is the people, and now wide awake,
> Honey is on the loaves of a rustic cake,
> And the tablecloth shows a bright pattern too.
>   For land and freedom, for earned bread
>   We march in arms to meet our foes!
>   Upon us enough they did tread!
>   Rush on to fight, to blows![22]

Klyuyev was interested in Lenin primarily from the religious, mystical point of view. To him, Lenin was another Archpriest Avvakum, but without Christ in his heart, and with the ptomaine of Marxism in his head; an embodiment of the Russian sacrilegious tendency, a heretic and a blasphemer, yet with the blood of Old Believer prophets in his veins—polluted, to be sure, but still prophets' blood. The very fact that Russia could produce such men as Lenin was, to Klyuyev, the consequence of the Old Believers' defeat. The Russian catastrophe, in his view, started with the Schism, not with the October Revolution.

The voice of God spoke somewhere in Lenin's innermost self, and his tragedy lay in the incessant discord between his reason and his heart. Hence his ceaseless oscillation between good and evil. In his poems on Lenin, written in 1918-1919 and republished in 1924 as part of the volume entitled *Lenin,* Klyuyev says:

> There is in Lenin something masterful.
> Like an old abbot, he speaks angrily
> In his decrees....[23]

Klyuyev often taunted the Orthodox clergy:

---

* A giant of Russian folklore; the reference to his awakening is taken from a popular ballad.

> The land is the peasant's at last,
> The church is no longer for hire,
> And red like a furnace blast
> Is the Word of the people's desire.
>
> . . . .
>
> The Khan of the Golden Horde
> Rings the brazen church bells on high,
> And Lenin today is the lord
> Of the storms that ravage the sky.
> Dark dungeons in the Smolny* are
> That smell of pine and cranberries;
> There stands a coffin, crudely made,
> And in it Holy Russia lies.[24]

In "The Land Beyond the Lakes" (about 1924) Klyuyev attributed the evil the revolution had brought with it to the decline in religiosity, and again blamed not the Bolsheviks but Patriarch Nikon and his successors at the head of the Orthodox Church for three hundred years:

> The little church in its old fur coat
> Angrily says of Nikon the stern:
> "It is his fault that a creaking rot
> Creeps through each rafter and beam in turn!"[25]

The peasant uprisings during the Civil War and their cruel suppression sobered Klyuyev. True to the humanitarian spirit of peasant literature, he appealed for an end to cruelty and the shedding of innocent blood. Work should be faced with love. In the "peasants'" revolution Klyuyev had already heard the "rumbling of an avalanche":

> The ant-like forces of evil
> Extinguish our songs and our flags.[26]

He regarded the future with apprehension:

> The red days are on the wane,
> The time of brimstone nears.[27]

---

* Headquarters of the War Revolutionary Committee and the Central Committee of the Bolshevik Party during the November Revolution of 1917 and until March 1918 seat of the Soviet government.

Klyuyev welcomed the NEP with a sigh of relief. During the following years he experimented with poetic form in his use of folklore. He proceeded rather like a clever well-to-do peasant buying himself a threshing machine, after much careful thought whether the farm would profit from the purchase.

Klyuyev needed a new form to clothe the new theme, that of the peasant's shattered and vanished way of life. He had written in the volume entitled *The Copper Whale* (1919):

> The tree of song lies broken in its pride,
> Marx has replaced the icon on the wall.
> The evening shakes a cracked old sieve outside
> And lets gray ashes, rime and darkness fall.[28]
> . . . .
> The mind may say "Republic," but "Mother!" cries the heart.
> I'll not deny you, Russia, though the very heavens part!
> Though I turn to a tree-stump, or to a mossy stone,
> My weeping and my sighing shall be for you alone![29]

Klyuyev's love of the past goes hand in hand with his loathing of the machine age. In this hatred, frequently encountered in that part of peasant literature known to the Bolsheviks as "kulak literature," a "Luddite* leaven" is sometimes found to be working. With Klyuyev, it was standardization that most repelled him in technological civilization. A muzhik might build a fishing boat lovingly or without love, lazily or with zeal, and his mood would be reflected in his work. A mass-produced, mass-producing machine always worked in the same cold, indifferent way, and everything came out alike.

> To the list of molecular weights
> Mendeleyev adds two or three . . .
> They know naught of saints and sinners
> In the Eden of industry.[30]

Klyuyev's hostility toward mechanization was also a transference of his hatred of Communists and their monopoly of the machine

---

* The Luddites, English industrial workers who in riots of 1811-16 systematically wrecked machinery, which they regarded as responsible for widespread unemployment.

Poets in the Ascendant

which enabled them to drive the peasants into the kolkhoz yoke. His anti-urbanism derived from his anti-Bolshevism.

During his last period, beginning in 1927, Klyuyev reached extraordinary heights in his harmonizations of the North Russian laments. He seems to be standing on a high belltower from which he saw the whole of rural Russia and all that would happen to it in the decades to come. His fear changing into wrath, he looked to the muzhik to sweep away with his beard the new Tatar yoke:

> Russia's day is drawing near—
> A new Tsar Ivan will appear
> To smite the Tatars everywhere.[31]

The long narrative poem "The Village," which miraculously rode through censorship and was published in 1927, is one of Klyuyev's best. It shows us Russia on the eve of the collectivization of agriculture:

> A brand-new tractor in the village—
> A walrus in the dining room!
> The folk besiege the manager:
> "What is it for, man? And for whom?"
>
> . . . .
> None but the fisherman Kondrati
> Saw how, without a backward look,
> The birches ran along the road
> To drown themselves in yonder brook.
>
> . . . .
> The swallows underneath the eaves
> Broke up their nests with angry cries.
> I wonder how the wheat will take
> To the industrial paradise![32]

In the same year Klyuyev published another openly anti-Soviet poem, "Lament for Yesenin." Almost as soon as the book containing it was put on sale, all available copies were confiscated by the government. Thereafter Klyuyev was hounded by the GPU and soon driven out of Soviet literature.[33] His last published work was *Cabin and Field,* 1928, a small collection containing only two previously unpublished poems.

His magnificent "Aftermath of Fire," a lament over the failure of the Revolution, far more daring than "The Village," was known to Soviet readers only in manuscript or from the poet's own reading in private homes and illegal meetings. In the poem Klyuyev rises to great tragic simplicity:

> The metal dragon from the West
> Of metal billows skims the crest.[34]
>
> . . . .
> The wheat field in its shroud of snow
> Gave up its ghost long months ago
> And rests beside the Devil's Mound.
> Broken the gaily painted sleigh
> And dead the lately prancing horse.[35]

In 1933, branded as a spokesman for the kulaks, Klyuyev was exiled to Siberia. He died in 1937, on his way back to Moscow for a verdict concerning his future, and the "suitcase full of manuscripts" which he carried with him vanished without trace.[36]

SERGEI KLYCHKOV (1889- ?)

"Beyond the high mountain, where the sun sets at night and rises in the morning, lies a fabulous azure-blue land," writes Sergei Klychkov, in his novel *The Sugar German*, introducing the reader to a muzhik utopia, a land of total, absolute peasant freedom:

They have no tsar. A cowherd ranks higher than a state minister. As far back as they can remember, the people have never paid any taxes. The muzhiks live and live and cannot get enough of living in that land.[37]

In Klychkov the real and the fantastic are interwoven, and his imagery is symbolic. It is not an easy task to separate the symbolic from the real. In this respect like Aleksandr Grin rather than his fellow peasant writers, he turned his rich and prolific imagination to romantic fantasy as a means of fighting Bolshevism.

Klychkov, whose real name was Sergei Antonovich Leshonkov, was born of peasant parents in the village Dubrovskaya, in the government of Tver'. The libretto writer Modest Il'ich Tchaikovsky, brother of the composer, guided Klychkov's first steps in literature. His early familiarity with the "operatic" vision of Russia left their mark on Klychkov's work. The folk tales and lyrical songs of the Tver' region were an even stronger influence.

I owe my language to Avdot'ya, the old woman who lived in the woods, to my voluble mother Fyokla Alekseyevna, and to my father's clumsy but often wise locutions—but most of all to our field just beyond the village line, and to the Chertukhino woods,[38]

says Klychkov in the foreword to his collection of prose *The Gray Squire*.

Klychkov's strange combination of earthiness and fantasy has its roots in the conflicting influences of folklore and opera, nature and stage props. The Russia he portrayed, however, is by no means an unreal, tinsel Russia, but a thoroughly genuine, muzhik Russia. The theatrical settings are merely a frame for the picture.

From the time of his first book of poems, published in 1910, his verse collections appeared at frequent intervals until 1923, when his best poems, carefully selected by himself, appeared under the title *A Wondrous Visitor*.[39]

Klychkov's early poems are often realistic nature descriptions without elements of fantasy. Often, too, in the early period Kol'tsov and Nekrasov are quaintly blended with an airy libretto style, and these poems abound in deities borrowed from Slavic mythology and in Russian folklore characters, such as Lel', Dubravna, Prince Bova, and Vasilisa the Beautiful. The mysteriousness of forests and forest brooks pervades Klychkov's early work and gives his landscapes a magic enchantment.

At times, repelled by the cruelty and coarseness of village life, the young Klychkov sought refuge in an imaginary world, fleeing into the woods, to Princess Dubravna, who had once stroked his head.

> I've dreamt of Eden all my life
> And all my life I've sung of spring.
> It is a twilight life I lead
> 'Twixt sleeping and awakening.[40]

The purely decorative quality disappeared from Klychkov's work as he grew older. His poetry gained in earnestness and began to throb with a premonition of irreparable disaster:

> Oft I dream of disaster at dawn—
> The horizon, I see, is ablaze,
> And the grief of the heart of the world
> Gathers over the fields like a haze....[41]

Unlike Klyuyev, Oreshin and Yesenin, he was never of a revolutionary temper. In his opinion, the peasant would have been better off if he had vented his elemental fury in labor rather than in revolt. The idealization of toil overshadows the revolutionary theme:

> In a pattern round the village
> Lie the fields of golden wheat.
> We will all have bread aplenty,
> We will take a glassful, neat.[42]

The revolution completely transformed the poet. His verse lost its melodious quality but gained in insight. Klychkov collected his most important poems of the Soviet period in the volumes *The Talisman*, 1927,[43] and *With the Cranes*, 1930.[44]

In the philosophy expressed in his poetry Klychkov was consistently a pantheist. Even Orthodox Christianity appeared valuable to him only insofar as it was, in times past, part and parcel of the Russian peasantry's elemental pantheistic conception of the world. According to Klychkov, the religious decline was due to the obtuse, shortsighted clergy's failing to notice that the pantheistic content had dropped out of the Orthodox Church ritual. Church rites and customs had been sacred just because the people's elemental pantheism had made them so. Deprive the ritual of its pantheistic roots, and it must wither and die, like any uprooted plant. To Klychkov the fact that the clergy turned its back on pantheism was one of the important factors of the peasants' revolution.

With the prevalence of godlessness Klychkov saw man at the mercy of his vile animal instincts. There was more than enough bestiality in the Russian villages even while the clergy was free to exert its influence. Klychkov was far from idealizing the Orthodox Church or the clergy, and his scrupulous matter-of-factness made his argument all the more telling:

> They quickly stripped me to the skin
> And with a single mind
> They fastened horns upon my head
> And tied a tail behind.
> They dipped me in a vat of tar
> And feathered me to boot,
> And sure I saw a wild beast's claws
> Come sprouting from my foot ...
> I don't believe in devils now—
> That much I've gained at least—
> Through having learned that man is worse
> Than any savage beast.[45]

This poem was written during the time of the ruthless campaign against kulaks. Klychkov opposed Communist agricultural policies and was reviled as an ideologist of the "kulak trend in literature." He replied:

> Do not in sudden tenderness,
> To pick a rose, let fall your sword,
> Lest you be trampled by the mob,
> That pitiless and surging horde!
> . . . .
> Experience is doubly bitter
> In its irrevocable flow,
> Anger is weak and protest futile,
> For I'm the victim and the foe![46]

He was arrested in 1937, when he was at the height of his powers, and sent to a concentration camp. Nothing has been heard of him since.

From 1925 to 1929 Klychkov published four novels: *The Sugar German, The Prattler of Chertukhino, The Last Lel'* and *Lord of This World*.

If Klyuyev may be called the theological realist of postrevolutionary peasant literature, Sergei Klychkov was its metaphysical romanticist.

As novelist, Klychkov follows Gogol in his symbolism and his treatment of the weird. He was one of the very few who penetrated the secret of Gogol's humor. He borrowed the warmth and humaneness of that humor, but he did not have it in him to borrow its malice. Gogol's influence on Klychkov's prose merges with that of Remizov. And Gorki once said that Klychkov was very like the Leskov of *The Enchanted Wanderer* and *Cupid in Bast Shoes*. To be sure, Leskov's influence is noticeable in plot construction and characterization techniques. Also, like a provident peasant, Klychkov stored up and used some bits of Aleksandr Grin's fantasy world. These literary influences are crossed with Tver' folktales for his own unique fiction.

The Sugar German, 1925, of which there have been several editions, is the most popular and widely read of Klychkov's novels. It opens in the trenches, and the soldiers' daily life and the rigors of war are shown in bold relief. The plot shifts to the world of secret illusions—among them dreams of a cabin, well-appointed and rich in good food—which had long been harbored in the Russian peasant's brain and which were the seeds that grew into the "peasants'" revolution. The plot develops in two dimensions, one realistic, the other symbolic. Klychkov deliberately mixes them, but when the real world is separated from the dream world born of suffering, it becomes clear that the collective psychology of the Russian peasantry during the First World War has been rendered with penetrating insight.

The unfortunate Zaichik, a peasant whom life has treated harshly, seeks solace in illusion, in dreams generated by a simple faith in Christ. Zaichik is a peacemaker who feels impotent before the growing rebellion, and his indolence derives from his aversion for the popular wrath and revolt. Failure stalks him even in his personal life; his love for the priest's daughter is not returned.

To Klychkov, collectivism was a distasteful idea:

As for the truth on earth, it is this—each tree rustles in its own way, each blade of grass speaks in its own voice, each bird sings in its own manner ... everybody lives out his own little truth....[47]

From the world of peasant dreams Klychkov moved to the world of folk myths, in *The Prattler of Chertukhino*, 1926, and brought into his story hearth spirits *(domovye)*, devils, watermaidens, and wood spirits *(leshiye)*.

"There are all kinds of devils in this world,"[48] he says. There is, for instance, the one who is supposed to do no other work than to bite peasant women at night and suggest lascivious thoughts. There is the congregate devil, the prince and overlord, so to speak, of all the other devils. Wood spirits and witches are something else again, not to be confused with devils. The wood spirit Antyutik, for instance, is a very positive character, one of the most admirable in the novel:

Nowadays people in our parts do not believe in wood spirits, and the spirits themselves have gone from the woods. . . . That must be why they have gone—because people don't believe in them any more. Yet there was a time when there were wood spirits, and the woods were the kind of woods just right for spirits to live in. There were so many berries in the woods you could eat till you made yourself sick, and so many beasts of all kinds, as if they'd been poured from a basket, and birds there were, such as now are found only in fairy tales and on pictures, and people believed in them and, in truth, the muzhiks' life was not any worse than it is now.[49]

In his watermaidens, wood and hearth spirits, Klychkov personifies his own pantheistic *Weltanschauung* and the elemental pantheistic world-perception of the Russian peasantry.

The pantheistic system of Klychkov's poems is further developed and concretized in his prose. In *The Prattler of Chertukhino* he carries on an argument with Orthodoxy and with the Dissent at the same time. He believes that the Schism strengthened, and not undermined, the muzhik's traditional faith. The Dissenters fled into the woods and became more than ever at one with nature. Indeed it was in their remote settlements that the lasting fusion of elemental pantheism with the Old Believers' rites was consummated. Klychkov considers that this gave the Dissenters an immense advantage over the Orthodox, from whose ritual pantheism gradually had disappeared.

On the other hand, to Klychkov both the Old Believers' dream of emerging from the woods into the world and their belief in the coming of paradise on earth, as visualized in the legend of Belovod'ye, are grave delusions. "Delusions have great power. The life of the whole world is disrupted by delusions."[50]

And "does it matter how a man crosses himself [with two fingers or three]?"[51] Faith resides much deeper:

Faith, in man, is the whole world. . . .
Nothing can kill it. But it may flicker out of itself, like an icon lamp choked with silly flies, flying in, on the wind, out of the dark toward the flame. . . . And when faith burns out, the . . . world may, too.[52]

To Klychkov, elemental pantheism is the origin and the foundation of faith, present in paganism and in Christianity. His wood and home spirits are a symbolic concretization of the pantheism of pagan times. The value of Christianity lies in the fact that it has immensely extended the frontiers of pantheism by turning the human heart toward heaven. Only in nature is it possible to glimpse a reflection of heaven. In pagan pantheism, or its survivals, these glimmerings were perceived but dimly, and as though on the surface of things. Christianity focused them and gave them perspective, directing the human heart toward the inner, not the external, life of nature. To Klychkov, a harmonious side-by-side existence of pagan survivals and Christianity is perfectly legitimate. There can be no heaven on earth, but the vision of heavenly paradise may help to illumine earthly life with the principle of good.

Klychkov rejects technological civilization because he sees in it the triumph of evil:

Not far off is the time when man will kill all the animals in the woods and all the fish in the rivers and all the birds in the air, and force all the trees to kiss his feet—cut them down with the screeching saw. Then God will turn away from the empty world and the empty soul of man, and the iron devil who is waiting just for this will screw some gear or nut from a machine in the place of man's soul. Because in matters of the spirit the devil is a pretty good mechanic. With that nut for a soul, man will live without noticing it till the end of time.[53]

Technological civilization originated in science:

Out of the gentry's yawn was born science, that boredom of the brain, that tombstone of the soul bereft of sight. Man's intellect plashes in that science like a blind kitten in a pail.[54]

The city is the citadel of technological civilization:

O City, City! Even the earth under you is not like earth. Satan has murdered her, trampled her down with his iron hoof, leveled her with his iron back, rolling around on her like a frothing horse in a meadow. That is why ships of stone have grown over her, that is why she has stretched out to heaven the red fingers of the city's outskirts, which neither storm nor tempest can bend and which are higher than churches and cathedrals, the red factory chimneys.[55]

In Klychkov's mind technological civilization was identified with the Bolshevik policy of industrialization at the expense of the peasantry. He realized sagaciously that what was being prepared was a raping of the peasantry by the state such as the world had never seen. As for the compliance of the peasantry, Klychkov says in *The Prattler of Chertukhino:*

The last muzhik will fall off the earth as off a wagon [only] when the earth itself will turn over on its other side. Between then and now, everything may go dead, but the muzhik will be a muzhik the same as always, on account of his staying powers.[56]

Pyotr Kirillovich Penkin, the hero of *The Prattler of Chertukhino*, is a more elaborate version of Zaichik. He, too, is a romantic dreamer, but he has shaken off his indolence and turned to work. And fate has smiled upon him. The miller Spiridon takes him into his affections and is ready to give him his daughter in marriage.

The symbolism of the novel relates to the NEP period. Klychkov interprets the NEP as mass repentance after revolt. The world is reorienting itself toward universal good. Consequently, Klychkov's hero is able to realize himself, to change from a peasant Oblomov* into the man he was meant to be, Mikula Selyaninovich.†

In *The Sugar German* the Russian peasant of the war period lives in a world of stormy dreams; in *The Prattler of Chertukhino* his imagination centers on work, as if in the quiet after the storm.

Actually, it is of no great importance at what time the action of *The Prattler of Chertukhino* takes place. The time is woven of blue

---

* Goncharov's passive hero in the novel of the same name.
† An epic hero of miraculous strength.

magic light. Moonlight plays a prominent part in Klychkov's novels.

In his third novel, *The Last Lel'*, 1927,[57] critics saw a return to the ornate, operatic manner of his early poetry. It is true that pagan deities, once more borrowed from Slav mythology, appear in the book, with Lel', the god of love, as the central figure. But here again the deities are used as symbols. In this novel Klychkov inveighs against the cruel and the brutish in peasant nature. Lel' is an expostulation against cruelty, grief over the passing of love.

There is an image of a woman that reappears in novel after novel of Klychkov's—a girl becoming pregnant out of wedlock, outside the law, and living in an agonized expectation of punishment. In *The Sugar German* she commits suicide, and in *Lord of This World* she nearly loses her mind. While not condoning a passion that sets itself above law and morals, Klychkov vigorously condemned savage mob justice. A great grief is in store for the peasantry, he warned—grief over the passing of love, which would come as God's punishment for the cruelty of the Russian peasant.

Klychkov's "homegrown" philosophy is by no means "mixed up" or irrational, or kulak "holy-foolishness" (*yurodstvo*), or an eclectic hodgepodge, a hogwash of Old Believer texts and vulgarized versions of philosophic theories, as official Soviet critics have charged. No, in its own way Klychkov's pantheism is well thought out and logical, just as, for instance, the architectonics of an Old Believer chapel, with its multitude of chantries and clusters of little cupolas, may be logical. Even as a philosopher, Klychkov remains first of all an artist—he thinks in images. Beauty in his novels is expressed in landscape, and the mysteriousness of nature is rendered through motion:

Everything seems to float as though cut off from the ground. . . .[58]

Only the Dubna steams and the mist floats curling like partridge tails in their mating haunts. . . .[59]

If you look long enough at that wheel and listen to the song of the Dubna's limpid water flowing through it, then the ground will float away from under your own feet, and the mill itself will move, and the birches after it.[60]

Klychkov's sadness turned into despair in his fourth novel, *Lord of This World:*

Little by little everything passes from life, from memory. ...
Memories flutter now in the long autumn night like the leaves of the weeping birch. It stands like a beggarwoman outside the window and weeps tear after tear. The wind sweeps the leaves against the fence and the rain flattens them against the ground.[61]

In this book moonlight disappears from Klychkov's novels; black-blue clouds cover the sky. The action again takes place at the time when the collectivization of agriculture was beginning. Smoke and a smell of burning fill the air. The village is engulfed in a forest fire. The fire scene strikes us as a grandiose symbol: "There was a roar of thunder overhead, and smoke spread over the porch like a black sheepskin."[62]

During the revolution the muzhik plundered landlords' estates. One reaps what one sows. The day is not far when peasant cabins shall be given over to rapine and pillage. Fall, then, on your knees before nemesis, for there is no escape—that is the burden of the novel.

Klychkov considered his first four novels only a beginning. He was full of vast and ambitious projects. The concentration camp robbed Russian literature of one more great writer.

PYOTR ORESHIN (1887- ?)

Pyotr Vasil'yevich Oreshin is the author of thousands of poems, some excellent, some very poor. He also wrote a number of stories and short novels.

In his writing Oreshin comported himself like a tough, prosperous farmer. He was not, however, labeled a "coryphaeus of kulak literature" by Soviet critics, as were Klyuyev and Klychkov, but held the somewhat lesser rank of "undisguised *podkulachnik*" (kulak supporter).

Oreshin was born on the Volga, and his verse sprang from the songs of the Volga region. In Klychkov's and especially in Klyuyev's work, we observed a blending of two cultures; in Oreshin's, we can see an attempt to blend folklore with modern literature. To the somewhat monotonous beauty of the Russian lyrical folk songs from which he draws his inspiration, he gives a modern, literary form, rather in the vein of Nekrasov, Ivan Nikitin, Pushkin and Lermontov.

In Oreshin's poems of the tsarist period a revolutionary note can be clearly heard. He was antimilitarist, unlike Klyuyev, who wanted to fight to the finish in World War I. Another important theme in Oreshin's early poetry—he began to publish in 1913—is the plight of the peasant who has been torn away from the soil and turned into something little better than a tramp. The bitterness accumulated in the heart of the uprooted finds an outlet in hatred of the city and urban life.

For a time after the revolution Oreshin expressed a new, never before experienced elation, as in "The Crimson Temple":

> Through the scorched wheaten waves
> I bring from the sun the Crimson Temple:
> Liberty to cots and hamlets
> Liberty to beggars and slaves.
> . . . .
> Away with sorrow's frown!
> Now I am joyous and bold:
> Over the abysses, the chasms and waterfalls
> The Angel of Freedom has flown.
> Over each hut, the bird of gladness!
> Over each hut, the fiery dream![63]

And in "Kvass":

> O native country mine, how beautiful thou art:
> The steppes of rye, the people of rye,
> The rye sun, and in thy songs
> There sing the earth and the rye.[64]

Oreshin's joy was like a beautiful apple with a worm inside. As soon as the revolution was in full swing, he was repelled by its senseless, unnecessary viciousness.

> Bright in the night the bonfires burn,
> Flame answers flame on field and hill.
> . . . .
> Brutality has drained my heart...
> The soldiers' song rings loud and clear.[65]

During the NEP years Oreshin rejoiced in the fact that the muzhik had been given a respite and had returned to his plow, but joy is again marred by realization that the respite will be brief.

At this time he wrote dozens of poems which became popular songs. Even now they must still be heard in out-of-the-way taverns. Who does not remember the hit song of the NEP period, "The Accordion Player"? Yet nobody gives a thought to the fact that the words are Oreshin's.

> In the truck garden after the rain
> The potatoes decided to bloom.
> The accordion's tender refrain
> Rang like bells in the gathering gloom.[66]

The words of "Komissarka" [The Woman Commissar], which incurred Bolshevik disfavor, are also Oreshin's. In common with most other peasant writers, he had nothing but contempt for the lower-echelon Party administration, though in "Komissarka" this contempt is expressed in a humorous vein. The song tells of a peasant who has set out to Koleno with the intention of buying some goods and bringing back a silk shawl for his wife. On the way he meets a woman commissar of a steppe village.

> And then my lady Commissar
> Invited me into her bower.

She is not averse to a drink and a good meal, and soon the peasant feels that the lower Party personnel is not so bad after all:

> Sweet is the dweller of the steppe—
> Her neck is sugar, her lips are honey.

All his money spent, the muzhik decided to return home.

> A carefree wind sweeps up and down
> The steppe with merry memories rife.
> I know I never got to town
> And bought no presents for my wife.[67]

Accused of "slander of the rural Party workers," Oreshin became more and more subdued. Sadness would suddenly overtake him even in his exuberant moods:

> We cannot help but drink and dance.
> Our very growth is violent,
> Our houses sweep across the steppe
> Breasting the snow with wild content.
> . . . .
> The peasants' woe, one hand upraised,
> Trips lightly through the ancient dance.[68]

The muzhik had come to mistrust the Soviet regime:

> Flooded are the copses, flooded are the dales.
> As the river rises, rise the people's wails.
> There a slender birch tree struggles with the flood:
> "Help me, good folk, help me out onto the road!"
> . . . .
> In the water flounder crosses, houses, poles,
> Through the Commissariat now the river rolls—
> As I see these wonders, I scarce believe my eyes—
> It's the strangest feeling to watch the water rise![69]

He deplored the trampling of Christ:

> Yet no man present crossed himself;
> Forsaken is the ancient sign.[70]

From the Bolshevik point of view Oreshin was long considered to be a spokesman for the steady middle-peasants rather than an inveterate kulak of the Klyuyev or Klychkov type; it was therefore important to convert him to the cause. It is true he tried to write verse praising the kolkhoz, but, consciously or unconsciously, he seasoned his praise with bitter, and sometimes biting, irony. In the final analysis his stand was the unequivocally hostile one taken by all the ranking peasant writers:

> My weary heart is torn with pain
> As this, my native land, I see.
> To love her is to grieve for her,
> And so to learn fidelity.
> She is not fair as others are—
> A yellow field, a dreary mound—
> But countless hopes lie buried here,
> And the fresh graves make sacred ground.[71]

During the twenty-five years of his literary career, Oreshin published dozens of volumes of verse. The most important ones are *Rye Sun*, 1923, *Straw Block*, 1924, and *The Spring*, 1927.

He worked hard on his long narrative poems, though with uneven success. "Rasputin," "The Ninth of January," and "Vera Zasulich," in which he belabored tsarist times, are long-winded and tedious, with a sluggish rhythm, lacking in originality, not worth reading. Of the long poems in which he ventured into the fields of philosophy and sociology, only "Mikula's Move" [*Mikulin khod*], which has the same beat as the Volga robbers' songs, deserves to be singled out.

Far more interesting are the long poems in which he renders the way of life of the peasants or of the motley "new intelligentsia" of the NEP period. His "Rural Correspondent Tsyganok," "Militiaman Lyuksha," "Teacher Chizh," and "The District" hark back to such classics as Lermontov's "The Treasurer's Lady" [*Kaznacheisha*], Pushkin's "Cottage in Kolomna" [*Domik v Kolomne*] and Turgenev's long poems.

In postrevolutionary Russian literature there is perhaps no better description of provincial life in the NEP times than the poetic yet very exact picture Oreshin gives us in "The District." He can portray the types of Soviet rural officials in a few telling lines, without malice. For example, he sketches the ubiquitous "boss" *(zav)* in charge of the district's "educational affairs":

> He wears the Lenin Order, and
> He's even read a book or two.
> . . . .
> For every one of his ideas
> He'll cite the Party for support—

> Stalin himself would not see through
> A clever scoundrel of this sort!
> . . . .
> And Lenin's portrait on the wall
> Raises an eyebrow when he speaks.⁷²

Several Soviet critics tried to interpret "Rural Correspondent Tsyganok" as a bid for collaboration with the Stalinists. The poem begins with a description of a steppe village:

> The steppe is soaking wet. You walk
> Through showers from each gate and tree.
> The autumn rain's monotonous talk
> Goes on and on unendingly.⁷³

In the homes of the poor villagers

> Of bitter wormwood smell the empty days,
> Of scallions and of burdocks dry as dust;

while for the prosperous there is "a plentitude of bread and all good things." ⁷⁴ Chalyi, the chairman of the local soviet, and militiaman Ivan Kapusta rule the village. Instead of assisting the soviet in robbing the peasants, both collect levies for their own profit. "Where tables groan, Kapusta likes to visit."⁷⁵ Rural newspaper correspondent Tsyganok, who comes from a poor family, sends *Pravda* an article on the corrupt village administration:

> The local chairman's always drunk.
> . . . .
> And the militiaman's no monk—
> Also a scoundrel and a drunk.⁷⁶

The article is printed, but Tsyganok pays for it with his life. He is murdered. Despite Oreshin's disapproval of Tsyganok—who had not stopped to think whether it was decent to inform, whether he might not do harm to himself—he stirs sympathy for the young fellow. As village correspondent he had only wanted to stand up for what was right. How could Tsyganok and the likes of him be expected to know that the people at the top were no better than Chalyi or Kapusta? Oreshin does not blame individuals but the system which makes them corrupt and vile.

"Militiaman Lyuksha" is the best of Oreshin's "everyday life" poems. It begins with a vivid description of a small provincial town during the NEP, formerly a thriving business center. The rows of shops now house cooperative stores. Lyuksha keeps the neighborhood in order.

> On duty he is firm, off duty pleasant.
> No need to fear a riot when he's present,
> And law and order strictly he maintains.[77]

Lyuksha works not so much in order to make a living as for love of his job. Although not a "materialist," he has been known to fill his pockets with free prunes and pears from the vegetable women's stands, when slightly "under the influence." Somehow this reaches the ears of the "incorruptible" chief of the militia, and Lyuksha is bawled out. It is hinted that the chief himself, on occasion, is not above filling his own pockets, though with money rather than prunes. Lyuksha now burns to redeem himself and becomes the terror of the market place. He catches his own wife selling apples without a permit and takes her to the militia station. He tells her in no uncertain terms that he represents the law—and that she better remember it. His "heroism" in dragging his own wife to the station earns him his superior's pardon:

> "But how dismiss a man so pure of heart?"
> And once again, in rain and wind and frost
> The worthy Lyuksha occupies his post.[78]

Surprisingly, Lyuksha's usually shrewish wife does not make a scene this time:

> Once more his wife, wrapped in her woolen shawl,
> Offers her produce in the market place.
> Of her arrest she does not speak at all,
> And when Lyuksha happens to pass her stall
> She gives him her best apples with good grace.[79]

For all anyone knows, Fedorka, who is quite a schemer, has engineered her own arrest in order to make her husband's job more secure.

Although the critics took little notice of Oreshin's "everyday life" poems, they were a great success with the public. When Oreshin's works were "purged" from Soviet libraries, privately owned copies of "Militiaman Lyuksha" were in great demand. These poems are, of course, not of great importance. They are amusing, juicy sketches from life, and their value lies not so much in their artistry as in the subject matter and in their good-natured if somewhat crude humor.

Only one of Oreshin's long poems is likely to remain in Russian literature for a long time—*On the Starving Earth*, 1922, dedicated to his grandfather, who died of starvation in a village street. In this poem, Oreshin courageously protests against the Bolshevik policy of silence about the terrible famine that began in 1921 in the Volga region. True, there had been drought and crop failure, but the real cause was the Bolsheviks' incapacity to organize rural labor and their callous disregard of the people's needs.

> Small village with your fields of rye,
> Your wormwood-scented countryside,
> How heavy on my spirit lie
> Your wordless grief, your broken pride![80]
> . . . .
> Here you cannot tell north from south,
> The carriage wheels drown in the sand.
> Someone's skull with its grinning mouth
> Is held fast by skeleton hands.[81]

There is not one weak line in the poem. From beginning to end it is written with the heart's blood and filled with bitter anger. The alternation between syllabic *(sillabotonicheskii)* and accentual *(tonicheskii)* verse is handled in a masterly way. This is Pyotr Oreshin's great achievement in technique, if his only one.

Many of Oreshin's short stories are prose versions of his poems. They are scattered in magazines and newspapers and have not been catalogued. A prolific writer, he used more than one pseudonym, and could not remember himself where some of his stories were published. It is left to future scholars to collect and evaluate Oreshin's prose.

Poets in the Ascendant

However, two "everyday life" stories, "A Slight Draft" [82] (the story deals with a timid character who wants to slip through life "like a slight draft") and *Wretched Little People*[83] should be mentioned. In them Oreshin sketches types of the new minor "intelligentsia"—bookkeepers, reading room managers, librarians, movie operators, agronomists, veterinarians, provincial actors—against a background of the Civil War and the NEP. To his usual debonair humor are added a frankness and truthfulness in which he has few equals in Soviet literature and which make these stories remarkable notwithstanding their second-rate craftsmanship.

Once at a reading by Oreshin in the offices of the *Krest'yanskaya gazeta* [Peasant Gazette] a critic taunted Oreshin for filling his poetry with commonplaces. Oreshin replied with great dignity that it was true he wrote about the commonplaces of compassion and love and elementary kindliness but, when these commonplaces were flouted, he took pride in trying to restore them. What grieved him was that others—the younger generation of writers—were not trying to do better than he. Those present jumped from their seats and gave him an enthusiastic ovation.

In 1937 Oreshin was accused of counterrevolutionary activities and sentenced to ten years in concentration camp without the right of writing or receiving letters. According to rumors which reached his son, Oreshin died there.

Oreshin never received the recognition he deserved. He is far from being a mediocre writer, as even the more objective critics of the 1920's, such as Gorbachov and Voronski, thought. Rather, it was Ivanov-Razumnik who was right when, during the revolution, he saw in Oreshin a "truly national poet" with a great future.[84]

The Russian village as Klyuyev and Klychkov knew it has been wiped off the face of the earth by collectivization and "dekulakization." But Oreshin's village still exists. Perhaps for this reason Soviet poetry has not followed the paths of Klyuyev and Klychkov nor the wide road of Yesenin, who had many imitators and no heirs, but has kept to Pyotr Oreshin's trails. His influence, both in form and in ideas, is still noticeable in Tvardovski, Isakovski and many other peasant poets.

SERGEI YESENIN (1895-1925)

Kornei Chukovski's mot to the effect that Yesenin is a "watered-down Blok" was caught up by Yesenin's detractors of the mid-1930's in their effort to discredit Yesenin and his poetry, especially with Soviet youth. The phrase was interpreted to mean that Yesenin lacked real culture. Mayakovski, too, once said to an audience of young people that even of vodka and passion Blok had written better than Yesenin and that only the unsophisticated admired Yesenin instead of trying to appreciate Blok.[85]

There can be no doubt that Yesenin owed a great deal to Blok, from the first lines he wrote to the last. Many of his poems even sound somewhat like Blok's. Yet a sensitive ear will immediately note a difference. Yesenin differs from Blok as a humble village church differs from a majestic cathedral, though it may follow the same architectural design in its lines.

Blok was the first writer whom the young Yesenin met when he went to St. Petersburg in 1913 with his unpublished poems. "As I looked at Blok, I was dripping with perspiration, because I was seeing a real live poet for the first time in my life," [86] says Yesenin in his autobiographical notes.

Yet Yesenin himself was a born poet. Vyacheslav Polonski observed that "Yesenin did not write in order to live, he lived in order to write poetry." [87] And he wrote little except poetry. One short story, "The Lone Man and His Dog, Pal" [*Bobyl' i Druzhok*], 1917 —a plaintive recitative rather than prose proper—the tale *The Brink* [*Yar*], 1916, and the study *Mary's Keys*, 1920, seem to be his entire prose output, except for the autobiographical notes and revealing letters.

The little book *Mary's Keys* alone suffices to discredit the myth of his "low-brow culture" and slavish imitation of Blok. It is high time to admit without reservations that Yesenin was a very perceptive and intelligent man. Written in an extremely economic style, this study traces the religious origins of various aspects of ancient Russian art and culture.

The little wooden horses on our roof edges, the roosters on our shutters, the doves on porch pillars, the flowers on bed- and body-linen and towels, all these are not simply ornamental devices but a meaningful part of the majestic epopee of the world and the destiny of man.[88]

... The dove over the porch symbolizes gentleness and charity. To the inarticulate Russian muzhik his handicraft is a kind of sacrament, and anyone who can understand this fact must feel deeply grieved by the outrage committed upon the true artistry of the muzhik by our commercial artisans and imitators. One has but to look closely at the colorful patterns of peasant sheets and pillowcases to become aware of the solemn symphony woven into these crosses, flowers and branches....[89]

From his research in the history of folk art and of Russian, especially Old Believers', religiosity, Yesenin concludes that "we have made almost all things around us live and pray." [90]

The second part of *Mary's Keys* is a lament over the disintegration of Russian religiosity and its inevitable consequence—the drying up of the very source of folk art and its eventual extinction. Yesenin believed that our forebears possessed a sixth sense by which they were able to "orient themselves" in the realm of cosmic mysteries.

The only remaining, if careless and wasteful, keeper of those mysteries was the peasantry, disoriented though it was by seasonal jobs in the city and by industrialization. This peasant world, which our hearts' memory is evoking here, we saw in its flower at the same time as in its death throes. It was dying like a fish thrown on dry land by a wave, desperately panting for water, but instead sand filled its gills and, like nails, tore its veins.[91]

The author displays a correct and very sensitive understanding of numerous scholarly studies of ancient Russian art. He was evidently familiar with the works of Buslayev and of Potebnya, and even with those of Rovinski, whose books are the fare of specialists. He also has an uncommonly thorough knowledge of those Russian crafts which are, or were until recently, kept alive among the Old Believers. Moreover, Yesenin knew folk art not as an outsider who had made a study of it but as a man who had lived with it since childhood. His approach differs from that of the learned specialists. For one thing, we find in *Mary's Keys* an interesting refraction of the views of Apollon Grigor'yev, who was able to see the spiritual beauty latent in the outwardly unattractive Russian life and scenery. For another thing, it is obvious that Yesenin had studied and applied the method that Blok had worked out for his research into incantations and spells, published while Blok was still a student at the University of St. Petersburg.

Yesenin's autobiography begins:

I was born in 1895, on September 21, in the government of Ryazan', in the village Konstantinovo. . . .
When I was a child, [my family] very much wanted to make a rural teacher out of me, and I was put into a special parish school, upon finishing which I was to enter the Moscow Teachers' Institute. Fortunately, this did not happen. . . . I enrolled in Shanyavski's University [an adult education center in Moscow], where I remained only a year and a half and then went back to the village.[92]

Yesenin began to appear in print when he was still very young, and his first collection of poems was published in 1916. His early poems resemble Oreshin's and Klyuyev's, although Yesenin's are perhaps more song-like, and their melodious quality more spontaneous.

His earliest work reveals an important trait peculiar to him which at once distinguished him from the other peasant poets. Klyuyev, Klychkov, and Oreshin—as well as Pavel Vasil'yev, who, as successor of the first two, was an anachronism in the 1930's—were all in a complex way bound up with their material environment and the peasant way of life. They were in intellectual bondage to the things which suggested their poems, or rather, let us say that these writers are inconceivable apart from their peasant environment, as a "squire" is inconceivable without an estate. In their poems the human soul is so inextricably entwined with the peasant way of life that they cannot be separated—the soul itself becomes an integral part of the material environment of peasant life. To Sergei Klychkov, for instance, even the elemental pantheism of the peasants is meaningful only because it preserves the intimate ties between nature and the peasant's daily life, and is itself an inalienable part of that life.

Sergei Yesenin is the exception. Even his earliest work shows the Russian peasant liberated from bondage to things and environment. Not that Yesenin disregards daily life and material values. But while all the others focused their attention on the environment, Yesenin puts man's inner life first. To the others it is things in their relation to man that are important. Yesenin looks at man in relation to things.

Serene spirituality of emotion and delicate purity of image are characteristic of his first poems. They seem to be written in the cerulean blue of a sunny early morning or a quiet evening and are filled with a prayerful love for the tranquil beauty of nature.

At fourteen the young poet tried his hand at a long story in verse, the remarkable *Mikola* (a folk variant of the name Nikolai), based on the popular legend of the cheerful and compassionate Saint Nicholas.

The Brink is less notable as a work of art than as Yesenin's first work striking a revolutionary note. Georgi Ivanov mistakenly accused Yesenin of being weak and of letting Klyuyev and Ryurik Ivnev drag him into Bolshevism almost against his will. Although his divided state of mind is already apparent in *The Brink*, what prompted him to exult in both the February and the October Revolution may also be discerned.

In June 1918 he wrote in "The Jordan Dove":

> The moon is the tongue
> In the bell of the sky,
> My country's my mother,
> A Bolshevik, I.[93]

There is reason for his playing up to the Bolsheviks, and peasant cunning may indeed have had something to do with it. Internationalism never appealed to him, and the idea of world revolution left him cold. To Yesenin, the revolution was Russia's own tempest which was not going to spread beyond her borders. Moreover, the tempest appeared to him to be of a religious rather than political nature. He thought that the Bolsheviks would soon be frustrated in their idea of the revolution and that the Old Believers' dream would then come into its own. In his "cosmic" poems of the early days after the revolution, Yesenin contrasted the vision of Belovod'ye—

as seen in his own reckless imagination—and the Bolshevik interpretation of Karl Marx's model society. The Russian, popular, peasant, religious idea of utopia as against the Marxist blueprint of Communist society—that is the tenor of Yesenin's revolutionary poetry. He wanted the revolution to change Russia into Belovod'ye, the paradise descended from heaven to earth.

> I see the horses grazing
> In meadows green and lush.
> St. Andrew the Apostle
> Is piping in the brush.[94]

At the beginning of the revolution, Yesenin thought it possible for heaven to become earthly reality if the muzhik would throw off his fear and servility. The long poem *Inonia*, written in January 1918, called for courage and daring:

> Today with my brawny arm
> I can turn the whole world upside down.[95]
> . . . .
> With my tongue I'll lick clean the icons
> Of saints and martyrs wan.
> In the City of God on earth
> We will worship the living man![96]
> . . . .
> Lo, another Saviour
> Comes riding on a mare.
> Our faith is in our strength,
> Our truth is everywhere![97]

In "Hymnal" [*Oktoikh*] he sounded irritated, even angered, at the fact that paradise seemed in no hurry to become daily life and went so far as to urge the muzhiks to use force if necessary to shake this reluctant world into descending.

The poem "Father" again indicates that Yesenin's cosmic poems have Old Believer roots.

> The dawn is a she-wolf
> With a wet red grin,
> But your two-finger crosses
> Banish all sin.[98]

In Yesenin's cosmic poems critics—Khodasevich, for instance—

have found that something of the animism of dark pagan times comes to the surface. It is common knowledge that the Old Believers' cult and, in particular, the apocryphal legends preserved by that cult are based on a syncretism of paganism and Christianity. This syncretism is exactly what Yesenin's cosmic poems express. Consequently, one cannot speak of the "paganism" of Yesenin's revolutionary poems apart from the "paganism" of Old Believers' apocrypha—a complex, grave and still controversial question.

These poems have also been called sacrilegious, since the Russian people, the "God-bearer," is made to appear blasphemous, and Yesenin himself seems to extol sacrilege. The Old Believers' church is bound by dogma and canon to a far greater extent than the Orthodox Church. But besides dogma and canon it has something far more important—fanatical faith and an elemental pantheistic conception of the world. In other words, there is the spirit as well as the letter. Yesenin rebelled against the letter but remained faithful to the spirit. It is a mistake to interpret this as a sacrilege.

"Humanizing" the saints and reducing all sacred things to an earthly scale were characteristic of Yesenin's religiosity. In this "debunking" the left-wing critics (Lelevich and, at one time, Rodov) discovered atheism, or at least the first sign of healthy peasant atheism which had not yet discarded the Church but had already outgrown servile submission to it. Yesenin was an "intuitive" atheist, critics have maintained, who arrived at his atheism without benefit of studying Marx. On this subject Yesenin himself wrote, with irony, toward the end of his life:

> Not even Lenin is a god to me.
> I know the world . . .
> On ritual I frown . . .
> Yet something makes me bow submissively
> Before the icon, ere I will sit down.
> "Well, sister, speak!"
> And Sister has her say.
> *Das Kapital,* her Bible, by her side,
> She talks of Marx,
> Of Engels . . .
> By the way,
> I've never read them—I've not even tried.[99]

The fact is, however, that in Yesenin's early cosmic poems it is impossible to define his religious convictions—or his political. They are lost in the welter of the poet's own confusion and vacillation. He may call himself a Bolshevik and a few lines later turn his back to the Bolsheviks. He may raise his voice in blasphemy and the next moment bow before an icon entreating forgiveness.

In any case, Yesenin's vision of Christ was very different from Blok's. Blok saw Christ in a wreath of roses; Yesenin in "The Coming" saw him flagellated and stumbling from exhaustion:

> Look at that meadow,
> Mown and cropped:
> Beside an alder
> Your Christ has dropped.
> Once more the soldiers
> Have raised their whips
> And shadows cover
> His bloodless lips.[100]

Yesenin was a poet of compassion and charity, and he never forgave the suffering caused by the revolution. Even in 1917 he was in despair, realizing that the revolution killed faith in Christ, and Christian compassion with it:

> A sudden burst of flame,
> The barking of a gun—
> A bullet through his heart,
> The Holy Child fell down.
> Now listen:
> There will not be another resurrection.
> They buried him without a genuflection.[101]

Unlike the cosmic poems of the period immediately following the revolution, two long poems written at the beginning of the 1920's, "Mares' Ships" and "*Sorokoust*" (in the Orthodox Church, prayers for the dead during the first forty days after death), are surrealistic —there is no clear line between reality and delirium, life and nightmare. The first expresses horror at the bloodbath of Bolshevik terrorism:

Poets in the Ascendant

>   With chopped-off arms for oars
>   You row into the future.[102]

Exultation in the bloody revolt has given way to remorse:

>   Soon the snow-laden tree will lose
>   Its last yellow leaf—my head.[103]
>   . . . .
>   I will not go back to men—
>   Better far I should die with you
>   Than that I should cast a stone
>   At a madman whom once I knew.[104]

The poem *"Sorokoust,"* written in 1920 when the peasant uprisings were at their height and when grandiose plans for electrification were being drawn up by GOELRO (State Commission for Electrification of Russia), expresses horror of technological civilization:

>   The dawn of electricity,
>   The metal dance of gear and lever—
>   The bellies of the peasant huts
>   Are shaking with dynamic fever.[105]

Yesenin feared that Bolshevik industrialization must lead to a war between the city and the country in which the latter would be the loser.

>   Rime, like whitewash, will cover tomorrow
>   The houses, the meadows, the lanes.[106]
>   . . . .
>   The peasant, smelling of straw,
>   Chokes on his slug of rotgut.[107]

Yesenin's wrath was directed at the Bolsheviks' control of machines and their use for evil ends, not at machines themselves:

>   Oh, Russia, give over dragging
>   Your wooden plough through the fields!
>   The birches ache, and the poplars,
>   When they see what the harvest yields.[108]

Formally, Yesenin belonged to the Imaginist school, but his poetry does not exemplify the principles of Imaginism—his method of superimposing layer upon layer of images harks back to ancient Russian literature.

Yesenin constantly improved the form of his lyric verse until he had reduced it to the extreme simplicity—"complex simplicity," as Yuri Tynyanov called it—which lends itself to expressing emotion.

In later years Yesenin often reverted to childhood memories in his lyrical poems, with increasing disappointment in the revolution:

> But the dream has gone up in smoke;
> From the tenderest dreams one must rouse.
> Peace be with you, O fields of hay,
> Peace be with you, my old frame house![109]

Soviet critics have accused Yesenin of wallowing in filth. To be sure, many of the poems in the *Tavern Moscow* cycle[110] are drenched in vodka, and conceal nothing, not even the most abject vices. At the same time they sound like a confession, utterly sincere and prompted by a longing to redeem himself.

In a poem of the *Tavern Moscow* period (1923-1924) he lamented the loss of his former simple faith in God:

> What a funny loss to bemoan!
> Life has many a joke like this:
> I'm ashamed that I once had faith,
> Yet that faith I bitterly miss.[111]

The most important poem of Yesenin's last years is "The Black Man," which deserves to occupy the same place in his work as *The Bronze Horseman* occupies in Pushkin's. It is both a confession and the frenzied, unchecked raving of an alcoholic who, in a lucid moment, has realized that he is sick. The poet is aware that his addiction to alcohol, his vices and unrestrained debauchery are a protest against the Soviet regime:

> This man, you see,
> Lived in a land
> Of truly appalling
> Cutthroats and charlatans.[112]

By now the Bolshevik Party had become in his eyes a party of cutthroats and mountebanks, and in *Tavern Moscow* Yesenin displayed his rebellious temper:

> They regret that unsparing October
> Misled them in merciless blizzards,
> And with fresh daring they've sharpened
> The knives they conceal in their boots.[113]

The Soviet critic Ye. F. Nikitina, pointing out that, in his *Tavern* cycle, Yesenin drew a contrast between the "Party-conditioned" man and the man who would rather be free, commented in 1926: "Yesenin is one of the victims, a great victim, of cold, implacable history which, at its crossroads, crushes the delicate, lyrical, individualistic soul." [114]

Trotsky, too, said in a letter made public at a commemorative meeting at the Moscow Art Theater soon after Yesenin's tragic death that a clash between this most intimate lyrical poet and "our unlyrical era" was inevitable.[115]

Curiously, Bukharin, even while berating Yesenin for pessimism, recognized to the full the significance of Yesenin's intention in setting Belovod'ye against the Marxist socio-economic scheme. The idea was not Yesenin's alone; it was latent in the whole peasant mass which had been rallied to the revolutionary cause. Yesenin, in confused and groping words, expressed what others could not articulate at all, but clearly felt. Bukharin, who advocated the gradual integration of the kulaks with socialism and looked to peasant resistance to force a radical change in Bolshevik agricultural policies, saw nothing dangerous or harmful in Yesenin's idea, as long as the peasants retained optimism and confidence. Belief in a bright future, if purged of mysticism and intelligently directed toward improving the standard of living, would, he felt, in time make the peasants forget Belovod'ye for Marxism. Yesenin's hope, of course, was for the exact opposite.

In Yesenin's pessimism Bukharin saw a sign of the peasantry's despondency, as well as an indication that they had given up hope of improvement by peaceful means, and admonished against loss of spirit.[116] Bukharin's broadside was used to discredit Yesenin's poetry.

Yesenin's two plays in verse, *Pugachov* (written in 1921) and "The Land of Scoundrels," which remained unfinished and of which only fragments were published, were also objectionable to the Soviet authorities,[117] although the first found admirers among the critics.

Pugachov was not written for the stage. It is less a play than a sequence of lyrical poems referring to the Soviet period rather than the past. The hero is not the Pugachov of history but resembles Gerasim Antonov, leader of the peasant revolts in the Tambov region. The NEP ended Antonov's movement by raising hopes that the situation might be improved by peaceful work, and this enticed the peasants into deserting their leader. Antonov gradually found himself in the role of a commander without an army. There is reproach in *Pugachov*, and resentment against the peasantry for not supporting Pugachov when he most needed support. Some Soviet critics, however, welcomed the play because it showed the peasants' reluctance to fight and their wish to exchange the gun for the plow.

P. S. Kogan wrote that in spite of "a touch of cloying Imaginism, *Pugachov* is one of Yesenin's best works." [118] Kogan was discussing only Yesenin's large-scale literary pieces, not his lyrical verse, and he may have exaggerated somewhat, but the great formal qualities of *Pugachov* are indisputable, though seldom recognized.

In the poem Yesenin combines Cossack battle songs and the rhythm of the *Tale of the Host of Igor'* [*Slovo o polku Igoreve*], with powerful effect, which cannot be reproduced in translation:

> Not disaster, but joy and triumph
> Will fall to the peasant's lot.
> The darkling plain with its silver haze
> Rings with sabers and shields that clash.
> The very forests,
> Like rebels, raise
> Their scarlet banners of mountain ash![119]

"The Land of Scoundrels," written soon after Yesenin's return from a visit to America during his short-lived marriage to Isadora

Poets in the Ascendant 129

Duncan, shows a strong influence of American movie thrillers. Not knowing foreign languages, Yesenin was influenced by Western culture mainly through films. It cannot be denied that he was deplorably "provincial," in the Western sense—one of the reasons why he did not become one of the greatest poets of the twentieth century.

The play has a bold plot construction and, had Yesenin finished it, would have been one of the most absorbing plays of the postrevolutionary theater. It has remarkable stage possibilities, in the hands of an imaginative director unafraid of bold innovations.

Yesenin displays mastery in drawing Communist "types." In a conversation between Rassvetov, the Trotsky type, and Charin, of the Bukharin type, the latter compares Communism with capitalist America:

> And have you forgotten, perchance,
> That we too are avid for gold?
> On us too the dark world of finance,
> Like a weasel, maintains its hold.
>
> . . . .
>
> Let us say it for all to hear:
> Our Republic is only a bluff.
> We're no better, my friend, than they.[120]

Charin is worried lest the people, having tasted socialism, might reject it, or even want to kill it for good:

> The peasants think we are thieves,
> Or are giving the thieves a free hand.[121]

Nomakh typifies the leaders of the peasant uprisings:

> I am mulling over a plan
> Of a nation-wide rebellion.
> . . . .
> I would like to challenge this crew
> Who grow fat on their Marx like Yanks.
> How their courage will bid them adieu
> When they're faced with our heavy tanks![122]

Bolshevik critics have written much derogatory nonsense about this play—for instance, that it was illiterate and silly, that Yesenin knew neither the theater nor life, that he was not equipped to write for the stage. Only Voronski was courageous and honest enough to defend it.

Anna Snegina, a long, more or less autobiographical poem produced during the last year of Yesenin's life, pictures a Russian village during the Civil War.

The poems written just before his death have indefinable affinities with Pushkin's last poems. In December 1925 Yesenin hanged himself on a radiator pipe, in a room of the Hotel Angleterre, in Leningrad, at dawn.

Georgi Ivanov wrote in the foreword to the Paris edition of Yesenin's poems:

Yesenin's importance lies in the fact that he happened to be in perfect consonance with the Russian people of "Russia's terrible days," utterly at one with it, and became the symbol of Russia's fall and of her striving for redemption. This is the secret of his "Pushkinesque uniqueness," which transforms his erring life and imperfect poetry into a fount of light and good. It is therefore no exaggeration to say that Yesenin was the successor of Pushkin in our generation.[123]

MINOR PEASANT POETS

Of the old generation, Spiridon Drozhzhin (1848-1930) and Filipp Shkulyov (1868-1930) offer striking examples of the effect of 1917 on the peasant intellectuals. Both poets were elderly men when the Revolution broke out, and both were spiritually rejuvenated. For a brief time their work took on new color and freshness.

Aleksandr Shiryayevets, Pavel Radimov and Pimen Karpov were contemporaries of Klyuyev and Klychkov. Shiryayevets (1887-1924) took his pen-name from his native village Shiryayevo, on the Volga (his real name was A. V. Abramov). Though the literary critics paid little attention to him, he enjoyed an esteem bordering on veneration among his fellow peasant writers who saw in him a modern Avvakum. Drudgery in government offices up to 1917 prevented him from fully developing his great natural gifts. There is a strong revolutionary note in his work of this period.

The most important poems of his remaining years were collected

Poets in the Ascendant

in *Volga Songs*, published posthumously. In them he defended the elemental forces of the revolution—the Pugachov and Razin spirit— but felt that the peasants should at all costs save the Orthodox faith from the Communists and that they should not tolerate the wholesale scrapping of the historical past.

> In a heart so truly Russian
> Russia's past can never die,
> And I well remember galloping
> With my heavy lance held high.[124]

Shiryayevets' last poems deal with the Volga famine of 1921:

> The thunder did not come; there was no sound,
> No drop of rain fell on the thirsty ground,
> No drop of rain . . .
> And Death was dancing its infernal round.[125]

Often his verse boils with a wrath in which other peasant writers found incitement to revolt against the Bolsheviks.

Pavel Radimov (1887-   ), on the other hand, is a poet of peace, of the static contentment of the old Russian village. Mayakovski made malicious fun of him and his antiquated hexameters. Radimov used this meter, however, very deliberately and with discretion. It was not unsuitable to his description of a patriarchal way of life which was doomed. To Radimov, rural life was inseparable from the Orthodox faith. He saw the work of the peasants as a kind of liturgy of toil. Monasteries, churches, pilgrims fill his poems.

> Here at the crossroads a chapel stands on a kerchief of lawn;
> In it Saint Nicholas bides, guardian of highways and by-ways.[126]

By 1923 his nostalgia and grief had become very poignant:

> Black is the pall over pasture, meadowland, coppice and field.
> Requiems sung by the wind float in the sky overhead.
> The land is a graveyard; by willows, birches and alders concealed,
> Lie in the desolate earth the summer's disconsolate dead.[127]

A painter as well as poet, in the early 1920's Radimov joined the artists Grigor'yev and Naumov in helping to organize the Association of Artists of the Revolution in Moscow. Thereafter he

devoted himself mainly to painting. In 1923 he was arrested but
soon released. He then published a few poems praising the kolkhoz
system, and fell silent.

Pimen Karpov (1884-   ), prerevolutionary poet and novelist,
is an interesting but neglected writer. In 1922 he published two
books of verse, *Stars* and *Russian Ark*, still in his former Symbolist
vein. His collection of short stories of 1920, *The Trumpet Call*
[*Trubnyi golos*] depicts the wretched situation of village intellectuals, affronted by the treatment accorded them under the dictatorship of the city and appalled by the rough-and-ready Party
recruits lording it over the countryside.

The label "muzhikites" *(muzhikovstvuyushchiye)*, a vaguely dis-
paraging term coined by Mayakovski, came to be applied to the
slightly younger peasant poets who were Yesenin's contemporaries
or later imitators.

Among the contemporaries, Pavel Druzhinin (1890-   ), Fyodor Fyodorov and Gennadi Korenev (1896?-   ?) deserve only
passing mention. Druzhinin was an unoriginal writer, a combination
of Yesenin and Oreshin, who never tired of describing peasant
"princesses" in cotton dresses, nibbling sunflower seeds and spitting
the shells out the window ("Beloved Russia, you live on,/Like your
black bread, you don't grow stale").[128] Fyodorov reveled in "fine,
flowery words," with "a weight attached to them," as Vyacheslav
Shishkov once told him. And the burden of Korenev's poetry was
that the Whites and the Reds should both go to hell and leave the
peasant alone, for he wanted to get on with his work.

The three followers of Yesenin who stand out as poets in their
own right all had their careers interrupted by political misfortunes.
Vasili Nasedkin (1895-   ) carefully polished his poems and
succeeded in rendering deep genuine feeling. Like many other
peasant poets of his generation, he could not quite make up his
mind between the kolkhoz and the traditional system of farming.
After his arrest and then release from prison in the late 1930's, his
poetry lost much of its vigor and charm. The poetry of Ivan Pribludnyi (1905?-   ) is more spontaneous, but also more careless,
than Nasedkin's. His favorite subject was the happiness of peaceful
toil no longer disrupted by civil war. His little book of verse *A*

Poplar on Stone, 1926, was his most important published work.[129] In 1935, Pribludnyi was arrested and disappeared from the literary scene. Konstantin Tyulyapin (1911-   ), too, found himself in a concentration camp before even having made a place for himself in literature.

6. The Imaginists

The Imaginist movement was of very brief duration. Its first manifesto was published in February 1919, and by the end of 1924 the group had formally dissolved.

VADIM SHERSHENEVICH (1893 -   )

Vadim Shershenevich, one of the founders of the school, was, like several other Imaginists, a former Ego-Futurist. There is no great difference, however, between his early theoretical work *Futurism Without a Mask* and $2 \times 2 = 5$, of 1920, a treatise dealing with Imaginism.[1] L'vov-Rogachevski, pointing out that Shershenevich derived his ideas from Potebnya (but overlooking Buslayev's *Influence of Christianity on the Slavonic Language*), accused Shershenevich of crude and arrogant dilettantism and of pontificating like a pretentious sophomore.[2]

There is some truth in Rogachevski's strictures, although he ignored Shershenevich's pertinent observation that scholars of literature, while aware that language was becoming specialized and no longer fired the imagination, did not know what to do about it; they recognized the disease but were unable to cure it. The Imaginists made it their job to work a cure.

Image and meaning, according to Shershenevich, are two distinct components of a word. Meaning is the product of ratiocination. In modern times, the image is not being destroyed, but it is being absorbed by meaning. (In this, of course, Shershenevich was wrong. Our vocabulary does tend toward extreme specialization, which, in the end, must result in total suppression of imagery.) He defines the cardinal principles of Imaginism as a return to thinking in images, subordination of meaning to image in poetry and, finally, victory of image over meaning, that is, words free of meanings. In $2 \times 2 = 5$, Shershenevich argues:

> The meaning of a word is fixed not only in the root, but also in the grammatical form. The image of a word is only in the root. In smashing grammar, we destroy the potential force of the meaning and preserve the earlier force of the image.[3]

Further, "a poem is not an organism but an agglomeration of images."[4]

The theory of Imaginism was weak and short-lived. The Imaginists did not succeed in restoring to words their lost imagery. The only exception was Yesenin, but his being numbered among the Imaginists was more or less accidental. He went back to ancient Russian usage for words still possessing their pristine freshness and emotional impact, words unimpaired by precise technical meanings.

The significance of the Imaginists is not in "thinking in images," as they tried so hard to do, but in the dramatic rendering of their impressions. They rejected the common aphorism that "when one person dies, it is a tragedy, and when millions die, it is statistics." To them, the death of millions was a tragedy a million times repeated.

Vadim Shershenevich has been described as "a man hiding a deep sorrow under shoddy antics and cheap witticism."[5] In his early prerevolutionary poems he foresaw the loss of man's individuality in the Communist social order, a prison of steel and concrete.

> We are the last of our caste
> Whose future fast declines;
> We are the peddlers of joy,
> The craftsmen of polished lines.
> Soon they will come to replace us
> Who look not below or above—
> Mechanics who hammer out glory,
> Cobblers who fashion love.
> They will calmly set aside,
> In the day they use so well,
> Seven minutes to fondle a bride,
> Three seconds to read a rondel.
> . . . .

> Women, make haste to love us,
> For we sing of wonders still,
> And we are the last thin cracks
> That progress yet has to fill![6]

In his later work he ceased to be critical of the regime and, like most of the other Imaginists, fell in line with the rest of the cowed intelligentsia.

ANATOLI MARIENHOF (Mariyengof)

Marienhof (1897-   ) created even more of a sensation with the obscenity and deliberate coarseness of language in his early books of verse (although these features are usually greatly exaggerated): *Showcase of the Heart,* 1918; *Pastry Shop of the Suns,* 1919; *Magdalen,* 1919; *Necktie of Hands* [*Ruki galstukom*], 1920; *Showing Off My Poems* [*Stikhami chvanstvuyu*], 1920; and *I Fornicate with Inspiration* [*Razvratnichayu s vdokhnoveniyem*], 1921. In *Buyan Island,* 1920, he defined his attitude toward Imaginism.

Marienhof's poetry is by no means devoid of talent. His early poems were Ego-Futuristic and lacked originality, but the revolution brought out new powers in him. L'vov-Rogachevski implied that the Imaginists attempted to make the revolution responsible for their delirious vagaries. Of Marienhof he said:

> His morbid, autumnal verse reveals a profound, pathological dislocation; and the tactless youth tries at all costs to connect his own sickness with the majestic, thunderous business of history.[7]

The fact is that Marienhof's early poems were filled with enthusiasm for the revolution ("I am naught but a happy madman/Who bet his shirt on October").[8]

Soon, however, the revolution appeared to him as a "bloody meatgrinder":

> Death is poking its broom into every single hole—
> All you prisoners, line up against the wall!
> The earth is stained with human blood
> As a butcher's apron with the blood of steers.[9]

His poems of 1922-1926 were collected in the volume *The New Marienhof,* published in 1926.

Marienhof was well aware of the power of the poet to make the revolutionary state fear the havoc it wrought upon the country. In his treatise on Imaginism he says:

> The mere touch of poetry congeals life, things and feelings. The artist stops the hoofs of a galloping horse; with a light touch of his brush he arrests the whirling wheels of a car. . . . The poet is the most redoubtable slayer of all that lives.[10]

Unfortunately his sound critical observations are marred by fatuous smirks in an imitation of Oscar Wilde's manner as he understood it.

The Shaved Man[11] and *A Novel Without Lies,*[12] 1927, are his own reminiscences in fiction form. In the first book, which was published in Berlin, he delights in obtrusive cynicism. *A Novel Without Lies* is largely concerned with Yesenin. The author insists that he is Yesenin's equal as an artist, and, besides, a much nicer man. The effect of this is rather comical. Shershenevich maliciously pointed out that Marienhof was, in fact, a model husband. His break with Yesenin was partly due to the fact that Marienhof could not carry his liquor well and did not really care for drinking. Shershenevich called him a coquette in pants, flirting now with alcohol, now with sex.

Marienhof's historical novel *Catherine,*[13] 1936, is more interesting and important, and it is a pity that only fragments of it have been published. To judge by the parts available, Marienhof restrained his taste for lurid eroticism and did not go into the details of Catherine the Great's amorous adventures.

His play "The Stranger" [*Postoronnyaya zhenshchina*] is a most amusing comedy. Although the play was produced by the Leningrad Comedy Theater and a film based on it was released in 1929 (from a scenario written by Marienhof and Nikolai Erdman), the text was never published. The comedy shows the failure of Communism to establish the much-vaunted new relationships among people. Hypocrisy and egotism prevail among Party officials, even in their private lives, in contrast with the simple kindness of the average man who has kept to the old Russian traditions. Both the play and the film met with a storm of protest and were withdrawn.

Marienhof tried, without success, to regain his standing by writing a few bombastically patriotic plays, such as *Shut Balakirev* [The Buffoon Balakirev], 1940.

OTHERS

Vyacheslav Kovalevski and Ryurik Ivnev are erratic poets, occasionally lacking in good taste and in sense of proportion.

Kovalevski is remembered now chiefly for the fact that he had his long poem *Plach* [Lament], 1920, printed in Church-Slavonic script—not merely an eccentric flourish, but a protest against the antireligious drive.

Ryurik Ivnev (pseudonym of Mikhail Aleksandrovich Kovalyov; b. 1893) was already a fully formed poet at the time of the revolution. His work centers on one theme, Russian Christianity. He rendered its due to the Orthodox Church which for centuries had kept evil on a strong chain, imprisoned by good. The revolution broke that chain and set evil free.

In the midst of the Civil War—the "black years of the plague" whose victims mistook hatred for love—he wrote:

> Arrest the world in its career,
> Your sunlit liberty remove,
> And give me back the somber years
> Of my pathetic, shameful love![14]

Of his novels, which are of uneven quality, *Love Without Love*, 1925,[15] is the best, and the best in it is inspired by Dostoyevski. In his Party hero, Kroner, Ivnev exposes the essence of the Communist system. Preaching a cold, abstract class hatred, it treats men as abstractions and thus does not hesitate to resort to terror, purge, prison, and execution in dealing with them. The tragedy of Kroner, a builder of the Soviet machine, is that his love for Nastya cannot develop into spiritual love because his world is built on hatred.

The Open House,[16] a sequel, is somewhat synthetic, and the Artsybashev motifs, also discernible in *Love Without Love*, are more prominent. Nastya, now Kroner's wife, meets Boris Ukatov, an "elemental" revolutionary whose hatred is living hatred and not a cold abstraction like Kroner's. Ukatov falls in love with Nastya, and his love leads to a violent revulsion against the cult of hatred. He feels that he is close to rejecting Communism which serves the wrong gods, but he also knows that he cannot recapture his lost faith in the old God. The inner conflict becomes so acute that he commits suicide.

The Hero of a Novel, 1928,[17] is a continuation of *The Open House*. It is Ivnev's weakest piece of work and reads like a poor version of Artsybashev.

Ivnev's writings were withdrawn from circulation in the U.S.S.R. in the early 1930's, and he has rarely appeared in print since.

Aleksandr Kusikov (1896-   ) published ten or eleven books of verse from 1917 to 1923, then fell silent ("Stranger to all who pass me by,/ Horseless and with broken lance").[18] Kusikov himself was from the mountains of the Caucasus, and the plight of the uprooted is his central theme.

On the whole, the formal achievements of the Imaginist movement are less interesting than its attitude toward the revolution.

7. *Dem'yan Bednyi*
(pseudonym of Yefim A. Pridvorov, 1883-1945)

During the First World War there was a Russian rhymester known as Uncle Mikhei who, in the style of sideshow doggerel and popular songs, ground out lines equally well suited for store advertisements and for propaganda in favor of the throne. With one stroke he made the nation love both the Don Cossack Kryuchkov, that killer of numerous German beasts, and the cigarettes manufactured by Asmolov:

> Kryuchkov chopped Germans into little bits
> Because he smoked Asmolov's cigarettes.

The masses took to Uncle Mikhei's vulgar, primitive rhymes and dirty jokes as to the cheap low-grade tobacco.

In Dem'yan Bednyi the Soviet propaganda machine found an

Poets in the Ascendant

Uncle Mikhei of its own, a Red Uncle Mikhei, who could make people laugh and at the same time appeal to the semiliterate in behalf of the Soviet government. From the time of the revolution through the mid-1930's he turned out a vast and steady stream of propaganda jingles on every topic of the day.

He interpreted the international situation in the style of the heart-rending songs favored by the working class:

> The birch-tree in the wind
> Shivers in every bough.
> The Entente's taken poison
> And is at death's door now![1]

In "Tocsin," 1919, he tried to hearten the Red fighters during the Civil War:

> The Whites by desperate courage are upheld,
> But our dispute is drawing to its close.
> For the last time our battle-ax we wield
> Against the slender swords of highborn foes.[2]

The peddler's pack is full to overflowing. What will you have, Comrade Commissar? Would you care to glorify the Committees for the Poor?* Certainly, Comrades—and in lyrical vein, to boot! A half-starved old pauper comes to Committee headquarters:

> Over the happy cabin
> Flutters the crimson flag.
>
> . . . .
> Clutching his brand-new sheepskin,
> The old man brushed off his tears:
> "To get to this point, my children,
> It took me seventy years!"[3]

His long narrative poem, *Muzhiks*, 1918, describes the impact of the revolution on the village.

"You alone have learned the secrets of Pushkin's verse form. Then why have you chosen to decorate fences with your verses?"[4] Vyacheslav Ivanov asked Dem'yan Bednyi.

His Civil War poems, in spite of their crudity, were heated by an

---

*Rural organizations set up in 1918 to confiscate foodstuffs and other necessities from the wealthier peasants, to redistribute them, and to aid requisitioning organs in obtaining supplies for the Red Army and urban areas.

inner fire and affected even educated people, much as raw alcohol would have done. During the NEP period, however, his verse lost much of its color and spirit, and there was nothing left but lewdness and bad taste.

As soon as he became convinced that Trotsky's career was over, Dem'yan Bednyi became Stalin's police dog; in obedience to his master's orders he would fling himself, growling, on the appointed victim. In addition to his printed poems attacking Stalin's enemies and glorifying Stalin's policies, he circulated pornographic poems—also with political overtones and of unimpeachable ideology—in manuscript form.

His militant anti-religious verse is marked by cynical hooliganism. An anonymous letter in verse to Dem'yan Bednyi protesting against his blasphemy which was copied by hand and circulated throughout the country contained the following lines:

> You've merely brayed at Jesus Christ,
> O Yefim Lackeyson Pridvorov.*

Georgi Ivanov has credited Yesenin with authorship of the letter,[5] although in the Soviet Union many thought that Andrei Platonov had written it.

In the second half of the 1930's Dem'yan Bednyi's *Ancient Warriors* [*Bogatyri*], was produced in the Moscow Kamernyi Theater. In it he scoffed at the Orthodox Church and treated with levity the introduction of Christianity into Russia—an event which, in the play, occurred because everyone concerned was drunk. At that very time—in the period of preparing for war—the Party's attitude toward the Church was under review, and in due course it was proclaimed that during its early stages the Orthodox Church had exerted a positive influence on Russia's development. Furthermore, Russian legendary heroes were restored to popular favor. Dem'yan Bednyi had miscalculated. *Ancient Warriors* was taken off the boards. Stalin's disfavor brought Dem'yan Bednyi's career and his prosperity to a sudden stop.

During the Second World War he was permitted to resume publishing, but he was unable to regain his stride.

---

* ["Pridvorov" literally means "employed at court."—Tr.]

3

The Proletcult and the Smithy

8. Bogdanov and the Proletarian Culture Organizations

"As soon as the Red Army soldiers return from the war, as soon as the workers and peasants overcome the famine, the development of our culture, of our art, will begin,"[1] proclaimed the working-class writer Bessal'ko in connection with the conference of the Proletarian Cultural-Educational Organizations (Proletcult), held in September 1918. Among its organizers were A. Bogdanov and A. V. Lunacharski, the first People's Commissar of Education.

A. Bogdanov (pseudonym of Aleksandr Aleksandrovich Malinovski, 1873-1928), Party official, philosopher, physician, sociologist, economist and literary critic, left a deep imprint on the history of the Proletcult as well as of the secessionist group called the Smithy [*Kuznitsa*], which differed only on questions of secondary importance.

According to Bogdanov, during the feudal and capitalist eras of its development, mankind was divided into two groups, the organizers and the executors. The Communist revolution was to heal this breach by obliterating the distinction between intellectual and physical endeavor.

When Bogdanov looked for concrete ways of transforming this dream into reality he was beset by doubt and hesitation, as in his two utopian novels, written before the revolution, *The Red Star* and *Engineer Menni*. Neither has any literary merit, but in both there is a depth of meaning and a fitful fire of restless thought which make up for shortcomings of form. Bogdanov was convinced that the revolution would precipitate undreamed-of technological development and that humanity would then launch vast projects which would change the face of the globe. But would not the complexities of technological development on a gigantic scale, instead of closing the breach between intellectual and physical work, deepen the rift betwen the organizers and the executors? Might it not lead to an engineers' state in which all power would be concentrated in the hands of a dictator, supported by an army of overseers who in turn would give orders to legions of executors tranformed into mere appendages of machines, into spare parts which, when unusable, could readily be thrown away and replaced? Bogdanov does not draw these conclusions explicitly in *Engineer Menni*, but sorrowfully foreshadows them. "Your triumph is a delusion!"[2] Life goes on, but love dies: "In the boundlessness of mighty being, only that will be preserved which you loved more than yourself—your work. But in it you lose yourself—that is the waste."[3]

Bogdanov is not a creative writer, but an intelligent, sensitive, and warm-hearted thinker. He thought of himself not as an artist but as a philosopher, and one whose vocation was not merely to take cognizance of, but to transform, the external world. The revolution would not be made, however, merely on the barricades and in civil war; first a revolution must occur in the soul of the individual and of the collective. As one of the organizers of the prewar Party school on the island of Capri—where, as part of the program, workers who had shown aptitude were trained to become writers—Bogdanov was "tainted" with the "God-making" of which Lunacharski, Gorki, and other founders of the school were accused by the Lenin faction. They were attempting, it was charged, to create a religion without a God through deification of the workers' collective. Gorki was even accused of worshipping a "demiurge-folk," of preferring the philosophy of Apollon Grigor'yev to the doctrine of Karl Marx. In any case, because of differences of opinion, Bogdanov left the Party during World War I. The initiative he took in convening the first conference of the Proletarian Cultural-Educational Organizations marked his return to active political work.

Bogdanov wanted to begin after the revolution to evolve concrete and practical methods of gradually eliminating the distinction between intellectual and physical labor, of bridging the gap between the organizers and the executors, of developing a spirit of comradeship, collectivism and solidarity. Such was the long-range aim.

In proletarians, functioning as both organizers and executors in production, Bogdanov saw the agency which would effect this reconciliation and bring about unity of experience. He argued that every problem of technology, economics or cultural activity is an organizational problem and that for performance of its eventual over-all organizational role the proletariat must first develop its own culture, a prerequisite to proper exercise of power. Proletarian art was to Bogdanov not only a representation of life from the proletarian point of view; it was a means of organizing the forces of the proletariat as a class for its historic mission of building socialism through collective labor.

Thus, the immediate purpose in setting up a network of educational and cultural centers—the Proletcult—was to educate workers and train new proletarian artists as the nucleus of a machinery of persuasion for gradual replacement of the machinery of compulsion. Bogdanov and the other founders of the Proletcult intended it to be an autonomous entity not accountable to Party or government; in fact, the implication was that the Proletcult was to hold itself apart from the government in order later to reconstruct it.

In 1918 Bogdanov published a small book entitled *Art and the Working Class*, which contains his three essays "What Is Proletarian Poetry?" "Criticism of Proletarian Art" and "Our Artistic Heritage."

In the last of these articles we once again encounter doubts and misgivings similar to those expressed in the novel *Engineer Menni*. How was one to find

a solution of the problem of organizing [through art] the human soul, which is split in two by the grave contradiction in our life between the desire for happiness and love of a harmonious existence, on the one hand, and the need to conduct a painful, stern and merciless struggle, on the other?

How are we to solve or reconcile this contradiction? How are we to keep the desire for harmony from weakening man for his unavoidable struggle, from robbing him of the necessary strength, firmness and self-control and at the same time prevent the required cruelty of the blows he strikes, the blood and dirt of the wounds inflicted, from destroying all the joy, all the beauty of living? How are we to restore the wholeness and unity of a soul which is torn in two by the bitter conflict between its deepest, highest needs and the imperative requirement to combat its hostile environment?[4]

The victorious proletarian must above all remain human, must preserve compassion and love. A soldier aiming the mouth of a cannon at a church or a palace was carrying out his duty, but in fulfilling his duty he must not take pleasure in the destruction of things once held sacred. Destruction was a temporary necessity. Accordingly, Bogdanov warned the members of the Proletcult against what he termed "the soldier psychology."

In short, Bogdanov combined his belief in the law of class struggle with the conviction that humanitarian principles must be preserved, that the class struggle, like any other struggle, might be ended by a truce or a peace. This opinion was later cited as evidence that his theory failed to distinguish proletarian culture from the classless culture of the future socialist society.

Before the end of the Civil War, Party leaders had blocked the attempt to foster a proletarian culture independent of the government and the Party. For several years, however, Bogdanov was in charge of the cultural development of the proletariat.

In 1920, there were about eighty thousand persons studying in "studios" of Proletcult organizations throughout the country. From 1918 to 1921 the All-Russian Council of these organizations issued its own policy publication, *Proletarskaya kul'tura* [Proletarian Culture], edited by P. I. Lebedev (V. Polyanski), F. Kalinin, P. Kerzhentsev, Bogdanov, and A. Mashirov (Samobytnik). Proletcult organizations published about twenty other magazines.

Through the initiative of Bogdanov and Lunacharski, such men as Belyi, Bryusov and Vladislav Khodasevich conducted courses for beginning poets and prose writers in Proletcult studios. Belyi was particularly successful in his efforts. A number of older industrial workers who had broken into print, or tried to, before the revolution also took part in the organization of the Proletcult. They studied their craft at the same time, going back to school with the youngsters, and a few of them became reasonably good writers and critics. On the whole, however, the work of the Proletcult and Smithy writers is weak. Its one good quality lies in its objectivity, in its combination of faith in the beauty of the future with a mercilessly exact portrayal of the ugliness and cruelty of the day.

9. Proletcult Poets

The hosannas to the Revolution poured out by mediocre workerpoets who had published before 1917 showed the salutary effect of their schooling in the Proletcult under major writers.

The volume of verse by the old glass-factory worker Yegor (Georgii) Nechayev (1859-1925) which was published three years before his death is his best book.

A. I. Samobytnik (pseudonym of A. I. Mashirov, b. 1884), a former foundry worker long active in the revolutionary movement, had been writing flat and colorless verse for years. Although the poems in his 1918 volume, *Under the Red Banner*, published by the Petrograd Proletcult, were still on a relatively low level, they had a new breath of passion and fanatical ardor.

> We've burst our barriers, one by one,
> Drunk with the savor of the earth.
> We who have never known the sun
> Do but precede a greater birth.[1]

The old Bolshevik Il'ya Ionov (1887-   ), who later became the head of the publishing house *Zemlya i fabrika* [Land and Factory] and who had long been scribbling revolutionary verse, also began to produce better work, as did the buoyant but wordy Il'ya Sadof'yev (1889-   ). In his compilation of poems entitled *Dynamo Verses*, which went through six editions in 1918-1919, Sadof'-

yev was obviously trying to translate Bogdanov's pamphlets into rhyming lines. This is his version of Bogdanov's views on the gradual transition from class struggle to the peaceful co-operation of collective labor and the bridging of the gap between the organizers and the executors:

> By dint of our collective effort,
> By laboring with might and main,
> We've raised a temple to Apollo,
> We have built cities on the plain.[2]

ALEKSEI GASTEV (1882-)

Of the older generation of prerevolutionary proletarian writers, Aleksei Gastev, a metal worker from his early years who had been publishing undistinguished verse and fiction since 1904, became by far the most original—and an uncannily clairvoyant—poet, despite his meager output and brief literary career after 1917. His reputation rests, and rests securely, on the volume *Shockwork Poetry,* published by Proletcult in 1918,[3] and on the thin sheaf of poems *A Stack of Orders,* first published in Riga in 1921 and later in the Soviet Union.[4]

Most of his work is free verse or prose poetry and shows the influence of Walt Whitman, Verhaeren and Marinetti. In the case of Marinetti, the influence is apparent in the form of Gastev's repudiation of his views.

Industrialization was Gastev's god. He did not, however, represent it as a strange blend of factory and church, as did many of the Proletcult poets. His "iron state" was built upon tense will power and by ruthless hands. The machine was the master of the world and commanded man, its creator. The poet rejoiced that the revolution had carried to power those who realized the necessity of building an "iron state."

> "We have come with new tidings,
> Reliable as steel, and spirited
> As the sound of an engine in the desert."
>   ... The speaker was still.
> The blast furnaces we build will speak for us,
> The beams we set in place will sing in our stead.[5]

The Proletcult and the Smithy

Himself an old revolutionary, Gastev minced no words in pointing out that the iron state required sacrifices, greater sacrifices than had ever been offered any deity. The fields would become a wasteland, grain would be found only in museums, and people fainting from exhaustion would be given still more work as their reward.

> Cram technics down the people's throats,
> Energize them with geometry,
> Beat them with logarithms,
> Kill their romanticism!
> Tons of indignation,
> Standardization of the word from pole to pole,
> Phrases based on the decimal system,
> Speeches like boiler works—
> Away with prosody,
> Let the tunnels give tongue![6]

Gastev's machine became a dehumanizing monster. In his theoretical prose works he spoke of the "mechanized collectivism" which would attend the vast industrialization of the future—movements of the workers synchronized with the movement of machines, individual human faces obliterated, individual thinking rendered impossible, a "normalized psychology" for the proletariat throughout the world.[7] For the deeper meaning of Bolshevik industrialization to the life of the nation, one may profitably study Gastev.

Great things had been expected from him, but after 1921 Gastev wrote little poetry. Thereafter, as founder and director of the Central Institute of Labor, he devoted himself to questions of labor management. In this capacity, Korneli Zelinski observed in 1935, his "mechanization ideas, which reduced the worker to the role of a machine part, affected his work in the field of scientific organization of labor and in the development of production training methods."[8]

COSMISM OR PLANETARITY

The careers of two of the most talented poets of the Proletcult—Kirillov and Gerasimov—justified misgivings which had troubled Bogdanov in recruiting the Symbolist poets as teachers. He feared that, while instructing their students in formal techniques, they might pass on to them their mystical and religious tendencies as well: "Any believer who seriously and attentively studies another religion runs the risk of conversion." [9] At the same time Bogdanov deprecated the derisive and destructive attitude toward the Orthodox Church. The Church, he held, was neither a royal palace nor a landowner's estate; it must not be razed by artillery fire or given to peasants to burn. The Church should be combated not by means of direct insult, injury and sacrilege, but by influencing the public conscience. A workingman employing the method of persuasion would be far more effective than a rabid atheist ranting that religion was a device of the priests for robbing the people.

Other influences to which the Proletcult writers were exposed combined with the teaching of the Symbolists to produce effects unforeseen by the sponsors of the Proletcult.

One of the most potent of these influences was that of Konstantin Tsiolkovski (1857-1935), the well-known scientist, inventor, visionary, and author. (In the mid-1950's Tsiolkovski was credited in Soviet sources with a prominent role in the development of rockets, with the proposal to create an artificial earth satellite, and with providing grounds—in his paper of 1903, "Exploration of Cosmic Space with Rocket Equipment"—for the possibility of interplanetary communication.) [10]

In the early stages of the Proletcult, Tsiolkovski was invited to lecture to the organization in Kaluga, where he resided. The general tenor of his efforts may be discerned from the meager records available of his association with the group. He is reported to have proceeded along the lines he followed in a book privately printed soon afterwards, *Outside the Earth,* a book setting forth in popular form the substance of his earlier scientific papers on rocket engines. In this book he writes:

> Usually we proceed from the known to the unknown, from the needle to the sewing machine, from the knife to the meat chopper, from the hand flail to the threshing machine, from the rowboat to the steamship. In the same way we have in mind moving from the airplane to jet-propulsion apparatus, for the conquest of the solar system.[11]

In another book of Tsiolkovski's he had taken his readers on travels through the ether, landed upon and taken off from planet after planet, and conversed with their imaginary inhabitants.[12]

Tsiolkovski was promptly, if tactfully, discouraged from further participation in the work of the Kaluga Proletcult—but not before Kirillov and many other Proletcult writers had been deeply impressed by his views. As a result of this influence in combination with the reading of certain scholarly works which were being recommended to them in their training program (such as Aleksandr Veselovski's essay "Giordano Bruno," Assanov's book *Galileo Before the Inquisition Tribunal* and Ferdinand Lassalle's treatise on Heraclitus) some Proletcult writers found their dialectical materialism giving way to "Cosmism," or "Planetarity," a trend which follows Tsiolkovski's lead in linking technological development with the conquest of outer space. V. Dubovskoi wrote derisively in 1924: "Planetarity is such a soaring flight of fancy that the scale of the earth, and even of the solar system, is lost from sight."[13] In the efforts to stamp out the Cosmism of Proletcult poets, Tsiolkovski was seldom, if ever, brought under direct attack. Attempts to impugn his standing rallied other scientists quickly to his defense. In 1923 the All-Russian Association of Natural Scientists protested in *Izvestiya* against the hushing up of the work of Tsiolkovski.[14]

VLADIMIR KIRILLOV (1889- ?)

Cosmism is particularly marked in the work of Vladimir Kirillov, one of the organizers and most active members of the Proletcult, as may be seen in his poem "Conversation with the Stars":

> One must be dull-witted in the extreme
> Not to see windows on infinity
> And fail to hear the music of the stars
> In lovers' kisses and art's unity.[15]

And again:

> Could we but grasp the purpose that we serve
> In being exiled on our little Earth,
> A spark of divine will we might preserve
> Against the shapeless dark that gave us birth.[16]

Bogdanov's misgivings were well founded: Kirillov and his fellow poets had combined Tsiolkovski's cosmism with the religious and mystical attitudes of Belyi and Blok.

Trotsky, with his barbed wit, made cruel fun of these "cosmic revelations." Bogdanov's and Tsiolkovski's ideas should not, he said, be interpreted in a primitive and simplified manner. In pointing to the need to overcome the breach between nature and human perception, Bogdanov expected the new era to open up new and hitherto undreamed-of prospects of harnessing nature to man's will. The Proletcult writers should see in Bogdanov's teachings an appeal to hard work. Collective labor was a miracle, but not one to be achieved by wordy revelations. The Proletcult writers, on the contrary, having decided that the universe was unknowable, had folded their hands and abandoned themselves to feeling at one with the cosmos. "In fact," Trotsky wrote,

Cosmism has some of the elements of desertion—of fleeing from the complex, art-defying state of things here below into interstellar spheres. . . . It is to be feared that the dubious tendency to stuff the gaps in one's world-view and artistry with the fine stuff of interstellar space may lead some of the Cosmists to that finest of all fine stuffs, the Holy Ghost, in which enough poetical corpses rest as it is.[17]

During the first few years after the Revolution, the Proletcult published three volumes of Kirillov's verse: *Poems,* containing work of 1914-1918; *Dawns of the Future,* 1919; and *The Iron Messiah: Verses of the Revolution, 1917-1920.* The poet had a modest but correct opinion of his work; he said that he was not capable of producing perfect poems, perfect images, memorable lines, but that he nevertheless regarded his poetry as of considerable importance in that it clarified the spirit and ideological objectives of the Proletcult.

Kirillov studied with Belyi and consulted Bryusov and Blok, not without effect. Advised to give up bombastic magniloquence ("O holy storm, convulse the air,/ Wreak havoc on the earth below"),[18] Kirillov took the exhortations to heart, and wrote of the revolution in his poem "October 25":

> Some days have the stature of ages.
> Bright in our memory grown
> This autumn day burns scarlet
> In the light of a deathless dawn.
>
> . . . .
>
> We were drunk, having no drink taken,
> And gay through a sleepless night.
> And each man walked more lightly,
> And each eye with spring was bright.[19]

Kirillov's poetry is saturated with worship of labor. In his early postrevolutionary poems, plants and factories resemble palaces or churches, and his proletarians swing their hammers as if they were so many censers.

With the introduction of the New Economic Policy in 1921 Kirillov gave way to doubt and disillusion. Like many proletarian poets, he had supported the new regime in the belief that it would radically change the conditions of labor and the general attitude toward labor. The economic retreat was to him a betrayal of the revolution, a desecration of the cathedrals of industry seen in his dreams.

Earlier he had written:

> Each heart within its burning dream
> Treasures the vernal name of Lenin.[20]

Then in January 1925:

> I was submerged in the noise and the shouting,
> While high in his tower, in awesome state—
> Neither God nor devil—a bald accountant
> Sat in majesty, ruling our fate.[21]

He inveighed against the deception practiced by the Soviet propaganda machine:

> We're filled with faith, we feed on legends,
> Falsehold and truth become as one.[22]

He himself had been guilty:

> I am a miserable wretch
> Guilty on many counts, I know.
> I failed to draw my shining sword,
> I did not call my foe a foe.
>
> . . . .
>
> I must confess another crime—
> Its heinousness I'll not disguise—
> I've written reams of foolish verse,
> And all it held was dreams and lies.
> Enough—there is no more to say.
> Condemn me, whip me cruelly.
> Your mercy I do not deserve—
> I am as guilty as can be.[23]

Early in the NEP period Kirillov handed in his Party card and later withdrew from proletarian literary organizations. As spokesman for disaffected workers, he came under heavy and prolonged attack by official Communist critics. Vyacheslav Polonski stated that poets like Kirillov gave expression to the illusions and disillusionment of that part of the working class which was "most eccentric, least disciplined, and most readily subject to dejection."[24]

Of the vocation of poet under such attacks Kirillov wrote:

> Nay, envy not the poets' fame.
> There is no harsher fate than theirs,
> Whose greedy graves in triumph claim
> The harvest of a few brief years.[25]

In his poetry after 1923, as Lelevich described it,

he plumps for roses and against steel, indulging even in the most reactionary attacks on industrial culture as having replaced the heart with soulless mechanism.[26]

Kirillov himself explains:

> If songs and flowers were destroyed
> Upon a sudden burst of thunder,
> Men would recoil in wordless wonder
> Before the horror of the void.[27]

After the adoption of the First Five-Year Plan, Kirillov's friends tried to bring him back into the mainstream of Russian poetry, in the vain hope that his illusions might be revived by the new policy. But his later poems on industrialization are remarkably bad. He is far more successful with themes of nature and friendship:

> In a little shack that smells of pine
> We will drink and sing till we are hoarse,
> Dream of spring—the spirit's anodyne—
> And blue flowers at the river's source.[28]

Kirillov's career was brought to an end by his arrest in 1937.

MIKHAIL GERASIMOV (1889- ?)

Gerasimov joined the Social Democrat party while still a boy, served a prison term for revolutionary activities, fled abroad to escape another arrest, and lived there for a long time, working in mines and factories. After the revolution he did Party and government work, in responsible administrative posts, but soon withdrew in order to devote himself to writing. In 1921 he resigned from the Party in protest against the NEP and against Party policies in respect to creative artists.

During the early Soviet years he was perhaps the most popular of the proletarian poets. His volumes of verse include *Mona Lisa*, 1918; *Springtime Factory*, 1919; *Black Foam*, 1921; *Unquenchable Strength*, 1922; *Electropoem*, 1923; and *Northern Spring*, 1924.

Gerasimov is frequently associated with "the relapse into Godmaking." This tendency within the Proletcult stemmed in part from Lunacharski's lectures in 1918 to Petrograd political-education instructors (later published in pamphlet form under the title *An Introduction to the History of Religion*).[29] Lunacharski made a sharp distinction between Christ's teachings and the "cult of Christ." Christ, he maintained, was one of the earliest "founders of utopian socialism," and the Church simply a derivative of the state, conserving pagan elements so changed as to be unrecognizable, and designed to make the masses forget the meaning of religion in mystical awe before its trappings.

Lunacharski's interpretation, coming as it did on top of Bogdanov's counsel against an uncouth and derisive attitude toward the Church, unexpectedly prompted several Proletcult writers to attempt to free the essence of Christ's teachings from the prison of church ritual. Gerasimov—in an otherwise arrogant and boastful poem exalting the proletariat as the force that made the wonders of the world (it laid the stones of the Parthenon and of the pyramids), the force that "shall take all," "shall know all," the force identical with all genius and sublimity ("we are Wagner, Leonardo, Titian")—asked:

> Were we not there in Judea
> When Christ taught all to love?[30]

The harking back to the Gospels on the part of Proletcult writers who at the same time rejected the Church took both Lunacharski and Bogdanov by surprise although it stemmed from the prevalent religious leanings of the Russian working class and from instinctive reluctance to accept wrath and hatred as a historical law, particularly after the violence and cruelty of the Civil War.

Gerasimov made a naive attempt to combine the cult of the machine with the worship of Christ by substituting plants and factories for the Church in his poetry. In a poem reminiscent of Blok's "I, stripling, light the candles,"[31] and beginning with the same words ("*Ya, otrok* . . ."), Gerasimov wrote:

> I, stripling, in a temple grew
> Where candles were of molten steel,
> And visions of a starry cross
> Before me rose and made me reel.[32]

Again, Gerasimov deliberately confused the Church and the factory by putting a factory or industrial plant in the place where a church ought to be. As every reader of 1920 knew, the most decorative feature of old Russian villages, even the poorest and the shabbiest, was the church, usually to be seen on the crest of a hill. Gerasimov gave a new twist to the scene in a poem of that year:

> Where swirls the incense of the fog
> The aspens weep, a sorry sight—
> But on the crest of yonder hills
> The factory with lights is bright.[33]

In due course the "God-makers" came under attack for their "lyrical prattle" about cathedrals of industry and complete ignorance of technology, and the Proletcult school was derided as "a breeding station for praying mantises."[34]

Gerasimov's *Black Foam*, published in the year in which the NEP was inaugurated, is a book of angry and bitter disillusionment.

> What pain,
> What pain.
> My poor head sways
> Like a street lamp,
> Gaping with broken glass.
> I see the injured sun of May.
> The fog in swirling clouds of moths
> Has eaten it away.
> The gilt has faded,
> The flags are torn,
> Rime and rust have eaten away the red.
> Once more is visible
> The brand
> Burned by the past
> On people's foreheads.
> . . . .
> And the worker poets have been crucified
> Upon the lamp-posts.[35]

Although technically Gerasimov was quite successful in *Electropoem*, 1923, a narrative poem dealing with the metamorphosis of the countryside through electrification, there is a forced quality in the exposition of his thesis. There is genuine poetry, however, in the passages in which, echoing Kirillov's neo-pantheism, he describes a lonely man who lives in a little cabin in the middle of a forest and who escapes his feeling of loneliness through communion with nature.

Gerasimov also tried his hand at prose. After an unsuccessful book of short stories, *Flowers Under Fire* (1919), in 1925 he published an interesting short novel, *Bee*. "Bee" is the nickname of the young woman manager of a sovkhoz, a Komsomol member. One day she encounters two men who are out hunting, Leonid, a young Communist, and Kolesov, an old Party member. They have stopped to eat and drink. In conversation with them she asks why they—evidently Party members—drink.

"How can you go hunting without drinking," Kolesov replied good-naturedly. ". . . We used to fight home-brew ourselves [and] now the . . . state sells vodka and brandy. It's all right for us to take a nip now and then, to help trade, as you might say."36

Bee is unable to accept the compromise of the NEP with the same aplomb. She is obsessed with the idea of building a new Russia and of throwing out all the bourgeois. She identifies membership in the Komsomol with heroic action and an ascetic mode of life. But Leonid, a locomotive engineer, is all too ready to forget world revolution and his fiancée Lida for the sake of the beautiful Bee. His crude lovemaking repels Bee. Little by little, through the vulgarity and cynicism of her proletarian comrades, she becomes disillusioned both in the Komsomol and in social work. The "new men" are no less ignoble than the old.

The old Communist worker Kolesov reproaches Leonid for hypocrisy—at meetings Leonid condemns petty bourgeois ideas and calls for a new way of life, but keeps right on lying and behaving exactly as in the past.

When Lida makes a melodramatic attempt to take vengeance on her unfaithful lover and her rival, Bee is finally disgusted with Leonid, the sovkhoz and the Komsomol alike, and goes away to study at an agricultural academy.

Like Veresayev's "Isanka," Gerasimov's story shows intelligent and morally scrupulous Soviet youth repudiating dialectical materialism in favor of an intuitive pantheistic philosophy.

Gerasimov continued to appear in print until 1935, although infrequently, but he too ended in a concentration camp.

10. The Smithy *(Kuznitska)* and Its Poets

Early in 1920 several of the leading Proletcult poets—including Gerasimov, Aleksandrovski, Kazin, Obradovich, and Sannikov—left the Moscow Proletarian Culture Organization and founded a section of proletarian writers under the Literary Division of the People's Commissariat of Education. This is the origin of the Smithy, a literary association the moving spirit of which, in the beginning, was Aleksandrovski. Later, Aleksandrovski yielded the leading role to Georgi Yakubovski, a mediocre poet and a far from brilliant, though well-intentioned, literary critic. The Smithy published its own magazine of the same name from 1920 to 1922, and later the magazines *Rabochii zhurnal* [Workers Review], *Zhurnal dlya vsekh* [Everyone's Review] and *Proletarskii avangard* [Proletarian Vanguard]. In May 1928 the Smithy became affiliated with the All-Union Organization of Associations of Proletarian Writers (RAPP).

The activity of the Smithy represents a desperate effort, sustained over a period of years, to preserve and if possible to add to what the Proletcult had accomplished in the early years after the revolution. At first boldly and then with increasing timidity as the attacks upon them multiplied, the "Smiths" insisted on their independence from the Party and its current line, asserting that the main concern of proletarian literature was by no means political.

Yet the Smithy's own beginnings show that this assertion was a mockery. The Literary Division of the People's Commissariat of Education was prepared to support only those proletarian writers who had no "God-making" leanings, or next to none. And at an All-Union Congress of Proletarian Writers which the Smithy called in the fall of 1920, Bogdanov firmly, although in tactful terms, condemned the God-making tendencies of proletarian writers. In other words, even during the period when the Smithy, which was constituted by writers of genuine proletarian origin, was dominant, proletarian literature was to a certain extent subject to Communist Party supervision. Gradually, through a succession of literary groups organized and supported by the Party itself—first, the group called

"October," to be discussed later—supervision was tightened into well-nigh absolute control.

The writers who remained with the Proletcult and the Smithy quite deliberately placed themselves in open opposition to the "political poster" in literature. For roughly a decade the Smiths maintained stubbornly that literature must not be made a propaganda weapon for Party policy. At times they recanted, acknowledged their mistakes and declared their readiness to bow before propaganda needs; but then, like Galileo insisting that the earth turned, they would go back to their old position.

With the exception of Semyon Rodov, who left them to join the October group, the Smiths conducted their literary disputes with restraint and with aversion for the purge tactics of their opponents.

Even before the Smithy was well under way, several of its founders and most prominent members, including Aleksandrovski and Gerasimov, broke with the Party. Kirillov, who had left the Petrograd Proletcult to join the Smithy, also turned in his Party card.

VASILI ALEKSANDROVSKI (1897 - 1934)

Although his work is very uneven, Aleksandrovski was one of the most gifted of the Smithy poets. He published several volumes of verse while still a member of the Proletcult, and then his more mature work in the volumes *Morning* (1921), *Scattered Lights* [*Rossyp' ognei*], 1922, *Sun's Way* [*Solnechnyi put'*], 1922, *Ring of the Sun* [*Zvon solntsa*], 1923, *Steps*, 1924, *Wind*, 1925, *Fettered Years*, 1926, and *Bonfire*, 1929.

Kornei Chukovski's remark that Sergei Yesenin is a "watered-down Blok" applies more fittingly to Aleksandrovski. Aleksandrovski's Russia is the Russia of Blok, with the difference that all the leaves have been blown off in the garden and all the colors have faded into a monotonous bleakness amid the heaps of ashes, burned-down manor houses, villages ravaged by the war and factories shut down.

The Proletcult and the Smithy

> The raw wind howls with laughter,
> The silent snow-drifts gleam.
> Who am I—poet or pauper?
> What are you—a wish or a dream?
> . . . .
> Where does your heart lie hidden,
> O whitefaced Russia mine?
> Where is your bearlike strength,
> Your fury's heady wine?[1]

Aleksandrovski welcomed the revolution as a release of creative energy:

> Eyes with a sterner light will flash
> And spring will come with stormy glee.
> The tumult of rebellious blood
> Will wake the world from lethargy.[2]

Over and over again he wrote of the two Russias, the one which had raised high a red flag and Orthodox Russia—two faces of the same nation:

> Two lives inside the chilly house,
> Two hearts—one gold, the other brass,
> One tempered in the heat of battle,
> The other putrefied at Mass.
> One could be buried in the snow
> And still maintain its resolute beat . . .[3]

To the other, sunk in its home-brew stupor and still as ice, he said:

> Go, chant your requiems,
> Who live in your dreams apart.
> But we, with our sun-bright eyes,
> Will pierce to the future's heart.[4]

In a transport of self-abnegation youth was ready to destroy itself for the sake of the general welfare, still vaguely perceived:

> Young men we have—yes, and young women too;
> Their eyes are bright, their guns in readiness.
> In their free time they hurry off to school,
> Swaying with hunger and with weariness.[5]

In his attitude toward the two Russias Aleksandrovski remained remarkably objective. Although he did not share the God-making delusions of his colleagues, he sympathized with what he saw as their attempt to overcome the tragic duality of the Russian people, to reconcile the revolutionary and the religious idea. The Russian intelligentsia had always lived by the mind, by rational thinking, whereas the workers and peasants lived by a blind irrational faith in God and a blind irrational faith in miracles. Like the Symbolist poets, from above, the proletarian God-making poets also tried to heal that breach, from below.

His own joy in the revolution had been mingled with misgivings from the start. He wrote in 1919:

> This is the limit of space.
> Beyond is a frozen waste
> And snow storms never still.
> On my lips a seal I will place.
> There has been too much hate,
> As chilly as ice is chill.
>
> . . . .
>
> A man gets used to anything in time—
> To fire and ice and snow.
> The North burns me upon its boreal pyre
> With the past I treasured so.[6]

His disillusionment came even earlier than Gerasimov's and Kirillov's, and for different reasons. For them, the NEP was a political betrayal. Aleksandrovski lost faith in the power of the revolution to effect a moral regeneration when concern for human worth was gone. In angry lines of 1923:

> The heavy hand of anguish
> Shall force no cry from me.
> They have no need of beacons
> Who sail the open sea.
> I'll set my course on madness,
> 'Gainst the deck my heart I'll stun;
> My verse, though hurt and bleeding,
> Shall not complain to the sun.
> Away with last night's visions,
> Too absurd for cherishing.
> From present pain and sorrow
> Grim fortresses shall spring.

> My lip will curl with derision
> For harbors safe and stale,
> For they cannot cast anchor
> Who are doomed forever to sail.[7]

Unlike Kirillov and Gerasimov, Aleksandrovski avoided the concentration camp; in fact, Soviet newspapers, including *Pravda,* printed well-disposed obituaries when he died, and he was buried with honors. For one reason, Aleksandrovski, a victim of alcoholism, had virtually stopped writing during the last years of his life. With his usual candor he had written of himself:

> The fog dissolves within the brain.
> One day I'll seek the open ways,
> But now beside a brimming glass
> I sit and stare with clouded gaze.
>
> . . . .
>
> Monotonous are the endless fields,
> Monotonous the snow storm's song.
> Was Stenka Razin but a dream,
> He and his freedom-loving throng?[8]

Aleksandrovski's hoarse-voiced poetry, despite its slovenliness, is gripping in its strong musical quality and its undisguised anguish. He had the makings of a superior poet.

VASILI KAZIN (1898-   )

Vasili Kazin caused a stir of pleasant surprise in Russian letters at the time when the Civil War was on the wane. Kazin wrote of artisans at work during the reconstruction period.

His first slim volume of poems, *Workers' May,* appeared in 1922, and another small volume, *Verses,* in 1925. In the following year his narrative poem *The Fur Coat and Love,* with illustrations by B. M. Kustodiyev, was published, and then *Confessions* in 1928. After a long interval, two more books were brought out, in 1934 and 1937, made up in large part of previously published poems.

Workers' May is an outstandingly sincere book, expressing with naturalness and genuineness the feelings of the man with the joiner's plane, and unmarred by the "Cosmist" excesses of other Proletcult and Smithy poets—in fact touched with irony in this respect, as in these lines of 1922:

> In my dream a freight train brought along
> Rainbows and sheet lightning by the bale.
> "I can work them," said the carpenter.
> "Why, my ax will split the sun as well!" [9]

There is a humorous note in Kazin's work that is entirely peculiar to him. His humor has a great deal of warmth and tenderness in it, and he can make fun without offense.

Kazin says of his origin and of his own work:

> My father was an ordinary plumber,
> But as for me, it is my fate to sing.
> . . . .
> My anapests and my iambics too
> Reveal the birthmark of my father's work.
> . . . .
> And so do I unfold the nets of song,
> And those I catch within them scarcely can
> Divine that in the poet with his art
> Survives the offspring of the artisan. [10]

Young Kazin was able to capture something of Tyutchev's elusive quality:

> I walk in happiness today,
> Though life, a few brief years ago,
> Led me along a crooked lane
> Into a world of pain and woe.
> The world I saw was passing strange,
> And strangely I my spirit fed,
> Spending my days in free-for-alls
> And reading Tyutchev's verse in bed.
> . . . .
> The air vibrated with desire,
> Trembling before my very eyes,
> As though all common household things
> I had been born to humanize.
> . . . .
> A face like any other man's;
> Distinctive features I have none.
> How often have I pinched myself:
> "A poet—me? My father's son?" [11]

The Proletcult and the Smithy

He saw the world of nature through Tyutchev's eyes and shared his pantheistic philosophy:

> 'Tis written by the hand of fate
> That Moscow shall be my abode.
> But there is lightning in my veins,
> And often, as the heavens glowed,
> I've watched in wonderment, the while
> The Universe about me flowed.[12]

The growing aversion for the city, its factories and machines which is evident in Kazin's poetry brought him into Bolshevik disfavor. *Workers' May* had given promise of a major proletarian poet. After the publication of *The Fur Coat and Love* and *Confessions*, critics saw in him a "petty bourgeois" wavering between the old pantheistic village and the proletariat. His "anthropomorphism" was stigmatized as typical of the patriarchal peasantry:[13]

> The radiant day saunters into
> My little chamber wreathed in smiles.
> The dust motes dance, the unswept floor
> Dreams of high Heaven's polished tiles.[14]

Kazin's preference of nature to the industrial scene was outspoken:

> Yours is an enviable lot—
> To resurrect what lay congealed.
> The very sidewalks that you tread
> Smell of the meadow and the field.
> You come—and every step of yours
> Is traced in verdant filigree.
> You leave—and I am doomed once more
> To dwell in urban misery.[15]

The most important of Kazin's narrative poems, *The Fur Coat and Love*, epitomized his unacceptable "petty-bourgeois" outlook. The hero of the story, visiting in the country, falls in love with a rich peasant's daughter. When he and his beloved kneel before her father asking for his consent to their marriage, the peasant refuses. In his opinion, a man from the capital who tries to make a living by writing poetry is simply an idler and a rascal. The stern father says to the poet, who has come a-courting, in the middle of a fierce winter, wearing a shabby cloth overcoat:

> "Are you as simple as you sound,
> Or are you cleverer than most?
> Before with girls you fool around
> And act as for the altar bound,
> Some decent clothes you might have found,
> The better to impress your host."[16]

All the other guests in the household wear fur-lined jackets or fur coats, and the host himself has coats of fox fur carefully hidden away in chests.

Lamenting that "as though only when wrapped in furs/Could love be kept truly warm,"[17] the poet goes out into the fields and implores the wild foxes to make him a gift of a fur coat until at last the absurdity of the idea dawns on him. He leaves the village, convinced that the men who rule there have the hearts of wild bears and that

> The beauty and joy of love
> Are idle chatter today.[18]

Back in the city:

> Bang on, bang on, bang on,
> Torment the ear as before,
> Tear my sorrow to shreds
> With your full-throated roar![19]

As he walks the streets of the capital, the poet catches sight of the imposing shop windows of the State Fur Trust:

> I saw in the shop window's glory
> A very flower bed of furs.
> . . . .
> There was the foxes' arctic gleam,
> Like a new ruble silver-bright,
> Opulent beaver, softest mink,
> And splendid sable black as night.
> Amid the black the price-tag shone.

> I looked and fairly staggered back,
> Renouncing sables in despair.
> The world itself looked very black . . .
> If the world's wisdom comes to this:
> Kill to be happy, live to kill—
> Small matter whether man or fox
> For this wise lesson foots the bill.[20]

Kazin's implication is that the fur trust managers were preparing to throttle the well-to-do, hard-working peasants who had fur coats stored away in chests, and that the violence of the Party would come to grips with the violence of the peasants. In practice, the slogan that the distinction between city and village must be obliterated meant that the villages were to come under the Party's domination. In the fighting, both the city and village would lose love and charity. The luckless man endowed with heart and soul never had anything to call his own and never would.

In this poem, as always in Kazin, solace is to be found in nature:

> The narrow lane was soft with grass,
> Luring on my wayward feet,
> As though green meadows had invaded
> The long familiar city street.
> Gay at the thought of meeting you
> As at a hurdy-gurdy's sound,
> Again I sought the open fields,
> Without a house for miles around.[21]
> . . . .
> Life's fitted me into a frame,
> But love, with its clairvoyant eye,
> Gave me a secret glimpse of space,
> And through the framework shone the sky.
> . . . .
> I watched its waves about me sway,
> And swung my sorrow like a hammer
> Against the footprints of the day.[22]

In his love lyrics Kazin was one of the very few poets in the early Soviet period to write of spiritual love and, moreover, to bring in moral and ethical elements derived from the Orthodox religion:

> I fear to fritter love away
> In weary passion's drunkenness.[23]

His strong musical strain often gives the impression that he has translated into words Russian folk dances or the songs of strolling accordion players. In addition, he had a remarkable way of portraying motion reminiscent of Pushkin's:

> The air was still. The weary wind
> Beside a fence lay down
> And yawned—as the accordion player
> Strolled into the sleepy town.
> He held the accordion in his hands
> As though his heart it were,
> And played—and all the window sills
> Now bloomed with flowers rare.
> The tall brick houses gently swayed,
> As if freedom were a breeze,
> While the dry ground began to dream
> Of small wild strawberries.
> People leaned out to hear the tune,
> And to its rollicking delight
> Raced barefoot through the dewy grass
> Of distant fields and meadows bright.
> The postman came and stood spellbound,
> Glanced at the letters in his hand,
> And saw that they were all addressed
> To woods and rivers and the land.[24]

In the Pushkin manner (it is doubtful that Kazin was following the suprematic theory of Churlyanis, Malevich and Belyi!) the landscape often rushes past in a rapid succession of images:

> Swiftly the trolley fled along its tracks
> Bearing us, chatting, off into the blue.
> Shop windows floated by in brilliant flocks,
> The very buildings fairly flew.[25]

Kazin's poetry was a barometer of the feelings and ideas of the average citizen of the Soviet Union, who, starting with faith and confidence in the government, developed mistrust. Kazin's optimism first became tinged by sadness:

> Combat to us is commoner than bread.
> Even in joy forgetting not to frown,
> We touch a woman's softness, and perceive
> Our hands are hard, and hard our eyes look down.[26]

He cried out against the painful death of love:

> I run, I race, I cry unheard:
> Stepmother Life, be thou our mother!
> Now spring is like a singing bird,
> Now that the earth to life is stirred,
> Oh, let us understand each other![27]

In the new world no man had individuality; there was no distinction between men save their occupation:

> Our iron age into the mold of reason
> Casts inspiration, wonder and delight;
> Now each man has his guild, and every flight
> Of fancy, each emotion is a treason.
> We're all trade-unionists—a sorry sight.
> . . . .
> And very soon we'll recognize each other
> By reading signs, and not each other's eyes.[28]

Was it to permit the Party to look on man as a unit of energy, as the cheapest and most easily replaceable part of a machine, that the revolution was made?

> Why do we not stop short and cry in scorn:
> Was it for this, these tiny screws and nails
> The eye can barely see, that we were born
> With our grand gift of speech that never stales,
> Our air of majesty, so lightly worn,
> Our thought that weighs the cosmos in its scales?[29]

The three narrative poems which Kazin wrote after *The Fur Coat and Love*—"Last Letter," 1935, "The Newspaper," 1931, and "The Bandit," 1936—are all in somber or bitter mood. In "Last Letter" the poet-narrator addresses a woman who has left him to marry an important and bemedalled Bolshevik official, not out of love but for the creature comforts available only to Party bigwigs.

> Far beside the River Don
> Your bemedalled legal mate
> Feasts his eyes upon your youth
> In your newly-wedded state.[30]
> . . . .

> Irresistibly your charms
> Smashed my happiness to bits,
> And in misery I nurse
> Broken verse and addled wits.[31]
>
> . . . .
> Trampling on the dreams of love
> With a thoughtless blasphemy,
> You fled into the arms of wealth
> From the ghost of poverty.[32]

The narrative poem "The Newspaper," only excerpts from which have appeared in print, records his reaction to an issue of *Pravda*. With the tightening of dictatorship, there had been a profound change between the Soviet newspapers of the NEP period and those of the thirties. What remained was transparent deception and utter tedium. Kazin's cryptic lines ostensibly describe the superiority of the Soviet press.

> If ever fate should wish us ill,
> And with its arbitrary might
> Install a loathsome parasite
> To rule and order us at will,
> The paper's comfort will be nil;
> Like death, its columns will be still.
> The fear of death your hearts will fill
> Before an idle master's spite.
> The dreaded, ruthless parasite
> Will dry the springs of your delight,
> And you will shudder in the chill
> Of endless slavery and night.[33]

The critics were sore perplexed in defining the object of Kazin's attack. The Communists or the capitalists?

> Stars or the sun—it matters not.
> To turn the spindle is your lot
> And eat the bread of slavery.
> And yet with us, by fate's decree,
> You'll set yourselves forever free
> From shame and bitter misery

> Where even stones with peace are blessed,
> And where the elements anew
> And to another world break through
> Where deadly strife is set at rest,
> Will shed their rage at your behest.[34]

In "The Newspaper," as well as in *The Fur Coat and Love*, Kazin revived the topical genre which Russian poets had rarely used after the nineteenth century (but in which Pavel Vasil'yev, Boris Kornilov and Nikolai Zabolotski now followed Kazin), and for it devised a mosaic, or kaleidoscopic, form combining different meters.

"The Bandit" as originally planned was also to be a mosaic in which the author's own basic meter was to be interspersed with fragments of underworld songs. Under pressure of criticism, Kazin was forced to give up this intention and delete all such passages from the published text, to the injury of the poem. Underworld songs represent a highly interesting branch of Russian folklore, and one which has been disdained by folklorists.

One of the most popular underworld songs is "Hop the Fiddle" [*Gop so smykom*], a Soviet epic describing the life and works of a confirmed Russian criminal and desperado undaunted by the devil himself. He describes his own imaginary arrival in the other world:

> Judas is a denizen of hell.
> All the devils know him very well,
> And my coming will be rued, as
> I will mop the floor with Judas,
> Teach the dirty bastard not to sing.

The few remembered lines following are from an adaptation of this underworld song which Kazin was reported to have made for inclusion in "The Bandit":

> Let them listen to this rhyme
> By a specialist in crime,
> The notorious Vas'ka Whatthehell.
> Here we live without a worry,
> Singing, drinking, making merry.
> But I've been in stir in every town—
> Not even Solovki got me down!

> Leningrad and Moscow know me well—
> One and only Vas'ka Whatthehell!

The raciness of the Russian lines is, of course, lost in translation, but even so it is obvious that "The Bandit" as first planned was far more interesting than the published version, which deals rather primly with the rehabilitation of criminals through labor in a concentration camp:

> You went to try
> With friends you had
> Your luck at a hold-up man's life,
> Now with a gun,
> Now with the mad
> Sweet sharpness of a Finnish knife.[35]

Rehabilitation by labor is no simple matter.

> The yawns of former
> Boredom faded
> As slowly,
> Stubbornly each day
> The metamorphosis
> Proceeded
> Of all your thoughts and all your ways.
> The Cheka men—
> The trained, the wise,
> The Soviet government's
> Patrol—
> Watched closely with discerning eyes
> The transformation of your soul.[36]
>
> . . . .
> And to the Cheka men
> In thought
> You came more closely every day.[37]
>
> . . . .
> And lovingly
> The Cheka men
> Now called you a
> Stakhanovite.[38]

Unable to continue such compromise, Kazin gradually stopped publishing. There was in him a certain neo-Tolstoyanism, a deep-seated conviction that one should not oppose evil with violence, and also a realization that, in the face of vastly superior strength,

The Proletcult and the Smithy

resistance was both senseless and hopeless. In "The Bandit" he portrayed the Cheka agents as endowed with a terrifying strength and absolutely unconquerable, then turned his attention elsewhere. He became very active as an editor, adviser to beginning poets, and compiler of anthologies, and escaped harsh reprisals for the courageous, and at times audacious, tenor of his earlier poems.

As a poet Kazin has been to all intents and purposes condemned to silence.

During the Second World War, like many other writers, he broke his silence for a brief time. The following lines are from "On Board the Steamer *Radishchev*," written in 1941:

> The peasant women in their *sarafans*
> Observed the painful ritual of farewell...
> That grievous war, in pity cruel still,
> Might bring their husbands back to them for good...
> And with their drawn-out sobs of parting, tried
> To make the river bank share in their pain...
> And, rising high, red with the native clay,
> The river bank watched as the motley crowd
> Pressed forward to their husbands, fell away,
> And in the ancient manner wailed aloud.
> The gulf of separation wider grew,
> As tears unheeded streamed from sightless eyes.
> Their riotous grief across the water flew,
> Swamped the departing with its agonies.
> Though each one was a drop of its blood-stream,
> The country said, commanding and intense:
> "Die if you must—but from the foe preserve
> Until the last your heart's wild innocence!" [39]

There is no need to exaggerate the importance of Kazin's work. His poems are too often marred by clumsiness and a tinge of sensationalism. Still they have a spontaneity and purity of emotion which assure him a place, albeit a modest one, in postrevolutionary Russian literature.

The poetry of many other Proletcult and Smithy writers, including Ivan Filipchenko (1887-   ), Nikolai Poletayev (1889-1935), Aleksei Dorogoichenko (1894-   ), Aleksandr Bagayev, Semyon Rodov (1893-   ), Sergei Obradovich (1892-   ), Grigori Sannikov (1899-   ), and Aleksandr Makarov (1898-   ), is best described by the malicious term invented by Vladimir Mayakovski, "massotonous landscape"—meaning both aimed at the masses and monotonous.

11. Prose Writers of the Proletcult and Smithy Schools

The older generation of the Proletcult and Smithy prose writers were mostly educated workers who had taken part in the revolutionary movement under the tsarist regime. Several of them had published before the revolution. By and large their guiding principle was objectivity, and their resistance to falsification of Soviet life in their work brought many of them into conflicts with the Bolshevik propaganda machine in later years. From the beginning, however, the proletarian writers frequently tended to idealize the working class, feeling that whatever was good in the common man came from the factory and the lathe, and whatever was bad was the result of peasant savagery, middle-class vulgarity and the baneful influence of the intelligentsia.

PAVEL BESSAL'KO (1887-1920)

Bessal'ko, for instance, who headed the Petrograd Proletcult in its early days, wrote about proletarians as if he were writing the lives of the saints. Long a member of the Social Democrat party (and a Bolshevik after the February revolution of 1917), he had written several novels and stories in exile in Siberia and Western Europe which were published by the Proletcult along with his new work. In 1918 publication began of the series of more or less autobiographical sketches and stories which were later assembled in the novel *Kuz'ma Darov*. In the same year his play *The Mason* appeared.

Bessal'ko was criticized because his heroes were revolutionaries on emotional rather than rational grounds. He had a contemptuous and rather bitter attitude toward revolutionary-minded intellectuals, and regarded as a true revolutionary only a man who acquired his hatred of the tsarist regime in a factory or plant.

Bessal'ko was one of the foremost literary theorists from the ranks of the proletariat, and from 1918 to 1920 produced many critical pieces and articles arguing the imminent cultural hegemony of the working class and denying the value of the art of the past.

MIKHAIL G. SIVACHOV (1877-   )

Sivachov, an old writer of proletarian origin and a member of the Smithy, had made a reputation before the Revolution with the novels *Procrustes' Bed* and *Twilight of War*, in which he foresaw the inevitable rebellion not as a triumph of liberty, equality and fraternity but as the coming of a new Peter the Great, armed with a big stick, who would force everybody to work.

The ideas which are only hinted at in these novels are given full development in his *Yellow Devil* of 1920. Ivan, the hero, a Bolshevik, is convinced that, if the revolution is to be victorious, people must be kept in constant subjection through fear of physical violence: "A rogue should be beaten to make him honest, and an honest man to keep him honest." His tactics are to "smash his face in, blacken his eyes, and pass a resolution."[1] Ivan is a man of enormous vitality, energy and will power—no snivelling intellectual, but a man who understands the revolution and the power of the fist. Sivachov with his bitter, skeptical mind recognized a characteristic national type brought into the foreground in 1917, and in the somewhat exaggerated characterization of Ivan represented those Bolsheviks who shouldered aside and later destroyed the idealists and romantics of the Russian Revolution.

After *Yellow Devil* Sivachov abandoned the naturalistic vein, made a clumsy and unsuccessful attempt at writing adventure stories, then turned to non-fiction. The collection of stories in his 1927 volume *Riot* (dealing with prerevolutionary incidents at the Bryansk plant) and the tale *Balakhany*, 1926 (dealing with the oil industry) celebrate the heroic past of the working class. In a bitter mood, Sivachov is a gifted writer, his talent being apparently a derivative of his bitterness, but when he takes an admiring attitude, he is a mediocrity. Nevertheless, *Riot* and *Balakhany* are important in that they represent the first attempts to record the history of plants and factories in novelized form, long before Maxim Gorki initiated large-scale efforts in that field.

BIBIK, DOROKHOV AND SKACHKO

Aleksei Bibik (1878-   ), another old worker and revolutionary, also continued to write of the pre-1917 workers' movement. His novel *The Black Zone* [*Na chornoi polose*], 1921, is a sequel to his earlier book *The Wide Road* [*K shirokoi doroge*]. One of the characters in the former voices the opinion of many early proletarian writers in asserting that the Russian proletariat still had such a long way to go before it was ready for its lofty mission, before it developed a sense of responsibility, and that nonetheless there were men dishonest enough to flatter it and insist that it was fully prepared to take the state into its hands.

Occasionally Proletcult writers produced "political posters" in which the Reds are painted in glowing colors and the Whites in black, as in Pavel N. Dorokhov's chronicle, *The Kolchak Adventure* [*Kolchakovshchina*], 1923, but usually they gave the political poster a wide berth.

A. L. Skachko, for instance, however mediocre a writer, faithfully copied events and people from life, frequently without realizing what the effect on the reader might be. His *Fellow Travelers*, 1923, is a story of Civil War partisans, on the side of the Reds, who make their way in a frail little boat from Astrakhan to Baku. The story shows the influence of Jack London, who was practically worshiped by many of the Proletcult writers. The characters are living men, with the good and bad qualities of real people. One, a sailor, ruthless and cruel, with bandit propensities, has joined the Reds not only because he has a fanatical faith in the revolution but because he realizes that, should the former order be re-established, he will be held accountable for his past crimes. On the other hand, Surovtsev, a military expert and former tsarist officer, who regards his comrades-in-arms with ill-disguised contempt but wins their respect, serves the revolution honestly, of his own free will. In his eyes the White armies have been bought by the British, the French and the Germans, and their leaders, without realizing it, have lost their national pride and dignity. Lenin and his henchmen have much that is murky, bestial and criminal about them, but they alone have taken over the idea of a great Russian state, an idea still no more than an intuitive feeling in rank-and-file Communists, but bound to become a conscious objective after a passage of years. In the bold idea attributed to Surovtsev, Skachko was simply making a conscientious reproduction of actual types and events.

N. LYASHKO
(pseudonym of Nikolai Lyashchenko, 1884-1953)

The old revolutionary Lyashko, who had been publishing since 1905, was one of the most prominent Proletcult and Smithy writers. The story entitled *The Breath of a Dove* is characteristic of his writing in the early years of the Soviet regime. Its hero, the old man Aleksei, is an unusual God-seeker from the lower depths of society. He finds his God not in the Church and its ritual but in the "joint truth" of human souls, the truth of the working collective, the mission of which is to endow the masses with "God's soul" and thus to establish peace and justice on earth through loving kindness, without fighting and bloodshed. Aleksei is killed in a fight between artisans and peasants, in a vain attempt to reconcile the two warring camps. The naive symbolic meaning of the death-blow struck by a peasant armed with a stake is that the infuriated peasantry kills the love and compassion of a working collective; the soil, with its mindless, bestial violence, conquers peaceful working-class wisdom.

In the story "The Rainbow" Lyashko, following in Bogdanov's footsteps, stressed that there had been enough blood, enough shootings, enough knifings. Embittered men set out to kill, and do not kill, look for their enemies and find their brothers.

During the restoration period after the Civil War Lyashko consistently idealized the proletariat as an ennobling influence on the cunning, mean, bestial, barbarian hordes of the Russian peasantry.

Both the story "Iron Silence," 1922, and the short novel *The Blast Furnace*, 1924, show the influence of Victor Hugo's *Toilers of the Sea* and Bernhard Kellermann's *Tunnel*, two books which the Proletcult and Smithy writers held in as great esteem as they did Ethel Voynich's *The Gadfly* and Raffaello Giovagnoli's *Spartaco*. The error which they were, however, inclined to find in Kellermann—that he made the engineers his main heroes and relegated the collective to the background—Lyashko corrected in *The Blast Furnace*; his workers are the ones who put the plant back into operation, treating the skeptical smiles of the engineers with proletarian contempt.

"Iron Silence" is the story of a kingdom of dead machines in a plant which had come to a standstill and been abandoned during the Revolution and Civil War, and of the dream of the impetuous, sincere hero, Stepka, of putting them back into motion.

In *The Blast Furnace* Lyashko moved from the particular to the general, from the single hero to the collective—in Soviet terms, he attempted to mold the chaos of life into an organized force. In this story the dead kingdom of the abandoned plant—surrounded by pigweed, high grass and thistles, rye growing next to the bin of the co-operative store—is transformed by herculean collective efforts into a paradise of machinery in motion.

> Labor cannot but win;
> He who denies it, lies.[2]

All in all, Lyashko painted a truthful, if naive, picture of the restoration period. Proletarian writers, Lyashko contended, were able to penetrate into the soul of metal, which remained closed to the factory owners and engineers—just as only the proletarian at the machine, with his work-worn hands, could give the beneficent, wonder-working power of metal to the world. Lyashko does not identify the factory with the Church, as do Kirillov and Gerasimov, nor does he deify the labor collective except in *The Breath of a Dove*; his divinity is the metal itself. This is God-making with a curious twist.

Like Kirillov and Gerasimov, however, Lyashko regarded the NEP as a return to capitalism, and wrote the short novel *Stirrups*[3] in an indignant frame of mind. Its hero, Pimen Morenets, a painter, sells a revolutionary painting to foreigners, at the insistence of his small-minded wife. This fraternization with capitalists destroys his talent, and he discovers that he has become an utter mediocrity. Laughable though the plot may be, the disillusionment and suffering of a revolutionary who does not believe in art for art's sake are described with great sincerity and truthfulness.

Lyashko was a prolific writer. The most popular of his novels was the melodramatic and banal *Breakup*, 1924, dealing with the tragedy of a family in which a doctor of worker class origin and his daughter are in the Red camp, while his wife and sons are with the Whites.[4]

In the second half of the twenties several volumes of Lyashko's short stories appeared, and a six-volume edition of his writings was published in 1926-1927. In 1930 he became a member of the Communist Party (he had been a Menshevik long before the revolution) and published a series of sketches dealing with socialist reconstruction, *The Sickle of Stars*.[5] His long novel of 1935, *Sweet Penal Servitude*, harks back to Russia's revolutionary past.[6]

During the Second World War Lyashko produced a volume of short stories entitled *Russian Nights*.[7] Many of the pieces are crude imitations of Korolenko and Garshin and abound in banalities.

PAVEL NIZOVOI

The "peasant fiction" wing of the Smithy was represented by Pavel Nizovoi, Vladimir Bakhmet'yev (1885-   ) and Feoktist Berezovski (1887-).

Pavel Nizovoi (pseudonym of P. G. Tupikov, 1882-1940) often wrote on the subject of the peasants' attitude toward the modernization of agriculture. The peasantry had split into two camps, some eager to adopt Western methods, others holding to the ways of their fathers. In the tale *Mityakino:*

Kuz'ma's vegetables are planted in tidy rows, all alike, all nicely weeded; the apple trees are whitewashed; poles support the branches of the cherry trees.[8]

Old Silanti, whose own plot is full of hollow trunks serving as beehives, disapproves of all this, grumbles that Kuz'ma plants by the books, not the Christian way.

The author himself cautiously advocates a middle road between tradition and the reckless extreme represented by the imminent collectivization of farming. This distrust of extremes, desire for balance, is in keeping with Nizovoi's entire development.

"My Spiritual Journey," of which only fragments were published (in the form of quotations given in the course of a critical discussion of Nizovoi),[9] tells of a religious quest which leads the hero, Stefan, like the author himself, from disillusionment in the Church not to atheism but to nature worship.

Nizovoi's pantheism is also reflected in the short novel *The Pagans*, 1922. For instance: "All is silent again, but I feel every inch of earth living a deep, wise, mysterious life, inaccessible to my hearing and to my sight." [10] And in a lyrical pantheistic passage from *Black Earth*, 1923, he writes:

The wedding party on its way from church filled the damp fields with a bubbling, cheerful jingle. The crystal air, the silk of the winter-crops, the lone pine tree on the knoll, all rang together like bells.

In a raiment of ribbons, scarlet, yellow and green, with chimes in her right hand and bells in her left, Spring swept through the fields, sowing healthy young laughter and heady joy.[11]

In 1930 Nizovoi published a romantic, deeply pessimistic novel, *The Ocean*. His later novels of the 1930's dealing with the industrial scene show a failing of his powers.

The major novelists of the older generation of Proletcult and Smithy prose writers, Fyodor Gladkov and Georgi Nikiforov, will be discussed later, in connection with the period when they were at the height of their powers, as will Mikhail Volkov, who from 1920 to 1922 was in charge of the literature section of the Moscow Proletcult.

4

The Pathfinders in Fiction

12. *Stylists and Stylizers*

YEVGENI ZAMYATIN (1884-1937)

During the Civil War the ascendancy of the poets was almost uncontested. Beginning in 1921-1922, the prose writers, a new crop as well as the re-emergent prewar names, asserted themselves in force, and within a few years restored Russian prose to vigorous life. For assistance in developing their craft, the young fiction writers owed perhaps more to Yevgeni Zamyatin than to any other one man. For several years after the revolution he lectured in literature and taught classes in prose writing at the Petrograd *Dom iskusstv* (House of the Arts), where Gumilyov lectured at the same time in the art of versification. Zamyatin also organized the "Serapion Brotherhood" (*Serapionovy brat'ya*), a group of highly talented beginners almost all of whom matured into top-flight Soviet writers. Of these years Zamyatin wrote:

We were all cooped up in the dark in a steel projectile whistling through space no one knew where. And in those years that flew like seconds toward death, we had to do something, to settle down to some kind of life in the speeding shell. Strange things occupied our minds —World Literature [the publishing house], the Union of Literary

Workers, the Writers' Union, the theater. . . . We had not yet realized that we were holding conferences while bolted in a steel shell.[1]

In his surrealist story "The Cave," of 1922, he described Petrograd during the period of War Communism, likening the houses to a herd of famished mammoths. Indoors the cavemen who had been Russian intellectuals clenched their teeth to stop their chattering and ate "pottery-like flat cakes from the stone age. . . ." "And in the center of this universe squatted its god—a short-legged, rusty-red, voracious cave god—the cast-iron stove,"[2] to which sacrifices must never cease, even if it came to stealing the wood. Rather than sink into an animal state, the hero chooses death.

Even under such conditions Zamyatin found it in him to be concerned for the future of Russian literature. When he warned of the dangers confronting it in the Bolshevik suppression of the individual, his words carried weight. Zamyatin's prewar work had at once put him among the foremost writers of the time. *Tale of a Country Town* [*Uyezdnoye*], 1911, *Alatyr'*, and *At the Back of Beyond* [*Na kulichkakh*], 1914, had satirized the dull, stagnant life of the provinces, provincial government officials, and the brutish or, at best, vegetative life led by officers at an out-of-the-way garrison. *At the Back of Beyond* was confiscated by the tsarist police, and Zamyatin came to be considered a dangerous malcontent, of revolutionary temper. He had always belonged to the radical intelligentsia. In his early youth he had been a Social Democrat, of the Bolshevik faction, but had left the party before the revolution because (to judge from indications given in his autobiographical notes published in 1929[3] and the story "Good-for-Nothing" [*Neputyovyi*])[4] of the bloodshed and regimentation implicit in its program. Still, he was by no means to be dismissed as a reactionary. Furthermore, he was one of the few mature, established writers not superannuated by the Revolution. He was only thirty-three years old in 1917. And, a master craftsman, original and lively critic and effective teacher, he held a large part of the rising generation of writers under his stylistic sway.

The apprehension for the future of Russian letters which he began to express soon after the revolution was therefore a serious affront to the authorities and in their eyes brought him into the category of troublesome inner émigrés.

Zamyatin's outspoken article "I Fear" appeared in the periodical named *Dom iskusstv* in 1921. He begins by quoting the following words of Payan, who in 1794 headed the French Revolutionary Committee for Public Education:

There are many agile writers following the fashion of the day; they know when to don the red bonnet and when to take it off. As a result, they profane literature and corrupt public taste. The true genius works from careful meditation and casts his thoughts in bronze; mediocrities, under the aegis of liberty and in its name, snatch at passing glory and pick the flowers of cheap success.[5]

In Russia, too, Zamyatin saw the same debasement of literature:

. . . I fear that, if we continue in this path, this whole period of Russian literature will become known as the "agile school"—because those who are not agile . . . remain silent. . . .[6]

True literature can be made only by madmen, hermits, heretics, dreamers, rebels, skeptics, and not by diligent, reliable government employees. . . .

. . . I fear that we shall have no true literature until an end is put to looking upon the Russian demos as a child whose innocence must be preserved. I fear we shall have no true literature until we are cured of a new kind of Catholicism which is as much afraid of any heretical word as was the old. And if this disease is incurable, I fear that the only Russian literature of the future will be the Russian literature of the past.[7]

In 1924 Zamyatin, deploring the spate of special-purpose literature, the tendency of writers to concentrate attention on the issues of the day rather than on the meaning of the modern age as a whole, saw his earlier prediction being realized:

Truth—that is what [current-issue] literature lacks most of all. Writers have become liars, cautious and fearful. Therefore, by and large, literature does not fulfill even its primary, simple . . . purpose—recording our astounding, unique epoch, with all that is horrible and beautiful in it, and exactly as it is. . . .

As soon as we glimpse on the stage the knee or the belly of truth, we hasten to cover it up with an opera cloak.[8]

In his own fiction Zamyatin disdained the compromises of writers who considered it expedient "to hatch a patriotic egg by gold-leafing it heavily [until] finally there was hardly anything left but the gold leaf."[9]

Zamyatin's most important novel, *We*, written in 1920 but never published in the Soviet Union (several translations and an abridged Russian version appeared abroad in the 1920's, and finally the full Russian text in New York in 1952)[10] described a totalitarian state of the distant future, headed by the "Benefactor." Elections exist in name only—all citizens invariably vote for the Benefactor. A superbly organized and vigilant "bureau of guardians"—in other words, an improved GPU—ensures unanimity of thought and undeviating observance of the regulations covering every contingency of human life.

We is written in the form of a diary. The narrator is an engineer, the builder of the "Integral," an interplanetary rocket intended to rescue the inhabitants of undiscovered worlds from "the savage state of freedom" and subject them to "the beneficial yoke of reason."[11] The hero accepts the principles of mechanized society, but cannot overcome the consciousness of his own individuality and finally reaches the point of revolting against the system. The story symbolizes the sharp conflict between the educated individual and the Communist dictatorship. With uncanny insight Zamyatin, an engineer and former Bolshevik, foresaw the inhuman nature of the future Bolshevik state, industrialized by ruthless methods. *We* was a political broadside in the form of a utopian novel.

When the rocketbuilder, D-503 (people have numbers instead of names), discovers that the girl he loves, I-330, belongs to a subversive group, he is flabbergasted at first:

"But that's inconceivable! It's absurd! Don't you see that what you are planning is, in fact, a revolution?"

"Certainly" [she replies]. "Why is that absurd?"

"Because it's impossible. Because our Revolution—I am speaking for myself, not for you—our Revolution was the last revolution and there cannot be any more revolutions. Everybody knows that. . . ."

"What do you mean, the last? There isn't any last revolution. Revolutions will never end."[12]

Zamyatin's thesis of an infinite series of revolutions—alarmingly akin to Trotsky's theory of permanent revolution—was alone sufficient to prevent publication of the book. Despite the ban, however, the existence of the novel was well known soon after its completion. Zamyatin referred to it by title in his study of H. G. Wells, written in 1921-1922, and the critic Voronski, in an article dated October 1922, even gave an account of the contents of "the still unpublished" book. It was, he said,

> not a utopian novel but a broadside on the present in fiction form and, at the same time, an attempt to foretell the future. . . . Zamyatin is an incorrigible pessimist: with him, inertia always wins; at best, it is only momentarily overcome. . . .[13]

Zamyatin remarked in *Herbert Wells* that Russian literature had a meager tradition of social and scientific fantasy and singled out the utopian novels of the nineteenth-century writer V. F. Odoyevski as rare examples of the genre. Certainly if Zamyatin is to be considered in relation to the Odoyevski "tradition," the label "incorrigible pessimist" is appropriate. To the extent that Odoyevski saw apathy as the most deadly danger of future generations and maintained that imagination and suffering went hand in hand and were liberating and constructive forces, Zamyatin agreed with him. In *We* the mathematically worked out happiness of the citizens of the new world is an illusion. What they call happiness is nothing but inertia and habit. The builder of the "Integral" is endowed with creative imagination, and it makes him suffer and, eventually, revolt. On the other hand, Zamyatin did not share Odoyevski's optimistic expectations that—in the words of the critic P. N. Sakulin—"science in Russia will reach such a high level that man will achieve almost absolute mastery over nature."[14] Zamyatin said in his study of H. G. Wells, written after the publication of Wells' book *Russia in the Shadows:*

> The laciest, airiest Gothic cathedrals are still made of stone; and the most marvelous, most fantastic fairy tales of any land are still made of the earth, trees and animals of that land. . . .
> Now imagine a land where the only fertile soil is asphalt, on which grow dense jungles, of nothing but factory chimneys, and herds of only one breed—motorcars. . . .

This mechanized land of stone, asphalt, gasoline and iron is twentieth-century London; it was bound to give birth to its own iron motor-car spirits and to fairy tales about mechanics and chemistry. . . . And indeed there are such fairy tales—Herbert Wells tells them; they are his fantasy novels.[15]

Zamyatin was well acquainted with Wells' work and admired his "gift of prophecy, the strange gift of seeing the future through the opaque curtain of the present,"[16] his socialist desire to reorder the world—not through Marxian class struggle, the way of bloodshed, of the surgical knife, but through the slower method of therapy—and his freedom from cant, from the doctrine of any particular party.

An artist . . . is always a heretic. An artist, like Jehovah in the Bible, creates for himself his own peculiar world with its own peculiar laws—creates it in his own image and likeness and not that of another. And therefore the true artist can never be confined to the ready-made, seven-day calcified world of any dogma. He will inevitably break out of the articles of this dogma; he will inevitably be a heretic.[17]

Wells' scientific romances strongly influenced Zamyatin's *We;* yet the book is a refutation of Wells' view which is implicit in his description of Soviet Moscow in *Joan and Peter*, 1918 (obviously based on observations during a prewar visit to Russia), and in *Russia in the Shadows*.

Wells rejected Marxism, but apparently thought that the industrialization of Russia under Communist auspices was a good thing—it might lift the masses out of ignorance and savagery and prevent the collapse of civilization in Russia which would drag Europe also into the abyss. In *Joan and Peter* he had summed up the opinion of a radical-minded English intellectual as follows:

We must now live like fanatics [in order to create a world state]—this rocking world of ours will not have a new birth. It will fall apart still more, and crumble. And then the race of Bolshevik muzhiks will tend their pigs among the ruins.[18]

And in *Russia in the Shadows* Wells had said:

I do not believe in the belief of the Communists—to me their Marx is a joke—but I respect and esteem their spirit, I understand it.[19]

In the regimented and numbed citizens of the future state, however, Zamyatin demonstrated the inevitable result of Bolshevik industrialization and collectivization. His satiric prophecy preceded by many years that of Aldous Huxley in *Brave New World* and George Orwell in *Nineteen Eighty Four*, both of which strikingly resemble Zamyatin's work.

Stylistically, Zamyatin was a many-faceted writer. In his prerevolutionary work he owed much to Leskov and Remizov and frequently employed the *skaz* form, in which the plot is related in the speech, usually vernacular, of the narrator. At the same time he often conducted the narrative on several planes, retaining the plane of the author himself, with his subtle psychological analysis. His stories *The Islanders*, 1918,[20] and *Fisher of Men*,[21] satirizing English smugness and addiction to tradition (Zamyatin had been in England during World War I, working on the construction of icebreakers for Russia) are highly stylized through a series of devices increasingly elaborated in his later work.

"The Cave," and "Mamai," for instance, are cunningly contrived narrative designs in which the action evolves, image by image, out of an initial all-inclusive metaphor. The metaphor which unifies "The Cave" has already been indicated. In "Mamai" the intellectuals of Petrograd during the period of War Communism freeze and die like passengers aboard doomed ships. The story opens:

At night, there are no houses in Petersburg, only six-storied ships of stone. Like a lonely six-story world, each ship speeds on waves of stone among other lonely six-story worlds.[22]

In his "Story of What Matters Most," 1924, somewhat similar to *We*, the plot develops on two planes, reality and fantasy. A kulak uprising leads to a fratricidal war. Muzhiks massed on one bank of a river exchange shots with muzhiks on the opposite bank. The Socialist Revolutionary Kukoverov, taken prisoner by the Bolsheviks, expects to be shot. His thoughts in the face of death are described in the Dostoyevskian manner in the stories interpolated in *The Idiot*:

This tin water mug. . . . As I looked at it, I thought that it would be exactly the same tomorrow. Over there, perhaps, there is nothing—a vacuum, a desert—and I thought [what a blessing it would be] if I saw this very mug over there.[23]

Kukoverov is questioned by Dorda, with whom he used to work in the revolutionary underground. Socialist Revolutionaries and Bolsheviks were brothers in tsarist times. After the October Revolution, they became bitter foes. As a man, Dorda is sorry for Kukoverov; as a Cheka worker, he must be ruthless. He "forgets" his gun on the table, hoping that the prisoner may shoot himself. But Kukoverov will not commit suicide. A curious psychological duel develops in which the victim torments the executioner.

On the other, the fantastic, plane of the story these events are paralleled by events on another planet, where air vanishes except for liquid air in bottles, and people kill one another for just a bottle.

The story is deeply pessimistic. Even eternal life offers no refuge; beyond the life on earth, new misfortunes and waterless deserts await us.

The theme of revolution and evil is developed in the story "The Dragon" and the short novel *Flood*, 1929. "The Dragon" is a Red soldier whose "cap crowded his nose and would have swallowed [his] whole head if it hadn't been held up by his protruding ears. His long overcoat swept the floor." Riding a streetcar, he boasts of his revolutionary feats:

"So I was taking him along—that mug, the intellectual. Just to look at him made me sick. And besides, he kept talking, the dog. Talking!"
"Did you deliver him?"
"I did, all right—straight to Heaven, direct. With my bayonet!" [24]

The Revolution has inculcated violence in the man who, following his inclination to pity, finds a frozen sparrow and warms it back to life.

In *Flood* the Revolution and famine have fostered lawlessness and turned men into savages. Sofiya, killing Ganka in a fit of jealousy, is a wild animal, starving and unable to distinguish between right and wrong.[25]

Zamyatin's gift for combining the tragic and the humdrum is unequaled. His "everyday life" stories, such as "X" [*Iks*], "The Watch" and "Comrade Churynin Has the Floor" [*Slovo predos-*

tavlyayetsya tovarishchu Churyninu] had a strong influence on Zoshchenko and Vladimir Vetov.

In his "parables" Zamyatin also attacked Communist ideology. In one of these the novice Erazm paints an icon of Saint Mary of Egypt, intended to lift people out of moral filth, but his icon, instead, inspires carnal thoughts and a wave of unbridled debauch.[26] In other words, even if the Bolsheviks were honest and sincere and wished Russia well, somehow their efforts always generated evil.

A master of dialogue and characterization like Zamyatin was bound sooner or later to turn to the stage. The setting of *The Fires of Saint Dominic*, 1923, is the Spain of the Inquisition, but the play was a courageous protest against Soviet terrorism.[27] *The Flea*, 1925,[28] is a dramatization of Leskov's story *Levsha*, and *The Society of Honorary Bell Ringers*, 1926,[29] is based in part on his own novel *The Islanders*.

Zamyatin finished his last play, *Attila*, in 1928. It was read, and approved, at a meeting of the Art Council of the Bol'shoi Theater in Leningrad, but permission to produce it was refused.[30]

The theme was taken up again in the unfinished novel *The Scourge of God*, written abroad.[31]

In the late 1920's Zamyatin's *We* had been published, in an unabridged version translated into the Russian language from Czech, by a Russian émigré journal in Prague. The Communist press attack upon him was soon intensified. After great efforts, including a personal letter to Stalin,[32] Zamyatin obtained permission to leave Russia in the early 1930's.

VIKTOR SHKLOVSKI (1893-   )

Viktor Shklovski has been an astonishingly versatile writer. Critic, essayist, literary theorist and historian, novelist, film scenarist, he was always experimenting, trying to work out in practice the theories that swarmed in his mind. He was active in one literary organization after another. Before the revolution he was associated with the Formalist movement and helped organize the group known as *Opoyaz* (Society for the Study of the Theory of Poetic Language). He was closely associated with the Futurists, and was a regular contributor to their journal *LEF* [Left Front of the Arts] and its successor, *Novyi LEF* [New LEF]. If not a formal member of the Serapion Brothers, he was one of the moving spirits of the group.

Shklovski is at his best in literary reportage, as, for instance, in "Petersburg During the Blockade," a description of the hardships endured by the rank-and-file intelligentsia in Petrograd during the Civil War, as Yudenich advanced on the city. Without fuel and food, they burned furniture and doors. They ate fodder and decomposing horsemeat. At the cemetery gates:

> I shall never forget the dismal squeak of the sleds on the snow. Death came simply and often. . . . In the dining room of the Writers' House, redolent of bad dinners, rows of people dozed along the walls, people who had fled from their apartments, people thrown into chaos by the darkness and the freezing cold.[33]

Shklovski's style, studiedly dry, laconic and offhand, served as model for many beginning writers of the time.

In his brilliant essays collected under the titles *Knight's Move*, 1923, and *The Hamburg Count*, 1928,[34] Shklovski protests against the use of literature for propaganda purposes:

> It is the greatest misfortune of Russian art that it is not allowed to beat naturally, as the heart beats in the human breast. Instead, it is being regulated like train traffic.[35]

Furthermore, he warns, the policy is ineffectual:

> When the air itself is saturated with propaganda, and the water in the Neva is thick with it, propaganda ceases to be effective. People become immune to it.[36]

Standardization is the curse of Soviet literature:

> . . . Are we not like the Selenites (inhabitants of the moon) who were put into barrels out of which only one tentacle, useful to the community, was allowed to grow?[37]

Very little of Shklovski's diversified talent survived the plowing under of the Formalist school at the end of the 1920's. In the thirties he published infrequently. After censorship difficulties he even gave up writing film scenarios for a long time. He broke his silence during World War II, with the series of stories "Partings and Losses." He had kept his deft touch, as in describing a scene of devastation: ". . . On the Minsk highway, a broad concrete bridge was lying, its back broken and the ribs in its chest exposed."[38]

But the destiny of the Soviet writer was still excruciating disorientation:

History utters a resounding sentence and I write it down, like a typist to dictation, not knowing how it is constructed, which words are proper names, where to put a period, or how the idea is resolved.[39]

ISAAK BABEL' (1894- ?)

Many of Babel's *nouvelles* which were later included in his well-known *Cavalry Corps* of 1926 appeared in 1923-1924 in various periodicals. When assembled in a single volume the separate pieces, combining into an account of Semyon Budyonnyi's Polish campaign, have something of an epic air; yet the historical events of the Civil War are used mainly as background for episodes from the daily life of soldiers and civilians. Budyonnyi's army, in which Babel' served as Cheka representative, is painted as a pack of mad dogs. Their White enemies are no better, and the war resembles a fight between wild beasts.

In "The Letter" a young Red cavalryman writes his mother that his father, serving with the Whites, has killed a son—brother of the boy—who served with the Reds; when the Reds occupied the region, a third brother killed the father. He had trouble carrying out his revenge, because of some Jews who tried to intercede. The young soldier concludes: "I cannot . . . describe to you exactly how Dad was finished off, because they sent me away."[40]

The fratricide, the filicide, the killings at every hand, which assumed the proportions of a national tragedy in Sholokhov's *Donskiye rasskazy* [Stories of the Don], published in the same year as Babel's *Cavalry Corps*, are treated by Babel' not as tragedy but simply as one more proof of Russian savagery.

His Jewish origin and personal experiences may have something to do with this tendency. As a child he barely escaped from a pogrom. His grandfather was killed by the mob. These episodes, described elsewhere (in the autobiographical tales "Story of My Dovecote" and "First Love"), had made a profound impression.

Repelled and frightened by the ruthlessness of the Civil War, Babel' resorted to irony over the discrepancies between revolutionary slogans and reality. Voroshilov and Budyonnyi

rode side by side on long-bodied red mares. They were dressed alike in military jackets and silver-braided trousers....
"Get us Warsaw!" yelled a Cossack in a bowler hat and bast shoes.[41]

The new "equality" is displayed in silver-braid pants for Budyonnyi, bast shoes and a cast-off bowler for the soldier.

Babel' rings endless variations on this device of incongruous contrasts. In another story a soldier shouts that the troops will die for a sour pickle and for world revolution.

The more intelligent and sensitive among Babel's heroes recognize that the revolutionary ideals have already been betrayed and that there is just as wide a gulf between the top Communist and the ordinary man as there ever was between the blood aristocracy and the people. The company commander Khlebnikov in "Story of a Horse" *(Cavalry Corps)* resigns from the Party. He cannot reconcile himself to the fact that Communism has become a mockery. (Babel' himself was a Party member for only a brief period during the Civil War.)

Among Budyonnyi's horsemen and in the regions they pass, Babel' kept looking for men who practice charity instead of hatred, and he found the old Jew Gedali. To him the voice of the revolution says: "You don't know what you love, Gedali. You will find out when I start shooting at you. And I cannot help shooting because I am the Revolution." He asks a Jew from the army, a student of the Talmud, "What kind of dish is the International, Mr. Comrade? What do you eat it with?"

"With gunpowder," replies the other, "and seasoned with the best blood."[42]

Gedali is crestfallen. Treated by non-Jews as barely human, he is ready to welcome a revolution, but if it proves to be nothing but shooting it must be the work of evil men, of no benefit to anyone, Jew or non-Jew. He had dreamed of an International of good people, who would not interfere with his going to the synagogue and who would let him listen to a phonograph and not take the phonograph away from him. His friend explains that an International of pious Jews is a utopian dream, and Gedali goes to the synagogue to pray.

In the story "The Song" a Polish peasant woman reasons in much the same way. Babel' had a touching respect for people of simple faith, whether Jews, Russians or Poles.

His narrator is sickened by the depredations in occupied Poland:

I grieve for the bees. . . . There are no bees left in the whole province of Volyn'. We have defiled the wonderful beehives. . . . Lacking bread, we used our sabers to get at the honey. . . . The chronicle of these little daily crimes oppresses me constantly, like a heart disease.[43]

A passage in "The Road to Brody" reads:

Everything is dust. Only mothers have eternal life. A mother, when she is no longer among the living, leaves a memory that no one yet has dared to defile. The memory of our mothers nourishes in us compassion, as the ocean, the boundless ocean, nourishes the rivers of the earth.[44]

But compassion was not the way of Bolshevism, with its cult of class hatred. In "The Argamak" (a breed of saddle horse), which is related to the *Cavalry Corps* stories but which was not published until 1932, the company commander Baulin is dressing down the narrator:

"I know your type," the commander interrupted me. "You aim to live without enemies. That's what you're always trying to do—no enemies. . . ."
A red spot appeared on Baulin's forehead, and his cheek twitched. "You know what comes of that?" he added, having trouble with his breathing. "Boredom, that's what! Get the hell out of here." [45]

The critic Georgi Gorbachov compared Babel' with Maupassant;

and the critic Lezhnyov, with Flaubert. Though these influences are undoubtedly present in *Cavalry Corps*, the critics failed to mention the "elephant"–*Tale of the Host of Igor'*, the influence of which is very obvious, especially in lyrical passages and landscape descriptions. For instance:

> Purple poppies bloom in the fields around us, the midday wind plays in the yellow rye; virginal buckwheat marks the horizon, like a far distant nunnery wall. The quiet Volyn' meanders, disappearing into the pearly mist of the birch groves, creeping through flower decked hillocks, fumbling with weak hands in the overgrowth of hop. An orange-colored sun rolls through the sky like a chopped-off head.
> ... The odor of yesterday's blood and of dead horses filters into the cool evening air.[46]

Babel's "physiological" style is both his strength and his weakness. His almost clinical language is very effective, though at times overdone and revolting. His eroticism, too, sometimes comes close to a pathological obsession.

The reactions to *Cavalry Corps* were mixed. Budyonnyi himself protested against the sections which were published in the magazine *Krasnaya nov'* [Red Virgin Soil] in advance of the book. In his article entitled "The *Babizm* of the Babel' of *Krasnaya nov'*" (the untranslatable Russian term *babizm*—from the uncomplimentary word *baba*, woman—conveys something of the meaning of "old-womanishness") he called Babel' a degenerate intellectual having nothing of a Marxist about him and belonging among the émigrés rather than in the Soviet Union.[47]

The critic Vyacheslav Polonski stated that, by playing down the "collective" and paying attention to the individual, the little man, Babel' had shown from a new angle the famous Cavalry Corps known only for its military feats. He had high praise for Babel's craftsmanship.

> The river of life flows by, the great events and the little affairs of men side by side. People kill and are killed, perform heroic deeds and commit crimes. Tears and blood flow—everything flows and changes; only the hero, like an invisible shadow, is the same on every page, from the first to the last. This remarkable book is not about the Cavalry

Corps—it is written about himself by a man who has gone through the fascinating and cruel torments of war. All that Babel' says of the Cavalry, and all that he manages not to say, tells his own story, reveals his own attitude toward life.[48]

But in the thirties, after the change in policy that came with the First Five-Year Plan, Babel's romantic individualism was considered harmful and few dared to defend the book.

Babel's total output was not very great. He published several books in addition to *Cavalry Corps*, but in them many of the same stories are carried from volume to volume. His *Short Stories* appeared in 1925.[49] *The Story of My Dovecote*[50] (containing the title story and "First Love," both autobiographical) and *Odessa Stories*[51] came out in 1926.

In the same year he published a film scenario based on a series of his Odessa tales in which the hero is the gangster Benya Krik, a kind of Jewish Makhno. In the screen adaptation, under the title *Benya Krik*, the hero becomes a Red commander, and then meets the same end as many other revolutionary leaders of the Pugachov-Razin type.

"The devil alone knows what these Bolsheviks want from me,"[52] he says.

"The workers' government, forgiving your past crimes, commands you to serve the proletariat honorably,"[53] explains a Bolshevik commissar in Odessa. Benya walks into a trap laid by his new commanders and is shot. The scenario is the work of a master.

In the late 1920's and again in the early 1930's Babel' lived in France, but he was in the Soviet Union during the campaign to collectivize agriculture and traveled through the country as a special correspondent for *Krest'yanskaya gazeta* [Peasant Gazette] observing the organization of the kolkhoz system. His observations soon led him to appeal to those of Jewish origin among the Party contingent of kolkhoz organizers to withdraw from the campaign in order to avoid a new wave of antisemitism.

Of his novel "Velikaya Krinitsa," describing the effects of collectivization on the peasantry, only a few fragments were published.

The first chapter, which appeared in *Novyi mir* [The New World] in 1931 under the title "Gapa Guzhva," suggests that Babel' foresaw the debilitating, oppressing influence of the kolkhoz system: "Silence descended over Velikaya Krinitsa, over the flat sepulchral ice-covered wastes of the rural night."[54]

After a silence of several years he published the play *Maria* in 1935.[55] It is in many respects a more important play than his first, *Sunset*, 1928, dealing with the decline of the patriarchal Jewish way of life.[56] *Maria* is concerned with the tragic fate of those whom the Bolsheviks consider "has-beens" or "ideologically alien."

The tsarist general Mukovnin, an upright man, has two daughters, one of whom grew up before the revolution and resembles her father. The younger daughter, forced to make her way in a country poisoned with class hatred, becomes morally degraded. The hero is a speculator named Dymshits, perhaps the first Jew to appear in an unfavorable light in Babel's work, and there were those who accused Babel' of antisemitism.[57] But he needed this character to develop his thesis that in an economically deficient country the people's wrath inevitably turns on those who handle supplies, particularly profiteers like Dymshits.

Maria demonstrates Babel's theatrical flair and his command of his medium. However, Soviet theatres did not produce the play.

In 1938, during the purges, Babel' was arrested and disappeared from the literary scene. In the following year he was released, only to be arrested again in 1940. In 1956 Babel's death was acknowledged by the establishment of a committee in charge of his "literary legacy,"[58] and later it was stated that, a victim of unjust treatment, he had suffered "spiritual death" in 1938.[59] The year of his actual death still remains unknown. It has been reported, unofficially, that in 1944 he was removed from a concentration camp near Rybinsk and that he died in the same year.

In his last published piece, a sketch entitled "The Beginning" (1938), he related a conversation with Maxim Gorki, who warned him: "A writer's way is littered with nails, mostly large ones, and he has to walk on them barefoot. He will bleed profusely, and more and more every year."[60]

BORIS PIL'NYAK
(pseudonym of B. A. Vogau, 1894- ?)

Boris Pil'nyak felt the revolution as a flood of stupendous proportions suddenly engulfing Russia, and most of his writing was an attempt at a bird's-eye view of that flood. He was obsessed with the race of time and the unique tragic color of the times in which he lived. It is significant that one of his collections of stories is entitled *Spilled Time* [*Rasplyosnutoye vremya*].

Pil'nyak's thinking was strongly influenced by Heraclitian philosophy. The critic Gurvich once remarked that Pil'nyak's copy of a Russian translation of Heraclitus served as his guide to life.

Throughout his work Pil'nyak's main concern was to distinguish between the essential, which would survive the new times, and the transitory, which would die with them. Everything else was of minor importance. His plots are chaotic, and his characterizations sketchy. The very chaos of his works, however, renders to perfection the catastrophic quality of the times and the impact of catastrophe on the human mind and on individual lives as well as on the life of the nation. Pil'nyak wove terror and disaster into his words and into the structure of his plots. His compulsion to be always in step with the times pushed him in the direction of brilliant reportage rather than imaginative literature.

Pil'nyak once described himself as a follower of Belyi and Bunin. The critics took him at his word and the label stuck. In point of fact, the influence of Aleksei Remizov is more marked in Pil'nyak's best writing. He has been called a master of analytical suprematism in prose, close in spirit and in style to the painter Filonov.[61] Strangely enough, his debt to Vlas Doroshevich and Aleksandr Amfiteatrov, the "kings of reportage" of the old Russian press, is never mentioned.

Pil'nyak appeared on the literary scene before the revolution, with variations on Artsybashev's theme. Even then it was clear to Pil'nyak that the breach between the masses and the upper social strata in Russia was serious enough to cause a revolution, and he proposed a novel way of bridging the gap—let all aristocrats fall in love with, and marry, peasant women, and all gentlewomen cleave to muzhiks.

The idea of merging the upper and lower classes through carnal union occupied Pil'nyak for a long time. In *Machines and Wolves*, an engineer with a fastidious, philosophical turn of mind is irresistably attracted to semiliterate Mar'ya, a broadfaced girl who looks after horses and smells of onion and oats. Their passion is described by Pil'nyak with inordinate gusto and an embarrassment of physiological details.

Voronski once said that "Pil'nyak's love stories sometimes border on the pathological." [62] There is something morbid, for instance, in the mystical sensuality of the hero's passion for an Egyptian mummy in the novel "Ivan Moskva." Very often Pil'nyak's characters suffer from venereal diseases.

On the other hand, nature appears in Pil'nyak's books in a halo of beauty. His descriptions sound like psalms:

At daybreak there rose a tart odor from the wormwood; and it came to Natal'ya that it was not only the dry dale in the month of July that smelled of wormwood, but all the days of the year nineteen nineteen—of wormwood, of its bitter and fabulous odor, the odor of life and of death. The times were bitter with the bitterness of wormwood.[63]

This passage is from *The Naked Year*, 1922, a book that grew out of the collection *Bygones* [*Byl'yo*], published in 1919. As a piece of literature it defies definition. The author described it as "material for a novel." It is, rather, a sketchbook giving a remarkably objective and vivid picture of the revolution from its first days.

The revolution meant freedom from all restraints:

. . . And into the cities the backroads Revolt of the people brought death. . . . Famine, syphilis and death roamed the city. Crazed motorcars rushed along the avenues, in the grip of mortal anguish. People went savage dreaming of bread and potatoes, people starved, sat without lights, froze, took apart fences and wooden buildings, to warm up the dying stones. . . . There was something eerie, in spring, about the smoldering fires in the streets, smoking like incense at a funeral.[64]

The first days of the revolution were days of wild rapture for the lawless. The anarchist Irina says:

"These days, as never before, mean only one thing, struggle for survival. . . . That is why there is so much dying. To hell with the fairy tales about humanism! . . . Let only the strong survive."[65]

In *The Naked Year* Pil'nyak saw the whole history of Russia as a struggle between the elemental, primary forces and the power that held them in check for centuries. In the revolution the elemental forces won, and Russia, smashing a two-hundred-year old civilization that nobody wanted any more, returned to the seventeenth century.

"Look around you," said Baudek to Natal'ya, "Russia is a living fairy tale. . . . Famine, death, as in a fantastic tale. Cities die, as in fairyland, receding into the seventeenth century, and, magically, factories spring to life." [66]

We see the "has-beens" doomed to death, the seething peasant mass, an anarchist commune, religious sects, and, finally, the "leather jackets," that is, the Bolsheviks. Nothing could save the weak. Pil'nyak fixed his gaze on the strong.

The strong were the Communists and religious dissenters. Pil'nyak found no great difference between them. Both movements originated in a decline of orthodox religiosity. Bolshevism was a perverted expression of Russia's yearning for God, for a great spiritual ideal. The Communists deified machinery. Because the factory was nearer at hand than God, they had carried the first victories, but it was still an open question who would win in the end, the Russian God or the machine in the wake of which the spirit of Karl Marx came from Germany to Russia.

When the storm calmed down, the anarchists were forced either to ally themselves with the strong or to go under with the weak. Where did the intelligentsia belong? Its salvation lay in spiritual freedom:

Because the present irrupted imperiously, and he, severed from time, was tossed about like a leaf amid raging elemental humanity, Andrei began to think of a different freedom—that which man can find within himself.[67]

Aleksandr Blok, too, had called it "inner freedom." Those who had it might survive; those who didn't would be lost.

Two forces pulled Russia in opposite directions—one, into the medieval past, the other toward modern technology and industrialization. To impose their ideas, the "leather jackets" were forced to resort to terror. Without the Cheka, it was impossible to tame the Pugachov-Razin forces and to save Russia from a return to the dark ages. In *The Naked Year* Pil'nyak was a frank apologist of Bolshevism.

In *Machines and Wolves*, written in 1923-1924, the wild license of the first days has given way to efforts at reconstruction. Pil'nyak compares the untamed elemental forces to a wolf roaming free, and the regimented proletariat to the same wolf in a narrow cage.

Mar'ya, the horse-herd woman, personifies Russia to her lover, the engineer, who says that she is unspoiled because she has not yet come in contact with machinery: "The machine, in throwing her into a factory, would have wiped out her uncomplicated morality and ethics, along with the bloom on her cheeks. . . ."[68]

The Communists have subdued the masses and herded them into factories.

> Russia, turn left!
> Russia, march!
> Russia, run![69]

The country has become a vast forced labor camp. Now, Pil'nyak is repelled and indignant.

In his diary for 1923 he had written:

I admit that the Communist power in Russia has been established by history and not by the Communists' will; and, since it is my purpose to trace (insofar as I can and according to the dictates of my conscience and reason) the historical destinies of Russia, I am with the Communists—that is, I am with them insofar as they are with Russia (right now, consequently, more than ever, because I cannot walk with the philistines). I confess that I am far less interested in the fate of the Russian Communist Party than in the fate of Russia. To me the Russian Communist Party is only a link in the history of Russia.[70]

The Naked Year and *Machines and Wolves* are the high points of Pil'nyak's work. Among his later writings, the outstanding ones are "Ivan Moskva," *Tale of the Unextinguished Moon,* and *The Volga Falls to the Caspian Sea.*

The relationship between the engineers—the so-called "technical intelligentsia"—and the Communists with whom they were obliged to work was long a subject of concern to Pil'nyak. In *Machines and Wolves* the engineer Forst says: "Only toil, only the accumulation of wealth can save Russia—the wealth that is consolidated by human toil and machinery."[71] The Communist Lebedukha replies: "History is on our side, and power, to us, is a means, not an end. Power is a terrible thing."[72]

Lebedukha, unlike Forst, worships machinery. Forst is a mechanized God-man; Lebedukha is trying to become a mechanized man-god. Neither can get along without the other. Lebedukha needs Forst, for without the engineer's knowledge the machinery will not run. Forst needs Lebedukha, for without the Communist organizer the machines will stop for lack of manpower. It is a marriage of convenience.

In "Ivan Moska," 1927, Pil'nyak returned to this theme.[73] The hero is a fanatic of industrialization who dreams of a complete fusion of the engineer's know-how and the Communists' fanaticism. His tragedy is that of the man who has too strong a personality to fit into the new system. Pil'nyak's treatment of Ivan's inner drama produces the effect of delirium and hallucination. He weakens the impact of the main social theme, however, by the stress laid on Ivan's personal troubles. His hero suffers from hereditary syphilis and avoids Aleksandra, the woman doctor who loves him. The plot structure of "Ivan Moskva" shows the influence of Hans Ewers.

In *Tale of the Unextinguished Moon*, 1926, the influence of Victor Hugo *(Quatre-vingt-treize)* and of Dostoyevski *(The Brothers Karamazov)* can be seen. The hero, army commander Gavrilov, who had distinguished himself in the Civil War and organized a revolution in China, dies on an operating table. Was it murder? Who wanted him out of the way? Here Pil'nyak alludes to the antagonism between the Party and the army and to the Party fear that the Russian Revolution might spawn its own Bonaparte. The intimation is that Gavrilov was removed because his popularity made him dangerous.

Pil'nyak dedicated the tale to Voronski and published it in the periodical *Novyi mir* [The New World].[74] Voronski answered with a letter rejecting the dedication and accusing Pil'nyak of patent reference to the death of Frunze—despite the denial in the foreword to the story—of insult to the memory of Frunze and vicious slander of the Party.[75] (It was rumored that Frunze, People's Commissar of Army and Navy Affairs, who died under chloroform, had been disposed of on orders from above.)[76] When Voronski's letter was published in the next issue of *Novyi mir,* the editors accompanied it with a note confessing their grievous error. The issue containing the story was confiscated after partial distribution to subscribers and has become a bibliographic rarity.[77] *Tale of the Unextinguished Moon* was, however, published in book form in Sofia later in 1926.[78]

Mahogany, 1929, which deals with the organized throttling of all private initiative at the end of the NEP and the beginning of the First Plan, was published only abroad,[79] and Soviet critics called it "a dirty libel of Soviet actuality."

In *The Volga Falls to the Caspian Sea,* 1930,[80] which incorporates large sections of *Mahogany*, reworked and given a different slant in an effort to rehabilitate himself, Pil'nyak resolved the conflict between the Communist organizers and the intelligentsia. The former had won. Professor Poletika, one of the main characters, an old-school intellectual and Party member, does not yet want to believe in that victory and still hopes for genuine collaboration. Although Pil'nyak ostensibly wrote this novel to celebrate the inception of the new period of "socialist construction," the picture which actually emerges is one of the Bolsheviks building anew with one hand and wantonly destroying with the other. Poletika, undaunted, continues to strive for balance, for an end to the policy of erecting factories on ruins at the cost of heavy human sacrifice. Other engineers in the novel, however, feeling enslaved, humiliated and doomed by the new system, choose death.

Okay, another of Pil'nyak's attempts to deflect the barrage of criticism from himself, was written after a visit to the United States in 1932. Ostensibly an attack on America's capitalist system, it managed to convey between the lines the impression that in the United States technology was man's servant, while in Soviet Russia man was enslaved by technology.[81]

In *The Roots of the Japanese Sun,* 1927,[82] another series of sketches based on a trip abroad, Pil'nyak described Japan, too, as industrialized but judiciously retaining its precious traditions. In 1934 he was constrained to retract many of his opinions on the subject in a new book on Japan, *Stones and Roots,*[83] which incorporated large parts of the earlier sketches.

The Ripening of the Fruit, a novel serialized in 1935, describes the cataclysmic clash between the old and the new in Soviet life. Among the Palekh masters, Pil'nyak observed antiquity's passionate will to survive. It is hard, however, to form a clear idea of them from Pil'nyak's description. While surpassing Vikhryov in talent and culture, he lacked his command of the subject. But he did render the spiritual beauty of the art of these followers of the ancient Russian icon painters:

The cabin was filled with an overpowering scent of lilies-of-the-valley. A fragrance of lilies-of-the-valley emanated from the nightingale's song. . . . And the glory of the world, gratitude toward this world and life, the majesty, simplicity, beauty, complexity and mystery of life —incomparably more imposing, beautiful, fresh, and blissful than all the nightingales, lilies-of-the-valley, raspberries and thunder—filled the mind and the senses. . . .[84]

In the early part of the novel Pil'nyak criticized Soviet literature for its lack of interest in individual human destinies. Its heroes, he complained, were not people but stereotyped "Party secretaries," and novels ended on

building a factory or organizing a kolkhoz, in much the same manner as English novels, or Russian novels of Turgenev's time, ended on the hero's and heroine's betrothal. A factory or a kolkhoz is the bridegroom, the people are the bride, and the opening of the new factory is the wedding.[85]

In his later years Pil'nyak, as if uneasy and wary, rarely wrote anything except in collaboration with others. With Andrei Platonov he wrote "Che-Che-O,"[86] with Sergei Belyayev *Meat* (1936),[87] and with L. Farid "Spring in Khorezm," 1934.[88]

During the purge years of the second half of the 1930's Pil'nyak was arrested and has not been heard of since.

13. *The Documentary Approach*

For the sociologist, the historian and the student of social psychology, the documentary approach of certain early Soviet writers to the Russian Revolution and the Civil War will often afford rewarding and reliable source material. These writers dealt with many subjects which have been carefully avoided or carefully distorted by the Soviet press, such as the endeavors of the Bolsheviks to master the Pugachov-Razin elements of the revolution, their maneuvering to prevent a Bonapartist period by close control of the tsarist military authorities engaged to help organize the Red Army, their intrigues to bring about a head-on collision between the latter-day Razins and the would-be Bonapartes.

DMITRI FURMANOV (1891-1926)

Furmanov has been officially retained in a place of honor in Soviet literature as chronicler of the Civil War period and one of the founders of proletarian literature. His deserved esteem rests not on literary merit—where form is concerned, all his writings, including the much-lauded *Chapayev*, are undistinguished—but on his inability to lie in his attempt to reproduce reality in fiction form. Occasionally, when called upon to express a critical opinion of other Communist writers of the propaganda-pamphlet persuasion, Furmanov would yield to the dictates of Party loyalty, as in his appraisal of the work of Serafimovich. For himself, however, he eschewed the political poster and produced a painstakingly conscientious album of graphic sketches, which Vyacheslav Polonski described as "living bits of life torn out of the stream of the past and fixed in literature." [1] Furmanov himself said: "I lay no claim to artistic form. I write, enlivening my notebook jottings by personal reminiscences." [2]

He was born in the village of Sereda in Kostroma province, of Russified German stock. Furmanov himself refuted Soviet attempts to build up a proletarian legend about him. He said: "We had a saloon." [3] He attended first a law school and then studied history and philology at a university, without graduating from either because of the war. Furmanov's early stories written at the front show him to have been a pacifist by temperament.

He was on the side of the Bolsheviks by chance. For a while he belonged to the left wing of the Socialist Revolutionary Party, then switched over to the anarchists. Finally, because of his personal friendship with Frunze, Furmanov joined the Communist Party, in June 1918. Equally by chance, the revolution bore him to the crest of the wave. He was made a member of the Provincial Executive Committee in Ivanovo-Voznesensk and then political commissar of the division headed by the Civil War hero Chapayev. Later, on charges of excessive kind-heartedness, Furmanov was removed from that post and put in charge of political work at the Turkestan front. He took part in the suppression of a peasant uprising in Semirech'ye. Finally he became head of the Political Bureau of the Kuban' army. After the Civil War, however, he was not retained in the army political organization; his incorrigible soft-heartedness stood in his way.

Furmanov spent his last years writing and doing political work among Soviet writers, in the latter activity again hampered by his congenital kindness and lack of self-confidence and unsuccessful in efforts to put an end to the factional strife around him. Toward the end of his life he was given the post as secretary of the Moscow Association of Proletarian Writers, but only as a reward for past services; he did not play an important part in the organization. Furmanov died just in time. In another ten years he would certainly have found himself among "Bukharin's brood," for he followed the same lines in literature as Bukharin did in politics.

Chapayev, published in 1923, deals with the attempt of the Bolsheviks during the Civil War—clinging to the Razin-Pugachov elements of the Russian people like a rider clutching the mane of a wild horse—to occupy as much territory as possible with a small number of armed forces. The action takes place in the southern Ural steppes.

Early in 1919, the forces which fought at Ural'sk—and which fought bravely, which fought well and heroically—were almost entirely peasant regiments, in which there were no Communists at all or very few.[4]

Chapayev, in command of the Red forces in the area, before the war had been an itinerant artisan, in every trade from that of carpenter to that of organ-grinder. He was not a Cossack, but one of the *inogorodniye* (persons who live in Cossack villages but are not of Cossack origin). In the distant past the Cossacks themselves had been in opposition to the tsarist government, sometimes to the point of unleashing peasant wars. When, having been granted various hereditary privileges, these traditional enemies of the throne became its stanch defenders, the *inogorodniye,* who lived among them, felt themselves almost outcasts, and were aroused to anger and bitterness by the Cossack enjoyment of privileges which they did not share. As a result the old freedom-loving spirit of the Cossacks passed from the Cossacks themselves to the *inogorodniye*. During the Russian Revolution a new type of chieftain arose among the *inogorodniye* who bore a much closer resemblance to the bold rascals of Razin's bands than did the Cossacks, who had betrayed their own rebellious past. Furmanov's record of the revival of this characteristically Russian rebel type after two hundred years is perhaps his most important contribution.

The reader is given the impression that Chapayev had very rudimentary notions of the nature of the new life for which he is fighting. At the same time he has certain well defined views. Chapayev shared the idea held at first by many Russian peasants that the new social order must immediately bring about a just redistribution of wealth. The rich must divide with the poor. For him there was no other method of doing away with private property. He also would brook no looting of churches by his men and once threatened them with his fist for stealing a priest's vestments.

The political commissar in the story, Fyodor Klychkov (who represents Furmanov himself), was faintly irritated and at the same time amused by Chapayev's frequent attempts to defend the Orthodox Church and by his habit of crossing himself, which Klychkov regarded as nothing but traditional Russian ignorance and superstition. Actually in the upsurge of religious feeling evoked in the people by the revolution there was a tendency among the latter-day Pugachovs to force the Church to correct its error in having rejected the living spirit in the name of the dead letter.

In his later *Rebellion*, another long chronicle, Furmanov relates the life story of the guerilla leader Mamontov, about whom a feuilletonist had written jocularly in *Pravda* in 1920 that he would sometimes force a priest to offer a public prayer for the Bolsheviks' victory and to preach a sermon on the same subject and that he had proposed engaging priests of the highest integrity as political commissars.[5]

Furmanov's ingenious and unpretentious tale of Chapayev—told by a man who considered himself an atheist and an opponent of the Church—combines with such episodes to bear out Aleksandr Blok's assertion that Christ was with the rebellious Red Army men.

The political commissar Klychkov had been sent to the division to tame the refractory and ambitious Chapayev, but, as it turned out, they influenced each other. In Klychkov's thoughts:

Chapayev is not run of the mill, he's not to be compared with the others—it's certain to be as hard to bridle him as a wild horse of the steppe, but . . . even [those] horses *are* bridled. But is it necessary? Might it not be better to leave this beautiful, original, vivid character to its fate, to leave it entirely untouched? Let it gleam, play recklessly and sparkle like an opalescent stone.[6]

Chapayev was a resounding success and went through more than ten editions.

Rebellion, a long documentary chronicle about the putting down of a peasant uprising in Central Asia, was first published in 1925.[7] Shortly before his death, Furmanov, in collaboration with S. Polivanov, turned this chronicle into a play by the same title. The hero is no longer an individual, a single person, but the group, and the impression is one of a great many characters rushing about like so many couriers. Fiction and plays in which this effect is cultivated A. Gurvich has dubbed "animated cartoon-film epics."

In the book Furmanov was disquieted by the fact that the unknown heroes of the revolution with increasing frequency ended either before the Special Section or before the Tribunal.

In the play those who made the revolution speak even more boldly:

"What have the Communists from the capital given us?"
"The Special Section, the Cheka, capital punishment and jails."[8]

Cheusov, one of the characters, demands: "Why don't you Party members try to avoid bloodshed? Do you want to shoot the whole people, or what?" [9]

Rebellion, a play no worse than other Civil War dramas still flourishing, was gradually dropped from the Soviet repertoire, for obvious political reasons. *Chapayev*, however, is kept to the fore.

SERGEI F. BUDANTSEV (1896- ?)

The candid-camera shots and sketches from life produced by other writers were less successful and less popular than Furmanov's. He was luckier than most. His path happened to cross that of a man whose life was like an epic song. In putting Chapayev into a book, it was enough for Furmanov to be a conscientious copyist, but an indifferent writer. The same windfall had not dropped on other writers who depended on their material.

The central theme of the novel *Rebellion*, 1923,[10] by Sergei Budantsev is the subjugation by the Communist Party of the Pugachov-Razin elements and the punishment meted out to the revolutionaries who defended those elements to the point of armed resistance against the Party. The hero of the novel is Kalabukhov, a Socialist Revolutionary who collaborates with the Bolsheviks

The Pathfinders in Fiction

and becomes an outstanding Red Army commander. He believes that the peasants, once they have sobered up after their bloody feast, will come to hate violence and death. When he realizes that the Bolsheviks are holding a knife to the throats of the leaders of the anarchic, freedom-loving mob, he accuses them of black ingratitude and takes it upon himself to fight for the people's interests. He has several military specialists, former tsarist officers recruited by the Bolsheviks to organize the Red Army, shot in front of the troops and places under arrest the commissars sent down by the Revolutionary Soviet. But the very people for whom Kalabukhov fights do not accept him; to them he remains an intellectual, a member of the upper class, a gentleman. It is the sailor Boltov who wins their confidence—a sly, self-assured careerist. Budantsev, a Party writer, frankly recognized the Bolshevik tactics of playing on the ambitions of soldiers and sailors who showed the qualities of leadership and of setting obedient commanders risen from the ranks against potential Bonapartes.

In a later novel, *Locusts*, 1927, Budantsev described with stark truthfulness the attempts to repair the ravages caused by the Civil War in Turkestan. The hero, Mikhail Kreisler, a former White officer and émigré, returns to his native land to earn pardon by honest labor. As he and his wife near their destination, he says: "I'm not looking for trouble, but we will stand up for ourselves, Tanya, and, if they let us, we'll begin a new life." [11]

A disastrous situation awaits them. The countryside is devastated, and the machinery of daily living broken down. Yet Party officials and bureaucrats, drunken and dissolute, carouse and misappropriate state funds, oblivious to the ragged misery which surrounds them. A locust invasion threatens, and wrath is rising in the people. Kreisler, who becomes a tireless fighter of locusts and builder of the new society, aids in bringing the corrupt band to justice.

During the NEP period and afterwards Budantsev wrote short stories and a play making fun of the futile concern of prerevolutionary commoners with their creature comforts and their obsolete traditions.

In the play "Collection of Copper Coins," portraying the crumbling of the family under the Soviet regime, the engineer Glebov's prattle of decency and conscience is merely a fig-leaf with which the commoner seeks to cover up his pettiness and his concern for his own welfare. Glebov's son says:

"To me, this life of ours can be broken down into the rooms of strangers and into pairs of lovers, but not into factory shops and meetings. I leave a conference or my work to rejoin my own woman, and that is where life begins." [12]

Glebov's opponents, however, are themselves a new type of self-centered, self-interested commoner, but hardier and less exacting, and the struggle is one of spiders fighting in a glass jar.

Budantsev's career, like that of other Bolshevik writers addicted to truth, ended in a concentration camp in the late 1930's.

ALEKSANDR AROSEV

Of the early practitioners of the documentary approach Aleksandr Arosev was the most advantageously equipped by background and experience. He was born in 1890 into a family of intellectuals, and was educated in Liège and at the Petrograd Psychoneurological Institute. He joined the Bolshevik faction of the Social Democrat Party in 1907 and, as a member of the Military Revolutionary Committee, played a prominent part in taking over the government in Moscow in 1917. Thereafter he was forced into the background and occupied progressively less important positions. His last post was that of chairman of the Society for Cultural Relations with Foreign Countries (VOKS), in the thirties. He was found to be an "enemy of the people," brought to trial for "counterrevolutionary activity," and, according to report, either shot or put in a concentration camp.

A character frequently encountered in Arosev's work is the intellectual who is painfully aware of his inner alienation from the revolution, although he is himself its creator and organizer.

Of his various first-hand accounts of the very early days of the revolution, his sketch *How It Happened*, in which he attempts to analyze the psychology of mass uprisings, is of particular importance.[13]

The best thing Arosev wrote is the short novel *Recent Days,* 1922,[14] which will have a permanent place in Russian literature not because of literary merits but because of its profound and truthful analysis of the psychology of a new national type born of the revolution.

The proletarian hero, Mikhail Andronnikov, becomes a Marxist before the Revolution, when he has done with the religious seekings in which he has engaged under the influence of his friend Fadeich. In exile Mikhail falls in love with Nastas'ya Palina, an ardent Socialist Revolutionary. Fadeich and Nastas'ya represent branches of the Russian religious urge growing in opposite directions. They are both seekers after God; the first follows Christ, and the second substitutes for the teachings of Christ the socialist doctrine of paradise on earth.

Mikhail, first under the tutelage of Fadeich and then of Nastas'ya, is spiritually alien to them both; there is in him something crude, wild, and at the same time grim and evil.

The beast comes to the fore during the revolution, in which he sees an opportunity of attaining great power, such as he could never have dreamed of before. In fighting, Andronnikov displays truly implacable energy and iron will. When Nastas'ya, whom he has loved after his fashion—but whom he nonetheless once attempted to take by brute force—is suspected of spying for the Whites, he unhesitatingly kills her.

The new national type produced by the revolution was a man whose mind and heart were held to a single purpose by a great tension of the will. He was conditioned to take practical action with great energy, but he was not used to independent thought. Accustomed to obeying the will of the Party without regard for consequences, he was too intent on action to consider a plan critically or to doubt for a moment the need for its execution. Without a dictatorship he could not function; under a democratic regime he would find no outlet for his energy. His driving will power was accompanied by an inability to enjoy freedom; more than that, by a feeling that freedom would pull him into a vacuum.

Rationally, Arosev, himself a Bolshevik, was on the side of Andronnikov. The writer realized that his hero's cruelty was a necessity for the Communists; had they not been ruthless with their enemies, they would never have stayed in power. For this reason he dwelt at length on Andronnikov's positive qualities, his practicality, endurance and organizing ability. Yet there was a duality in Arosev's attitude toward his hero. He was unable to reconcile himself to the fact that the Andronnikovs were charged with energy and will power from the dynamo of hatred.

The practitioners of the documentary approach in the literature of the Civil War period have given us two equally representative types in Chapayev and Andronnikov—the former with the sturdy, grass-roots beauty of his personality, in which good and evil, cruelty and nobility conflict; the latter with his implacable hatred.

The hero of Arosev's *Memoirs of Terenti Zabytyi*,[15] a story told in the first person, is a man of the people, an idealist who had devoted his life to the revolution and worked in underground societies but who found himself an unwanted outsider once the cause had triumphed—he was too kind, too generous, too soft-hearted toward his fellow men. The tale was clearly influenced by Dostoyevski's *Poor People*. It has greater literary finish than Arosev's other writings, although its composition and style are still old-fashioned.

Nikita Shornev, 1924, is the story of a neurotic Party member tortured by the conflict between revolutionary duty and the normal concepts of honor and decency.

The men who planned the revolution experienced a flowering of their personality. The men who made the revolution underwent a withering dissolution of their ego. Arosev mapped out an epic cycle dealing with the lives of revolutionaries and showing this process. The first book of the cycle, and the only part which Arosev was able to publish, is entitled *The Roots*.[16] It is a broad and truthfully drawn panorama of the life of the revolutionary-minded intelligentsia under the tsarist regime, in particular of the workings of the Bolshevik underground organization. The character of Vano, a silent, sullen man, eternally smoking a pipe, was apparently intended to represent Stalin. Vano's pride suffers because he is merely one of many instead of the top man, and this injured pride breeds distrust, bitterness, and contempt for others.

The grace period for the objective documentaries of the Civil War was brief.

In 1926 N. Yarov published a novel entitled *The Year 1919*, in which the hero, "Daddy" Chubary, is another latter-day Pugachov, whose spirit the Bolsheviks succeed in breaking. Chubary feels that, so long as he quarrels with the high command and protects his boys from the sharp eye of the Special Section, the people are on his side and he himself is one of them. He is aware that "the closer his relations with the Commissar, the further his brethren draw away from him."[17]

The critics' censure of the book signalized that the Civil War documentary had outlived its usefulness:

> This book is just nine years out of date. . . . Two subjects are interwoven in it: the transformation of guerrilla detachments into disciplined army units and the change in the peasant mentality which came with the beginning of collectivization. In 1919 both these subjects were of vital topical interest, but today they are history, material for the archives.[18]

14. The Political Poster

Side by side with documentary writing, which had inherited at least some of the ethics of Russian classical literature, if not the mastery of form, there developed a literature of propaganda which was to letters what the political poster was to painting. During the revival of prose in the early NEP period the line taken by writers who studied the literary heritage of the past in an effort to overcome the spiritual and esthetic impoverishment of Russian literature may be called Voronski's line. An opposite line was pursued by those who, like Serafimovich, regarded their writing as primarily a means of promoting Communist Party policy. In the end Voronski's line petered out, while Serafimovich's line triumphed and served as the basis for the present cultural policy of the Party.

The outstanding representatives of the political poster school of writing during and immediately after the Civil War were Serafimovich, Larisa Reisner, Libedinski, Malyshkin, and Dem'yan Bednyi.

ALEKSANDR S. SERAFIMOVICH
(pseudonym of A. S. Popov, 1863-1949)

Serafimovich, an old Marxist long associated with revolutionary organizations, a member of Gorki's *Znaniye* group, a writer and journalist of established reputation, joined the Communist Party in 1918. Lenin recognized the value of this acquisition. He wrote to Serafimovich in 1920: "Your writings and what my sister has told me have given me a deep liking for you and I am anxious to tell you how much the workers and all of us need your work." [1]

Serafimovich's early work was interesting and at times original, particularly the novel *City in the Steppe*, 1912.

He made only one major "contribution" to postrevolutionary Russian literature, his novel *The Iron Flood*, 1924, which—although from the point of view of form greatly inferior not only to Serafimovich's own prerevolutionary work but also to the writings of Yakovlev, Furmanov, Budantsev, and Arosev—was proclaimed a classic of proletarian literature. Bolshevik critics exulted in the appearance, at long last, of a novel in which the hero was not the individual but the masses, and gave praise to Serafimovich as creator of a modern epic. Thanks to these accolades, Serafimovich was able to live on the interest from his capital for the remainder of his life. In 1933 he was awarded the Order of Lenin. Later the village Ust'-Medveditskaya was renamed Serafimovich in his honor. In 1943 he received a Stalin Prize.

In sober fact, the hero of *The Iron Flood* is neither the masses—which, incidentally, are shown as a dull, submissive herd—nor any individual character, but the Soviet government.

The novel tells the story of how the Taman' Army of Cossacks, under the command of Yepifan Kovtyukh, broke out of encirclement by the enemy and marched up through the northern Caucasus, with their families, to join the main forces of the Red Army. In the book Kovtyukh is portrayed under the name of Kozhukh.

More than half the book, in the usual manner of Civil War writers, is devoted to descriptions of scenes of fighting, and these descriptions are the work of a craftsman skilled at his trade. When Serafimovich writes of the diapers hung up to dry on rifles and cradles slung under cannons, of cows munching side by side with artillery horses, and of women hanging their cooking kettles over the fire, we see and hear the scene. For the remainder, *The Iron Flood* is a fictionalized propaganda pamphlet, a social falsification which wears an air of complete verisimilitude. When the leader Kozhukh addresses his army, it is with a strong Ukrainian accent, as it should be, but the content of his speech is that of a demagogic speech made by an experienced Bolshevik agitator who had his political theory down pat and knew what line to take with the people, incongruous from the lips of Yepifan Kovtyukh, formerly a Cossack officer in the tsarist army:

"Then why did thousands, millions of people suffer such torments, why? . . . For one reason only—for the Soviet Government, because it alone is for the peasants and workers; there's no one else." [2]

Serafimovich himself made no secret of the fact that Kozhukh was an idealized (read "Communized") Kovtyukh: "I was often forced to sacrifice some salient features, traits of character, customs, relations with the family, etc." [3] It is of passing interest to note that after the fifth edition of the novel, published in 1930, Serafimovich was obliged to sacrifice even his character's Ukrainian accent, which was gradually eliminated in subsequent editions.

Kovtyukh himself remarked about his fictional reflection: "That's not me, that's some kind of saint. There are no real people like that." [4]

For an account of the real Kovtyukh and his activity during the Civil War, one does well to turn to Furmanov's sketch "Yepifan Kovtyukh." [5]

In 1937 Kovtyukh was arrested for treason and participation in the Tukhachevski conspiracy, and, it is rumored, was shot. Thereafter *The Iron Flood* was removed for a time from libraries and school book lists. Later Serafimovich regained his prestige. He cleared himself by pointing out that his character Kozhukh was differerent from Kovtyukh, and that he, Serafimovich, had endowed Kozhukh with traits lacking in the actual man precisely because he had sensed that Kovtyukh had something up his sleeve, that he was not "one of us."

Serafimovich was an early exponent of the style which still dominates Soviet literature—illusory realism, later known to Soviet critics as "socialist realism" and canonized as the sole method of Soviet literature. The whole trick lies in fitting together bits of real life and propaganda so cleverly that the reader is unable to distinguish between the two.

LARISA REISNER (1895-1926)

One of the most prominent women Bolsheviks, Larisa Reisner was given wide publicity for her Civil War sketches, in which she drew on her own experiences as political commissar on the Czechoslovak front in 1918-1919. Her writing has, however, long since dropped into oblivion.

The collection of sketches entitled *The Front*, 1924, was in large part political propaganda aimed at enlisting the intelligentsia on the Bolshevik side. She minced no words in admitting that pity and the revolution are incompatible:

> The revolution wears out its professional workers unconscionably. It is a harsh master with whom there is no use talking about a six-hour day, maternity benefits or higher pay. It takes everything—men's brains, wills, nerves and lives—and, having sucked them dry, having wounded and exhausted them, deposits them on the nearest scrap heap and recruits splendid new soldiers from the vast reserves of the masses.[6]

At the same time she assured her readers that cruelty and terrorism were only temporary evils unavoidable in the building of a bridge to the bright new world:

> The new men are on the march . . . who in a few swift years must master all of the old bourgeois culture and, more than that, recast what is best and most useful in it into new ideological form.[7]

Although Larisa Reisner's writing was on the level of that in prerevolutionary provincial newspapers, her persuasive powers were enhanced by sheer feminine charm and influenced such seemingly hopeless and incorrigible individualists as Boris Pasternak and Vsevolod Rozhdestvenski,[8] to name only two. Pasternak even dedicated a beautiful poem to her.[9]

Libedinski's and Malyshkin's Civil War writings, to be discussed later, are also little more than political posters in the form of fiction.

15. Revolutionary Naturalism

ALEKSANDR TARASOV-RODIONOV (1885-1938?)

Although the name of Tarasov-Rodionov has been expunged from Soviet annals of postrevolutionary literature, his contribution, in retrospect, takes on more and more significance. At a time when prose was still in eclipse, when the few genuine fiction writers appearing in print were for the most part confining themselves to short staccato stories and sketches and were largely preoccupied with form, Tarasov-Rodionov produced a solid sustained narrative, a thesis novel, which had the effect of a severe electric shock. The book was his *Chocolate* of 1922, the prototype of such books—decades later—as Arthur Koestler's *Darkness at Noon* and Victor Serge's *The Case of Comrade Tulayev*.

As an idealistic young man, Tarasov-Rodionov joined the Party in 1905. During the Civil War he was a brigade commander and special investigator with the High Tribunal. An abrupt break in his Party career occurred probably in 1921, when he took a modest post in the State Publishing House and began to devote himself entirely to literature. During his trial in 1938, when he was sentenced to death, he was accused of having assisted in the release of the White General Krasnov who had been taken prisoner by the Reds, after making Krasnov promise not to fight the Communists again. The general did not keep his word.

The motivation for Tarasov-Rodionov's quixotic action—if the charge had any basis in fact—is seen in his work. Aversion to violence is the keynote of the two tales we know, *Chocolate* and *Linyov* (entitled *Grass and Blood* in the second edition). He probably wrote other tales in a similar vein, but his papers were confiscated at the time of his arrest.

In *Chocolate* the head of a regional Cheka, Zudin, an old Party member, is moved by pity to save a dancer, Val'ts, who has been arrested on suspicion of espionage. He doubts her guilt and, instead of having her tried, gives her some work in his office. To forestall gossip about himself and the ballerina, Zudin takes her home to meet his wife. The women become friends, and Val'ts gives Zudin's wife a pair of stockings and some chocolate. This present eventually leads to Zudin's execution for accepting bribes and "selling out" to a counterrevolutionary organization. Even the prosecutor at the trial does not believe in the truth of the accusation, but it is necessary to make an example of Zudin to frighten other soft-hearted idealists among older Party members, as well as provide one more scapegoat for the masses.

On the night before Zudin's execution, one of the judges of the special commission which has heard Zudin's case visits the former Cheka official, to have a heart-to-heart talk with his old Party comrade. He admits candidly that the question at issue is not whether Zudin is guilty:

"There's no guilt at all! But on the other hand, we can't leave things as they are! Something must be done, something harsh, frightful. Otherwise, our whole cause will be lost. You understand! . . . It was the devil that made you take pity on that woman."[1]

Party members had already ceased to speak of truth and justice. The one aim was to hold their power.

The controversy over *Chocolate* was of long duration. In 1925, when the story was republished in book form, Leopol'd Averbakh, already displaying the tactics he would later employ as literary dictator, wrote in a review that Zudin should have prosecuted Val'ts whether she was guilty or not and that the shooting of an innocent person did not matter very much if it increased the authority of the Party.[2]

Many of the old underground revolutionaries, especially the intellectuals, however, strongly disapproved of Cheka methods ("I blush for your torture chambers," wrote Larisa Reisner. "Opinions on terror may differ," said the old Bolshevik Ol'minski, "but what is going on now is not Red terror but common crime"),[3] and it is this attitude Tarasov-Rodionov expressed in *Chocolate*. Despite his grim thesis, however, the author looked forward to better times.

The action of *Linyov*, 1924, is set in Siberia, during the Civil War. The hero, Linyov, who looks like Lenin and is sometimes mistaken for him, behaves almost like a priest of some mystical cult of which Lenin is the god. Tarasov-Rodionov tried to show the difference between the real Lenin and the myth created by popular imagination and diligently fostered by the Party, and made it clear that fanaticism harmed the revolutionary cause.[4]

Tarasov-Rodionov's contribution to memoir literature is the "chronicle" *The Heavy Tread*, in three parts, *February*, *July* and *October*, only two of which were published. It is an impressive picture of the period from the fall of the monarchy to the October Revolution. The author obviously grieved over the degeneration of liberty, for which all the Russian revolutionaries had fought for decades, into its direct opposite, despotic totalitarianism. In *February* he says:

Often a strange desire overtakes me—to stop looking at life. Usually at such moments I close my eyes, bow my head and cover my face with my hands, and this immediately gives me a better sense of my real self. But the world around me does not wish to leave me.[5]

Whatever his formal shortcomings Tarasov-Rodionov commands respect for his refusal to embellish reality to suit the Party propaganda line and for his insistence on the stern truth in recording events and Party practices of the early postrevolutionary period.

ALEKSANDR YAKOVLEV (1886-1953)

Lobov [the hero of Yakovlev's novel *The Victor*, a newspaperman and writer] recalled the promising beginning of a bad novel: "I take a piece of life—drab and coarse—and create a delightful legend." . . . He would now take a piece of life—only far from drab, because all life in Russia was ablaze—and reproduce it. However, if that life were to be reproduced literally, photographically, his novel would lack charm and meaning. Any piece of writing is a work of art only if it is well written, has an interesting plot, and, what is most important, when it conveys an important idea.[6]

Yakovlev must have had his own writing in mind. The value of his work lies primarily in the novelty and topical interest of his subject matter, but, unlike the other practitioners of the documentary approach, he was able to cast his material into literary form, even though the form remains of minor interest. Yakovlev is a colorful and original naturalist. Emile Zola was one of his favorite writers and in a sense his master. Yakovlev's *Victor* also shows the influence of Theodore Dreiser's novel *The Genius*. (Yakovlev knew no foreign languages and read the works of both writers in translation.) An old Socialist Revolutionary, he had been sent into exile in 1905 for his opposition to the tsarist regime.

Bolshevik literary critics never weary of repeating that in Russian Civil War literature the central character was no longer an individual, but the collective, the masses, and never cease to praise contemporary writers for this new achievement. Serafimovich's *Iron Flood* is usually cited as a model.

But it is Yakovlev and none other who is to be credited with the discovery of this gold-bearing vein; his *October,* published in 1923, is the beginning of the device in postrevolutionary Russian art. N. Agadzhanova, working on the scenario of the film *Potyomkin,* adopted Yakovlev's method, and Eisenstein, the director, won world-wide fame by fixing this method on the screen.

In his novel about the Bolshevik Revolution Yakovlev attempted to convey the whole through the part, that is, by describing the moods and emotions of individuals to portray the complex feelings and thoughts of the collective. *October* is a gallery of mass scenes and episodes, in the foreground of which are presented the experiences and actions of single persons.

In an instant madness swept the street. The crowd, terrified, huddled against the walls and swayed convulsively, hiding behind corners, projections, entrances. The soldiers hugged the walls, nervously raising their rifles, getting ready for defense and murder.[7]

And so the battle is joined.

An officer jerked his head backward, dropped his rifle, took a step sideways, tripped over his army overcoat and fell. . . .
A workman in a blue cap was writhing on the window sill, trying to get up. His rifle thumped against the wall.[8]

Yakovlev is very good at describing skirmishes. One of his mannerisms is to stress the contrast between the peaceful scene of yesterday and that same scene in an atmosphere of battle. This device is particularly successful in a scene in which he describes a crossfire in front of a food shop, with bullets whistling past signs which read "Fresh meat and game," "Cabbage, cucumbers, onions."

The author strove for objectivity by seeking out in the crowd its typical representatives. The mob was split into three camps—some for the revolution, others against, and the majority, helplessly marking time.

Among the embittered and the dissatisfied the Bolshevik coup was merely the detonator by means of which potential energy was converted into kinetic energy, accumulated anger into revolutionary action.

Leonti Ryzhov, a blacksmith, a nasty, lively and stupid muzhik, yells to the crowd, "Why do you stand still? They're giving out rifles at the city gates. Let's kill the cadets!" [9]

A swaggering soldier pronounces "amen" over the bourgeoisie. "We'll smash them all. The intelligentsia has been in the saddle long enough." [10]

They are joined by a proud and self-important proletarian with a sparse red mustache and sunken cheeks who, because of drunkenness and petty pilfering, never held a job long.

Akimka, fond of singing, fighting and adventure stories, who sees himself as a sort of mountain eagle and who represents the young stalwarts captivated by the romanticism of the revolution, takes up his rifle, too.

Among those on the other side, a working-class mother says to her son, "Some revolutionaries! First they drove out the Tsar, and now they are starting to fight each other." [11]

Yasy-Basy, an intelligent shoemaker, who is fond of philosophizing in his hours of leisure, thinks there is no sense in the revolution. "The main thing is, nobody knows the real truth. I've listened at some of your meetings. . . . How can I go and shoot at living men, when I don't know the real truth?" [12]

Yakovlev was especially concerned with the third sector, the silent onlookers.

The alarmed crowd stood still, talking in low voices and staring into the distance with frightened eyes in which there was little understanding, as though the men were still in the grip of a nightmare.[13]

Vasili Petryayev, a Socialist Revolutionary and an educated workingman, is a spectator rather than a participant in the revolution. His lonely, perplexed figure wanders through the whole gallery of pictures of which Yakovlev's *October* is composed. An idealist dreaming of universal brotherhood to be achieved through love and charity, Vasili realizes that he is of no use to the revolution, that he is superfluous, and commits suicide.

Yakovlev was concerned with human values and shunned propaganda. His description of the revolution is scrupulously veracious. He shows that the people sincerely rejoiced at the victory of the revolution, not because the Communist idea had come out on top, but simply because the whole bad business was over at last. Once more free of the fear of death, they could now turn to reconstructing what the revolution wrecked.

On the whole, Party-minded critics at first received *October* with approval, partly because certain of Yakovlev's observations could be used to bolster Leninist doctrine. He had noted, for example, that the revolution redeemed many men who were thought to be worthless or finished and gave them new faith in themselves. Occasionally drunkards and loafers from the industrial suburbs shook off their lethargy and moral decrepitude and fought the enemy day and night; the apparently stupid developed at times into clever military leaders.

During the early and mid-1920's Yakovlev wrote a great many stories and novels of the Civil War and also of the period during which capitalism was developing in Russia. Among the most interesting of these is "Freebooters," 1922,[14] in which he describes the tragic fate to which the peasant Razins and Pugachovs were doomed at the hands of the Communist fanatics, their recent comrades in arms.

The story *Zhgel'*, 1925,[15] and the novel *Man and the Desert*, 1926,[16] deal with the series of defeats suffered by progressive capitalists in their struggle against the inertia, conservatism and greed of the Russian merchant class before the revolution.

The Pathfinders in Fiction

The Victor, Yakovlev's last novel to attract general attention, was published in 1927. In it he turned from rebels in the thick of revolution to a tamed penitent. The hero, Lobov, is a talented newspaperman from the provinces who is hired by a Moscow newspaper. In Moscow he feels alone amid hostile crowds and buildings. His fellow workers on the newspaper strike Lobov as smart-alecky, clever men without principles, out to make a career. They tell each other anti-Soviet stories, which reflect their own views, while in print they vie with each other in praising the Soviet regime.

Lobov becomes a feature story writer. He is successful and highly thought of, but he is very lonely. In time, against his natural bent but driven by circumstances, Lobov develops into a calculating egoist. Olga, a woman even more lonely than Lobov in the big city, becomes his mistress after a casual meeting. Less well educated, she is his superior in that she is capable of genuine, selfless love. Under its influence Lobov begins to change for the better.

Olga dies suddenly. At her deathbed Lobov realizes for the first time in what miserable circumstances she has been living and feels at fault because he has not taken care of her. "This was love—a great love without self-interest, and I have let it go by without taking notice of it." [17]

His personal grief makes him aware of the general suffering and of the prevailing social inequality covered up in the Soviet press with sanctimonious, lying prattle about the state's concern with the needs of the common man. Emotionally upset, Lobov can no longer write as he used to.

He begins an affair with Lyudmila, a ballet dancer, who proves to have no use for a suffering, lonely man, turned into a failure by meditation and his inability to write the well-phrased lies of his colleagues. One day Lobov finds Lyudmila in bed with Bernshtein, a fat bald man who has bought the dancer's affections with money and valuable presents. In a fit of rage Lobov kills her and is arrested.

Fyodorov, a peasant who shares Lobov's cell and who has been arrested on charges of beating up the chairman of the village soviet—he is innocent but has decided to atone for another man's sins—advises Lobov to repent, for repentance will give him the strength to bear his punishment.

"What are you, a dissenter?" Lobov asked.
". . . I believe in life—with all the stars, the sun, the moon, the trees, and us, in our gladness," the peasant replied.[18]

Fyodorov's pantheism is that of the simple folk, a result of dissatisfaction with the Orthodox Church for stressing ritual to the exclusion of faith, in contrast to the pantheism of Veresayev's Isanka, dissatisfied with dialectical materialism.

Through the efforts of a woman journalist who has influence in Party circles, Lobov is released pending trial and accepts the invitation of Fyodorov, set free earlier, to visit him in the country. Here Lobov's moral regeneration, which is the focal point of the novel, takes place.

Toward the end of the NEP period there was a wholesale return of the peasantry to the Orthodox faith. In *The Victor* the peasant Svishchev, in a transport of fury, shouts, "Give me the truth! You've hidden the truth! The Antichrist rules the land! The seventh phial [of wrath] pours down on Russia!" [19] As a sign of protest, he breaks the windows in the houses of the chairman of the village soviet and the local militiaman. He lands in jail three times but continues to fight with undiminished zeal.

Lobov discovers meaning in life by sharing in the nation-wide repentance and by coming to revere the people's conscience, although in the past he thought of religion as a sign of ignorance and stupidity. Lobov no longer cares what he is going to be tried for, or how; he has already given himself a fair trial.

Stylistically Yakovlev was very uneven, falling under the obvious influence of various other writers, first Zola, then Dreiser and even Artsybashev. As he worked on his style, however, he learned to blend the two opposed elements of folk speech (large doses of which were dictated by his material) and the literary language of the intelligentsia in the Remizov manner, and his originally rather crude writing took on considerable beauty. Furthermore, Yakovlev was a good psychologist. The trouble is that he had no sense of proportion, and for this reason he never went beyond naturalism, never developed his potentialities to the limit. Nonetheless, Yakovlev was one of the best and most objective writers of the Civil War period.

In the late twenties and early thirties he came under attack by Soviet critics. *The Victor* was denounced as preaching obscurantism and the peasant "mystique," and was removed from libraries. As a former Socialist Revolutionary, the author was accused of sharing the ideology of the anti-Communist kulaks, and was censured for "slander" of the proletariat in speaking of its Luddite tendencies.

Yakovlev ceased to publish for a few years. When new stories and sketches began to appear in the mid-1930's—*Great Volga*,[20] *Lights in the Field*[21] (about collective farms) and *Pavel Morozov, Pioneer*[22]—his unpolished but genuine literary talent was gone. His last novel, *Steps*, was published in 1946.[23]

ALEKSANDR NEVEROV

The naturalist peasant writer Aleksandr Neverov (pseudonym of A. S. Skobelev, 1886-1923) reproduces peasant speech almost stenographically, yet concisely, and gives an objective picture of the peasants' thoughts and attitudes toward the Soviet regime.

In his short novel *Tashkent, City of Bread*, 1923,[24] Neverov deals with the Volga famine from the point of view of those who managed to outwit it and survive. He paints the smart, resourceful youngster Mishka, who travels from a Volga village to Tashkent in search of bread, with warm sympathy and humor.

Geese and Swans of the same year describes the peasants' division into conservatives (geese) and progressives (swans) on the question of agricultural methods.[25]

Although Neverov's best work is free of propaganda, the novel *Andron Good-for-Nothing*, 1923,[26] the story of a peasant who fights for the new Soviet dispensation in an effort to reform the dark and savage life of the peasants, has a tendentious tone.

Neverov also wrote for the stage. Of his various plays *Laughter and Tears*, 1922, a comedy satirizing a commissar who has become a village autocrat, is the best.[27]

5

Rival Camps of the NEP Period

---

16. *The Serapion Brothers*

The group of young writers who called themselves the Serapion Brothers was formed with Zamyatin's assistance in 1921, when the Civil War was almost over. The group included Lev Lunts, Mikhail Zoshchenko, Konstantin Fedin, Veniamin Kaverin, Nikolai Tikhonov, Nikolai Nikitin, Mikhail Slonimski, Vsevolod Ivanov, Il'ya Gruzdev, Yelizaveta Polonskaya, and Vladimir Pozner. To the question whether they were with or against the revolution, Lunts replied in 1922 that they were with the hermit Serapion (a character in E. T. A. Hoffmann's stories).[1] This defiant declaration signified that each of them intended to keep his individuality as an artist in spite of the political pressures of the time.

LEV LUNTS

Lunts' independence of thought—in Gorki's words, "a fire that burns out only when the man has been consumed"[2]—also marked his controversial paper "To the West!" which he read to a meeting of the Serapion Brothers and in which he urged Soviet writers to adopt Western techniques. "We Russians do not know how to handle plot . . . and therefore we despise it."[3] Gorki's journal *Beseda* [Colloquy], which printed the article, commented:

The Serapion Brothers, urging us to turn "to the West" and to a literature of plot, are themselves drifting away from the West. Never before has Russian literature been so full of folk ways, folklore and "stylization" as are the writings of Zoshchenko, N. Nikitin and Vsevolod Ivanov, and this reduces it to something of merely local interest and mades it inaccessible to the Western reader.[4]

Gorki had expected Lunts, with his "audacity of mind," to develop into a great playwright: "Had he lived and gone on working, I thought, the Russian stage would surely have been blessed by plays of a kind it has not yet had."[5]

Lunts wrote four plays, "The Apes Are Coming," "Outside the Law," "Bertrand de Born," and "The City of Truth." The last is the most significant of the four. It was published abroad posthumously.

"City of Truth" is a boldly constructed utopian fantasy which combines features of the Soviet scene immediately after the revolution with features of the "ideal" Communist state of the future on Blok's principle of the "oneness of time."

A commissar is leading a crowd of people from somewhere in the Far East to Russia. He extols Soviet Russia in the most extravagant terms—a place better than paradise, now that the Tsar and Kerensky have been overthrown.

But the road to paradise leads through violence and death. After the panegyrics, the Commissar turns to his immediate job:

"The first one who complains, I'll kill him! And I'm telling you once more, I'll kill anyone who stumbles! Only the strong shall arrive. The sick are as good as dead." [6]

The Doctor does not believe in the Commissar's paradise and says so. Other characters chime in, and are silenced by one of the characteristic methods by which the Communists drove the people into the Civil War:

An Old Man: We should say a prayer, brothers.
A Morose Character: To the devil with you. What are you going to Russia for? There is no God in Russia.
A Cheerful Character: Don't mind him. His goose is cooked anyway.[7]

There are moments of tension:

Soldiers' voices: Baloney! Let's turn back! We won't go! I'm hungry! Stinker! You can't fool us! We won't go!
The Commissar: Quiet! . . . All you think of is food. Hungry? There, eat your fill! (Shoots the Morose Character.)[8]

The action shifts to the City of Truth, similar in many ways to Zamyatin's totalitarian state. "We all work alike and live alike. You are looking for justice, happiness and work. Come, live and work with us,"[9] the inhabitants of the City of Truth say to the Russians. Here passion has been supplanted by machines, feelings are attuned to their rhythm. Man, creator of the machine, has put himself beneath his creation and is trying to imitate it. Everyone senses the impoverishment of the mechanized man, even the Commissar, who says to the Doctor: "I cannot go on like this. Am I robot, a machine tool?"[10]

The Doctor: What now? A commissar crying! And what about? Because all that's sacred in life has been spit upon. By whom? By yourself! You were looking for the truth, now you've found it.
. . . .
What are you going to do now, Commissar? Go on deceiving them and yourself? . . . I no longer believe in anything. I hate those who believe.[11]

The Commissar has lost faith in the cause, but he cannot relinquish his power. Hostility and cruelty to those who have discovered his weakness and challenged his authority arise in him. He decides to continue the journey and arranges to have the Doctor murdered.

The Doctor: Why? Why?
The Commissar: Because you did not believe. We do not need people like you. . . . We who believe will make our destination without you.
The Doctor: And find a land of the dead, like this one! A land of machines.[12]

Lunts' play has been underrated, both in the West and in Russia. There is no more courageous and pungent anti-Bolshevik play in modern literature.

Lunts had the makings of a great playwright. He emigrated from

Soviet Russia and died abroad in 1924, at the age of twenty-three, from a disease caused by nervous exhaustion.

VSEVOLOD IVANOV (1895-   )

The most talented writer among the Serapion Brothers was unquestionably Vsevolod Ivanov. In regard to form, his work can be divided into three periods. In the first he was something of an Imaginist, though not a "modern" one like Shershenevich or Marienhof but one rooted in ancient Russia, taking his imagery from old epics, in particular *Tale of the Host of Igor'*. Even his titles served to characterize his early writing, for instance, *Colored Winds*, 1922, and *Blue Sands*, 1923. The second period was marked by a dimming of his gaudy colors, less ornateness and increasing simplicity and restraint. The third period was a long-drawn decline, in spite of Ivanov's attempts at recapturing his old vivid manner.

Vyacheslav Polonski writes of Ivanov's early work and its heroic romanticism:

He unrolled the picture of the peasants' revolution before the readers' eyes, seared their faces with the heat and smoke of conflagrations, opened up to them a new world....[13]

Ivanov's *Armored Train 14-69*, published in 1922,[14] a tale of the Civil War and Japanese intervention in the Far East, was later adapted for the stage and in play form has the well-nigh unique distinction of having remained in the repertory of the Moscow Art Theatre since the NEP times until now, with unvarying success.

In Ivanov's perceptive portrayals of national types he depicts both the White officers and the Red guerillas as capable of selfless heroism. The White officer in command of the armored train, Nezelasov, is conscious of the estrangement between the ruling class and the people, between the officers and the soldiers, and is eager to repair past mistakes before it is too late. In the play he says: "We are like pus draining from a wound. Our country has thrown us out. . . . But I am not the kind that can be thrown out."[15] He wants to make friends with the peasants before taking the train through the Siberian forests, but he is alone in his desire to find a common language with the masses, and his efforts are doomed to failure.

Ivanov is at his best in the remarkable novel *Blue Sands*. Vas'ka Zapus, the hero, a Party commissar, is an exception to the stereotyped revolutionary "fine fellows" who abound in Soviet literature. In this book Ivanov destroys the myth of the "elemental anarchism" of the navy men. In the service they had been subjected to grueling training and the strictest discipline. They were part and parcel of the steel bodies of their ships. In a decisive battle with the Whites, the old habit of discipline and organized action returns to Zapus—"more and more strongly, his body vibrated with the beat of a huge and silent machine" [16]—and makes him a leader, and a terribly dangerous man. In addition to his naturally powerful personality, ingrained discipline turns Zapus into a legendary figure whom people call "a scoundrel, a savage beast. But a dream and a flame. A man capable of great heroism." [17]

In *Blue Sands* Ivanov took a great deal from Zamyatin.

The samovar on the table hummed and glittered, hurting the eyes, as though it were jumping up and down, about to explode—a golden bomb.[18]

This is Zamyatin, even to the syntax and the cadence.

The treatment of nature in this novel is especially good. The reader can almost breathe the scent of flowers described by Ivanov. For an example of his richly suggestive writing, take the short sentence "The smoke of the campfires smells of grass." [19]

Ivanov, like many others, grieved over the end to the heroic period of the revolution which came with the NEP. Pykhachev, a character in "The End of the Iron Division," says:

"What kind of country is this? Can one imagine that anywhere in Europe, with their respect for the individual, they would bury a man in a swamp and make a profit on the funeral besides? And they write: beautiful scenery, lovely surroundings. . . . Disgusting." [20]

Although forced to relinquish his revolutionary romanticism, Ivanov remained romantic even in the NEP years. In this "second period," though, the romanticism was that of despair, as in the collection of short stories *Mystery of Mysteries*, 1927.

"Runaway Island," in this volume, contains many lyrical passages reflecting hopelessness and premonition of disaster, as, for instance, the following epitome of the peasants' mood:

The war has worn out our souls and made our hands shake like the hands of a tyrant squire when he stakes his estate at cards. . . . It takes a great effort and much gunpowder now to hit a sable in the eye. We have become poor and use birch-bark bowls for dishes.[21]

"In every story of *Mystery of Mysteries*," says Vyacheslav Polonski, "we come face to face with futility, frustrated hopes, and the triumph of destructive forces beyond man's control."[22]

In the story "Khabu" the Bolshevik Leizerov embodies the utilitarian philosophy of life.[23] The man is depressingly practical, so absorbed in the details of various industrial processes that the beauties of nature make him think of how to avoid "waste." At the same time, he is very sentimental. His personality is entirely uncongenial to Russian peasants, who, it is indicated, will never accept him.

Ivanov's last period may be described as slow extinction. In *The Adventures of a Fakir*[24] he tried to whip up some of his former zest for life, then turned to history, with the play "Twelve Strapping Fellows from a Snuffbox,"[25] concerning the assassination of Paul I. His work during the Second World War, in which he made an effort to recapture the heroic romanticism of his early period, lacks vigor and color.

The other Serapion Brothers who reached their full stature as writers toward the end of the NEP period will be considered in the final section of this book.

17. LEF (Left Front of the Arts)

In 1923, on Mayakovski's initiative, the Cubo-Futurists who had "accepted" the revolution formed the group known as LEF. Other original members included Nikolai Aseyev, Boris Arvatov,

O. Brik, Boris Kushner, Sergei Tret'yakov, and N. Chuzhak. They were later joined by Semyon Kirsanov, Dmitri Petrovski, Mikhail Levidov, V. Pertsov, and others. Shklovski was also closely associated with the group.

From 1923 to 1925 the LEF group published its own journal of the same name, and from 1927 to the end of 1928 the journal *Novyi LEF* [New LEF].

For several years the Futurists of LEF continued to cherish the idea of *komfut* (an abbreviation signifying an alliance of Communism and Futurism), but they were unable to hold their ground against Party-sponsored contenders for literary hegemony in the 1920's and, after various reorganizations and shifts of position, went out of existence in 1930, when Mayakovski capitulated and became a member of RAPP (Russian Association of Proletarian Writers).

The Communists were out to make all culture serve their political aims, and, on the whole, the new forms of art fared badly under the Soviet regime. The Party favored conservatism, and for good reason—modern art was unintelligible to the masses and had little propaganda value. Moreover, many of the Futurist innovators boldly criticized Soviet practices and disputed Party dogma.

In their bid for an alliance with Bolshevism, however, the Cubo-Futurists often deliberately "went primitive" —a technique which considerably impoverished the art of Mayakovski, Aseyev, Kirsanov, and Tret'yakov.

NIKOLAI ASEYEV (1889-   )

Aseyev's early work was influenced by Severyanin and the Ukrainian poet Pavlo Tychina. Passages in *Oceania*, 1916, such as the one in which Aseyev describes the seashore as an all-night café in the sky where "the moon reclined half-naked on a dark blue chaise-longue," while one of the "attendant stars served oysters,"[1] recall Severyanin very distinctly.

After the revolution Aseyev tried to attune his small but pleasant voice to the new music—a lyric tenor singing a dramatic aria. Khlebnikov became his model.

Aseyev identified his own rebellion against dead routine and petrified art with the revolutionary cause. His narrative poem *Budyonnyi*, 1922, celebrated the battle exploits of the famous Red commander.[2] Like other early romantics, he interpreted the NEP as a sign that the revolution, begun in fanatic dedication to an ideal, had ended in vulgar stupidity:

> How can I sing for you,
> You Communist breed,
> When the age is russet
> That you're calling red?[3]

Soon, however, Aseyev realized the dangers of criticizing Bolshevism and became a "Stakhanovite of literature." Many of his mass-produced poems, such as the long narratives "Storm in Sverdlovsk" (1924), "Electriada" (1925), "Fire" (1925), and "Semyon Proskakov" (1926), are frank potboilers.

The cynicism dropped away in his long poem *Mayakovski Emerges* of 1940, re-creating, with nostalgia, the atmosphere in which the "left" forms of art came into being and giving warm portrayals of Mayakovski and his associates in the days before the new forms were brought to bankruptcy and their creators lost their illusions.

> In those early days
> There was wonder and pride,
> And horse-drawn trolleys
> On the avenues ran.
> My friends clustered round me
> On every side;
> Wherever I looked,
> I saw a man.[4]
> . . . . .
> He walked along,
> Broad-shouldered and lean,
> An improbable guest
> From another world,
> Tall as a banner
> Against the screen
> Of a pure June sky
> In splendor unfurled.[5]

Aseyev's latest poems betray his discouragement and regret over a talent frittered away on propaganda hackwork.

SERGEI TRET'YAKOV (1892- ?)

During the early years of LEF, Sergei Tret'yakov wrote verse which cast him into the role of a political commissar of Futurism. Over and over he reiterated that the building of a better future required sweat and blood and sacrifices.

> The famine has convulsed the land,
> Conveyor belts have got the jumps—
> But iron men give stern commands:
> Plug up the holes there!
> Man the pumps![6]

Tret'yakov's plays of the LEF period, although schematic, all have well contrived plots and are excellent theater. *Roar, China*, a verse play published in 1924,[7] was a great success under Meierhold's direction.

In "Gas Masks," a prose melodrama,[8] a gas main bursts at a factory and must be immediately repaired, but there are no gas masks. There is a tense clash between those who believe that human lives are more important than a factory, and those who hold the opposite view. Of the seventy volunteers who rush into the danger area and succeed in making the repair—each man working three minutes before being taken to a hospital—sixty-four are poisoned. Objectors then demand criminal court action against those who had called for volunteers. Who was right? Tret'yakov gives no direct answer. The play exemplifies his distinctive ability to present a general social problem in concrete terms. The play was produced by the First Proletcult Workers Theater under the direction of Sergei Eisenstein.

The prose play "I Want a Child," 1927, deals with the problem, again unsolved, of a Communist woman agronomist who, dominated by a healthy maternal instinct, rejects the current free-love theory.[9]

Tret'yakov was accused of Trotskyism, then of espionage for the British, and, in 1938, was arrested. It is not known whether he was shot or died later in a concentration camp.

OTHERS

Semyon Kirsanov (1906-   ), who joined the LEF after its formation and who is considered to be a disciple of Mayakovski, was one of the most talented poets of the group. His work of the twenties displays a strong ambivalence toward the Soviet regime. Finally he made up his mind, at the beginning of the First Five-Year Plan, became a Stakhanovite of propaganda and topped even Aseyev's record for quantity production.

Occupied as he was with pedestrian and shallow propaganda work during the 1930's, he nonetheless continued to write fine lyrical poems. His two best poems, both inspired by his grief over the death of his wife, are the very moving *Thy Poem*[10] and the fairy tale *Cinderella*.[11]

The LEF and the New LEF groups took a lively interest in filmwork, and it may be said that they raised the movie script to the level of literature. In addition to Mayakovski himself, Boris Brik, Natal'ya Agadzhanova and Aleksandr Rzheshevski are outstanding in this field.

18. October and the On-Guardists

At the end of 1922 several members of the Smithy group broke away and joined forces with other "proletarian" writers to form the group known first as October and then as On-Guardists—from the name of their periodical *Na postu* [On Guard], after 1925 called *Na literaturnom postu* [On Literary Guard]. With the appearance of this organization, under the militant leadership of Semyon Rodov, Yuri Libedinski, G. Lelevich, Aleksandr Bezymenski, and Leopol'd Averbakh, the theoretical dispute over the development of a proletarian literature became a violent political struggle. The membership of the new faction was composed almost exclusively of Communists, relatively few of working-class origin. The "manifesto," published in the first issue of *Na postu*, amounted to a declaration of war on "reviving bourgeois literature and the wavering fellow travelers," on "the stagnation and self-repetition of several groups of proletarian writers and the excessive pursuit of form," on "those . . . who distort and slander our revolution by the attention they pay to the rotten fabric of the fellow travelers' literary creation, in their attempt to build an aesthetic bridge between the past and present," on "those desperate people who, in search of the new, support all the acrobatics of literary juggling and propound theories of the 'future,' forgetting the present and sinking into the slime of flowery phrases." In other words, their purpose was to eliminate the Serapion Brothers, the Smithy, the Voronski-defended fellow travelers, the Futurists—all other literary schools. "We shall stand firmly on guard over a firm and clear Communist ideology in proletarian literature," the manifesto declared. "[We] count principally upon the attention and the sympathetic interest of the wide mass of the Communist Party and of the working class, of the Communist youth and proletarian students." [1]

Throughout the 1920's this group, without scrupling as to methods, fought to entrench itself as the sole keeper and arbiter of Soviet letters. In 1928, after various reorganizations, the group emerged victorious and, under the name RAPP (Russian Association of Proletarian Writers) and with the unmistakable if not acknowledged authorization of the Party, constituted itself a political commissar for literature.[2]

The preceding struggle for power was long and bitter. The challenge issued by the On-Guardists sharpened the debate on the very nature and existence, or possibility of existence, of the proletarian culture, for which they claimed the right of sole guardianship and on behalf of which they demanded preference, both in ideological support and material aid, from the Party and government.

Trotsky vigorously opposed the arguments of the On-Guardists. He wrote in *Literature and Revolution:*

> During the period of dictatorship there can be no question of creating a new culture, which would involve construction on a vast social scale; the cultural construction, not comparable with anything known in the past, which will come when the need for "the iron grip of dictatorship" is over will no longer have a class character. We therefore arrive at the general conclusion that proletarian culture not only does not exist,

but will never exist; nor is this to be regretted. The proletariat has taken over power precisely in order to make an end of all class culture and to clear the way toward human culture.[3]

Both sides sought and found support in the writings of Lenin. There was aid and comfort for the On-Guard adherents in Lenin's 1905 article "Party Organization and Party Literature," in which he argued that "the socialist proletariat must promote the principle of Party literature. Away with non-Party writers!"[4]

Opponents of the October group had the advantage in that Lenin had said in the last article he wrote before his death, "Quality Before Quantity":

... We cannot help entertaining [mistrust and skepticism] when we hear people expatiating too much and too frivolously on "proletarian" culture. To begin with, we could do with some real bourgeois culture.
... In matters of culture there is nothing worse than haste and sweeping strokes. There are many of our young writers and Communists who would do well to get this through their heads.[5]

Voronski, critic and Party member, in his article "Proletarian Art and the Art Policy of Our Party," 1923, took a stand against the Party bureaucrats in literature who reasoned that

We have our own Sovnarkom [Council of People's Commissars] and our own Sovnarkhoz [Council of People's Economy]—why shouldn't we have our own Sovnarkoms and Sovnarkhozes in literature?[6]

Voronski himself stated flatly, "There neither is now nor can be any proletarian art so long as we are confronted with the task of assimilating old culture and old art,"[7] and advised Soviet writers to take the classics of Russian and Western literature as models, after serious and profound study, not on the basis of superficial imitation.

In its fight for hegemony the October or On-Guard group had only one powerful weapon at its command. The other organizations had, by and large, a corner on demonstrated talent. Furthermore, the October platform on the nature and role of literature differed little from that of the groups of genuinely proletarian membership, such as the Proletcult and the Smithy. The October platform merely echoed Bogdanov's theories in calling upon the proletariat to develop its own class culture and declaring:

In a class society literature, as well as other things, serves the interests of a particular class and only through that class does it serve all humanity; therefore proletarian literature is such a literature as organizes the psyche and the consciousness of the working class in the direction of the final tasks of the proletariat as the creator of a Communist society.[8]

Despite the ideological kinship, the October group was particularly vitriolic in its outbursts against the organizations of proletarian writers. The Smithy, repeatedly upbraided, was forced to reply that the October attacks compelled proletarian writers to give up studying the theory of literature in favor of Communist doctrine and thus gave an esthetic advantage to the fellow travelers—while the proletarian writers studied Karl Marx, the fellow travelers pursued their real work, and wrote good novels and poetry.[9]

Still surrounding themselves with enemies of their own making, as yet publishing little of importance, claiming to represent the interests of the proletariat although themselves of nonproletarian origin, the leaders of October wielded the one weapon that assured final victory—the insistence that literature be brought under the control of the Party.

The stamp of the proletarian writer became not working-class origin or employment as a worker, as in the definition formulated by the old Proletcult member Bessal'ko, but "a sound proletarian outlook," that is, blind adherence to the Communist Party cause.

YURI LIBEDINSKI (1898-   )

Libedinski was one of the few October writers to make a name for himself during the early 1920's. His short novel *A Week* (1922),[10] ideologically sound from the Party point of view but of political-poster quality, brought him immediate acclaim as a proletarian writer, although he was not even remotely connected with the proletariat, being the son of a physician and himself a secondary-school graduate. One of his intentions in writing *A Week*, Libedinski once said, was to counteract the false interpretation of the revolution by other writers, such as Pil'nyak.[11]

The setting is an isolated small town in the provinces. The spring sowing is not far off, but the peasants have no grain for seed—the Bolsheviks have been a mite too zealous during the grain collection for the government. It is up to the local Party members to procure seed elsewhere in order to prevent famine. The Red Army troops normally stationed in the town have been sent away to collect firewood for the branch railroad over which the seed must be hauled. At this time a peasant uprising occurs, and most of the Bolsheviks lose their lives defending the town.

In representing the Party as the source of all wisdom, courage, initiative, and heroism, Libedinski succesfully discharged his propaganda assignment, but, as he himself admitted later, his characters are more like romantic symbols or ideas than typical human beings. "The general tone of the piece," Libedinski stated, "was derived from the deep impression which Party meetings made on me at the time." [12]

In a forced attempt at lyricism in his bare tale the author wrote many of the chapters in rhythmic prose.

His next short novel, *Tomorrow*, 1923,[13] began the series of Libedinski's mishaps in backing the wrong political horse. He put his stake on Trotsky, expounding the idea that the building of socialism was impossible in a single country and that the flames of revolution must spread throughout the world in order to rescue Soviet Russia from the NEP slump. Later at a Party purge Libedinski defended himself against charges in this connection by stating that the reaction of the top Trotsky clique to *Tomorrow* was: "An officious fool is more dangerous than an enemy!" [14]

Libedinski then curried favor with the Red Army political commissars and recaptured his reputation for a time with *The Commissars*, 1925, written to demonstrate the need of reindoctrinating the Red Army command politically at the beginning of the NEP period.[15]

With the inception of the First Five-Year Plan to industrialize the country, Libedinski produced a timely propaganda piece in his play *Heights*,[16] designed to illustrate the validity of Lenin's warning against the dependence of Party officials on trained, old-regime engineers and the attendant risk of being led instead of leading. The ambitious engineer of the play gets the upper hand in his relations with his Communist chief, but is finally unmasked as a wrecker.

As a political speculator, Libedinski suffered his most serious failure with the novel *Birth of a Hero*, 1930.[17] In it an Old Bolshevik, Shorokhov, questions to himself whether the revolution has justified the hopes once reposed in it. At the end he overcomes his own doubts and waverings, and the revolutionary fighter is reborn in him. Again Libedinski chose the wrong side. He approached the problem under the manifest influence of the Deborin school of philosophy which was soon supplanted by the group of young Marxists of the new, or Stalinist, persuasion, led by Yudin and Mitin.[18] In the process Libedinski lost the entire political capital which he had amassed.

In the early 1930's Libedinski was temporarily expelled from the Party, but was later taken back into the fold. He published a book of short stories in 1933,[19] and then nothing for a long time. During and immediately after the Second World War a few stories[20] and a novel—*Mountains and Stones*, 1947, dealing with the revolutionary movement in the east of Russia[21]—appeared. In 1952 another novel, *Sky Glow*, came out.[22]

ALEKSANDR BEZYMENSKI (1898-   )

The poet Bezymenski, one of the October ringleaders and noisiest of the so-called "Komsomol poets," produced his major work after the NEP period and thus is outside the bounds of this book. His poetry of the 1920's, however, should be mentioned as an interesting record of unstinting oblation of youth and vigor to the Party. In a poem of 1923 he wrote:

> First of all
> I'm a Party member
> And a rhymester—afterwards.[23]

He was strongly influenced by Mayakovski, in spite of a ludicrously patronizing attitude toward the latter. Mayakovski, as Bezymenski once described him, was "a giant" at romantic verse but "a complete failure at epic narrative."[24] Mayakovski, in turn, compared

Rival Camps of the NEP Period

the poetry of Bezymenski and other Komsomol poets to ersatz coffee made of carrots.

Bezymenski's comedy in verse, *The Shot [Vystrel]*, a propaganda piece, published in 1930, rose to a somewhat higher level than most of his writing because it was composed with the assistance of Meierhold and Tret'yakov.

THE "ZHUTKINS" AND OTHER KOMSOMOL POETS

The two Komsomol poets Aleksandr Zharov (1904-   ) and Iosif Utkin (1903-1944)—for whose ilk Mayakovski combined their two names and coined the disobliging nickname "Zhutkins" —also belong, in the main, to a later period.

Zharov's early poems extolled Komsomol activities, yet betrayed a hidden distaste for political work. His long poem *The Accordion*, 1926, is remarkable chiefly in that it represented common human feelings as normal and compatible with the obligations of Komsomol youth.

Utkin's poems are saccharine imitations of Blok or Yesenin, and at times of Mayakovski. One of his poems, however, the long narrative with the amusing title *Tale of the Redhead Motele, Mr. Inspector, Rabbi Isaiah, and Commissar Bloch*, 1926, is a corker.[25] The tailor hero, a Jew like the author himself, feels a pariah among the Russians until the revolution gives him a chance to be accepted as their equal. Here Utkin's raptures over the revolution, though couched in humor and even occasional irony, were patently sincere.

Two other Jewish Komsomol poets, Mikhail Golodnyi (pseudonym of N. S. Epstein, 1903-1949) and Mikhail Svetlov (1903-   ), took a more pessimistic view. In Golodnyi's poetry may be sensed a fear of a new flare of antisemitism, due to irreconcilable differences between the Jewish and the Russian temperaments.

Svetlov's long poem *Bread*, 1928, reflected a sincere desire for mutual understanding, as well as disappointment with the revolution. Svetlov is a genuine poet, if a minor one. His long poem *Grenada*, 1926, throbs with poetic feeling, although the piece by no means justifies the inflated praise of some Soviet critics.

Far superior to these officially lauded writers are the Komsomol poets Nikolai Ushakov (1899-   ) and Boris Likharev (1909-   ), to whom Soviet critics have never been well disposed. Ushakov has been upbraided for pessimism, for pantheism, for lack of revolutionary fervor; and Likharev for being a follower of Gumilyov. His long poem "Central Asia," of which only fragments have been published,[26] was undoubtedly influenced by Gumilyov; perhaps for that reason it is the best poem produced by any of the Komsomol poets.

19. Pereval

The original members of the *Pereval* group, organized in 1924, were young men, newcomers to literature. Many of them had taken part in the Civil War. They had something to say, but lacked training and craftsmanship. Recognizing the need for knowledge and polish and opposed to the rigid dogmas, self-interest and squabbling of other cliques of writers, they banded together for the purpose of learning how to write well, with sincerity, observing literary amenities the while. It was by no means merely a group of "fellow travelers" or Party opponents which announced such aims. On the roster of *Pereval* from its early days were a good number of Communist writers who had formerly belonged to October or its affiliates—for instance, Svetlov, Golodnyi, Artyom Vesyolyi, Nikolai Kutznetsov and Aleksandr Yasnyi. Among other Party writers who belonged to *Pereval* at various stages were Pyotr Pavlenko, Anna Karavayeva, Andrei Novikov, and Ivan Katayev.

ALEKSANDR VORONSKI (1884-1935)

The Communist critic and editor Voronski was the organizer and guiding spirit of the group, which took its name *Pereval* (Mountain Pass) from the title of one of his articles.[1]

In the eyes of latter-day Soviet Marxists, Voronski was at best a heretic. He has been reviled as a Bergsonian, a Freudian, a Trotskyist. In point of fact, he was a follower of Tolstoi and Dostoyevski, and, as a literary critic, of Georgi Plekhanov and Apollon Grigor'yev.

In his article "Art as Cognition of Life, and the Present,"[2] Voronski looks at science and art as two ways of studying life and points out that great writers often discover truths long before science does, through the power of intuition.

Voronski's theory of "the shedding of the veils" *(snyatiye pokrovov)*, synthesized from Tolstoi and Grigor'yev, meant, in practice, rejection of political propaganda in literature and insistence on utter sincerity. This stand led to serious conflicts with the Party. Himself a Marxist, Voronski disdained a dogmatic interpretation of Marxism. His broad-minded tolerance distinguishes him among the critics of note in the postrevolutionary period.

His best essays are collected in the volume *Literary Notes, 1926*,[3] in which he deplored the poverty, shallowness and provincialism of Soviet writing. Thanks to Voronski, the best in postrevolutionary literature appeared in the periodical *Krasnaya nov'* [Red Virgin Soil], which he founded in 1921 and directed until 1927, when he was dismissed as editor and expelled from the Party.

As a creative writer, Voronski received recognition with his two volumes of memoirs, *Live Waters and Still Waters*.[4]

His fiction is little known, although the tale *The Eye of the Hurricane*, 1931, for instance, like Tarasov-Rodionov's *Chocolate*, anticipates such political novels as Arthur Koestler's *Darkness at Noon*. A quotation from Elisée Reclus serves as its epigraph:

Amid the darkness, there appears in the sky a whitish space, which the sailors call "the eye of the hurricane," as though they really saw in the hurricane a merciless deity descending from the skies to seize and drown them.[5]

War is the hurricane, the October Revolution the eye of the hurricane. Against an apocalyptic background, Voronski describes the despair of Valentin, a disillusioned revolutionary. The story is, apparently, a fragment of an unfinished work.

In 1933 he published a volume of stories,[6] the most interesting of which are "The Exhibit" and "Fedya Gveril'yas," both dealing with men whom the revolution had used, broken, and discarded.

Three short stories printed in a periodical in 1934 are Voronski's last published writing.[7] They were written during his exile from Moscow as a Trotskyist, and conveyed his yearning to return to active work in the capital. He did return, in the early thirties, but was arrested in 1935, and died in the same year in prison.[8]

After the "incubation period" of *Pereval*, as one of its members has called its first years,[9] two other good critics joined the group and served as mentors to the young writers—Abram Lezhnyov (pseudonym of Z. A. Gorelik, 1893- ?) and Dmitri Gorbov (1894-   ).

Even during the "incubation period" two major talents of Soviet literature had made their appearance in the early "almanacs" published under the name *Pereval*.

ARTYOM VESYOLYI
(pseudonym of Nikolai Kochkurov, 1899- ?)

Vesyolyi was one of the founders of the *Pereval* organization. Like Andrei Platonov, the second to emerge as a writer of distinction in the early *Pereval* publications, Vesyolyi remained a member for a relatively brief time.

He occupies a special place in peasant literature as a modern Robber Nightingale *(Solovei-razboinik,* a folklore character) glorifying the elemental Pugachov-Razin forces of the revolution. Peaceful toil and problems of farming lie outside his interests.

Rivers of Fire, 1923-1924, is his best-known novel. Its two heroes, nicknamed Van'ka Gramofon and Mishka Krokodil,

rolled off a cruiser in the memorable year 1917. . . . Had Van'ka and Mishka been dressed in clerical garb, everyone would still have known them for navy men, by their dashing manner and ponderous juicy oaths.[10]

Mishka boasts of having personally "stirred up the revolution." He and Van'ka are "big-time fellows. . . . In their breasts, like a dog on a chain in a backyard, raged a huge, fanged, sailor's God." [11] To them the revolution is a new kind of religion.

Five years have gone by. The Civil War is over. Mishka and Van'ka are back in the navy. Again the enlisted men are treated no better than before, and the officers put on the same old airs. The "revolutionary guys" are disgusted. The Red God has gone up in smoke.

Mishka and Van'ka are wholeheartedly on the side of the peasants' rebellion. They are born rioters and anarchists, and there is a streak of banditry in their nature; yet they yearn for justice and freedom for all, not merely license for the Communists. Vesyolyi had a sure understanding of the "elemental" revolutionaries almost unmatched by other Soviet writers.

Other excellent short stories followed *Rivers of Fire* in quick succession, notably "Pride," "Quick Justice," "Sky-Glow of Courage," and *The Wild Heart*.[12]

The Red Army commander who is the hero of "Pride" has contempt for the political commissars who, in his view, are stupidly trying to get inside men's souls with a propaganda leaflet. He has his own methods. When a Chechen-Ingush regiment refuses to fight, Chernoyarov taunts them into a suicidal charge on the enemy: "So you want to take a rest. . . . You're not soldiers but a bunch of old women. I'll give orders this very day to have you sent to the rear, to an old people's home."[13] A straightforward word born of fury and despair served the revolution better than a thousand propaganda leaflets.

In the story "Quick Justice" a tsarist colonel, convinced that only fanatics and lunatics die for a lost cause, joins the Bolshevik camp. Made director of a Red munitions plant, he drinks and rapes factory girls. Because of the desperate need for trained personnel, he gets away with such behavior until two Red Army soldiers, the father and the brother of one of the girls, come to visit her. When she complains to her father, he administers "quick justice" by shooting the colonel. Father and son hurriedly return to their unit. Cheka investigators follow them, but all the soldiers testify under oath that the two men had not left the camp.[14]

The revolutionary mob, though cruel, had its own ethics and an instinctive sense of justice. "A certain contrast is drawn between the fair and brotherly spirit of the partisans and the dry, impersonal and merciless Soviet law-enforcers, stirring up the dust in their cars," the critic M. Charnyi pointed out.[15]

The novel *Native Land*, 1926, Vesyolyi's largest canvas, portrays the peasant mass turning in rebellion against the Bolsheviks after their short-lived alliance. The village is for the revolution but against Communism. Mit'ka, a leader, starts a revolt: "A rising in Yelabuga. Risings all over Simbirsk province. In Saratov too. Water in the boat and water under the boat," [16] he tells his peasants. He is not at all sure of success, for, although loath to admit it, he cannot help feeling that the peasants have had enough of wars and revolutions. Along the way, some villages meet the insurgents with icons, some with bread and salt, and still others with grim and sullen faces. The old peasants are of the opinion that the government may be bad, but it is their own. The revolt fails because the muzhik's craving for peace is stronger than his desire to reform the world.

From the far North, in clattering freight cars, crossing the bread transports on their way, Red regiments poured down. . . . On the dirty walls of railroad stations, the paper appeals quivered under the wind like expectorated blood. . . . The city overran the village, the grass-roots resistance collapsed, and the insurgents fled, throwing away their pitchforks, pikes and guns along the roads, galloping, crawling, scattering to all sides, wild and terrible to see, as after the Mamai rout . . . my native land . . . smoke and fire without end.[17]

In a few broad, easy strokes Vesyolyi makes all his characters three-dimensional and alive. The reader cannot help feeling that Vesyolyi draws an invidious comparison between the peasants and the Party. His Communists, workers as well as Party officials, are people with withered, or withering, souls, whereas the village, still with its weddings and church holidays, dances and fairs, is painted in rich, vivid colors.

The Socialist Revolutionary Boris Ivanovich, who organized the revolt, and the school superintendent Yelena Sudakova oppose Communism precisely because they are acutely aware of the sterility and flatness of the Communist idea.

"In these days, when bare subsistence is such a crucial problem for most people, our inner life has grown dreadfully shallow, and there is no time for soul-searching," [18]

Yelena writes in her diary.

Vesyolyi's character Mit'ka might have rivaled Sholokhov's Grigori in *The Silent Don*, if the author, having been accused of "incorrigible anarchism"—he had once been an anarchist—had not deliberately subdued his colors in painting anti-Bolsheviks.

In 1932 Vesyolyi published the novel *Russia Washed in Blood*, made up of the stories "Pride," "Quick Justice" and "Sky-Glow of Courage," now worked into one plot with a revised version of *Native Land*, again hastily and not very thoroughly cleansed of "anarchist leanings."[19]

In the thirties, Vesyolyi, like Chapygin, sought refuge in history and wrote *Volga Rampage*,[20] a novel about Yermak.

Vesyolyi's style is rough and careless, but vivid and bold, with an impetuousness that gives a rhythm of wind to his prose.

Despite his concessions to the demands of Bolshevik propaganda, his early work, especially *River of Fire*, continued to be held against him, and during the Yezhov purges he was dispatched to a concentration camp. The date of his death is not known.

ANDREI PLATONOV (1896-1951)

Andrei Platonov was one of the most remarkable of Soviet writers, again less because of literary skill than because of moral qualities. Although his stylistically most mature work came long after he had left the *Pereval* organization (he was a member for only a short time and then struck out as a lone wolf), he spoke from the beginning in his own distinctive voice. The germs of his later work, with its intense strain of compassion for luckless, fear-ridden men were already discernible in his first stories and soon invited the disfavor and vilification which he was to suffer throughout his life.

In his prose of the mid-1920's (he began as a poet) Platonov followed in the footsteps of Leskov, although he was also under the influence of Gogol and Remizov. Over and over again the same characters recur in Platonov's stories—the grandsons of Leskov's Levsha, that uncrowned king of self-taught men, the craftsman who shod a mechanical flea. His descendants have come down in life and become hoboes, tramps, drunkards, failures and crackpots of all sorts, but have inherited their grandfather's audacity, innate intelligence and conscience. But whereas Levsha made no mistakes and aroused universal admiration by his craftsmanship, his grandsons experience one failure after another and let their work fall from listless hands. Kondrov, eager to help his collective farm, enters into socialist competition with the sun and invents an artificial sun, the only trouble with which is that it gives no light. Makar builds a merry-go-round which is to move by wind power, but the merry-go-round stands still. Levsha's descendants are not stupid or lazy, nor have they lost their skills, but they rebel against dull, senseless labor which calls only for muscular strength without intelligence. They refuse to be an appendage of the machine.

They had believed in the revolution because they expected it to give them the opportunity of exercising their native inventiveness in organizing the processes of production. But when they were not permitted to work in freedom and have a hand in the technological revolution, Levsha's grandsons lost heart, had no more interest in their work, and often, in bitterness over this unexpected defeat, descended to the level of tramps.

Soviet manufactured products, with their defects, bear the impress of the physical and spiritual suffering of their makers and designers, men whose imagination has been atrophied under the whip. The worker is a "nameless man who has lost his way in the intricate order of the world, among men as cold as machines,"[21] says a worker in "Che-Che-O," 1928. The group of sketches under this title, which Platonov wrote in collaboration with Pil'nyak, describe the dissemination of Communist doctrine and practice in the outlying areas.

Platonov took an original view of the relationship between man and machine; his machines grieve, weep, freeze—behave like living human beings with a heart and a soul. Emmanuel Levin, chief of a railroad depot somewhere out in the Far East, telephones to Moscow, thousands of miles away, and "both men listened to the suffering of energy, trembling through space."[22]

It has been said that in Platonov's *The Making of a Master*[23] the cult of the machine reaches its apogee. On the contrary, it seems

Rival Camps of the NEP Period

that here and elsewhere in Platonov's stories, the cult of the machine reaches its nadir, for the writer deliberately replaced it by a cult of nature (notably in "An Adventure," 1928)[24] and the human heart.

The theme of protest against the depersonalization of man, against the callous and contemptuous attitude toward man that underlies the Soviet system—a theme hinted at in the satiric *Town of Gradov*[25]—is fully developed in "Doubting Makar," 1929.

Makar Ganushkin is a typical representative of Levsha's scions, victimized by the "organizers" and their army of overseers who have turned the "doers" into slaves. In the story Gleb Chumovoi represents the organizers who do not know how to work themselves but are experts at fining and speeding up rebellious workers, and who describe their function as leadership, "a progressive moving of the people along a straight line toward the general welfare." [26]

"The First Ivan,"[27] 1930, is a sketch, written with painful and distorted humor, of an amateur inventor, a diamond in the rough, whose audacity of thought might have led to imaginative inventions but, beaten down, degenerated instead into megalomania.

The short novel "For Future Use,"[28] 1931, is a panorama, in terms of caricature and grotesquerie, of the Russian countryside during the early stages of forced collectivization, with its impoverishment of the peasantry and breakdown of agriculture. There is not one superfluous word in it; Platonov's writing is as laconic as it is honest.

"Che-Che-O," "Doubting Makar," and "For Future Use" brought Platonov under virulent and extensive critical attack at the end of the twenties and beginning of the thirties. The affair was of such political importance that Leopol'd Averbakh's assault of 1929 was printed simultaneously in two reviews, *Na literaturnom postu* [On Literary Guard] and *Oktyabr'* [October].[29] Aleksandr Fadeyev's article entitled "A Kulak Chronicle," referring to "For Future Use," appeared both in the newspaper *Izvestiya*[30] and, in expanded form, in the magazine *Krasnaya nov'* [Red Virgin Soil].[31]

The journal *Proletarskii avangard* [Proletarian Vanguard], the last stronghold of the Smithy, joined in the abuse of a former member, now disavowed as having been only a "casual member."

Pavel Berezov in his "Behind the Mask"[32] was even harsher than Averbakh himself, who called Platonov a "petty bourgeois run amok," but one entitled to leniency because of his proletarian sympathies. Nonetheless, Platonov was put under arrest and exiled from Moscow.

Platonov thereafter adopted a new manner. This buffoon and merry-andrew of popular speech, this modern village fool, this peddler of old saws, proverbs, clever cracks and caustic jokes, now appeared before his readers in his true guise—champion of the failures and unfortunates in the country, the injured and dispossessed, the victims of hunger and fear.

In this second period Platonov modeled himself primarily on Dostoyevski and Pushkin.

In 1937 Platonov published an article entitled "Pushkin Is Our Comrade" which indicates that his starting point in guiding his own work into new channels was Pushkin's *Bronze Horseman*. This poem is a monument both to the bold sweep of Peter the Great's creative genius and to loving kindness, compassion for ordinary, unremarkable people. Pushkin brings into conflict the two hostile forces of the state and the individual, the first symbolized in the superhuman figure of Peter, and the second in a man who has nothing but love to keep him alive. In this conflict lies the age-old, living contradiction of Russia.

Platonov saw Dostoyevski as inheriting from Pushkin the gift of compassion for the individual but not that of differentiating between the suffering of single human beings and the destiny of the nation: "He laid emphasis to an extreme degree on the pathetic aspect,"[33] on the misfortunes befalling the individual, on man's impotence to heal the suffering of another through love.

Basing himself on Pushkin's poem, Platonov evidently resolved to compose his stories so that the wretchedness of his characters should not interfere with the glorification of Stalin's feats. He planned, it seems, a double projection: from Peter the Great to Stalin, and from Yevgeni to the living victims of the Revolution and the Civil War. He failed in this effort, however, for, like Dostoyevski, he fell into the trap of the pathetic, the fatal misfortune, the impotence of human beings, and therefore tried in vain to justify the destruction of hundreds of thousands of indivduals by the might of the superman who had become their absolute ruler.

Platonov's masterful historical tale *Floodgates of Epiphany*,[34] published in 1927, had foreshadowed his later attitudes.

The hero of the tale, Bertrand Perry, an English engineer, is invited to Russia by Peter the Great to direct difficult operations intended to make several shallow rivers navigable. Perry is a highly gifted man but hampered at every step by his innate decency and kindliness, and in the end falls victim to his own trustfulness and honesty. When he disappoints Peter's hopes, the Tsar has him executed on charges of having attempted to prevent Russia from becoming one of the world's leading naval powers.

The plan which Perry undertakes to put into effect has been drawn up by clever charlatans—although leading engineers held in high esteem by the Tsar—who have done their surveying not in the field but on paper. That the terrain is very different from the data given in the plan Perry discovers only after the work has begun. It is not yet too late to suspend operations and to send a letter to Peter denouncing the engineers who prepared the plan and asking that they be brought to justice. But Perry is no informer; in mid-operation, without letting the Tsar know, he hastily alters the entire course of a project in which tens of thousands of serfs are engaged. By taking this decision Perry undermines his own authority, but he is not yet lost. Peter has made him a general, and has given him the right to flog, and, at his discretion, even to hang the men under his command. Perry fails to exercise this right. He is filled with compassion for these common people who have been rudely torn from their plows and harrows and put to unfamiliar work. It is his stubborn refusal to punish his subordinates which drives Peter into a fury, and in the final analysis brings Perry to the executioner's block. In essence, he dies merely because he is incapable of hating and oppressing small miserable people whose only fault is that they are small and miserable.

The writer, like his hero, was incapable of subordinating his sympathy with the common man to admiration of the superman whose role in history is to create a new state regardless of the suffering and sorrow inflicted.

With Platonov's attempt to remake himself as a writer, a marked change in style occurred. He gave up his former stylization of popular speech in favor of brevity and utter simplicity.

In 1937, at the very height of the purges and terror, at the time of the greatest spiritual and esthetic impoverishment of Russian literature under the yoke of censorship, Andrei Platonov published a book of short stories entitled *The River Potudan'*, in which he found the courage to step forward in defense of the oppressed and miserable—beggars, slaves, homeless children, and orphans. The critic A. M. Gurvich wrote of Platonov shortly after the appearance of the book:

Platonov feels an imperative need to speak of and for those who are weak and mute. Helplessness exerts a powerful attraction on him. He is always drawn to unfortunate, homeless people. . . . Wherever a lonely, forgotten man may wander, Platonov follows him like a shadow, as though he feared that someone's grief might die unknown and unshared.[35]

In "Takyr," one of the stories in *The River Potudan'*, the Persian woman Zarrin Tadzh had been kidnaped by Kirghiz when she was a small child. She was a mother at fifteen, and an old woman at twenty. "She tried her body with her hands; the bones stood out everywhere, her skin was dry from fatigue, her hands were sinewy from hard work. She understood that life was slowly leaving her."[36] She does not live, she vegetates, forgetting herself in daily cares. Her whole life is a slow and monotonous journey toward death, which finally comes from the plague.

Zarrin Tadzh's daughter Dzhumal' is eager to embrace the new way of life. After the revolution she makes her way to Tashkent and enters an agricultural college. According to Soviet dogma, Dzhumal' should now find fulfillment and happiness. Instead she is profoundly unhappy. The new order offers women only the same misery as did the old. The daughter's experience is to be a repetition of the mother's. Dzhumal' yearns for the desert, where bones turn to dust and the dust is blown by the wind.

Other stories in the volume—"The Third Son," "Immortality,"

"Fro"—dwell on the regime's demands for abnormal "labor, under pressure, to the point of suffering,"[37] and for the sacrifice of love and family life to the needs of "socialist construction."

"Like his own heroes, Platonov not only does not detest suffering, but embraces it greedily, like a religious fanatic who seeks the soul's salvation in burdening his body with fetters,"[38] wrote Gurvich, complaining that Platonov offered not help, but consolation.

Further, Gurvich charged that Platonov attacked Soviet socialist society and sought to correct reality by creating an unreal world of his own. He portrayed ideal Communists resembling Christian martyrs and alien, possibly hostile, to the real Communists who were really building a new world.

There was basis for these charges. What has been termed Platonov's abstractness, his world of eternal twilight, was in reality a method of universalization by which he made the fate of a lonely individual stand for the tragedy of Russia. And his Bolsheviks who were not true to life represented an attempt to clothe an impossible ideal with flesh and blood.

After a silence of several years Platonov reappeared in print during the Second World War with two volumes of short stories, *Tales of Our Country*[39] and *Toward the Setting Sun*.[40] These stories are marked by a certain lassitude, and are much weaker than his previous work. Nevertheless, they are an honest treatment of the psychology of the Russian people at war. Levsha's descendants stop being failures and become the successful defenders of their country. Their initiative has at last found a purpose they can embrace and a point of application. Platonov's interpretation of the psychology of the Russian troops is a striking one. They face combat as but another form of difficult and ungrateful labor, such as was exacted from them in peacetime, yet with the realization that the fate of the nation depends on the success of this particular job.

His new work brought Platonov only further trouble. The critics were particularly displeased by the story "Armor" in the volume *Tales of Our Country* and by "Ivanov's Family,"[41] one of his few postwar pieces. His last book, *The Magic Ring*, a volume of stories drawing heavily on folklore, was published posthumously.[42]

KEY MEMBERS OF *PEREVAL* AND STANDPATTERS

Among those who made a little stir in the early almanacs published by *Pereval* were Vladimir Vetrov and Boris Guber. Vetrov's short novel "Breath of Cedar," 1924, is comparable with Artyom Vesyolyi's tales in its bold conception, but indifferently written.[43]

Boris Guber (1903- ?) attracted attention with his story "Sharashkin's Office," a disquieting picture of village life after the Civil War when, in the guise of Party commissars and "organizers," a new and more rapacious breed of vultures replaced the hereditary merchants and kulaks.[44] The savage struggle for power and money serves as background for the main theme, the loneliness of a woman hungry for love who finds only lust and hardness.

Guber's best story, "Chips," 1928, deals with a Civil War hero who is expelled from the Party when the "restoration" period begins and idealists become a hindrance.[45] His humorous story "The Notorious Shurka Shapkina," about a provincial *femme fatale*, was very popular for a time.[46]

Along with the hordes of speculators, the NEP produced also a good type of kulak, peasants who had adopted new farming methods and owed their prosperity to honest work and personal enterprise. The right kind of cooperative effort, from the ground up rather than imposed from above, had begun to take shape under the leadership of such men. Guber's story "Office Manager," 1928, develops this theme and foreshadows the indiscriminate liquidation of kulaks, the good with the bad.[47]

In the thirties the *Pereval* writers were forced to compromise. Several of them turned to reportage. In 1931 Guber published a book of competent sketches about a sovkhoz.[48] His short novel "Indian Summer" of 1934 is a wistful, subdued picture of resigned kolkhoz peasants who have learned that rebellion is useless.[49]

Ivan Katayev's first well-known work "The Heart," 1928, is the story of a humane Communist who believed in the millennium to be brought about by cooperative effort, and saw his dreams betrayed.[50] He published two other tales in the same year, "The Wife" and "The Poet."[51] Katayev had enough individuality as an artist to absorb the conflicting influences of Dostoyevski and Boris Zaitsev and produce a style of his own.

The publication of "Milk," 1930,[52] was an act of great courage on the part of Katayev. Himself a Party member, in the story he exposed the strong-arm methods employed by the Party in collectivizing agriculture and "liquidating the kulaks." One of the two central characters is an upstanding, prosperous Russian Baptist, Nilov, who runs a model milk farm on a cooperative basis with his sons and sons-in-law. He has lost two other sons who fought for the Reds in the Civil War, and is friendly to the Soviet regime. His fellow villagers look up to him, and the "instructor" sent down by the People's Commissariat of Agriculture is more or less forced to enlist his help in "organizing" the peasants. He also approves of Nilov personally, and they make a promising start. To the higher authorities, however, Nilov is just another kulak. The instructor receives orders to finish him off, and obeys, though he feels very sorry for him. Katayev's open sympathy for the victims of the campaign was not expressed with impunity, although punishment was deferred for several years.

He continued to be indiscreet. The collection of sketches published in 1934, *Man on a Mountain*, was in its entirety a veiled protest against the reduction of men to the role of mere cogs in a machine.[53]

His story "Encounter"[54] and the beginning of "Khamovniki"[55] (name of a Moscow suburb) appeared in the same year. "Encounter," which deals with the political sections of machine tractor stations, contrasts the living conditions of Party workers and of ordinary peasants. Katayev touched warily on the peasants' hatred of their Party bosses, and on this occasion was at pains to make it clear that the latter were not particularly to blame. They were average, often decent men who enjoyed their privileges without thinking whether they deserved them or not.

Nikolai Zarudin's two volumes of undistinguished verse, *Cherry-Blossom Snow*, 1923,[56] and *Through the Fields of Youth*, 1928,[57] which show some influence of Blok and Yesenin, are far less interesting than his prose. In fact, he is a better poet in prose than in verse. His story "Antiquity," recreating old Russia and the loveliness of nature unpolluted by factories, reads like a lyric poem.[58]

In 1932 Zarudin published a documentary novel "Thirty Nights in a Vineyard,"[59] and in 1936 "In the People's Wood."[60] The latter, defending cooperative as against collective farming and deploring the ruinous consequences of mass "dekulakization," took more courage to publish than either Guber's or Katayev's writings on the same themes, since it appeared when the kolkhoz system was already in full swing.

In the following year (1937) Zarudin paid for his daring. He and other former members of *Pereval* who had remained friends after the breakup of the organization—a long-drawn-out process beginning with the persecution of Voronski—were arrested in a general roundup. Zarudin, according to report, was shot, and Boris Guber and Ivan Katayev were sentenced to long terms in concentration camps. Lezhnyov disappeared without a trace. Others were interrogated and released.[61]

Pyotr Slyotov (1897-   ), one of the most polished prose writers of the *Pereval* group and one of the few who stayed the course to the end despite the unceasing attacks on the organization, inexplicably escaped reprisals, as did the critic Gorbov.

The careers of several junior members of *Pereval* were adversely affected by the fact that they remained to the end—in addition, of course, to the universal handicap in the lack of creative freedom. The gifted poet Gleb Glinka (1903-   ), for instance, was deflected from his natural bent, but made a name for himself as author of sketches and student of prosody.

YEFIM VIKHRYOV (1902-1935)

Vikhryov's early death in 1935 permitted him to pursue his single-minded course in literature to the end. He was a writer with one love, and all his work centers about it—Palekh, a village in the Shuya area of Moscow Oblast, where for centuries the peasants painted icons, while also engaging in agriculture. His writing on the subject obliterates the distinction between a research paper and a literary essay.

All Vikhryov's work speaks of his passionate desire to preserve the ancient art of icon painting at the Palekh colony, which was even in his lifetime on its way to annihilation.

After the revolution the art was severed from its religious source. The painters frenziedly sought a solution which would enable them to continue practicing their art and to adapt it to the new conditions.

Vikhryov's essays, stories and articles of the 1920's about Palekh, published in *Pereval* and elsewhere, were assembled in the book entitled *Palekh*, 1930. It is an alternation of portraits and landscapes.

In the description of nature there is usually a note of elegiac sorrow over the disappearance of Russia's former beauty: "Rye, cornflowers, thickets of young trees, the singing of larks accompany you along the road to Palekh." [62] But, "through the open windows of the community house comes the warning whisper of the graveyard birches." [63]

In the gallery of folk artists, each portrait is set against the background of the Palekh landscape. For example, the following passage precedes the description of the craftsman who painted his wife's portrait: "Like the frozen waves of some strange ocean, snow surrounds Palekh on all sides. Rising in crests, ripples and billows, it gleams everywhere—virginally pure and blindingly white." [64] The oldest of the painters, Ivan Bakanov, is "ochre and cloud wisdom." Ivan Vakurov's work has a "leafy sadness." Ivan Golikov is all "joy of ornament" and "color in motion."

In most monographs on icon painting and other arts and crafts, the thing created usually overshadows the creator. Vikhryov, however, concentrated first on the artist, then on the work of art. In his time he was still able to talk to people who told him stories of the old masters.

The old men themselves who were still around were not inclined to talk. One of them had once had Maxim Gorki as an apprentice. Vikhryov hoped that the old painter would share his memories, but he was vouchsafed only the one brief remark that once upon a time there was vodka to drink and apprentices to beat. Obviously he did not trust Vikhryov, a Communist, if a thoroughly untypical one.

Vikhryov returns again and again to the drunken binges of the painters—an ancient tradition surviving after the revolution: "The icon and vodka, neither conquering the other, shared their lives. Palekh is saturated with drying-oil and alcohol. Palekh is shot through with both the holy and the satanic." [65]

In the early days after the revolution the peasants attacked two agitators from the city; one they did to death with their pitchforks and scythes, while the other, beaten and bleeding, managed to escape on a bicycle. Until the agitators attacked God, all had been well. But to the hereditary icon painter, religion was more than a spiritual problem—it was a question of existence.

The portrait of the father of the community house librarian, done by one of the former icon painters, especially aroused Vikhryov's interest:

Eyes in which genius lived side by side with madness . . . behind those eyes one could see all of life. Behind them was wild carousing, thousands of miles of space, unrelieved poverty, blinding wealth, doom, a lost soul, a cascade of daring ventures, pride, strength and vulnerability.[66]

In the old days the icon painter was the creator of the individual work of art. Later, individuality bowed down before accepted patterns. The tragedy of the icon painters is that they were unable to reconcile themselves to their art becoming a craft. They wished to preserve their individual talent and, by bringing fresh forms into religious painting, to provide a new current in religious perception of the world. This they were forbidden to do by the Orthodox Church. Thus Vikhryov ascribed the standardization of icon painting methods to the bigotry and dogmatism which made the Church unable to withstand the onslaught of Marxist-Leninist doctrine.

In the end the Palekh craftsmen found an outlet for their dying-out tradition. True, their solution, like the method of collapsing the lung of a tubercular patient, could merely delay the hour of death, not cure. They turned their hand to decorating boxes and cigarette cases and illustrating books. Inevitably they changed from religious to secular themes, treating the new subjects in the ancient manner. Despite the makeshift nature of this resort, the masters were able to introduce into their work that which before they had been forced to keep out of it—their artistic individuality. In their particular case individuality was not a rule but an exception to the rule and was used to sustain traditional forms. The problem of preserving individuality through the conservation of traditional methods of work transferred from icon painting to the applied arts is stated by Vikhryov in his portrayal of present-day Palekh painters.

IVAN YEVDOKIMOV (1887-   )

Yevdokimov withdrew from *Pereval* after the first serious threat to the organization, but not before he had been recognized as an artist of considerable stature with the publication in 1926 of his "chronicle" novel *The Bells*.[67] It is a large canvas of Russian life—villages, country estates, city slums, industrial suburbs, the revolutionary underground, factories, meetings, strikes, and finally the 1905 uprisings and barricade fights. Yevdokimov resisted the temptation to prove a thesis and wrote as a genuine artist giving play to his lyrical talent. *The Bells* tells the truth about the revolutionary movement in Russia which cannot be learned from the writings of Bolshevik historians.

Yevdokimov's is a many-sided talent. Among his works there are excellent hunting stories; an interesting tale of two adolescents, *North Wind*, 1925;[68] the very good novels *Chistiye prudy* (the name of a section of Moscow), 1927,[69] and *The Land Beyond the Lakes*, 1928;[70] a volume of short stories, *Green Mountains*, 1928;[71] a fictionalized biography of the painter Boris Musatov;[72] a study of the painter Isaak Levitan, 1941;[73] and the play *The Last Old Woman from Semigor'ye*, 1934.[74]

The heroine of the play, Feodosiya Mitrofanovna, spiritedly defended her cottage from being included in the kolkhoz. She wanted to preserve the ways of old, and Yevdokimov saw profound human drama in her struggle. The Party line required that such old women be portrayed as feebleminded relics, but the author made the kolkhoz activists appear small and stupid next to her. It is a pity that this play is not suitable for the regular stage. An ethnographer rather than an actress would be required to render all the folk tales and ancient songs contained in the text.

Yevdokimov's later chronicle novel, "The Firebird," 1936, which was published only in part,[75] is inferior to *The Bells*. He had begun to conform to the Party line.

PEASANT WRITERS

The main value of peasant novels—naturalistic almost without exception—lies in the subject matter and in the objectivity of the narrative. One of the most objective peasant writers was Rodion Akul'shin (1896-   ), author of numerous sketches of Soviet rural life. *What the Village Whispers*, 1925, is his best book. "My native village," he wrote, "showed me its ugly face, and I do not want to conceal it. . . . To cover it with make-up would be harmful and vain."[76]

Like so many other writers, he painted the lower Party executives in the darkest colors. His Vyrypayev terrorizes the peasants with his gun and his Party card. He and the drunken windbag Arsen'yev are almost the only supporters the Party has in the village. Details such as these make Akul'shin's sketches valuable documents for historians. He now lives in the United States and continues to write.

Leonid Zavadovski (1888- ?) provided something more than mere photographic records. A romantic strain relieves the naturalism of his stories.

His *Chaff*, 1926,[77] belongs to the postrevolutionary trend described as "sex literature." The Orthodox Church had held the peasants' animal instincts in check, and the sanctity of marriage and family was strictly observed. But the younger generation, free of the restraining influence of religion, had a lax moral code. *Chaff* deals with the fathers-and-sons conflict on matters of marriage and sex. The drama of Lyubka, who has become pregnant by another man than her husband, is meant to show that so-called "free love" can bring only misery to the woman.

The short novel "Enmity"[78] evoked much adverse comment

from critics. The conflict in village life as Zavadovski saw it was not between the rich and the poor, or kulaks and Communists, but between decent people and scoundrels—and the latter always won. The past was more acceptable, if only because religion made it more romantic.

"My ear catches the distant sad ringing of church bells,"[79] he wrote in the story "On the White Lake." Soon there would be no bells at all:

The forest grew thinner under our eyes, while the village on the banks of the great river was growing. It seemed as though the larches and pine trees were turning into people. There are more and more people, and the forest recedes farther and farther, swinging its branches as though it were running for its life.[80]

ALEKSANDR MALYSHKIN (1890-1938)

Aleksandr Malyshkin, first a member of the Smithy, then of October and finally of *Pereval*, discreetly resigned from *Pereval* in 1930 when the Party-organized campaign against the group reached its climax. By this time, like many other members, he had found his stride as a writer.

In *The Fall of Dair*,[81] 1923, he had turned out a political-poster story which is the equivalent of speeches made by members of the State Duma at the front during the First World War exhorting the soldiers in lofty vein: "Doughty knights of Russia! Smite the bloodthirsty Teuton with your swords!" The soldiers were, of course, not prepared to cope with this high-flown style, but when they heard the word "Teuton" they guessed readily enough that the reference was to the Heinies.

Malyshkin's "epic" style in this account of the Red Army victory in the Crimea toward the end of the Civil War was not always comprehensible to the unsophisticated reader for which it was intended, but it is imposing and impressive.

For ornamentation of his propaganda piece, Malyshkin borrowed freely from *The Tale of the Host of Igor'*, *The Story of the Azov Siege of the Don Cossacks* and Gogol's *Taras Bul'ba*.

In his novel *Sevastopol'*, 1929,[82] an album of scenes from the early period of the Revolution, Malyshkin gave up his abstractions in the epic vein and adopted a manner similar to Yakovlev's. The hero is the intellectual Shelekhov, a failure and a bore, who, as a seaman in the Black Sea fleet, sides with the Bolsheviks not for ideological reasons but as the only salvation for a weakling without hope of making a career for himself after the collapse of the February revolution.

Malyshkin's last book, *People from the Sticks*, 1938,[83] portrays construction work in the Urals, on a large canvas crowded with characters.

20. The Constructivists

IL'YA SEL'VINSKI (1899-   )

In "Our Biography" Il'ya Sel'vinski wrote:

> We blundered, untutored in party distinctions,
> We followed Lenin, Kerensky, Makhnó,
> Then in despair we went back to our schoolbooks—
> But to obey when the leaders said "Go!"[1]

If Sel'vinski shared the confused state of mind of educated youth immediately after the revolution, he had recovered from it by the time he wrote his long narrative poems dealing with the chaos of the Civil War, "Stetsyura's Execution" and *The Ulyalayev Adventure*, 1927. In them he observes history as if from a comfortable seat in a theater box, watching the rifle carriers of the revolution, rather than the intellectuals, as they swung from Lenin to Makhno and back again. The émigrés accused him of cynicism, and Soviet critics of "objectivism." He defended himself against the latter by insisting that Communist propaganda would gain by accepting the principle of neutrality in literature.

Sel'vinski wrote *The Ulyalayev Adventure* intending to unravel the knot of the relationships of the social classes during the Civil War. The two heroes, the Communist Gai and the anarchist Serga

Rival Camps of the NEP Period

Ulyalayev, are mortal enemies. One is a fanatical Leninist, the other an "elemental" revolutionary of the Pugachov-Razin type. Gai has a kind of metallic, single-minded energy and purposefulness. To achieve his aims, he will stop at nothing. In his inmost self, he is tragically conscious of losing touch with humanity.

> Gai thought, "I'm tangled up in Party lines
> Like a conducting rod. I speak in every hall,
> I am a teacher, organizer, guide.
> I have no right to think of love at all!" [2]

Serga Ulyalayev is reckless enough to measure himself against this man:

> Dear Communist bastards,
> I order you to cut out grain collections.
> Yours truly, Ulyalayev of the People. [3]

He is a criminal type, a robber and killer, with a following of desperadoes like himself, but, listening to the anarchist Shtein, he is inflamed with a genuine desire to establish social justice for the peasants, even though by criminal means.

> The thrifty peasant who toils and sweats
> And who makes the two ends meet
> Is no kin to either the rich or the poor,
> And his land he will fight to keep.
> . . . .
> The collective is only a grand façade
> For the idler to hide behind,
> Or the thief, perhaps—for the working man
> It's the worst of traps you could find! [4]

Ulyalayev is capable of kindness and love as well as ferocity, and his fierce passion for Tata is more than animal desire.

> The icy wind with its breath of steel
> Blew gusts of snow against her cheek,
> And opening her eyes she saw
> His dolorous face, like a carven saint's. [5]

In the end Ulyalayev is killed by his own men, in whom the fire of rebellion is extinguished by the peasant proprietary instincts.

Sel'vinski's demonstration that irrational, elemental Ulyalayevism had no chance against the cold, scientific Communist machine might well have served as a warning to rebellious spirits.

> Serga fought fiercely, like a boar
> Cornered by hounds. They got him down.
> They trussed him up, and in a cart
> They took him to the nearest town.[6]
> . . . .
> He is immune to lead and steel,
> Though there's a bullet in his skull. . . .
> He may be dead, but from his grave
> Terror, miasma-like, will rise.
> . . . .
> There in the field they killed Serga
> And drove the cart over his head.[7]

The theme of his verse *novella* "Stetsyura's Execution" Sel'vinski defined as the fate of the waverer caught in the iron grip of the revolution. Stetsyura is a former Communist who has become an inexorable foe of Communism. His motto is "The Soviets minus the Bolsheviks." He wants an end to senseless persecution so that the muzhik may work in peace.

In this poem Sel'vinski outlined the incipient rift within the Party as the idealists began to realize that their dedication to the cause was being used by Party careerists for selfish ends.

The commissar's motives are purely materialistic. He thinks of the medal he will receive for the campaign against counterrevolution, of promotion, of an unofficial increase in his food ration, and of a new apartment in Moscow.

> At dawn the happy Commissar,
> Proud of the victory he'd scored,
> Dreamed in the train that rushed through the woods
> Of his glittering reward.
> And that same night, in the gloomy woods
> That cared nothing for politics
> That villain Stetsyura was put to death
> Under Article Seventy-six.[8]

The play *Second Army Commander*, 1929, develops the Ulyalayev theme.[9] The outlaws' desperate resistance is broken, and they are eventually incorporated into the Red Army, to be taught iron discipline and obedience.

"Stetsyura's Execution" and parts of *The Ulyalayev Adventure* were first published in the Constructivist anthology *A State Plan for Literature*, which was edited by Sel'vinski, Korneli Zelinski and others.

The Constructivist group was formed in the early twenties, with the assistance of the critic A. N. Chicherin, who rather soon broke away because of ideological differences. In 1924 the group organized formally under the name Literary Center of Constructivists (LTsK). Its "manifesto" of the same year was signed by Il'ya Sel'vinski, Korneli Zelinski, Vera Inber, Boris Agapov, Yevgeni Gabrilovich, Dir Tumannyi, and Innokenti Oksyonov. Accepting the Marxian premise that ideological concepts were influenced by the nature and requirements of modern industry, they argued that writers should concentrate attention on current developments in that area. Subject matter, meaning, was the dominant factor. The chief principle of procedure laid down was the so-called "local principle," the constructing of a theme strictly in terms of the subject matter. Thus, any figure of speech or other device employed should be drawn from the milieu described. For example, in a poem dealing with a government office, Boris Agapov described "brows like the signature of the director of the trust."[10] Such "intensification" was intended to match, in literature, the increasing efficiency in industry attained through modern technology. Through technological progress the unit of force was gradually decreasing in weight and material consumed and increasing in efficiency, as in the case of an airplane engine. In the same manner, literary effectiveness was to be achieved through "loadification" of the word, "maximum load of meaning per unit of material."[11] Technical expressions, the jargon of engineers and foremen, were invading the common vocabulary and were of necessity to be used in literature. Instinct with pure meaning, stripped of emotion, mood, nuance, these prosaisms would heighten the effect of poetry in which meaning was to be dominant. Finally, the group stood for "the identity of sound and sign."

Put into actual practice, the cryptically phrased principles of the Constructivists involved little more than acceptance, however reluctant, of the Bolshevik methods of industrialization.

In *A State Plan for Literature* Zelinski, comparing the LTsK and the LEF policies, predicted with considerable acumen that the alliance between the Bolsheviks and the Left Front of the Arts would not last long. The LEF was always in a state of ferment, prone to objections and polemics. The Constructivists, on the other hand, were averse to endless altercation and ready to take a friendly view of the situation.

In Sel'vinski's work we can observe both a tendency toward prosaism and an inner rebellion against it. Lyricism attracted him, and he was especially fond of Russian lyrical songs. He experimented with "stylization" of Cossack songs and gypsy love songs, though not very successfully. His gypsy songs are decidedly banal.

He adhered closely to the tenets of Constructivism in his poetry written during the First Five-Year Plan.

Elektro-News, 1931, tells how an electric bulb is manufactured. The author succeeded in poetizing the transformation of matter, but he failed to make factory work sound poetic. When the "neutral observer" in him reasserted himself, he found much to criticize:

> What madness! The workers' own
> Government now conspires
> To go through its workers' pockets,
> To screen their thoughts and desires![12]

Fur Trade, 1929, concerns the status of intellectuals in the Communist Party. The unusually gifted and sincere Poluyarov is contrasted with another Party member, an aggressive and unscrupulous mediocrity named Krol', who exploits competent intellectuals without the slightest compunction and manages to get credit for all Poluyarov's achievements. When Poluyarov tries to lay claim to his own work and retain initiative, Krol' humiliates and persecutes him until he is driven almost to the point of suicide. Politics is not Poluyarov's forte. He is "the last of the intellectuals."[13] Sel'vinski gave the Krol's their due: they knew how to handle business and Russia.

Rival Camps of the NEP Period

> Antediluvian Russia, with
> Its icons and its priests, today
> Sets foot on an untrodden way,
> Each province bursting into song.[14]

A similar theme is developed in *Chelyuskiniana*, 1937-1938, the first two parts of which celebrate the courage and will of Otto Shmidt, the famous Soviet Arctic explorer. In the third part Sel'vinski reversed his position to glorify the Communist "doers" for whom dreamers like Shmidt merely opened the way. The reason behind this about-face was the arrest of Bergavinov, Shmidt's political commissar in his capacity as director of Glavsevmorput' (Main Administration for Northern Sea Route). Shmidt himself was later removed and replaced by Papanin.

Sel'vinski's foreword to the poem reads like a complaint against the enforced conformity of writers to the Party line:

> Where find the marvelous simplicity
> Our time demands? We fought a goodly fight
> For our new poetry—but having won
> We stand deserted in the desolate night.[15]

In the verse play *Umka, the Polar Bear*, 1935,[16] the theories and actions of the confirmed Bolshevik Kavaleridze strike the intellectual Peshkin as fantastic nonsense, a kind of socialist obscurantism. Yet the Chukchi tribesmen get along much better with Kavaleridze than with the kindly, broad-minded Peshkin who tries to defend their patriarchal way of life. *Umka* is the story of "technological primitivism" of a half-savage tribe.

In Sel'vinski's later period he wrote several historical tragedies, in verse, which are much weaker than his earlier work. They are more like movie scripts than plays, and resemble Cecil DeMille's historical films in their showmanship and romanticism. The artificiality is somewhat redeemed by a warm lyricism and an extremely skillful stylization of popular songs, as in *From Poltava to Gangut*:

> Where an island rises
> In the Neva River,
> In our mighty river,
> There a shipyard stands

> Where the carpenters
> Built a goodly ship,
> Fit to breast the waves,
> Fit to ride the storm.
> Twelve white sails it had
> Of the stoutest cloth.
> Sails upon the masts,
> Catch and hold the breeze,
> Don't you rip in twain!
> Don't you sink in battle,
> Russian fighting ship![17]

In this play and in *The Livonian War* Sel'vinski faithfully followed the Party line, but in *Knight Ioann* and especially in *Babek* he returned to his old theme of the clash between elemental individualism and totalitarian despotism. The hero of *Knight Ioann*, based on the seventeenth-century peasant rebel Ivan Bolotnikov, is another Stetsyura, dressed in an ancient caftan.

> Take up your axes, pitchforks, hunting knives
> And follow me! We will dislodge the tyrant
> And put the man we choose upon the throne—
> A peasant, though he be of royal blood![18]

Babek in the play of the same name is the leader of a revolt against the successors of Harun al-Rashid. The moral of the play is that despotism of the eastern Asiatic type carries its downfall within itself. In the effective ending of the tragedy Babek is crucified. From his cross he sees the despot's soldiers shooting arrows at an elephant and laughs aloud as the elephant, unscathed and unconcerned, merely shakes off the arrows.

Sel'vinski is a poet of great range, but his talent has been crippled by his surrender to the Party line.

VERA INBER (1890-   )

Vera Inber, who has a prominent place in Soviet literature, produced her best poems while a member of the Literary Center of Constructivists. During the 1920's she published the verse collections *Words Are Dust* [*Brennye slova*], 1922, *The Goal and the Way*, 1925, and *To the Son I Do Not Have*, 1927.

In her early poetry she usually took a neutral attitude and spoke objectively of her country's ordeal:

> She holds them all—vast fields of rye,
> Clouds, rivers, mountains, firmament;
> Upon the surface of the globe
> She covers half a continent...
> Naked she lies beneath the sky,
> Twice victim of the tempest's blast,
> A beggar with her gold and wine,
> Just as she was in ages past.[19]

Vera Inber reacted to the revolution in a purely feminine way, less concerned with politics and social questions than with the stuff of daily living, with the hardships and lack of joy in the life of the "machine builders." Her hopes of the future centered on warmth and comfort and the home. Paradoxically, however, her outstanding work of the LTsK period, "Vas'ka Svist in a Jam," 1926,[20] deals with the Soviet criminal underworld, a product of dissatisfaction with life and rebellion against the heartless social system, an ugly means of reasserting one's individuality.

In her early prose work, too—notably the short stories and sketches contained in the volumes *The Nightingale and the Rose*, 1925, *An Equation with One Unknown*, 1926, and *The Comet Hunter*, 1927—Vera Inber was not afraid of the truth.

In time, like Sel'vinski, she too capitulated. She began even in the 1920's:

> A mother, lifting up her child
> So he can gaze upon
> That face, will murmur, "This is Lenin,
> My son."[21]

And she was merely clinging to her status when she wrote of the vast shelter belt undertaken toward the end of Stalin's life:

The power that is in water, the windbreak sturdiness of trees and shrubs, the abundant heat and light of the sun—all these will be used for the welfare of the people in our Stalin epoch.[22]

Her long *Pulkovo Meridian*, a vivid picture of the terrible days of the siege of Leningrad, contains lines of rare excellence, for instance:

> Between two hospital pavilions, where
> The trees stand radiant in their autumn pride,
> With birds atwitter in their golden hair,
> A bomb, bearing one ton of death inside,
> Fell down to earth, but it did not explode,
> Kinder than they who blind destruction sowed.
>
> . . . .
> With blood and iron did the Germans come—
> And all was lost. The quiet wards were now
> A hell convulsed, chaotic, noisome;
> The wounded hero who with peaceful brow
> In combat turned the enemy to rout
> Pales as he sees death come to seek him out.[23]

Yet even in this poem, as in its companion piece, the collection of prose sketches entitled *Almost Three Years*,[24] the "neutral observer" had changed into the callous egoist whose rejoicing in personal survival while others starved and froze is somehow excessive and faintly distasteful.

The work of the other writers who signed the Constructivist "Manifesto" belongs almost entirely to the literature of the thirties.

6

Prose During the Uneasy Truce (1925-1929)

21. *The New Realists*

To outward appearances, the resolution of the Central Committee of the Russian Communist Party (Bolsheviks) dated June 18, 1925, "On the Policy of the Party in the Field of Belles-Lettres," was intended to end the strife of the early NEP period among the various literary factions. The resolution denied the claims to hegemony of the On-Guard group on behalf of the proletariat and took a conciliatory stand toward fellow travelers. Peasant writers were assured friendly support while being set "on the rails" of proletarian ideology. Fellow-traveler "literary specialists" were to be accorded tactful and considerate treatment, and a thoughtless and disdainful attitude toward the "old cultural heritage" was to be avoided. The Party committed itself to forbearance in regard to the transitional ideological forms and tendered "patient" assistance to writers in ridding themselves of these old forms in the process of increasingly close cooperation with the cultural forces of communism. Although it declined to grant a monopoly of literary production to any one literary organization, even to the proletarian group itself, the Party at the same time acknowledged its obligation to help the latter writers to earn for themselves "the historical right to hegemony."

Just as the class struggle in general has not come to an end in our country, so it has not come to an end on the literary front. In a class society there is not and cannot be a neutral art, although the class nature of art in general and of literature in particular is expressed in forms infinitely more varied than, for example, in politics.

Thus, the outcome was made abundantly clear—Communist ideology would ultimately hold sway in Soviet literature—but for the time being coercion was repudiated as a means toward that outcome.

The resolution was a compromise, a deferring of the decision in favor of the "proletarian hegemony" demanded by the On-Guardists. The very ambiguity of policy apparent in the prolix paragraphs of the resolution provided a few years of relatively free competition in literature, when both the militantly "proletarian" faction and the fellow travelers asserted their prerogatives.

During the later NEP the traditional genres of Russian literature re-emerged in the camps of both the fellow travelers and the Communists, but, within the genres, the ideological cleavage remained as conspicuous as before.

The full-scale realistic novel, the revival of which is usually considered to be signalized by the publication of Fedin's *Cities and Years* in 1924, established itself as the leading genre during the years before the inception of the First Five-Year Plan. However, the writers who contributed most to the revival of the realistic novel —for example, Sholokhov, Fedin and Aleksei Tolstoi—displayed their powers to the full at a later time; only those who produced their major work during the NEP period are discussed in this chapter.

MIKHAIL SLONIMSKI (1897-   )

Mikhail Slonimski, one of the Serapion Brothers, is a thoughtful, if somewhat dry and rationalistic writer. His early work, as defined by Anatoli Gorelov, traces the course of the intelligentsia through the fire of the Revolution. "The fire consumed some, and tempered others." [1]

Slonimski made a name for himself with the collection of stories

The Sixth Rifle Regiment, 1922, in which he shows how the First World War led to the revolution.[2] The Russian intelligentsia, which made up a large part of the wartime commanding staff, had an inherent aversion for killing, not so much out of humanitarian conviction as out of the confusion of floundering minds and weak wills.

The impact of the attempts at industrialization after the Civil War is analyzed in the *novella* "The Emery Machine," 1924. The hero, Oleinikov, Communist manager of a salt mine,

> thought that it would be a good thing if man could be completely mechanized—his feelings, sensations, desires, everything but his brain —so that the machine would not only be working for him but also rejoicing and suffering in his place.[3]

Gorelov says: "To the author, Oleinikov symbolizes the stiff, straight-line system knowing no mercy but perfectly aware of its goal."[4]

Oleinikov is an automaton. Yet when he hears that a catastrophe has happened at the salt mine and that his wife is probably among the victims, the machine breaks down and he faints. Although he had been cold and formal with his wife, there must have been love in his heart, carefully hidden even from himself. In Slonimski's interpretation, the Bolsheviks have, through will power, made themselves well-nigh immune to suffering.

In *Srednii Prospekt* (the name of a street, literally translated *Middle Avenue*), a novel of the NEP period, when life became insipid and barren to revolutionaries, a former Civil War hero is the leader of a criminal gang. The real hero of the novel is the epoch, in which man merely floats, as on a vast sea, with a life belt around his body, for the ship on which he had long traveled has been sunk.

The novels *The Lavrovs*, 1926, and *Foma Kleshnyov*, 1931, are somewhat sluggish and long-winded. In the first, the intellectual Boris Lavrov tries to develop his will power, not, however, in order to affirm his independence but in order to adapt himself to the new times, since the Bolsheviks have no use for softies. The novel, in fact, is a rationalization of compromise and a vindication of "conformism."

The Communist Foma Kleshnyov, who appears in this novel, is

the hero of the later novel which bears his name, one of the iron men forged by the revolution.

As was the case with several other Serapion Brothers, Slonimski's talent showed signs of weakening during the thirties. In his novel *Engineers*, 1950, he is but a shadow of his former self. He had always been something of a dry rationalist, and the Bolshevik cultural policy brought out the least attractive traits in this penetrating, observant and intelligent writer.

PANTELEIMON ROMANOV (1884-1938)

In *Property*, one of Panteleimon Romanov's last novels, the painter Bol'shakov overhears, at an exhibition, the following remarks about himself:

"He thinks he can pull it off with good old realism!"
"I don't know how his pictures come to be here at all. He must have been asleep all these years. Or, worse, he ignores the new times. After all, this is an exhibition of Soviet art, and there is nothing Soviet about him. This is a heroic era, and he paints landscapes in the old lyrical manner, and with a churchy smell besides." [5]

Bol'shakov is a modest man, but he knows his worth. "My paintings will remain," he says, "while theirs will be thrown out in a month." [6]

"You are a free artist, and the Revolution needs artists who are ready to serve it," [7] reply his critics.

Romanov resembled his hero; he met with the same kind of criticism and reacted to it in the same way.

It was Romanov's habit to interlard his realistic narrative with philosophical digressions about the underlying causes of the revolution and the changes it had wrought in human personality and relations. For this reason he, too, has sometimes been labeled, unjustly, a "dry rationalist." These digressions, which show the strong influence of P. L. Lavrov and Freud on Romanov's thinking, clarify the general trend of his novels, even if they somewhat impair their artistry.

He distinguishes two simultaneous processes in human society: a slow one, clearly visible only in historical perspective, resulting in reforms or in revolutionary changes, and transforming the face of a nation; and the daily movement of life, with its tedious struggle for survival. The average person is so absorbed in his little affairs that he does not notice the trend of the first process and usually finds himself quite unprepared when confronted with the change.

Romanov's characters are often Chekhovian intellectuals living in postrevolutionary times. Their homes, if they have not been burned down, are more neglected, dreary and dirty than before; and the people, too, have deteriorated. Some are paupers, others have become despicable "conformists." If Romanov showed that life had made them worse than they were, it does not follow that he was biased, unfeeling or malicious, though émigré critics were inclined to think so. He had Bunin's love of truth and naturalness, but he sometimes shrank from Bunin's harshness and adopted the milder, kindlier manner of Zaitsev.

Romanov is a great master at drawing national types. Characters in the long novel *Rus'* are pitiful but recognizable descendants of Tolstoi's Nikolai Rostov and Goncharov's Oblomov or even of Pushkin's Onegin and Lenski.

The first volume of *Rus'* was published in 1923. Romanov had begun work on the book long before, in 1907, and he died without completing it. It was to consist of three parts, dealing, respectively, with prewar Russia, with the First World War, and with the Revolution and the Civil War, and each part was to consist of three volumes.[8] Romanov was an excellent reader, and he read the first chapters of *Rus'* at a Moscow Art Theater studio in 1922, greatly impressing Lunacharski, who praised the "truly Russian sweep" of the parts he had heard.[9]

Rus' describes the rift that had been growing with the years between the aristocracy and the peasantry until they had nothing in common. Romanov's peasants are ignorant and coarse, and sometimes savage, but the author had a sincere affection for them. He felt that the landowners should have helped the people, if only by teaching them better agricultural methods, instead of humiliating them with ineffectual compassion or charity. But the gentry were not able to manage even their own estates, let alone help the peasants. Like Miten'ka Voyeikov, hero of *Rus'*—filled with anger at the futility of life, "in despair over the mess and filthiness of his life, over the peasants who were always bothering him, over everything around him"[10]—they enjoyed abstract discussions but had no real wish to improve their country.

All these enthusiastic dreamers and melancholy whiners and lazy talkers—part and parcel of their estates—are depicted by the author with a profound knowledge both of the way of life of the landed gentry and of the literature about them, and they all bear the stamp of doom,[11]

wrote L'vov-Rogachevski about *Rus'*.

The gentry in the novel are a collection of disappearing national types, with the possible exception of Valentin Yelagin, who shows a certain amount of initiative. The peasants, on the other hand, are full of energy, though they do not know what use to make of it. It is this elemental drive that will sooner or later burst out in revolt.

Another theme of *Rus'* is the conflict between sensuality and love. The first is personified by Olga Petrovna, the second by Irina. Miten'ka is attracted now to the one, now to the other woman, and the reader feels that he is not worthy of either. He is a young man, but he seems to have been born with a sclerotic soul.

Even before he started *Rus'*, Romanov had worked on the tale *Childhood*, which he finished in 1920. It took him seventeen years to write this book, which also grew out of his respect for a way of life that had vanished forever.

Romanov's short sketches of everyday life give an objective picture of the Civil War and the NEP periods. He is a keen psychologist. His approach is never superficial. A striking trait of all his short stories is the optimism of the characters. No matter how badly life treats them, they remain cheerful and believe in a better future, especially the common people. The intellectuals are somewhat less sanguine, but they learn from the masses to take hardships in their stride. Soviet critics ascribed the optimism of Romanov's characters to the fact that the average citizen felt sure life would improve after a short period of adjustment, when the Soviet regime became well established. The impression is inescapable, however, that the optimism of Romanov's characters means, rather, that they expected the downfall of the regime.

He had a deep understanding of the peasants and did not idealize them. One of his frequent themes is the consternation caused by the Bolsheviks' demagogic tactics. In "Fishermen," peasants receive orders to "return all plundered property to soviet jurisdiction. . . . Those who conceal anything shall be brought to trial." The peasants wonder: "How come? They said everything belonged to the people." [12]

In "The Voice of the People," a demonstration that the "people's rule" was nothing but a farce, peasants are frightened into electing to their soviet a candidate they do not want.[13]

Nor did Romanov spare the peasants themselves. They had made the revolution but did not know how to benefit from it. In "Calamity" an enormous yield of apples from the former landlord's orchard is left to rot.[14] The same story of inefficiency and waste is told in "Good Lands," in which the peasants ruin formerly well-kept fields.[15]

Romanov became even more popular when he turned to "sex problems" in a series of novels and stories dealing with the new amorality.

In the story "Spring" a girl and an engineer strike up an acquaintance in an empty railroad car.

"Open your mouth, can't you," breathed the engineer with annoyance.
She obeyed, and suddenly, with a moan, pressed her body against his.[16]
She continued to stand without moving. Then she moved her lips as people do when they are in great pain, and said in a barely audible voice, "I don't have any money . . . for my return ticket."
"Oh, that's what it is!"
. . . For some reason the engineer looked at her clothes more attentively. Then he took out his wallet, extracted a ten-ruble bill, put it back, pulled out three rubles and gave it to her, then hurried away. . . .
The girl remained standing where she was, with the three-ruble bill in her hand.[17]

The hero of the story "A Secret," a dashing, bemedaled Red Army officer, seduces a girl on a train and then tries to console her with a bit of ideology. Chastity, he says, is a capitalist prejudice, and there is no reason to grieve over lost virginity—on the contrary, she should be glad. The girl is disgusted. "What was the matter with her? A boor had insulted her, and she hadn't the pluck to defend her dignity."[18]

Both the Bolshevik and the émigré critics pounced on Romanov for these stories. The former maintained that sex abuses were a remnant of tsarism and that Romanov showed incredible arrogance in presenting them as something new, brought in by the revolution. The émigrés were indignant at what they considered slander of Russian men, who, they implied, had always been and remained models of decency, revolutions notwithstanding. In this case the Bolsheviks were closer to the truth; in Romanov's view the revolution had freed animal instincts previously held in check.

He portrayed the lover in the revolutionary period as a coarse, foul-minded nonentity, who discarded fidelity and spiritualized love as harmful, sentimental, petty-bourgeois notions.

The effect of current mores on adolescents is considered in the story "Trial of a Pioneer."[19] Young Andrei Chugunov courts his fellow Pioneer, Maria, in a chivalrous, not the proletarian, manner. He is very naive, and very appealing in his purity. The other Pioneers frown on such a state of affairs. To be sure, it may be a little early for a fellow to have sex relations before even being a member of the Komsomol, but if he happens to be precocious he could ask the girl to satisfy him, like a good comrade, instead of resorting to prostitutes. Sentimental slush is the last thing a progressive young Soviet citizen should be guilty of—that kind of love is the same as religion, opium for the people. The court decides to expel Chugunov from the organization, though many of his friends feel that the punishment is too severe. Vyacheslav Polonski called this story a bad joke giving a totally false impression of Soviet youth.

Best known among Romanov's "sex stories" are "Without Cherry Blossom" and its sequel "The Big Family." In the first an affair between two students results in the girl's pregnancy. She yearns for real love, but the hero, as usual, is a crass egoist, concerned only with the satisfaction of physical desire. "What do you want?" he sneers. "Nice surroundings? It's not 'poetic' enough for you?"[20]

Prose During the Uneasy Truce 277

The heroine can forget the ugly surroundings but not the need for tenderness. As they walk along the river, she stops to buy a spray of flowers.

"So you can't manage without cherry blossom?"
"Yes, I can, but it's nicer with some cherry blossom than without." [21]

She is the narrator of the story.

I have, in the window of the dormitory, a bottle with its neck broken off, and in it a small, drooping branch of bird cherry blossoms. . . . And when I look at that bottle, for some reason I feel like crying.[22]

. . . .

Our contempt for all that is beautiful, pure and wholesome leads to brashness and boorishness in our intimate relations also—to a fear of showing any human tenderness, understanding and kindness. . . . We have no love, we have only sexual relations.[23]

"Without Cherry Blossom" is the story of a Russian woman's struggle for a stable, affectionate family life in the old tradition.

Its sequel, "The Big Family," shows that not all traditions were worth preserving. The heroine, now the mother of an illegitimate child, meets with contempt in her parental home but finds a new family, "the big family" of the title, in her friends at the university who help her to care for the child and continue her studies. In a sense, the revolution has had a salutary effect, in sweeping away much that was bigoted and obsolete.

These two stories had a great deal in common with Veresayev's "Isanka" in their appeal for moral purity and unselfish love.

Toward the end of the NEP period the civic themes in Romanov's writings became more and more pronounced. One of his best tales, "The Right to Live," deals with the problems of non-Party people. The hero, Leonid Ostankin, a writer, embodies the mood of the Russian intelligentsia during the NEP. He thinks:

"If I am still alive, that means I've been lucky enough to slip through the Revolution and now have a right to live—on account of seniority, so to speak." [24]

The NEP made him feel that life had, at last, settled down, and no one would stop people in the street just to ask why they were so well dressed and what their social class origin was. [But] now and again he suddenly felt afraid that things might go wrong—that there might be some change, for instance, in the policy toward writers. He lived in a state of vague apprehension.[25]

In conversation with another writer, Gvozdyov, he says:

"Russia is the kind of hapless country that will never have real freedom. But it's beyond me how they can fail to see that they kill all culture when they seal up the sources of creative art. The U.S.S.R. is the only country in the world with preventive censorship. When a writer doesn't know what will happen to him tomorrow, how can you expect him to speak his mind? No wonder none of us cares what he writes, as long as it gets past the censor. . . ."
"That's right."
"In the old times a writer fought for his convictions. They were sacred to him. The government was something alien to him and hostile to freedom. Now we've got to look on the government as on our own. To dislike it would denote conservatism, not liberalism as before. But what convictions does a writer have now? If he's told that his line is 'unsuitable,' he blushes like a schoolboy who has made a mistake, and is ready at once to rewrite everything and to say 'white' for 'black,' just because he is terrified. We are so steeped in lies that we even fear one another." [26]

Ostankin's existence becomes a struggle between honor and fear, and he decides to take his own life. "Comrades," he says in a last letter, addressed to writers in general,

". . . here are a few words from a man who does not need anything any more. . . .
"Out of shortsightedness and cowardice, you betray your true selves, you are faceless, indifferent journeymen paid to do what you are told. . . . I prefer to leave with a ray of consciousness. . . . I had only enough courage to understand. And once the truth has become clear, there is nothing left but to die." [27]

Romanov's most important work is the novel *The New Table of Commandments*, 1928, about a Soviet marriage. Sergei, the husband, a Party member in charge of a workers' club, is a self-educated man. Lyudmila, the wife, comes from a good family. She does not want to be a square peg in a round hole and tries to adjust to the new life. Most of all, however, she wants love. "You are trying to wipe out the things which for centuries have made life worth living," she once told the Communist Sergei:

"You discard love and beauty as you have discarded religion. . . . You have made a desert out of life, tarnished all its color, destroyed the family. . . . But worst of all, you have killed love, the most sublime thing on earth." [28]

Sergei was attracted by this frank and unusual woman. Not only Lyudmila's beauty and refinement impressed him, but also her complex inner life. Soon they began living together, postponing official marriage till Sergei obtained a divorce from his first wife, a peasant woman. At first, it seemed to Lyudmila that she and Sergei would both benefit from their union.

Sergei worries about the rowdyism and the low morale among the younger members of the workingmen's club. The same young people who had been unselfish and heroic were now "lazy and careless."

Their morale flopped when, after the great days of enthusiasm, they found nothing to do. . . . They proved unable to adjust themselves to a world at peace. . . . [29]

His outlook broadened by Lyudmila's love, Sergei becomes aware of the dangers of such states of mind. At a club meeting, he makes a speech on the importance of overcoming destructive instincts.

But the marriage which started out so well is soon on the rocks. Sergei has the peasant's tyrannical attitude toward women and believes that a wife is her husband's chattel. He tires of Lyudmila's romantic love but expects his educated wife to help him in the fields. Lyudmila is quite willing to do so but wants her husband to be a friend, not a boss, and to treat her as a human being. "Woman, with all her rights," she says, "will have to go begging for crumbs of love and warmth . . . trample her dignity into the mud and yield where she never would have yielded before." [30] She feels "discarded, like a useless rag." [31]

"You fear being alone more than you fear death," says Sergei, "because, to you, loneliness means death." [32]

The revolution had raised from the lower classes a domineering type of man, steeped, moreover, in the synthetic hatred of the class struggle theories. It was Lyudmila's tragedy that she had given her love to the new man of will for whom love had no place in the scheme of things.

The novel *Comrade Kislyakov, or Three Pairs of Silk Stockings*, which describes the end of the NEP period, is more interesting as a historical record than as a story of marital unfaithfulness. The hero is a cowardly opportunist.

The huge museum where Ippolit Kislyakov was employed was, as before, quiet and clean like a church. [It] was an island that had not been submerged by the waves of the new times.[33]

The picture changes with the arrival of the new director Polukhin, a factory worker, who, in his rough-hewn, angular features, resembles a stone idol. He complains:

"It is hard to work with people I'm not used to . . . especially as I'm new on the job and can't make head or tail of these things. . . . I see it is the intelligentsia that sets the tone here. A bit of purging is indicated. I'll tell them so right away. I'll make them see who is boss here, the proletariat or they." [34]

Kislyakov has only contempt for him, but hastily agrees. Polukhin brings in other proletarians. Churikov, who sides with him, says: "If they don't understand the requirements of the new times, we'll throw them out. But we will take science out into the street." [35] The museum is no longer a museum but a hotbed of class hatred.

Romanov was accused of slandering Russian women in this novel by the intimation that under the circumstances of the times they could be bought by luxuries and creature comforts.

Svetlana,[36] a sequel to *Property* and Romanov's last novel, published abroad in 1934, shows the deterioration of culture that had occurred in Soviet Russia. Art had become a propaganda weapon. The painter Viktor Bol'shakov, who in *Property* still fought for his independence, is a broken man in *Svetlana*.

As a playwright ("Free Love" and "Earthquake"), Romanov has little originality.

The Russian intellectuals were Romanov's main concern. His writings always expressed regret over the intelligentsia's lack of heroic qualities, energy and will power.

A conflict between the author and the Soviet machine was inevitable. In 1927 Lebedev-Polyanski accused him of daubing the new Soviet structure with tar.[37] For approximately two years in the mid-thirties Romanov was forbidden to publish. The ban was lifted thanks to Bukharin's intervention, and in 1936 a brief sketch on an industrial subject appeared in the magazine *Novyi mir* [New World].[38]

Romanov died in 1938, from a heart attack. The Writers' Union printed an announcement of the funeral but did not risk even an obituary notice.

LIDIYA SEIFULINA (1889-1954)

The peasantry's obscure yearnings are Lidiya Seifulina's main theme. Her Virineya, in the 1924 novel of the same name,[39] one of the most convincing positive heroines in Soviet literature, has a wishful belief in the Revolution.

The peasants who turned against the regime are well represented in the character Alibayev in the 1926 tale "Kain kabak" (name of a place in Siberia). He is head of the local soviet, and he approves when Kudashev, head of the neighboring soviet, simply arrests a Party man sent down to "strip the muzhiks." Kudashev, with many others, is sentenced to death, and Alibayev wants to be shot with them but is given a short prison term because of his former services to the Party. He takes Kudashev's place when the rebels are led out to be shot. The substitution is discovered. "I only wanted to correct your mistake,"[40] says Alibayev to the president of the local Cheka.

"Kain kabak" is Seifulina's best work. The characterizations show an influence of Gorki, especially of *Foma Gordeyev*; and the style, that of Remizov. Her Alibayev is akin to Artyom Vesyolyi's and Aleksandr Yakovlev's reckless heroes—and less contrived.

Like Tarasov-Rodionov in *Grass and Blood*, Seifulina, in *A Muzhik Legend of Lenin*, 1924, distinguishes between the real Lenin, who bid on the proletariat, and the myth of Lenin as the protagonist of a muzhik kingdom.

In her other early writings, too, Seifulina is observant and skilled. Her tales *Lawbreakers*, 1921,[41] *Four Chapters* (from an unfinished short novel of prerevolutionary Siberia),[42] "Noah's Ark," and "Humus," 1923,[43] belong in the so-called documentary fiction. *Lawbreakers* deals with the *besprizornye* (bands of homeless waifs), and "Noah's Ark" with a small town's resistance to the police methods the Bolsheviks tried to impose. "Humus" shows how the interference in peasant life of the city proletariat, who neither liked nor understood peasants, led to a violent clash.

Seifulina submitted to the Party's propaganda requirements, but with many reservations.

"There has been too much cheering,"[44] she wrote in a critical article. Gradually, with such an attitude, she became one of the "superfluous" writers in Soviet literature.

ANDREI SOBOL' (1888-1926)

Andrei Sobol' stands out among Soviet writers for his original style—in general, Russian literature after 1917, rich in documentary material, has little originality of form, the best in it being patterned after Blok, or Bunin, or Remizov, or some other prerevolutionary master. Sobol' was no mere copyist, although the influence of a strange assortment of teachers—Gogol, Korolenko and Zamyatin—may be discerned.

A Jew, a Zionist in his youth, a political exile in Siberia where he made friends with Socialist Revolutionaries, Sobol' began publishing before the revolution. The temperament he displayed in his work, even in that dealing with his term of penal servitude, was such that he was once scolded for endowing even jailkeepers with kindliness.

Sobol's first piece dealing with the 1917 upheavals was the story "Lounge Car," published in 1922 in a book of the same name. The revolution had exerted its force through the masses and trampled the dignity of the individual. Sobol' raised the question whether everyone would not in time learn to do the same thing, whether the revolution would not end in callous disregard of the masses.

After the February revolution a distinguished tsarist general writes to Pyotr Gilyarov, a commissar of the Provisional Government:

I am a war-hardened general . . . decorated with the St. George cross for bravery, yet I cried like a newly inducted conscript, and I am not ashamed of it. But I do not wish my tears to be misunderstood and misrepresented. They were not tears of fear for my life, nor did I shed them because my beloved brigade had demanded my removal, even though I have never mistreated a single soldier, even before the revolution. But why, why is it that living men seem to be already dead? Why are we inexorably sliding into an ever deepening pit?[45]

The posters and slogans of the time described all old-regime generals as beasts, and even the generals who were living denials of these tracts were killed in the senseless bloodshed to which the propaganda against an abstract evil led. The story is an impassioned protest against such gratuitous carnage. With the next revolutionary spasm—the Bolshevik Revolution—Gilyarov's violent death, too, becomes a matter of course:

The next day . . . the lounge car was carrying the chairman of the Revolutionary War Committee of the N. . . Army to headquarters at the front. The tall mirror as calmly and dispassionately reflected the image of the new occupant—his stocky, vigorous figure, the brown forelock from under the fur cap worn at an angle, the holsterless gun tucked in his belt, the military tunic on the bulging chest, and the arched eyebrows over his alert, youthful, somewhat foxy eyes; but, because the mirror had two crossed cracks—it had been hit when the soldiers had rushed into the car after killing the commissar—the image was crooked and ugly, as though cut into pieces.[46]

Always Sobol' condemned the cruelty of the revolution. In "The Princess," the heroine, Princess Muravlina, working for the White intelligence service, takes a job in the Cheka, under the name of Natasha Toropova. The Cheka director is a blend of criminal and inquisitor, "an abstraction framed in a pair of broad shoulders.

A formula, crammed into a mighty thorax. . . . Tears? The very earth may cry, the towns and cities may weep—but never he." [47] The author obviously shared Natasha's horror of all that goes on at the Cheka. Her death is symbolic of his own inner drama.

Thus an unquenchable love takes hold of the soul.
Thus you have taken hold of me—my country, my Russia, land of iron and wax.[48]

The hero of "A Man and His Passport," a former White officer, returns to Russia on a secret mission with faked papers. A patriot and an idealist, he realizes that the ruling class to which he belonged was as much responsible for the revolution as the Bolsheviks, but he can see that the new masters will be far more ruthless. Already the Communists are deceiving the people. His despair aggravated by lack of faith in the Allies, he commits suicide.

The meeting of the exile with his native land is moving:

At the Russian frontier, at the sight of the first Red Army soldier, there was for the first time a tremor of life in the gray eyes, and for the first time they closed, as if in pain. Then they again gazed, unmoving, at the poor Russian fields, the unlovely towns, the monotonous net of dirty roads, and the wide [Soviet] railroad. . . .[49]

After long absence he is in Leningrad again:

In the shimmering light of its lamp posts, the Avenue of October 25 [date of the Bolshevik Revolution according to the old calendar] shimmered and trembled, at once real and unreal, as always, as in Gogol's days, rising like a mirage out of the fog, from the depth of the Finnish marshes. . . .[50]

With a casual remark, a minor detail skillfully used here and there, Sobol' recreates the atmosphere of life under the Soviets. A few sentences overheard in a school dining hall, and we know who the students are and what they live by. The hero dies because he is unable to hate:

I do not know why I no longer have my old determination, nor . . . even my old hatred.
When I walk in the streets of Moscow, why do I feel that every corner of the city reproaches me?[51]

Prose During the Uneasy Truce

The two heroes of the mournfully humorous *Memoirs of a Freckled Man* also have returned to Russia illegally, simply to live at home. Both are pitiful derelicts. One becomes a small-time swindler; the other, the freckled man, is unable to shake off the old Chekhovian ideas of decency and honesty. Both are failures, not "enemies." Out of an old-fashioned conviction that writers are champions of the downtrodden, the freckled man turns for help to a Soviet writer and is sorely disappointed when the latter admonishes him:

You do not understand the Marxian principle in literature. Human souls aren't worth a copper. Daily life, local color, that's what we need —and you keep harping on the soul.[52]

His faith is restored by a "kulak poet" in a saloon who sympathetically buys him a meal and a drink and confides his own troubles:

I'm a bird of the fields, and they want to clip my wings; I'm suffocating because of this inhuman attitude of the Soviet government toward a proud peasant poet. Where is the liberty we shed our blood for?[53]

In Sobol's interpretation, the elemental cruelty of the mob was mitigated by compassion, but not the mechanical cruelty of the system. The hero of the tale "When the Cherry Tree Blooms," ataman Dzyuba, a midget Makhno, gives orders not to hang Jews on cherry trees but in the synagogue yard—nearer to their God. His men bring in a Jew whose life they have spared because something about him baffled them. The prisoner turns out to be an anarchist, and a discussion develops between him and the "natural" anarchist Dzyuba. Though the man behaves with pride and independence, something like pity for him stirs in Dzyuba: " 'Get out of here,' snarled Dzyuba. 'Leave this town at once. I've given my word—but hurry . . . I don't vouch for myself.' "[54]

Dzyuba's mistress, Marina, a former opera singer, had had romantic ideas about the Civil War but cannot stand its savagery. She begins to hate her lover, and he shoots her.

The tale "Shadow Play" describes Moscow during the NEP— at once a European metropolis and a sprawling village steeped in antediluvian traditions.

... In every direction throughout its length and breadth, [Moscow] is studded with dynamic slogans, such as "Time Is Money," "No Handshakes," "Get It Done and Leave," and with signs of trusts and syndicates, and less blatant, more modest signs of agents for the South, the North, the Don region, Turkestan—cotton, black gold, the tart wines of Crimea, sable fur, Amur-river salmon.

Yet in the very heart of the city there is an islet—the waves of Moscow surround it on all sides but cannot submerge it, and the Mother of God behind the little blue lights of the icon lamp remains undisturbed.

Blue is the light—and in the stillness a friendly and funny wooden cuckoo calls on the threshold of its little wooden house, from which flows dreamy, placid, unruffled time.[55]

The NEP had brought back prosperity and a European look to Moscow, but it was an uncharitable prosperity. The revolution had awakened Russia's energies and passions, and had at the same time destroyed its conscience and its capacity for love. "I don't want big dinners with 1884 Hungarian wines," says one of the women characters. "But I want love of the 1884 vintage . . . Love free from caution and from fear."[56] In Moscow saloons, fist fights were a release of pent-up hatred of the regime and stifled initiative: "Suddenly you can see a patron beat his fists on the table and shout . . . sprinkling saliva on the neighbors' beer mugs."[57]

A man says:

Inside me, Nadezhda, everything is burned to ashes. Not even Moscow exists for me, not even Russia. All I can do is lift my hand and press a gun to my temple.[58]

In 1926 Sobol' himself committed suicide. "Must go. Superfluous man," runs his laconic last note.[59]

There are perhaps more talented, more important writers in Soviet literature, but none more humane than Sobol' among the ranking authors.

YURI SLYOZKIN (1887-1947)

Scant attention has been paid Slyozkin by critics, but his books are in great demand in public libraries and their popularity is well deserved. Unlike most Soviet writers, Slyozkin rarely touched on politics, and seldom referred to the revolution except obliquely, in terms of the personal tragedies of his characters. The superfluous man of Soviet society was his hero.

With *Phantasmagoria*, 1924, the earlier influence of Bunin began to wane before that of Gogol, Leskov and Zamyatin. In the book lyricism frequently gives way to mild irony, a kind of caricature done in pastels.

The novel *With Different Eyes, or A Basket of Letters*, 1926, contrasts the genuine intelligentsia and the upstarts who owed their rise to Party loyalty. The economist Pechonykh writes to his wife: "They have no use for true scholars, but try more and more to get by with half-baked 'experts.'"[60] Ambitious and incompetent, the latter are fearful of losing their jobs, fall into savage careerism, intrigues and mutual mistrust. Sergei Porosha writes to the columnist Semenetski that there are two kinds of Russian intellectuals,

the pre-October intelligentsia and the quick modern product. They are two different worlds, two peaks of the same mountain range—Russian culture, the Russian spirit. . . .
How can the little man . . . the ordinary, average, kind Russian man arrange matters with his conscience? . . .
I meant to discuss the intelligentsia, but what I have said applies to every Russian, to all the Russians who at last after all the strain and struggle and hardships had a moment of rest, looked round—and fled from the great world into the world of their own souls.[61]

The more gifted among the pseudo-intellectuals, if they tasted real culture, began to lose faith in Communism, as in the case of the young Communist doctor, Zhdanov, in the novel. As a rule, the semi-intellectuals were content to build their personal success on other people's ideas, and for that reason the Bolshevik leadership found them very convenient.

The novel *A Goat in the Garden*, 1927, is Slyozkin's most important work of the NEP period. The scene is laid in the provinces, recovered from the Civil War and not very different from what they have always been, except for increased poverty and dreariness.

To tell the truth, our town can hardly be called a town. . . . There are a good number of such in the vast U.S.S.R., as alike as loaves of bread from a communal bakery. As soon as you drive up the hill, you can see it all as in the palm of your hand—lazy smoke rising from its chimneys, leafy cherry trees leaning on ramshackle fences, yellow sunflowers sleepily gazing at the sky . . . white down frothing in the goose pen, while the clay-coated cottages and the blue onion-shaped domes of the little churches look on.[62]

The inhabitants feel that they are no longer their own masters. They may affect a somewhat ironical view, but they chafe under the new order.

The League of the Godless has sent a former priest to give the townsmen a lecture, "Do We Need a Church?" "The Reverend knows very well what pays best, and when—under the tsar, pray to God at the altar, and under the Soviets, bark at God from a platform."[63] Even the pro-Communist mailman, Klunya, is disgusted; he feels that the ex-priest should at least have the decency to keep quiet.

The revolution raised many half-educated people to important posts. In the Ukraine, as Slyozkin shows, these people had strong nationalist leanings.

The bright hopes kindled by the revolution had failed to materialize, but an obscure longing for something new and great remained in the heart of the common man. Shady characters exploit these feelings. The hero of the novel, Kozlinski, posing as a movie director, fleeces the officials of the department of political education but makes the mistake of marrying a pretty girl and lingering too long in the town. He is an amateur Ostap Bender, the fabulous swindler in the novel by Il'f and Petrov.

Slyozkin planned a cycle of novels, somewhat on the lines of Romanov's *Rus'*, but only the first part, entitled *Before the Storm: Summer 1914*,[64] was published, in 1928.

During the Second World War he wrote a novel about the Brusilov campaign,[65] a somewhat contrived, listless and drab piece.

FYODOR GLADKOV (1883-   )

Gladkov's novel *Cement* was serialized in the review *Krasnaya nov'* [Red Virgin Soil] in 1925. Soon afterwards it was published in book form.[66] By mid-1927 it had already gone through ten editions. Bolshevik publicists were making the most of the novel as evidence that a genuine proletarian literature was at last arising to outweigh the efforts of the fellow travelers.

The critic Lebedev-Polyanski hailed *Cement* as a true reflection of reality, "a living refutation" of allegations that proletarian literature was tendentious, focusing only on the facts which justified Soviet policy and rejecting those which contradicted its preconceived ideas.[67]

P. S. Kogan maintained that after the revolution the literature of emotional experience was being replaced by the literature of practical action. The "new man" had not yet come into being, but new relations betwen men were being established where labor was concerned. This labor wholly absorbed man's spiritual life; since in life emotional experience was being replaced by action, literature could not but follow suit. To Kogan the significance of *Cement* was that Gladkov had presented in it a romantic view of the social necessity for practical action.

Each opinion contains a grain of truth. Gladkov did indeed reject the principle of passing over certain facts for the sake of propaganda—he even brought into his novel Party members who are vicious men—and in this respect he compares favorably with Libedinski and Serafimovich. Gladkov's treatment of the Cheka agent Chibis, a ferocious sadist, also bears out Kogan's interpretation. Chibis' fanatic devotion to the Communist idea is portrayed so that his personal character seems to be unimportant or, in any case, excusable. It seems of no significance whether a man was noble or vicious by nature—the system obliterated his individuality. By aggrandizing the system, which conquers man's personality, Gladkov was able to forego the usual idealization of individual Bolsheviks and still produce ideologically acceptable fiction.

Cement is an account of the reconstruction of a partially wrecked industrial plant in the period following the Civil War. Gladkov devoted far more attention to Party meetings and planning than to actual scenes of labor and industrial processes. The Proletcult objected to his method, and on this count compared *Cement* unfavorably with Lyashko's *Blast Furnace*.

Gleb Chumalov, protagonist of *Cement* and rebuilder of the plant, is the hero of *Toilers of the Sea* (that working bible of the Proletcult school) turned Russian Communist. He is filled with romantic enthusiasm, and he comes to life. Gladkov is in general unsurpassed among postrevolutionary writers in portraying workers.

Chumalov's activity as organizer and Party member is in dramatic contrast to his private life. As an organizer he profits greatly by the revolution, but as a man he is even more unhappy than under the tsarist regime, which he fought to overthrow. The contradiction between public and private life which Gladkov saw besetting the makers of the revolution in general exemplifies the philosophy censured by Soviet critics as "an unnatural blend of Marxism and Freudianism."

It is true that Gladkov was perhaps more deeply influenced by Freud than by Marx. Gladkov saw the unbridled sexual instinct asserting itself in an endeavor to offset the effects of the revolution. The lust of the flesh translated man's attempt to make the loss of his ego, swallowed up in the storm, relatively painless, to rob it of its sting by indulging in a feast of the senses. The reverse side of the medal was the elimination of spiritual love, and the resultant suffering on the part of women. But sensual passion might also be transmuted into dynamic energy and thus lead to creative activity. Such a transmutation facilitated the process of dissolution of the personality and permitted the individual to become a small but integral part of the storm which raged about him. It is on this basis that the characters Dasha Chumalova, Gleb's wife, and Bad'in in *Cement* were evolved.

Gladkov was haunted by the image of the same woman. Marina in *Steed of Flame*, Nastya in the play *The Gang* and Dasha in *Cement* are all variations of that image. This woman is a slave to household drudgery who tries to fight her way to freedom and becomes the captive of a man's sensual passion, caught in a vicious circle.

Bad'in, the chairman of the executive committee, is a proletarian Sanin, who makes his prototype look like a callow youth, a sniveling intellectual. After seducing the teacher, Sanin at least makes some attempt to set her mind at peace. Bad'in rapes Polya Mekhova, but when she is expelled from the Party he will not raise a finger to help her. Gleb Chumalov, a Communist of moral decency, turns on Bad'in in disgust. At the same time Bad'in is an energetic and able executive and does a good job for the Party. In recompense, Gladkov granted him a remission of all his sins and whitewashed him precisely as he did Chibis.

In the character of Sergei Ivagin, blood brother to Yuri Svarozhich in Artsybashev's *Sanin*, Gladkov criticized the intelligentsia and portrayed it as merely pathetic and downtrodden.

From the point of view of style and its system of imagery *Cement* is a mediocre imitation of Andrei Belyi's *St. Petersburg*. What Belyi turns into a symbol, Gladkov tried to interpret in a materialistic and realistic way. Stylistically *Cement* suffers from the author's attempts to achieve epic scope. The value of the novel lies not in Gladkov's craftsmanship but in his powers of observation and in the story he tells.

Gladkov is not a very important writer, but he has brought home with force—if only by virtue of dogged repetition—the important theme in postrevolutionary Russian letters of the dissolution of the individual personality in the storm of the revolution and the subsequent attempt of those carried to power—the organizers who had retained the storm's dynamic energy—to impose their will, to suppress and obliterate the individuality of the executors, who had lost their energy and strength of will.

Gladkov, born of peasant parents, is a typical self-made intellectual. As a boy, he worked for a pharmacist; later he became a typesetter and then a teacher. He had been a provincial newspaperman for a long time before the revolution. Soon afterwards he joined the Communist Party and was an active member of the Smithy.

An early story "The Fallen" [*Izgoi*], written in 1912 but not published until after the revolution, described the life of political exiles in Siberia and introduced one of the themes to which Gladkov was to return again and again. He contrasted doubting and vacillating intellectuals with the proletarian Ivanyuk, who is able to suppress his own doubts and to devote himself wholly to revolutionary work. *Old Secret* [*Staraya sekretnaya*], a short novel written in the mid-1920's, repeated the same theme, greatly elaborated, apparently for the purpose of tracing the current outbreak of doubts and vacillations—rightist and leftist deviations—to roots in the past and of showing it as an organic outgrowth of prerevolutionary contradictions.

Gladkov's prominence came with the novel *Steed of Flame* [*Ognennyi kon'*], 1923, a story of the Civil War in the Kuban'. The Cossack Andrei Guzi vacillates between the Reds and the Whites and finally sides with the latter. His death is a foregone conclusion. His friend, Gmyrya, another Cossack, is torn between hatred and pity for Andrei and tortured by passion for the Cossack girl Marina, who welcomes the revolution as liberation from domestic slavery and fights against Gmyrya's passion for fear of falling into another captivity, but in the end unwillingly succumbs. The Bolshevik Globa deludes his own reason with talk about the "Scythian element" in the revolution; but his disquisitions are merely a way of quieting the unease he feels over the incipient shipwreck of the human ego.

Gladkov's strong point is revealed in this novel—his acute sensitivity to, and dramatic presentation of, the new forms of life after the revolution. Stylistically, however, he lacks originality. He has always imitated other writers. In *Steed of Flame* the influences are those of Andreyev and Artsybashev.

Gladkov's intellectuals have decency and integrity, but an inner emptiness and an acute awareness of their own maladjustment and impotence. They have lost contact with the soil and lack the strength which comes from it. Already half dead, the intelligentsia as a class faces inevitable extinction in the new world.

Gladkov's play *Uprooted by the Storm*, 1921, dealing with the inadequacies of the Russian intelligentsia, even those who laid the groundwork for the revolution, is reminiscent of Artsybashev's play *Jealousy*, particularly in the characterization of the hero. Ugryumov, a former Party member and political exile, now a teacher, can find no safe place for himself under the new order. "The intelligentsia," says another character, is nothing but "the remains of outdated formations, and its whole life is spent in continuously looking for a safe harbor."[68]

All Gladkov's negative qualities are concentrated in his plays, which are very poor theater. They suffer from an amorphous and overburdened composition, a confusion between the personal and the social planes, and a crude naturalism of speech. *The Gang* [*Vataga*], 1923, is the most chaotic of his plays, so confused that it is not always comprehensible. Several conflicts are presented, but none of them is fully thought out and developed. In the character of Shatalov, Gladkov intended to portray a transcendental peasant rebel, a modern Sten'ka Razin, but Shatalov remains no more than a red flag waving over a drab fishermen's village.

Pride, 1935, is an unsuccessful dramatization of his novel *Power*.

Gladkov intended *Power*, 1932-1938,[69] to be a sequel to *Cement* and reintroduced the character of Gleb Chumalov, but there is little connection between the two books.

Power is an archipelago of scenes of industrial life vaguely and unconvincingly related. The scene is the construction site of the hydroelectric power plant Dneprostroi.

Osip Brik once said about *Cement* that Gladkov was a slave to "the heroic cliché." The defect is far more obvious in *Power* than in the earlier novel. *Power* is, generally speaking, Gladkov's greatest failure. The defects are more conspicuous in later editions than in the original version, for the author was compelled to revise the novel several times to meet new censorship requirements. A comparison of the original form of *Power*, as serialized in *Novyi Mir* [New World] in 1932 and 1937-1938, with the edition of 1939 shows that the book suffered considerably from the changes. The 1939 version omits Chumalov's conversation with the German workers' delegation—the anti-Fascist attitude expressed in the incident had already become embarrassing. Further, the author excised a chapter entitled "The Tournament" *(Turnir)*, in which the engineer Khabi was unmasked prematurely and too crudely. In this excision—dictated by the fall of Yezhov and the rise of Lavrenti Beriya, who eliminated some of the excesses of his predecessor—Gladkov was toeing the Party line and abandoning any claim to truthful representation.

There are a great many characters in *Power*, but few living people. The brains of the organizers act as so many dynamos, producing the energy and will power needed to set into motion thousands of robots. The charcter of Kostya Gromov, a gypsy, a free son of the steppes, natural and spontaneous, stands out in contrast to his mechanized environment: "I've traveled all over the whole country. Everyone working, fuss and bother everywhere. Not like before. And I don't like it—it's shameful." [70]

Gladkov is an unusually prolific writer, but only a few of his remaining works deserve attention—the stories *Drunken Sun* and *Lyubasha's Tragedy*, the sketch *Heart's Blood*, and the two satiric tales "The Cephalopod" and "Inspired Goose," from *A Little Trilogy*.

In *Drunken Sun*, 1927, Gladkov managed to shake off Artsybashev's influence and indeed to argue and joust with his former mentor. At first glance Akatuyev, the protagonist of *Drunken Sun*, a high Party official, has a good deal in common with Bad'in in *Cement*, but the resemblance is merely external. Akatuyev is ashamed of the beast in himself, and, repressing his lust, transforms it into energy, action and leadership.

The setting is a rest sanatorium surrounded by people who hate the guests—a symptom of the growing antagonism between the common man and the privileged class. It is the NEP period, and the country is going through a crisis. The executors are weary unto death, not merely in body. They have lost faith in the cause and interest in their work, and seek oblivion in drunkenness and license.

Among the young people at the sanatorium not all are depraved. Marusya, the heroine, and Yasha are repelled by the heartlessness of the new order. Marusya, a new feminine type for Gladkov— the woman who forces men to accept her not as a female but as a human being—is another Isanka, not so highly educated but with the same instinctive protest against the crudely materialistic attitude and with an inclination toward a naive and touching pantheism:

From the unreachably far horizon, where the sea merged with the sky and was as ethereal as the sky, came an endless series of small and rhythmical ripples and a distant sound of deep and piteous sighing. It was a siren-buoy out in the harbor, and Marusya liked to think that it was the depths of the sea moaning, tired from doing some mysterious important work somewhere far out in the blue inhuman distance. . . . When she was alone, she felt sad and a little frightened, and was obsessed by vague thoughts about the unknown distances that she would never attain.[71]

Lyubasha, the heroine of *Lyubasha's Tragedy*, 1935, one of Gladkov's best pieces, represents a further development of Marusya and yet is a type known in Russia since time immemorial, the peasant-woman whom Nekrasov called "the regal Slav" and of whom he said that, although she walked in the selfsame road as all, the dirt of the shabby surroundings did not stick to her.[72]

After the devastation of the village such peasant women went off to work in factories. But wherever they went, nothing could break their pride and independence. *Lyubasha's Tragedy* is a tale of the inevitable conflict of one of these Russian women with the Soviet regime.

Lyubasha is a weaver, a Communist. She wins respect not through making speeches at meetings or currying favor with her superiors, but through stubborn and inspired hard work. The habit of working and of doing everything well is in her blood, a heritage from her ancestors. Suddenly Lyubasha begins to turn out poor-quality textiles. The department in which she works is being supplied with poor yarn. To explain away defective output—the deterioration of flax, cotton and silk as a result of the collectivization of agriculture is of course not to be hinted—scapegoats must be found. Lyubasha is one of the victims. The foreman says to her:

"You are not here as a decoration, this is no glasshouse. Turn your soul inside out, if you have to, but turn out stuff that does the heart good."
"Do you expect me to feed myself into the machine?"
"If that's good for production, go right ahead!"
"A human being is nothing to you—you judge him by the quality of the cloth." [73]

Indignant at the callous treatment of human beings, Lyubasha comes into conflict with the Party and her fellow workers. A secret agent in the factory resorts to forgery to deliver her over to the OGPU on charges of "plunder of socialist property." She is alone in her trouble. Even her husband fails to understand what she is going through—to him she is merely a source of sensual pleasure.

Like Marusya, Lyubasha unconsciously turns from Marxism as a religion to pantheism:

> She listened to her heart, to the blood singing in her ears, and it seemed to her that her heart was everywhere in this far blue sweep of space. . . . The sparkling lake, the wood and the sky were filled with the ringing of distant bells.[74]

The long-drawn out happy ending is altogether unconvincing. As often, Gladkov set his sights on a bold idea but suddenly lowered his rifle, afraid to press the trigger. His work in general is crippled by fear of the censor.

Lyubasha's Tragedy is refreshingly free of the deliberate crudities and clumsy language with which Gladkov's style is frequently pock-marked. The "cosmic" imagery of his earlier work—Gladkov had frequently done in prose what Kirillov and Gerasimov did in poetry—has also become less stilted in this story. When the weavers' looms remind him of "harps clad in grey work-clothes," the second half of the simile suitably tones down the first.

One piece of Gladkov's written during the NEP period is remarkable for its blunt speaking. Gladkov chose to call his "Heart's Blood" a short story, but it is a piece of literary criticism nonetheless. At the end of a literary soirée given by a workers' club for a popular writer, the writer is taken to the club's library to have some tea and to indulge in a friendly discussion. One of the workers listens unobtrusively to the discussion for a long time. Finally the librarian introduces him to the writer with the remark that Comrade Chizhov is a typesetter and the library's most faithful reader.

"How strongly are you aware of the responsibility your fame carries with it?"[75] Chizhov asks the writer without preliminaries.

The writer is a connoisseur of men. He understands instantly that Chizhov is one of those rare readers who open a book not for a pleasant pastime but in order to find an answer in its pages to the question of what is worth working and living for.

The writer admits to himself that he does not deserve such a reader, that he is weak in spirit, a coward, like other Soviet writers given over to hypocrisy and self-delusion. Chizhov realizes that his question has seriously disturbed the writer, who is already torn by doubts and vacillations, and seizes the opportunity to pour out the grievance he has on his mind. The greater part of "Heart's Blood" consists of a monologue in which Chizhov berates Soviet literature, accusing current writers of failing as prophets and teachers, of being cringing little men:

"You are too poor and mediocre to make us follow you. . . .
"Where is the inextinguishable fire that people used to have? . . . The classics stirred in people a spirit of indignation, protest and rebellion. What did you learn to understand from them? Nothing. You are ignoramuses and pitiful imitators. . . .
"Are we to believe that the wooden images you describe . . . were the makers of . . . the revolution? Are we to think that this dreary and obscure existence which you praise to the skies is indeed the nucleus and foundation of the human society of the future? . . .
"And you, you bureaucratic scribblers, you kill the living spirit of protest in man. You waste paper by covering it with patent lies: We are so wonderful! We live in a paradise! We are unique . . . in the universe! . . . You get drunk on self-praise to the point of not noticing how blind and nauseating you are. . . .
"You try to make even art live in a barracks. . . . You oversimplify until you reach the level of primitives, of illiterates. You forget that the creative act is a glance into the future; its whole point is in depicting not what is, but what must be. . . .
"You forget that the path we have traveled is strewn with the corpses of the fallen, with the dirt and abomination of our struggle." [76]

The writer has nothing to say in refutation.

During the NEP period there were still among the highly skilled workers self-educated men who thought for themselves and were not afraid to offer harsh criticism of the new regime. Gladkov's "Heart's Blood" might now be fittingly retitled "In Memoriam."

A Little Trilogy, published in the thirties but containing three stories written earlier, can hardly be called true satire. Gladkov imitates Shchedrin, but the Shchedrin of *The Golovlyovs* [*Gospoda Golovlyovy*], which is also not a satirical work.

The hero of the first story in *A Little Trilogy*, "The Cephalopod," is a wire-pulling careerist capable of any immoral action, of any crime, if it will win him a promotion.

Comrade Budash, hero of "The Inspired Goose," is a type which fills the ranks of Soviet editors, agitators and propagandists—men without principles or original ideas but with a "practiced agility of mind." Through the efforts of men like Budash, "the Press . . . has a wonderful way of transforming a mediocrity into a hero . . . you may kill a talent that the Republic could well use—but no matter!"[77]

The remaining story of *A Little Trilogy*, "The Immaculate Devil," relates the adventures of a fool obsessed with sex. The whole thing sounds like a dirty story and lends a tinge of vulgarity to the entire book.

After *Lyubasha's Tragedy* Gladkov's powers began to decline. During the war, he published a series of patriotic stories, all inferior to his earlier work.

Gladkov's postwar books *Story of My Childhood*, 1949,[78] and *Free Men*, 1951,[79] each of which was awarded a Stalin Prize, are novelized reminiscences, in which the reader senses the suffering of a spiritually depleted man. Galdkov's philosophy, his peculiar combination of Marxism and Freudianism, is still shallow and incoherent.

Nevertheless, to pay Gladkov his due, he was a keen observer and in his accurate recording of characteristic national types after the revolution he has few rivals.

22. The End of Prose Romanticism

YURI OLESHA (1899-)

Olesha once wrote:

. . . Despite the existing order, despite everybody and everything, I create a different world, ruled by no other law than my own . . . feeling.

What does this mean? There are two worlds, the old and the new! But the third one—what's it? It is the world of the artist.[1]

Aleksandr Grin and H. G. Wells also created worlds of their own. Their worlds, however, were sheer fantasy. Olesha could not, or did not want to, turn his back on Russia and her problems. His third world was created to preserve human personality from the deadening effect of the real Soviet world.

Many Soviet writers strive for extreme simplicity. Olesha always had it. The admirable limpidity of his style reveals another attractive characteristic, his intellectual honesty. Like Pasternak, he was not a revolutionary in art but believed in a gradual development of new forms.

Olesha's heroes are tragically conscious of the disharmony between their dreams and reality, and suffer from loneliness. But if they were not lonely, their lives would have no value or meaning. A passage from "I Look into the Past" applies to many of his characters:

A forever isolated life, the destiny to be alone everywhere and in all things, that is loneliness. People call him a dreamer, laugh at him, and he lets them, and even laughs with them, and they think that he makes up to them and despise him. He walks on alone, shoulders hunched, his head full of vanity, arrogance, self-abasement, and contempt for people, alternating with affection. Thoughts of death ceaselessly storm his mind.[2]

Olesha's *Envy*, 1927, the novel which brought him fame, explains his need to create his own world. Olesha knew that the changes in prospect would disfigure beyond recognition the face of the country and produce an entirely new breed of men. This new generation would, perhaps, possess nerves of steel and be able to grow roots even in a desert, but it would also become incapable of compassion and love.

The hero of *Envy*, Nikolai Kavalerov, is an odd mixture of the Chekhovian intellectual with the sad tramp of American movies. No wonder that Igor' Il'inski, the Russian counterpart of Chaplin, wanted to act the part of Kavalerov on the screen.

Kavalerov is obsessed with a desire for fame, not merely out of vanity but out of a longing to make some great spiritual contribution to posterity. He hopes for a miracle, though he knows in his heart that it cannot happen. "In our country, the roads to fame are barred. . . . Even the most outstanding man counts for nothing."[3] Kavalerov is not a genius, but he is a gifted man. Meeting with one failure after another, he turns into a nonentity. He dreams of a great love, such as Dante's for Beatrice.

You rustled past me like a bough full of flowers and leaves. . . .[4]
She was lighter than a shadow. The lightest of shadows, the shadow of falling snow, could have envied her.
"Valya shall be mine [thinks Kavalerov], my reward for everything —for the humiliations, for my frustrated youth, for my dog's life."[5]

But Valya is a practical girl, and dreams of a man like her uncle Andrei Babichev, a big business executive. Kavalerov is no match for her, because he will never make a career.

The romantic dreams do not prevent Kavalerov from becoming the lover of fat, common Anichka Prokopovich. One day he finds Valya's father, Ivan Babichev, in Anichka's bed. Babichev is not a bit embarrassed, and tries to put Kavalerov at ease: "I have something pleasant to tell you. . . . Tonight it's your turn, Kavalerov, to sleep with Anichka. Bravo!"[6]

Envy is built on grotesque contrasts. Kavalerov tries to build his own "third world," but his idealism founders against the dull meanness of daily life and he sinks lower and lower into filth.

Kavalerov is somehow overshadowed in the novel by the struggle between the two brothers Babichev.

The Soviet critic A. M. Gurvich has said that people like Andrei Babichev are "the soul of the Revolution."[7] A man of indomitable energy, dictatorial, buoyant (he sings in his bath), Andrei Babichev is a super-executive in charge of food processing and distribution, ruling over a vast network of kitchen factories. He is "the great sausage-maker, pastry cook and chef."[8]

Kavalerov despises him:

"Andrei Babichev, the great man . . . feels happy simply because a fine quality sausage has been produced. What is so wonderful about that? Is that fame? Why am I not in the least thrilled by that kind of fame? It makes me sick. . . . Biographies, monuments and history tell of a different kind of glory."[9]

Andrei is a happy man, but he can be inhuman. With sadistic satisfaction, he delivers his own brother, the alcoholic Ivan, to the GPU.

Ivan is an engineer and could have made a brilliant career. Instead, he is driven to drink by his disillusionment in industrialization and his hatred for it. Fundamentally, he is an inventor, and he would have liked to preserve the imaginative, creative spirit of earlier years, when machinery was a dream of the future. Imagination had created the machine, and then the machine killed imagination.

Ivan Babichev is a typical Russian. He hates his practical brother because he represents energy and action without any of the finer perceptions. Through him Olesha flouted Bolshevism as action minus imagination. Gurvich said of Ivan Babichev that he "defends the great and disappearing human values which have come to be considered trite and worthless." [10]

Ivan has the courage to maintain that Andrei is not really liberating woman in freeing her of kitchen drudgery with his ready-cooked foods. In fact, he is robbing women of family life and trying to abolish the family. Eventually everybody will become the property of the state.

To halt the process, to avenge the insult to human emotions, Ivan invents a machine which will confound the "mechanizers." It is a marvelous machine. It will level mountains. It can fly, lift loads, crush ores. It will serve as stove for the kitchen, as a child's cradle, as a heavy gun. One machine which can do everything, the answer to the quest of the new age. And then Ivan realizes that the invention gives him the power to avenge the wrong done to humanity by the machine worshippers. So that his machine may never serve the new men, who would use it to devour human beings, he deliberately "humanizes" it, turns it into a "vapid, sentimental, prevaricating, unscrupulous woman" singing "old-fashioned silly love songs." [11] He makes a mockery of the godhead of the new men in the name of personal emotion.

In the brothers Babichev, Olesha depicts two faces of Russia, the machine and the beast. He saw the great Communist reforms as a struggle between these two. The animal man was superior to the mechanized man in that he might realize his degradation and change into a human being again, while the "machine" could only run down and stop.

Olesha's stories of the twenties show highly original modernist leanings. The following passage from "Love," 1928, bears an elusive resemblance to the painting of Filonov:

The architectural lines in the flight of birds, of flies and of bugs are illusory, yet one could distinguish a pattern, outlines of arcs, bridges, towers, terraces—a delicate, swiftly moving, continuously changing city.[12]

Sometimes, Olesha resembles the early Marc Chagall, as in "The Cherry Stone," 1929:

But what is happening to this man walking along placidly? He sees his shadow before him. It moves along the ground, stretching out far ahead; it has long pale legs. I cross a vacant lot, the shadow scales a brick wall and suddenly loses its head.[13]

Olesha chose his colors with method: gay, sunny shades for childhood memories, happy dreams and things that happened before the revolution; ashen grays for the Russia of the end of the NEP period.

The hero of "Cherry Stone" wants to plant a cherry stone, but cannot find a place where a cherry tree would have a chance to grow. The entire country is being clothed in asphalt and concrete; everywhere trees are being felled, to be replaced by factory buildings.

At first glance, this looks like a simple tale for children. Then we realize that the child in Olesha has bared the deepest, most complex contradictions inherent in the Communist system.

In *A Writer's Notebook*[14] and in "Bits from the Secret Notes of the Fellow Traveler Zand,"[15] Olesha argued with the Communist Party, maintaining that, by treating intellectuals as potential enemies, the Party destroyed a reservoir of brainpower it might tap with profit. It was a loss to push waverers—as likely to turn toward Communism as against it—into the opposite camp.

Olesha is a good playwright. The play *Three Fat Men*, based on an earlier novel of the same name,[16] is a fantasy representation of revolution, marred from the Soviet point of view by the fact that the enemies of the working class have something engaging about them. "The author used the bourgeois social structure as one would a Christmas tree," wrote Gurvich, ". . . to hang all sorts of balloons, stars and flickering lights on it."[17]

In *A List of Blessings*, 1931, the heroine, Yelena Goncharova, a famous actress, plays the role of Hamlet, with astonishing success. After the performance, there is a question period, and somebody asks:

"You are a famous actress and make good money. Why are you dissatisfied? Why do your eyes have such a troubled expression in your photographs?"
"Because it is very hard for me to be a citizen of the new world,"[18]

answers Goncharova.

To the question why the theater has staged *Hamlet* instead of a modern play, she replies, "Modern plays are schematic and lack sincerity and imagination. . . . " Her answers frighten the director of the theater. He keeps ringing his bell for order, and Goncharova makes fun of him: "Comrade Orlovski, have your bell ready, I am going to say something subversive."[19]

The very truthfulness and sincerity which make her a great actress set her at odds with the regime. In a dialogue with the up-and-coming Communist Fedotov:

Goncharova: The Revolution has robbed me of the past without showing me the future. . . .
 A normal life is possible only when thought and feeling harmonize. Intellectually, I embraced Communism . . . but my feelings were against it. . . .
 I am an actress, which means that I must be human above all. An actress is great only when she embodies a theme universally understandable and affecting.
Fedotov: You mean socialism?
Goncharova: No.
Fedotov: Then what is it?
Goncharova: Human loneliness.[20]

The actress keeps a diary in two parts, which she describes as "the two halves of a single conscience, a mix-up which drives me crazy." In the first part she lists the "crimes of the revolution," and in the second its "blessings." When a friend suggests she had better hide it, Goncharova replies: "Don't worry, these aren't common complaints about food shortages . . . I record crimes against personality. There are many things in our government's policy that I cannot accept." But she notes the good points too. "I am not a counterrevolutionary," she says. "I am a person of the old world, arguing with myself."[21]

In the end she leaves Russia for Paris. But the decadent, pleasure-seeking West disillusions her and makes her homesick. After deciding to return to "the land of the Soviets" she is killed trying to save a Communist leader from an émigré assassin. She dies regretting that she had been unable to become completely at one with the revolution.

Was this ending a concession to Bolshevik propaganda under cover of which Olesha permitted himself to discuss the conflict between the intelligentsia and communism? It was more than that. The country had been severed from Europe, and the Russian intelligentsia, ignorant of the West, idealized it. The play smashed such illusions. *A List of Blessings* is hopelessly pessimistic. It is also one of the best plays of the postrevolutionary theater.

The hero of Olesha's movie script "A Stern Young Man," 1934, is Grisha Fokin, who draws up a "moral code" for a Soviet youth organization featuring, among other things, modesty, sincerity and magnanimity, and defending the role of individual sentiment.

"Those are bourgeois virtues," objects one boy.

"No, they are human,"[22] says another.

The central problem is that of equality in socialist society, the rights of the especially gifted as against the prerogatives of the collective. For various indiscretions in the script—one of the characters, for instance, says, "I see much suffering around me. . . . Abolishing capitalism does not necessarily mean abolishing misery"[23]—Olesha was thereafter effectively silenced. A film was produced on the basis of his scenario, but it was never exhibited.[24] He did continue to do a little film writing and editing, but even this work was interrupted by a term in a labor camp. He reappeared on the literary scene after the war, with a few insignificant short stories and newspaper articles.[25]

LEONID LEONOV (1899-   )

Leonid Leonov, now well known as author of realistic psychological novels, started out with Hoffmannesque romantic stories and with fairy tales in the style of Andersen or of *The Arabian Nights*. In this group belong the three stories contained in his first small book of 1923 ("The Wooden Queen," "The Knave of Diamonds" and "Valya's Doll"),[26] as well as the short novels *Tuatamur*[27] and *Khalil'*, both of 1924.

Sergei Klychkov's influence is apparent in the feeling for the earth and its magic powers in Leonov's early stories on Russian themes, such as "What Happened to Yakov Pichunok,"[28] "Yegorushka's Death"[29] and especially "Buryga."[30] The last title is the name of an engaging little wood-devil who goes to live with people when the ax disturbs the peace of his forests. After some upsetting adventures in the households of a count, a merchant and others he returns to his native haunts.

Even in the more realistic early tales, the romantic strain persists in the descriptions of nature and of patriarchal peasant life, as in *The Petushikhino Breakthrough*,[31] *The End of a Little Man*,[32] and *Kovyakin's Journal*.[33] All three describe the struggle between the old order and the new in which the latter won by virtue of its youthful, vigorous drive and tenacity.

Leonov's first full-scale novel, *The Badgers*, 1924,[34] deals with a peasant uprising against the Soviets. The revolt fails, because the Bolsheviks are far better organized and because they play shrewdly on the peasants' desire to return to peaceful work, which is stronger than their wrath. Leonov's approach was completely impartial. In a letter of September 8, 1925, Gorki wrote to him about the novel: "Not once in the three hundred pages did I notice or feel that maudlin, prettifying manner that has long been the rule in Russian writings about the peasantry."[35]

Leonov's second novel, *The Thief*, 1927, is his best to date. A Civil War hero, Vekshin, devoted to communism though an anarchist at heart, finds himself at loose ends when the fight is over. He has a chance of using his particular talents in the service of the GPU if he can forego his scruples. But it is one thing to kill an enemy in open battle, and quite another to kill him in a torture-chamber. Vekshin prefers a career of private crime and becomes a "safe-cracker" of legendary reputation in the underworld. He feels that in adopting the New Economic Policy the Party has monstrously betrayed the people, that nothing is left of the revolution except shadows of an old fire playing on the wall. Velkshin's counterpart, the successful NEP businessman, Zavarikhin, is also, in the end, ruined by the Party. Leonov derided the notion of solving social problems and putting an end to suffering through mechanization of the human being and standardization of thought. One of the characters says:

"If I were in charge of the world, I'd attach some sort of telegraph-tape machine to everybody's head. In the morning a designated official would [examine the recording] and write down a decision." [36]

The novel is an indictment of communism for its inhumanity to man.

In *Sot'*, 1930,[37] Leonov's third novel, he again related a highly dramatic clash between the old and the new with the utmost objectivity. A paper-mill is to be built near an old monastery deep in the woods. To the monks it means the end of the world. The two Bolsheviks in charge of the project, fairly ordinary men who rise to the challenge of a superhuman task, are remarkably true-to-life portrayals of dynamic Communist "builders." The reader is left with the impression that the new order could not but win, if only because it had the steely grip and the drive that the old one lacked.

The hero of the short novel *The Locusts*, 1931,[38] is another typical Communist leader. No disaster abashes him. Whatever the faults of the Bolshevik characters, they have organizing ability—and that, implied the author, is what the country needed most.

Leonov's next two novels, *Skutarevski*, 1932,[39] and *Road to the Ocean*, 1935,[40] marked his capitulation to the Party line and a decline in his art. Of *Skutarevski* Leonov said:

In the complex process of political reappraisals generally known as the reorientation of the intelligentsia, I distinguish two phases, very different from each other. One, long drawn-out and not in the least dramatic

—the scientists' and technologists' progress from total denial of the revolution's constructive forces to recognition of the stern necessity of working for the Soviet power. And the second, much shorter but more highly charged and arduous, with all the attributes of a cataclysm —from the old, largely illusory and forever discredited philosophies to the realistic and practical *Weltanschauung* of the working class. . . . *Skutarevski* is a novel about the second phase in the reorientation of the Russian intelligentsia, the one in which they grasped the meaning of the greatest of revolutions.[41]

The hero, however, is a conformist rather than a convert, and the novel, in the last analysis, is a glorification of opportunism.

In *Road to the Ocean* Leonov was even less outspoken and remained very cautious in his condemnation of terrorism. Many of his characters are demoralized by fear. In Leonov's interpretation, the intelligentsia had no choice but to work for the Soviet regime. Resistance was futile and merely intensified terrorism. To the authorities, however, he suggested in this book that in many cases reconciliation might be forfeited by excessive harshness. Significantly the hero, a political commissar, does not carry through the "unmasking" of a counterrevolutionary. *Road to the Ocean* explains Leonov's own motivation in coming to terms with the Party, and it must be said that it was of a higher moral order than either Ehrenburg's or Tolstoi's.

In *Russian Forest*, 1953,[42] Leonov made an effort to return to his former objectivity. The novel treats the problem of the stripping of the natural resources of the country and efforts to put an end to such practices.

He has written a number of plays: "The Orchards of Polovchansk" (1938),[43] "The Wolf"[44] (also known as "Sandukov's Flight"), *Invasion* (1942),[45] "Lyonushka,"[46] *An Ordinary Man* (1944),[47] and "The Golden Coach" (1955).[48]

In Leonov's works, for the most part unbiased, readers may profitably study postrevolutionary Russian life.

Like Leonov, two other Serapion Brothers, Nikolai Nikitin and Veniamin Kaverin, at first wrote in a highly romantic vein. Both, however, produced their distinctive and most mature work at a later period.

BORIS LAVRENYOV (1894-   )

Lavrenyov began, before the revolution, with moderately Futurist, unoriginal verse. Even in his later poems, there are echoes now of Konstantin Fofanov, now of Igor' Severyanin. As a poet he is at his best, however, when he writes in Gumilyov's virile style.

Lavrenyov fought in the First World War and then served in the Red Army until 1921. He wrote of this experience:

War is a wonderful school! It cleanses the world of scum, filth and muck and, in the crucible of spirit and of will, tempers the best and the bravest and the most worthy of life.[49]

Although his hopes of a military career were not realized, his participation in the Civil War provided him with a wealth of material which he used in his *nouvelles* "Wind," "Starry Blossoms" and *The Forty-first*, all of 1924, and *Story of a Simple Thing*, 1925.

The style of his early stories is often extremely ornate and, indeed, awkward. But he caught the romantic spirit of the revolution which many other writers, absorbed in its more sordid aspects, overlooked. His portrayals of revolutionaries are particularly successful. Even when idealized, they are not lifeless puppets.

In "Wind" Lenin is seen through the eyes of the sailor Vasili Gulyavin:

Stocky and vigorous, he was tossing words—no, not words but chunks of iron into the human sea, throwing out his short, powerful arm in measured movements....
... Listening to him, Gulyavin felt the iron words pounding against his skull and kindling dark fury in his breast ... and he surrendered to the sweeping fire.[50]

Lenin may seem to have stepped down from a propaganda poster, but Gulyavin is made lifelike:

Stone-hard cheekbones sticking out like boils, and impudent brown eyes. Two black ribbons, like tails, at the back of his head, and "Petropavlovsk" in gold letters across his forehead.[51]

Lavrenyov's sailors resemble Fyodor Bogorodski's paintings of revolutionary "fine fellows" in their brazen yet good-natured cynicism and their reckless daring.

No less picturesque is the woman ataman Lyol'ka, with her bold, devil-may-care good looks. The critic Shteinman's reproach that Lavrenyov had been guilty of cheap sensationalism in drawing Lyol'ka is unfounded. She is lawless and dissolute, but endowed with an indomitable spirit which redeems the coarseness in her. Gulyavin orders Lyol'ka to be shot, though he has been her lover, and literary critics interpreted the theme of the story as a conflict between passion and revolutionary duty. It is, rather, a conflict between friendship and love, more human than political.

The theme of passion versus duty is treated in *The Forty-first*. A Red girl sniper, Maryutka, and a White officer who has been taken prisoner are stranded alone on an island and fall in love despite their political differences. She is impressed by his mild, well-bred manner, different from the casual roughness to which she is used. He is thoroughly tired of the Civil War, but when he suggests that they both should drop out of the struggle she is indignant— she cannot abandon her people while they are "fighting for truth and justice."[52] When the Whites approach, she obeys her orders not to give up the prisoner and kills her lover. He is the forty-first White officer she has "sniped."

In *Story of a Simple Thing*, a Bolshevik, disguised as a Frenchman, Léon Couturier, remains in a city occupied by the Whites and carries out dangerous underground work. When the Whites discover his identity and order him to be shot, he says: "I overplayed, like a fool, and fell into the paws of your henchmen. . . . The cause entrusted to me is lost through my failure. Now I must make amends if only with my death."[53] The story loses somewhat from being written in standard "thriller" style.

In the novel *The Seventh Satellite*, 1928, a tsarist general, Adamov, is so impractical and unable to adjust himself to the new times that soon after his release from a Bolshevik prison he begs to be readmitted: "Take me back, please take me back. Or shoot me. I've nowhere else to go. No home, nothing. Everywhere I've gone I've been thrown out, and I don't want to die in the street."[54]

He is given a job first as jail laundryman and then as a "specialist" in the army. He "accepts" the Revolution but feels uncomfortable in the role of Bolshevik collaborator. In the end, he is captured and shot by the Whites as a renegade.

The feeling of the book is grimly realistic, very different from the romantic enthusiasm of Lavrenyov's early stories:

It was impossible to quench life. Out of every crack in the ruins, it looked at the sorry present with thousands of mocking, resolute eyes. . . . It laughed at the times and, oblivious of the destroyed past, was building anew, clutching a broken hammer and dented pliers in its hardened, stonelike hands.[55]

Disillusionment is also apparent in the plays *The Break*, 1927,[56] and *Enemies*, 1929.[57]

The NEP period convinced Lavrenyov that all the destruction had been futile. Thousands had perished in the Civil War to build a new world, and, instead, the old was being hurriedly and clumsily patched up. The following passage is from "A World in a Bit of Glass":

You who live in the great noisy world with vast horizons . . . and limitless space, who love the brass music of thunder and the flares of cosmic lightning, you, the people of the macrocosm, have for a moment taken a tiny crystal ball into your hands—the hands made to rule the earth—and you can see a tiny, scintillating microcosm, created by me, a toy world enclosed in a bit of glass. . . . In that crystal ball, as in your own colossal world, which you are rebuilding usefully in sweat and blood, dwell the same constant sister-companions of man: Love, Hate and Death.[58]

This is very characteristic of the Lavrenyov of the NEP period. As he had formerly admired the common man exalted and made heroic by the revolution, so he now loved him for his suffering and his plight.

In "The Woodcut," a story of 1928, Lavrenyov posed the problem of art in the new society. The hero, Kudrin, who had given up painting for administrative work in the Party, decides to return to his real calling—it is not clear whether from love of art or under the necessity of putting his art at the service of the new regime.

There are indications of a conflict between Kudrin's artistic conscience and Party requirements: "In a socialist society, the artist has a different task. He must not discourage and depress people with pictures of suffering and grief."[59]

In Lavrenyov's 1947 play, *For Those at Sea*,[60] there are unexpected flares of the old romantic fire, but it is a dying fire.

In addition to the usual difficulties, Lavrenyov may have been handicapped also by the fact that much of his time was devoted to administrative work in the Union of Soviet Writers. The nature of the post he occupied in the mid-1950's—editor of the magazine *Druzhba narodov* [Friendship of the Peoples]—indicates that, belatedly, he had become a member of the Party.

ALEKSANDR GRIN
(pseudonym of A. S. Grinevski, 1880-1932)

Aleksandr Grin's brand of romanticism is an anomaly in Soviet literature. In dealing with him, Communist critics have customarily resorted to a curl of the lip and summary dismissal of his writing as frivolous, trashy adventure thrillers. This is underestimation with a vengeance. It is true that Grin's work consists almost exclusively of fantasy yarns of adventure and romance which can be read, with pleasure, for the sake of their exciting plots alone. Yet at the same time these yarns are often veined with provocative meaning. He is something of an Acmeist in prose.

Grin once said of himself that he was in constant need of a living fairy tale. A public in need of the same fare made him one of the most popular Soviet writers during his lifetime and afterwards. He had begun to publish a decade before the Revolution, and had brought out perhaps ten books before 1917. Then he fell silent for several years. From the time of his reappearance in print, in 1922, he produced another prodigious body of fantasy fiction, all of it in direct opposition to the vogue of "flat-bottom naturalism"—a term of Grin's own coinage for the documentary approach.

Grin himself had enough imagination to create a whole new continent, accessible only by climbing high mountain ranges or by sea, dotted with towns and villages and large ports bearing such exotic names as Zurbagan, Liss, Gel'-G'yu, and populated by sailors, dreamers and good and loving women, with a proper admixture of scoundrels, brutes and ladies of easy virtue—a continent on which Grin and his readers escaped from bleak reality into a world of freedom, romantic love and high adventure.

The exotic flavor of his stories and their extraordinary vividness gave rise to various rumors about the author. He was often taken for a foreign writer, usually an Englishman. It was said that he had stolen manuscripts from the captain of a foreign vessel on which he had shipped and that he was now translating them into Russian and passing them off as his own. It was whispered that he was an agent of the British Intelligence Service.

His *Autobiographical Tale* (1929) dispelled these rumors. It tells of an extremely hard life which drove him to escape from the chronic dreariness of everyday in romantic and bizarre dreams.

Grin was born in Vyatka, the son of a Pole who had been exiled to Siberia for participation in the Polish rising of 1863 and of a Russian mother. The boy was poor in his studies and was suspended on several occasions for laziness and bad conduct. But he read enormously. His favorite writers were Mayne Reid, Fenimore Cooper and Gustave Aimard, and later Conan Doyle, Jack London and Rider Haggard. He was constant in his admiration for Lermontov, Ivan Bunin, Edgar Allan Poe and Hamsun, however, and it is from them that he learned the art of the short story.

As a schoolboy he dreamed of running away to America. With an old hunting rifle his father had given him he wandered about the woods and the nearby villages, acquiring the reputation of an idler who would come to no good. He shipped as a sailor in the merchant marine, out of Odessa. Narrow-chested and sickly, he was a bad sailor. He then hired himself out to scrape off paint from old ships, led a hobo's existence, sleeping in empty boilers, under boats and beside fences, joined a company of fishermen, and finally, with the help of Kuprin, made his debut as a writer.

In *Autobiographical Tale* Grin gives a very detailed account of his life up to this point; then half-truths and omissions occur with increasing frequency, apparently for political reasons. He had joined the Social Revolutionary party and had been sentenced to two years'

Prose During the Uneasy Truce 313

imprisonment for engaging in subversive activities, but soon abandoned the movement because of ideological differences.

During his service in the tsarist army he was known as a fine shot and a rotten soldier. While fighting with the Red Army after the revolution he came down with typhus. Later in Petrograd, still weak from his illness and penniless, he was rescued by Maxim Gorki, who found work for him.

Grin was an alcoholic and went on periodic binges. He would be found lying in the gutter, covered with mud, or in fits of rage, he would throw bottles and plates of food.

The last two years of his life, when reviews and publishing houses no longer accepted his work, were a period of constant humiliations. He tried to become a geography teacher in Theodosia, but was turned down on the grounds of political security. For a livelihood he carved toy frigates and caravels, fashioned wooden boxes and bark skiffs. He died in poverty.

In his own life Grin seldom left his imaginary Zurbagan and Gel-G'yu to return to Soviet Russia. He refused to be imprisoned in a totalitarian state.

In defiance of minds which deal with life in a logical and niggardly fashion, minds which have raised their little gray flag over the majestic vastness of the world with its insoluble mysteries in the short-lived and ludicrous belief that all men will direct their footsteps toward that little flag—in defiance of all that, I say, there are occasional lives the mission of which seems to be to tune themselves to the majestic and enigmatic whisper of the unexplored.[61]

"Grin looked at the pallid and melancholy woods of the mute North and painted them as brilliant and marvelous landscapes,"[62] said Konstantin Paustovski. In the north of Russia Grin had encountered Old Believers who still preserved legends of Belovod'ye, their paradise on earth. Although he took a skeptical view of the ritual aspect of their religion, he appropriated their dream of a new world and transformed Belovod'ye into his romantic Zurbagan.

He knows no peer in conveying the feel of Russia's turmoil in apparent aloofness from social and political issues. His ostensibly unpolitical imaginings, when combined with his skillful psychological treatment, however, may sometimes have been less innocent than they seem. Even in those stories in which Grin brought himself back to the world of actuality, the reader is kept constantly guessing whether what is taking place is fantasy or reality.

In "The Ratcatcher," the first version of which was published in 1924, fantasy is used to reveal the true meaning of totalitarian ideology. The action takes place in the Petrograd of Civil War days. Grin's description of the life of the city is entirely realistic:

I have seen a stove kept going with a sideboard, a kettle brought to the boil on a lamp, horsemeat fried in coconut oil and wooden beams stolen from collapsing buildings.[63]

The food shortage was especially hard on the intelligentsia, impractical and unable readily to adjust itself. Susie, the heroine of the tale, has been selling books from her father's library:

"I don't steal them; I take them from the shelves when Father is asleep. My mother was dying. . . . We sold everything then, nearly everything. We had no bread, no wood, no kerosene. You know what that means?"[64]

The hero, who has been seriously ill and has left the hospital too soon, finds shelter for the night in the abandoned building of the old Central Bank, where two hundred and sixty rooms stand

like water in a pond, still and dead. . . . The silence which we always hear inside ourselves, was luring me, like a forest, with memories of the sounds of life; it was hiding behind the half-shut door of the next room.[65]

Life has fled from the building but the objects left preserve a memory of bustling activity. There are piles of documents,

a broken desk, a door torn out of its hinges and stood against the wall . . . a cupboard, an abandoned chair. . . . Now and then I came across a steel safe, its heavy door standing open, like that of an empty oven. . . .[66]

It seemed to me that I was walking along the bottom of an aquarium which had been emptied of water or among wastes of ice or—an impression which was the clearest and most sinister of all—that I was wandering through past centuries which had somehow penetrated into the present....[67]

Finally, in delirium, the hero comes to the brightly lighted central hall, spared in the revolutionary conflagration, and sees a company of elegantly dressed men and women whirling in a mad dance. He later discovers that the scene was an apocalyptic hallucination brought on by fever.

Given shelter by Susie and her father, the hero opens an ancient book and reads that the world will soon be filled with rats in the shape and semblance of men. The dancing figures had been not ladies and gentlemen but rats, a swarm of horrible rats:

> These perfidious and grim creatures have the intellectual powers of human beings. They are abetted by pestilence, famine, war, invasions and floods. Then they gather under the sign of mysterious transformations, acting like people, and you will speak to them and not know them for what they are.[68]

The assemblage of rats is headed by a rat with the enigmatic title of "Liberator."

From the beginning of his literary career, in 1906, to the day of his death Grin had a standing quarrel with revolutionaries. He had left the Social Revolutionary Party because—as he clearly indicates in his first volume of stories *Cap of Invisibility* [*Shapka-nevidimka*]—his fellow members, embittered and full of hatred, were intent on an orgy of destruction in which he declined to share. He remained faithful to the revolutionary dream of freedom, but not "a poisoned freedom," without love.

Many years later, in "A Tale Ended Thanks to a Bullet," Grin recounted the substance of his first quarrel with the revolutionaries. A writer is working on a story about two anarchists, a man and a woman, who are planning an act of terrorism. He is all action and resolution, while she is full of doubts and hesitation. Kolomb, the writer, is at a loss to explain to himself the behavior to which his heroine is impelled:

> The mysterious laws of the spirit, contrary to her resolution, convictions and philosophy, bring the heroine to a salutary last-moment re-

treat from her plan. . . . She steals the bomb and hides it in a place where it will not endanger human lives; she thus changes from a destroyer to one of the common crowd and leaves her lover in order to lead [its] simple, ordinary, but essentially profoundly human life. . . .[69]

Only as Kolomb himself faces death, wounded during a visit to the battle zone, does he realize that the fierce desire to live is made up of the need to love as well as of animal instincts and thus comes to an understanding of the woman anarchist.

After 1917 Grin's running quarrel with revolutionaries was continued in his resistance to Marxist cosmogony and dialectical materialism. In one of the discursive passages to which he is given, he writes in "The Enemies":

I know of no more ugly habit than judging "by appearances." One of the chief defects of the thinking apparatus is its inability to pass beyond the limits of the apparent. This could be applied to the least details of existence, but through necessity I shall confine myself to but a few examples. We often speak of a man's face, a man's appearance, that bulk which is apprehended only by the senses and which conceals his true spiritual essence, frequently even from himself. Fully half our actions are subconsciously conditioned by our idea of our personal appearance—[moral] lapses, suicide, self-deception, megalomania, and self-appraisals so mistaken that they might be likened to forming an impression of oneself by gazing into a concave or convex mirror. Our attitude toward others is at best a mixture of two kinds of impressions: those produced by their actions, words and thoughts, and those arising from the qualities with which we endow them on the basis of their physical appearance.[70]

The flaw in Communist ideology, according to Grin, was that it treated wealth born of men's minds as though it had an existence independent of the will and organized action of its creators; the created thus became the master of the creator, who was sacrificed to it. Grin regarded this situation as absurd; to him, the machine and the state alike, before becoming reality, were seen by man in his imagination. Worship of material things resulted in man's disowning both God and his own soul. In Grin's fantasies the physical world is always subordinated to the inner world which exists in each man's mind. By acquiring the habit of living in the world of imagination, he believed, man might prevent his "I" from dissolving in the "we." The secret of the extraordinary charm and great popularity of Grin's stories among Soviet readers, living under conditions which suppressed and degraded the human personality, lies in the strong assertion of their individuality by his audacious and romantic heroes.

In 1939 Paustovski wrote:

Had Grin put his unbridled imagination to use in writing books about real life—life as it really is—he might have won a place for himself in the foremost rank of writers, those whose names are spoken with love.[71]

To this, the number of Grin's readers and the posthumous publication of his *Fantastic Tales*, despite Communist disapproval of his work, are the best retort.

Paustovski also regretted that "when the revolution held before Grin on its outstretched hand the very world he had long dreamed of, Grin refused to believe in it."[72] It is not that Grin mistook the world he was offered; he rejected it, and he was willing to pay the price of his rashness. Frank, in Grin's novel *The Road to Nowhere*, 1930, says:

The lowest abyss and the highest peak are the two extremes of the same chain. A rejected tramp, I rejected everyone myself. Let my women be dirty and drunk, my wine cheap, my gambling for low stakes, my traveling done in the open, on a deck or on the top of a boxcar, these are the same things that a millionaire enjoys, this too is living, damn it, and if one looks at it from the esthetic point of view, it really has a certain colorfulness and originality, as proved by the predilection of many writers for descriptions of dives, paupers and prostitutes.[73]

Despite the cavalier treatment of Grin by orthodox critics, he had many admirers among other Soviet writers. In the 1920's his work and the personality of the man himself laid hold on the imagination of Konstantin Paustovski, who portrayed Grin in the character of the writer Gart in his *Black Sea* cycle of stories. Paustovski's own work also displays a strong romantic bent. His most significant writing, however, was done at a much later period.

23. Naturalism Bidding for Trouble

LEV GUMILEVSKI (1890-   )

Gumilevski has been unjustly classified as a "dime novel" author. He did write a few thrillers, such as *Kharita* (1926), "The Land of the Hyperboreans,"[1] and science fiction stories, but the novel with which he made his name, *Dog's Alley* (1927) is an objective picture of the sexual life of Soviet young people in the 1920's. Because of its stress on the cynicism and dissoluteness prevalent among Komsomol groups, efforts were made to discredit the book. Tarasenkov wrote in the *Literary Encyclopedia*:

This novel, which undeservedly brought fame to the author, in a quasi-literary form attempts to find orthodox solutions to the sex and morality problems facing the postrevolutionary younger generation.[2]

Out of the Civil War came a generation of young animals— people who had not known gentleness but had seen plenty of blood. The Soviet system did nothing to mitigate the consequences of their training in violence.

Khorokhorin, a Komsomol member who has come to the university from the GPU, asserts aggressively:

"We deny that there is such a thing as love. That's nothing but bourgeois nonsense and it interferes with work. An amusement for the rich, that's what it is!"[3]

When he takes a fancy to a woman, he wants her to hurry and undress, because he has no time to waste on ridiculous sentiments and unnecessary preliminaries. "No complications, no love tragedies,"[4] is his creed. To him the sex act means no more than smoking a cigarette.

The instructor Burov challenges him:

"Have you any idea what love is? ... Love is a terrific creative force to which we owe a great many works of art ... and heroic deeds. ... A superficial acquaintance with biology sometimes leads to theories such as yours ... that intercourse is all there is to it."[5]

Zoya Osokina, too, daughter of a former priest turned criminologist, has a strong aversion for the current practices. Her fainthearted father may have given up the priesthood, but Zoya pays dearly for having an unsuitable "class origin":

For the first time, she felt isolated, unwanted, a stranger. "The regional committee has rejected me!"
"Why?"
"Because father used to be a priest, of course! . . . They have expelled me from the university, they won't let me join the Komsomol." [6]

The book inspires profound distaste for the cynical repudiation of moral standards among Soviet young people of the mid-1920's. Gumilevski is a prolific writer, but he remains known chiefly as the author of *Dog's Alley*.

In recent years he has published several biographical novels and sketches, mainly for young readers—*N. Ye. Zhukovski* (1943), *Russian Engineers* (1947) and *A. M. Butlerov*, 1951.

SERGEI MALASHKIN (1890-1941?)

In spite of a politically impeccable background—son of poor peasants, Party member since before the revolution—Sergei Malashkin's standing in the Party was shaky. His books provoked angry strictures, but he showed no readiness to reform. "An author should write only of things he has seen with his own eyes and felt with his own heart," he asserted in the introduction to his story "Moon on the Right-Hand Side, or An Extraordinary Love," 1926,[7] and he followed this course.

As characterized in the Soviet *Literary Encyclopedia*, Malashkin "depicts the revolutionary era with an exaggerated, unwholesome interest in the darker aspects and perversions of life."[8] And his pictures are somber—he was a candid writer.

In "Moon on the Right-Hand Side" he laid bare the selfishness and bestiality of Party bureaucrats whose disproportionate privileges and indifference to the people's needs betrayed the whole meaning of the revolution. The heroine is psychologically crippled by having been the mistress of twenty-two Komsomol members. Malashkin was accused of representing the entire Komsomol organization as depraved. Actually, the book was a plea for moral regeneration, and attacked the Party elite for setting a bad example.

"The Sick Man"[9] was obviously influenced by Dostoyevski's *The Double*. Malashkin's understanding of Dostoyevski was neither deep nor subtle, but the fact that he chose him for a model was, in view of the official attitude toward that writer, one more proof of his independence.

The "sick man" is a former commissar, Zavulonov, now insane. He began to lose his balance after shooting a White Army sergeant, who met death with dignity and courage. Gradually Zavulonov came to see all the killings in the revolution as unjustifiable murders. The sergeant's doubles appear to him everywhere—and the doubles occupy high Party posts. They are prosperous, important, overbearing. Malashkin can only be saying that all Russia had become a camp run by sergeants. Zavulonov also has visions of a great bird; he wants to reach it but cannot. The bird symbolizes the spirit of integrity and charity that has gone out of the revolution.

To escape the stoning of the critics, for a time Malashkin avoided topical subjects. Going back to the beginnings of the revolution, he produced the long tedious novel *Two Wars and Two Kinds of Peace*, which remained unfinished, and the more interesting war story *Anani Zhmurkin's Notes*, both of 1927.

With his next novel, *Yevlampi Zavalishin's Paper About a People's Commissar and About Our Times*, 1928, he returned to the subject that troubled him most deeply, the rift between Party members and the common people. As a satire, the novel harks back to Saltykov-Shchedrin's *The Town of Glupov*.

Among his later works, the novel *The Columns March*, 1931,[10] is fairly well known. Here again Malashkin proved to be an observant chronicler—in this case, of the life of kolkhoz peasants. While stressing peasant resistance to collectivization, he conceded that the kolkhoz system, no matter how unpleasant, was the quickest, if not the only, way of solving pressing economic problems. To that extent, Malashkin submitted to the Party directives, but he tried to be objective at least in his description of the life and feelings of the peasantry, and thus spoiled the propaganda value of his book. After this novel he was finished as a writer.

His last published work was a sketch entitled "Sasha Rozhkov" [11] which appeared in 1941. It has been reported, unofficially, that he died in the same year while taking part in the defense of Moscow.

MIKHAIL KOZAKOV (1897-1954)

Mikhail Kozakov applied Dostoyevski's methods more ingeniously and forcefully than Malashkin. His short novel *Little Man Adameiko*, 1927,[12] is frankly patterned on *Crime and Punishment* but given an utterly dissimilar political twist. The hero observes, with a mixture of malice and regret, that neither the material circumstances nor the morale of the common people have improved since the revolution, which began as an effort to promote general welfare. He comes to the conclusion that everyone should develop his creative drives and steel his will power—in an individual, as opposed to collective, effort—and then apply his new strength first of all to helping the weak and injured, if necessary by liquidating the parasites still left after the revolution and using their possessions to relieve the plight of the deserving. Adameiko plans to kill a rich woman in order to help a poor family, but induces another man to commit the actual murder.

One of Kozakov's best things is the story "A Party Affair," [13] about disenchanted Communists.

The novel *Nine Points*,[14] in several volumes, intended as an epic-scale treatment of the prerevolutionary and immediate postrevolutionary period, remained unfinished. Kozakov's talent was not suited to the long novel.

LEONID GRABAR' (1896-   )

Leonid Grabar' insisted on a candid presentation of life "as is." In an "author's digression" in the novel *Selwynites* he wrote:

> Public opinion has seen in my work willful slander rather than an attempt at cleaning up, and literary critics have accused me of depicting our society as a crowd of leftovers and misfits. I grumbled in anger, surprised at people's lack of perspicacity, and insisted on my right to sweep the dirt out of the house.

[For] there was a time when people vacillated, took to drinking, made mistakes, lost their way, degenerated. I have known that time....[15]

Grabar' has been maligned as a sensation hunter and a third-rate Artsybashev. While not an outstanding talent he had sincerity and the courage to speak the truth.

His short novel "Bricks" traces ironically the careers of two Soviet doctors. Yegor Timoshenko, reared in the tradition of "serving the people," goes to work as assistant physician at a brick factory. Right away he incurs the displeasure of his chief, Dr. Uspenski:

"Are you crazy? Sending this guy to the dispensary? A vacation for this bird?"

"But, Andrei Osipovich, his left lung is affected. . . . He is sick. He coughs," Yegorushka tried to make his point.

"Sick! Of course he's sick. So are you and I. What of it? Give him some codeine . . . or, better, the Daver pills, that's less expensive. We really can't go on like this—yesterday you signed thirty-five releases from work. You know very well there should never be more than fifteen, and none for more than two days."

"How can I give a man only two days when I know he won't be able to get up even in a week?" said Yegorushka in anger.

"This is a factory, not a rest home, young man," [16]

replies his superior, and explains in a friendly enough way that the days of the liberal intelligentsia are over; nowadays only the Party has the right to say what is good for the people. Yegor, however, is not easily dissuaded.

At the quarry, looking at the sweaty backs of the clay diggers up to their ankles in water, Yogorushka asked, "Aren't the workers supposed to have watertight boots?"

Glyants [a technician] tugged at his shirt and mumbled, looking at some point in the sky, "Yes, they get shoes."

A bearded workman, putting down his spade for a moment, gave Glyants a sidewise look . . . and murmured, as if to himself, "Yeah, we get them. Military issue. One pair for two people."

Yegorushka was shocked. "But the regulations call for watertight boots. . . . No wonder there are so many cases of rheumatism." [17]

Prose During the Uneasy Truce

He appeals to the Party boss, Klimov, who is doubtful. "It's a big expense. The factory can't very well manage it. However, you can try. Send in a report." [18]

Surprised at the Party man's indifference, Yegor decides to take the initiative in applying for proper boots for the workers. The bookkeeper Sinitsyn, seeing that the young doctor is a well-meaning but unpractical man, advises him to drop the matter. "Nothing will come of it anyway, believe me. You'll only jeopardize your position. . . ." [19]

Since Yegorushka does not give up, the factory director calls him in and says: "I hear from Sinitsyn that you incite the workers against the administration. . . . Watch your step, Doctor. Don't forget that there is the GPU." [20]

Finally Yegor has to leave the factory "at his own wish, and with the Administration's consent." Disillusioned, penniless and hopeless, he returns to his native city and learns, from a newspaper advertisement, that his friend Bakhrushin has opened a swanky office and is apparently flourishing. He specializes in syphilis and gonorrhea.

Bakhrushin's philosophy is cynical and simple: "Good old venereal diseases will always see me through. Who knows when your socialism will make good, but there will be enough gonorrhea for my lifetime." [21]

Grabar' himself was a Communist, but usually in his stories the characters who are on good terms with the Party are cynical careerists, while the misfits and "superfluous men" are decent and idealistic.

The story "Notes of a Hanger-on" deals with the transition from the Civil War period to the NEP and the bitter realization that the revolution had failed to live up to its promise.

Near the signal lights, in the ditch, sat a young snub-nosed fellow with a shaved head, carefully removing the star from his grimy helmet.

"Getting ready?" asked one of the retreating soldiers, dressed in a torn military shirt, barefoot, his face bristling with brown stubble.

"Why not?" the other replied indifferently, tearing off the fourth point of the star.[22]

One of the Party dissenters says: "It hurts . . . here I am, a

Bolshevik since 1904. And all of a sudden I find that everything has been wrong and that I no longer belong." [23]

In his stories "Kuvandyk," "Cranes and Buckshot" and "Lakhudrin Alley," Grabar' contrasted the heroic, romantic Civil War times and the materialistic, practical NEP. A passage of "Lakhudrin Alley" reads:

It's a moot question which is easier—to work day and night running a Cheka district office, keep a tight hold on oneself and subsist on millet from a rusty tin plate, or to manage a chemical trust, grapple with trade unions, keep in line those who are irreplaceable, count the pennies, and hide a stinging, vicious hatred behind dark glasses.[24]

The thirties were unlucky for Grabar'. First he was run over by a train and had one leg amputated. Then, implicated in the Zinoviev opposition, he was arrested in 1935 and disappeared. The last thing he published was a play called *The Big Poker Game*, 1933.[25]

GEORGI K. NIKIFOROV (1884- ?)

Nikiforov, one of the older proletarian writers of the Smithy group, began to publish only in 1923. He was a serious, intelligent and circumstantial writer, who combined a journalistic approach with a Remizovian manner ungraced by Remizov's brilliance.

He first attracted general attention with the short novel "Ivan Brynda," 1925,[26] and a volume of stories entitled *Either—Or*, 1926.[27]

Ivan Brynda is a workingman who has degenerated during the years of economic collapse and who finds himself again during the restoration after the Civil War period. Labor is second nature to Brynda, and it matters little to him who has put the plant back into operation—a private owner or a fellow-proletarian who won the director's post through possession of a Party card. The important thing is that a man go back to the kind of work to which he is accustomed. The characterization of the worker Brynda is one of the most truthful in Soviet literature.

In 1927 in the review *30 dnei* [Thirty Days] Nikiforov published excerpts from a novel then entitled "Denis Ramzayev," which, apparently, was later reworked–in order to play down the political and ideological implications—and published under the title *Beside the Street Lamp*, 1928. Despite the modifications, the novel remained palpably an attack on the Bolshevik practice of inventing armies of class enemies where none existed. For Nikiforov, inasmuch as the Civil War was over, the enemy was conquered. He opposed purges and dismissals on the grounds of "undesirable" social origin or a dubious past.

Denis Ramzayev is a nobleman and a former adherent of the Whites who has concealed his social origin and has secured an important position in industry. In the passages of the novel first published under the title "Denis Ramzayev" he is extraordinarily honest, high-minded and energetic, capable of valiant efforts and service in the rebuilding of the country, a man whom, Nikiforov implied, the Party had no moral right to cast aside in retaliation for his past. In the novel as published in book form Ramzayev is a much less heroic figure.

After the discovery of his identity a full investigation is made by the Central Control Commission.

"And you did not know who was hiding under the name of Denis Ramzayev?"[28] a highly-placed Bolshevik asks Golandina, Ramzayev's wife, a Communist.

An avenue of escape opens before her—she can blacken her husband and get off scot free. But she refuses to take that course. "I cannot accuse him, I cannot,"[29] she cries, pale and choking with emotion.

Even an old woman Communist who is a member of the Central Control Commission sympathizes with Golandina. "Ah . . . good, very good,"[30] the old woman says when Golandina refuses to furnish evidence against her husband.

Between the two versions of the novel there is a marked difference in the handling of the conflict which develops between those at the top and those at the bottom of the Soviet hierarchy. In the first version the men at the bottom rebel against their leaders who are planning to destroy Ramzayev. The rank and file think that Ramzayev is an excellent worker and respect the combination of practical mind with a kind heart which they see in him. They feel that, in concealing his past, Ramzayev's intentions were good, that his purpose was not to harm the working class but to serve it to the best of his ability. For the second version this conflict between the higher and lower echelons was expurgated. Nevertheless Nikiforov still conveyed the idea that the Russian people, good-natured and forbearing, did not want to elevate anger, hatred and vindictive retaliation to the status of law and, ready to let the dead past bury its dead, demanded that the principle of Party discipline be subordinated to humanitarianism.

Orthodox critics accused Nikiforov of turning everything upside down in characterizing the nobleman Ramzayev as a decent man while making the Communist Chuvyakin, a Civil War hero, a dull, self-satisfied bureaucrat and idler who has found himself a snug harbor not because of ability but because of Party membership. In the novel Chuvyakin is in fact offset by the Communist Tsepilov, a man of energy, decision and intelligence, who, although he is not interested in Ramzayev as a person, deems it irrational to refuse to make use of his abilities.

With high-tempo industrialization and collectivization in the offing after the decisions of the Fifteenth Party Congress, Nikiforov expressed his misgivings concerning the threatened growth of Soviet bureaucracy and the army of overseers in an allegorical story entitled "The Sparrow," 1928. The Soviet regime is presented in the guise of a bird state in which the blackbird is the philosopher of bureaucracy, suggestive of top-level Party officials. He is surrounded by admiring chaffinches, ordinary officials, to whom life without the blackbirds is unthinkable. The bullfinches are the common men, the goldfinches the careerists, the starlings the experts, and so on.

"Through the fine plumage of beautiful canaries on to world revolution!" [31] is the motto of the feathered community.

The sparrows are apparently the proletarian writers, failures to a man, who vainly try to learn from the nightingales how to sing. The drab little sparrow born to cheep can never trill like a nightingale, no matter how long he studies: "Be firm, my friend, keep alive your hatred of the past, preserve your truth from the corroding dust." [32]

Prose During the Uneasy Truce

As a whole, "The Sparrow" was a protest against the transformation of the Party into an exclusive caste of new exploiters. The end of the story, in which the blackbird perishes, may be interpreted to signify that the Party would be destroyed, but no final victor emerges from the struggle.

Nikiforov was admonished, and became somewhat more cautious. In his next novel, *The Woman*, 1927,[33] he toned down his protests and concentrated on the question of woman's role in the Soviet system. Sonchika, a pretty woman whose whole aim in life is to be a decorative "bedroom accessory" for some man, is contrasted to Faika, a highly educated girl with a background of the old intelligentsia who goes through a process of social regeneration.

Faika's solution of the "woman question" also raised the larger issue of the relationship between the old and the new intelligentsia. Nikiforov developed the thesis that it was imperative for the new semi-educated intelligentsia, composed of former workers and peasants, to raise itself to the level of true intellectuals, through study and friendly contact with the old intelligentsia, that toward this end the old group must cease to assert its superiority and the new group must recognize that assertion as mainly a method of self-preservation. Faika, who is characterized with great warmth and sympathy, is regenerated when she swallows her pride and takes the first step to establish contact with the new intelligentsia.

In 1931, upon publication of his novel about collectivization, entitled *Into the Wind*,[34] Nikiforov was taken to task for "underestimating the kulak opposition." Once more, he paid for being faithful to the truth. Nikiforov saw no difference of kind between the kulaks, the poor peasants, and the in-betweens. For him, the Russian Revolution split the peasantry into two groups: those who continued to till the soil, and those who, carrying Party cards as a reward for their services during the Civil War, were given posts in the Soviet government. Thus, Nikiforov regarded the process of collectivization as a struggle between the "conservatives" (that is, peasants of all levels—the kulaks, the poor and the in-betweens—who continued to work on the land as before the revolution) and the "progressives" (that is, all peasants who abandoned the land to take part in state administration).

In the fight the kulaks, both conservative and progressive, gave no quarter. The victors destroyed the vanquished. On the other hand, the in-betweens on both sides were prepared to compromise. Both sides resorted to perfidy, cunning and treachery. The fratricidal struggle undermined the nation's strength and, in Nikiforov's opinion, bore no relation whatsoever to the class struggle described by Marx.

Apprehensive and cautious, Nikiforov developed the thesis of *Into the Wind* in a roundabout way, frequently by mere hints. The meaning must be read between the lines. For this reason the value of the book is greatly impaired.

Nikiforov was nonetheless severely taken to task for daring to hint. His offense was all the more reprehensible in that he was not a peasant writer, but an old worker in the revolutionary movement and a Communist since 1917, and yet had gone even beyond many kulaks in his ideas.

To restore his reputation Nikiforov hastily wrote an extremely bad novel, *Unity*, 1933.[35]

The accusations against him were given some weight by his writings which deal with the history of the labor movement in Russia, including *Gray Days*,[36] *Thirty-three Adventures*,[37] "Belated Spring,"[38] and a novel, *The Master Craftsmen*.

In all these Nikiforov's excursions into the past run counter to the Bolshevik attempt to falsify Russian history, particularly history of the revolutionary movement. In *The Master Craftsmen*, 1935, he made use of the past for a critical appraisal of the present. A story told by Alfei, one of the characters, was obviously meant to be a description of Stalinist Russia at the time when Nikiforov was writing:

> The important thing in this story is that there was a dark country where people never laughed and from their birth were beset by great dejection, as though, you might say, they found themselves in a graveyard on a rainy day—the clouds droop down to earth and hang from the trees, the dead, as is their custom, are silent, the birds are all hunched up, the wind hangs its head and hides in the mountains. . . . Everybody has a gray face and bitter eyes. . . .[39]

Nikiforov emphasized the fact that the workers who fought

against the tsarist regime made no distinction between Bolsheviks, Mensheviks and Socialist Revolutionaries but, motivated chiefly by desire to better their living conditions, at times fell in with the ambition to change the entire social order.

In 1937 his intellectual independence put Nikiforov into a concentration camp.

Soviet critics have called him "a bad Remizov" and "a less intelligent Zola." It is true that his work has no stylistic distinction. His strong point is his familiarity with and honest rendering of the Russian worker's psychology, way of life and aversion to Bolshevism. Nikiforov's contribution to postrevolutionary Russian literature has been underrated.

24. *Satirists and Humorists*

MIKHAIL A. BULGAKOV (1891-1940)

Among the writers of the NEP period who were still faithful to the classical tradition of Pushkin and Tolstoi, one of the most important was M. A. Bulgakov.

Like Sholokhov's *The Silent Don*, Bulgakov's novel *The White Guard, or The Days of the Turbins*, 1924, is the chronicle of a Russian family disintegrating under the impact of war and revolution. The family tragedy epitomizes the national tragedy. Sholokhov took his characters from the Cossack peasants and Bulgakov drew his from the gentry intelligentsia. The action is set in Kiev during the Civil War, first under the rule of Hetman Skoropadski, then under the occupation of the Petlyura forces and finally of the Bolsheviks. In a daring departure from conventional Soviet treatment of the Civil War, Bulgakov looked at events through the eyes not of the victors but of the vanquished. With manifest sympathy for his high-principled and heroic White officers he shows the hopelessness of their cause, due to the rift between the ruling elite and the people. A sense of futility and doom pervades the novel.

Skoropadski's administration is pictured as a grotesque provincial imitation of the Russian monarchy. Bulgakov saw an ironic prank of fate in the fact that Skoropadski was proclaimed hetman in the Kiev circus building. Against this background the assassination of the Imperial family assumed a particularly tragic significance.

"They have all been murdered," says Myshlayevski, "the Tsar and the Tsarina and the Heir."

The Whites are slow to accept the unbelievable news. Yelena raises her glass and cries hysterically: "Even if that is true . . . It does not matter, I toast them, I toast them!" [1]

Skoropadski's rule crumbled for the same reasons as the Russian monarchy. The Hetman was a typical country squire, and the Ukrainian peasants had no more use for him than the Russian peasants had for their squires. In Bulgakov's novel one of the characters, Aleksei Turbin, gives his impression of what is in the back of the peasants' mind:

"All land to the peasants."
"Three hundred acres to each."
"No landlords for evermore. And a good formal deed, properly stamped, for every piece of land, clearly saying that it is given in perpetuity, to be passed from father to son, from son to grandson, and so forth."
"No riff-raff from the city to come and demand grain. The grain is ours and we keep it. What we can't use up ourselves, we hide in the ground."
"Kerosene to be brought from the city." [2]

Bulgakov satirized the idea of an effective peasant revolution. The muzhik was the backbone of the nation, but there was no need to idealize him. It was futile to expect great things of him. Bulgakov saw that the opponents of Bolshevism carried their defeat in themselves, and his pessimism on this score served in the eyes of certain critics as an antidote to the anarchic individualism of writers like Artyom Vesyolyi.

Skoropadski's farcical reign was followed by the equally farcical and more bloody reign of Simon Petlyura. The ruling elite had nothing acceptable and constructive to offer.

As Bulgakov characterized them, the Whites were always heroic at the front, but at the rear, where the situation also demanded sacrifices, the only thought of the upper classes was how to preserve a pleasant, easy life. Their hatred of Bolshevism was not open, fighting hatred; it was a cowardly hatred hissing from a dark corner. *The White Guard* is the story of the gradual transformation of heroes into frightened little people in the face of the terrible power of Bolshevism.

After *The White Guard* Bulgakov turned from realism to fantasy and satire—a logical application of his flair for combining laughter and terror. "The Fateful Eggs," 1925,[3] is a fantastic tale in the manner of H. G. Wells' *The Food of the Gods*. It castigates the Bolsheviks' mania for launching projects without regard for consequences and their practice of hanging the blame on some scapegoat when the results were an unpleasant surprise to themselves.

In "Fateful Eggs" they decide to counteract a calamitous epidemic of poultry disease with the "life rays" discovered by Professor Persikov. The miraculous stimulation of procreative powers through the use of these rays is expected quickly to rebuild the poultry population. The job is assigned to a "man of action," Rokk (whose symbolic name accounts for the pun in the Russian title; the pronunciation is the same as of the word *rok*, meaning "fate"). In vain, the professor protests that the rays have not been sufficiently studied, the apparatus needs testing, and so on. To complicate matters, Rokk in his hurry uses eggs from the wrong incubator. Instead of the oversized hens anticipated, giant snakes, lizards and crocodiles hatch out and multiply with such speed that the army has to be called in to exterminate them. This is finally achieved, though not without the aid of Russia's most ancient and reliable ally, the winter frosts.

At the height of the "war," the enraged and frightened populace smashes up Persikov's laboratory and kills the professor. The police fail to prevent his murder, though they had been most efficient in protecting him from the lucrative offers of foreigners to come and work on his invention abroad. The Party evidently was only too glad to have the mob visit its fury on Persikov.

Professor Persikov typifies the great scholars whom the Bolsheviks used despite their opposition to Bolshevism. Rokk represents the new Communist elite, who, as Bulgakov foresaw, were going to kill the NEP, if only because they would have nothing to do if it became firmly established. Bulgakov had a rare gift for revealing a man's nature by simply describing his mannerisms and appearance.

In the swift action of the tale "Devilry," 1924,[4] we can see the modern variant of the hapless heroes of Gogol's *The Overcoat* and Dostoyevski's *The Double*. Korotkov is a frightened office worker, victim of the inhuman Soviet bureaucracy and continuous purges.

As a satirist, Bulgakov is akin to Gogol; his humor does not resemble the angry, bilious humor of Saltykov-Shchedrin.

Facets of Bulgakov's fiction writing may well be still completely unknown. He was singularly unlucky in publishing. His first volume of stories, "Notes on the Cuff," was purchased by a Berlin organization for publication in May 1923 but was never put on sale.[5] The novel *The White Guard* was withdrawn from the market almost immediately upon publication in the U.S.S.R. And it is thought that Bulgakov wrote many other pieces which could not appear in print after the end of the NEP and the tightening of censorship. Ivanov-Razumnik has mentioned a satirical tale, "Sharik," which he read in manuscript,[6] and the existence of another unpublished tale with the unmistakable Bulgakov touch has been reported. In the account given, the story deals with a bookkeeper arrested in the late 1930's and used as a guinea pig in the NKVD experiments with hypnosis. As a result, he comes to believe that he really is a spy for the British Intelligence Service and sets about his job in good earnest. It is to be hoped that the story will come to light during the course of the Soviet research begun in 1956 in connection with the posthumous rehabilitation of Bulgakov. No doubt other interesting works will also be uncovered in time.

As a playwright, Bulgakov is assured of an important place in the history of the Russian theater, despite continual difficulties in the production and publication of his plays. He adapted *The White Guard* to the stage, under the title *The Days of the Turbins*.[7] Dr. Turbin was changed into Colonel Turbin. The author made other revisions to suit the different medium, but these are all of a technical nature. The message remained the same. *Days of the Turbins* played for many years at the Moscow Art Theater. Early in the 1930's, however, other theaters were forbidden to produce it.

Bulgakov's play "Flight" [*Beg*], dealing with émigrés, is thematically a sequel to *The Days of the Turbins*. It was written in 1927-1928 but not published or produced. In 1956, however, it was announced that the Vakhtangov Theater would soon offer the play.

The comedy "Zoika's Apartment"[8] played with great success in several theaters, but was taken from the boards in 1928. It depicts a brothel where the new "Red aristocracy" indulged in drunken revels.

Bulgakov called "The Crimson Island" a "satiric lampoon." The satire concerns the collapse of Communist hopes for world revolution. There are overtones of tragedy in the portrayal of Bolshevik control of art. The play was banned after a brief run in 1928,[9] and the text was never published.

During the 1930's Bulgakov served as consultant to the Moscow Art Theater and the Bol'shoi Theater. When his comedy "Molière" was banned in 1936 just before the opening, he wrote to Stalin asking to be allowed to leave Russia. No visa was granted, but Stalin took a personal interest in the persecuted author, and Bulgakov received the Red Banner medal for his services to the Soviet theater.[10] His adaptation of Gogol's *Dead Souls* had a successful run in 1938-1939, and his last play, about Pushkin (*Last Days*), remained even in the postwar repertory.

Bulgakov is one of the outstanding figures in postrevolutionary literature.

NIKOLAI ERDMAN (1902-   )

While Malenkov, at the Nineteenth Party Congress in 1952, was calling for Soviet Gogols and Shchedrins, the ablest of living Russian playwrights and the only one, perhaps, with the true Gogolian touch, Nikolai Erdman, was employed as hack writer on the script of a propaganda film concerning China. Then a gaunt, white-haired revenant from concentration camp, his plays banned and his name all but forgotten, Erdman had had his hour of success in 1925, when his masterpiece, "The Mandate,"[11] was produced by Meierhold and played to the unceasing laughter of the house. The dialogue is very funny, and the comic situations are excellent theater. A playwright in the Western European tradition, Erdman was at the same time a master of the typically Russian grotesque. His sharpest barbs were aimed at petty-bourgeois vulgarity. He enlarged the well-worn theme, as Mayakovski also did, to include the rising Party caste, whose mentality, except for their delusions of grandeur, was the same as that of the "has-beens." The latter were harmlessly absorbed in their own trivial affairs, but the Communist philistines held dangerous power and abused it. Meierhold, in his brochure *Reconstruction of the Theater*, 1931, called Mayakovski's and Erdman's plays "magnificent." Their satire, he said, pointed out the worst sores of Soviet society, in a way that prevented the public from becoming discouraged.[12]

"The Mandate" makes fun of the efforts of a lower-middle-class go-getter to obtain a Party card and thus join the ruling caste.

Production of another of Erdman's plays, "The Portrait," was evidently prevented by his first arrest, in 1931.[13] On his return he wrote the script for the well-known film *Jolly Fellows*, 1934, directed by Grigori Aleksandrov. It is hard to tell how much of the scenario is Erdman's, and how much the editors' and the censors' work. It lacks Erdman's sardonic humor but nevertheless makes a brisk, funny and entertaining film. It had a great success with the public but did not escape censure from the critics.[14]

Erdman was again arrested at the time of Meierhold's disappearance in the late 1930's and was sent to concentration camp. Once more released, he resumed film work. A film based on one of his scenarios was produced during the war. The 1951 film *A Sportsman's Honor*, made from a comedy which Erdman wrote in collaboration with M. Vol'pin, was soon banned as harmful, though the plot seems innocuous enough—a young Stakhanovite, who is also a soccer star, makes ridiculous mistakes at his work and in an important match because he has fallen head over heels in love. In sheer craftsmanship, the film is far superior to the majority of Soviet screen comedies. Erdman was accused, however, of attempting to smuggle Meierholdism into Soviet films,[15] and was put to work on animated cartoon movies. This excellent playwright was not even present at the Second Congress of the Union of Soviet Writers, which convened in December 1954.

MIKHAIL ZOSHCHENKO (1895-   )

In the favorable conditions of the NEP period satirists and humorists mushroomed and prospered. Towering above the rest was Mikhail Zoshchenko, one of the Serapion Brothers and a follower of Zamyatin.

He had been a law student, a volunteer in the First World War, and had tried a number of trades after the revolution, from professional card player to detective. His checkered career provided much of the material for his humorous stories.

Lacking, perhaps, Zamyatin's fastidiousness and depth, he surpassed his teacher in "stylization," that is, relating the story entirely in terms of the idiosyncratic speech of his "narrators," usually drawn from the lower middle class of suburban Leningrad.

Professor Vinogradov found Zoshchenko's *skaz* form less natural than Zamyatin's, on the ground that the spoken idiom is mixed with deliberately misused bookish expressions which, he said, make the author's presence obtrusive.[16] Professor Vinogradov lost sight of the fact that after the revolution the urban vernacular did become a fantastic hodge-podge of factory slang, regional expressions brought in by peasants who had come to the city to work, revolutionary neologisms, and the jargons of political pamphlets and dime novels, with the added grotesqueness of pretentious, "cultured" turns of phrase.

Zamyatin urged the writers of the Serapion Brotherhood to learn from Leskov. He himself often used the Leskovian *skaz* manner, though he gave it a twist of his own. *The Left-Handed Smith* [*Levsha*], one of Leskov's best tales, is full of admiration for the Russian artisan's skill and intelligence, and most of his *skaz* stories are cheerful. Zamyatin's are often gloomy with the fear that the Bolshevik industrialization would bring only misery to Russia. Zoshchenko followed Zamyatin's lead—for instance, in "Propagandist" [*Agitator*], in which a guard at an aviation school tries to persuade his fellow villagers to donate money for the advancement of aviation because every flier is a candidate for the other world and is courting death.

Zoshchenko's charm lies in the realistic, meaty telling of funny stories on subjects of widespread current interest. Hundreds of the pieces in his many collections of stories are based on common jokes, all told in the same preposterous style, somewhat resembling Damon Runyon's.

Their mood gradually underwent a marked change. At first the hero cheerfully puts up with his many worries and misadventures—poor food, inadequate housing and threadbare clothes, quarrelsome neighbors, troubles at work, and so on—and never loses his confidence in the Soviet authorities. They will make up for everything, given a little time, and then the life of the working man will be one of ease and plenty. This optimism pervades the numerous volumes of short stories published through 1927, the most important of which are *Short Stories* (1923), *Respected Citizens* (1926) and *Nervous People* (1927).

With the years the confidence of Zoshchenko's characters evaporated. Life became worse instead of better. In most of the later stories the hero is discouraged and skeptical—and the author more sympathetic.

Even in 1927, in the volume of longer stories entitled *What the Nightingale Sang About: Sentimental Tales*, Zoshchenko began to speak as a social philosopher or, at times, as a serious literary critic, in lengthy but pithy digressions. At the beginning of "A Gay Adventure," contrasting Russian and foreign writing, he said:

Let us take, for example, our dear Russian literature. The weather, in most cases, is nothing much—either a blizzard or a storm, or a wind blowing in the hero's face. And the heroes chosen, to make matters worse, are unattractive. They gripe all the time. They are badly dressed. Instead of gay and merry adventures, bloody encounters in the Civil War are described, or just something that's apt to put the reader to sleep. No, this author is not in favor of that kind of literature! Granted that it is full of books of genius, and that these books are full of heaven knows what profound ideas and assorted words—but this author can find in them neither peace of mind nor joy.[17]

In a foreword to the volume Zoshchenko was even more outspoken:

> Of course, the reader has a right to expect from the author a revolutionary approach—great themes, projects of planetary dimensions and heroic pathos, that is, the whole gamut of lofty ideology. . . . This book, however, is written about people as they are. . . .
> This author . . . simply describes how people live, what they do, and what, so to speak, they strive for.[18]

In this outwardly flippant manner Zoshchenko accused Soviet literature of having forgotten about man. The narrator of the title story of the volume, "What the Nightingale Sang About," protests:

> In some three hundred years, how people are going to laugh at us! What a strange life, they will say, those people led. They had something called money, they'll say, and something called a passport. Civil acts, whatever that may mean, and square feet of living space.
> Well, let them laugh if they want to. It's too bad, though, that they won't understand half of it. How could they, when maybe they will have the kind of life that we do not even see in our dreams.
> What that life will be like the author does not know and does not want to guess at. Why should he frazzle his nerves and ruin his health for nothing, since he isn't going to see that wonderful future life anyway.
> Besides, who knows whether it is going to be as wonderful as all that.[19]

Deploring the current fashion of denying the existence of love, the narrator recalls a girl he had loved in his youth.

> Now, when fifteen years have passed and the author is going slightly gray from various illnesses and the tribulations of life and from worrying about making his living, when, indeed, he simply does not want to lie and has no reasons for telling lies, and when, finally, he wishes to see life as it is, without any lies and artifices—now, at the risk of appearing to be a funny character out of the last century, he wants to state that the academic and Party circles are quite in error on the score [of love].
> To these lines about love the author can foresee vehement strictures from public figures.
> "Your own case, comrade," they'll say, "is irrelevant. . . . Personally, you are unattuned to the epoch," they'll say, "and, altogether, it is a mere accident that you are still living in these times."

"Accident, hell! I mean, may I ask why you think it's an accident? Do you want me to throw myself under a streetcar?"

"That," they'll say, "is up to you. Under a streetcar or from a bridge, as you wish, but the fact is that you have no excuse for living." [20]

The narrator refuses to be silenced.

The author wishes to make this frank and honest request: "Let me finish, comrades! Let a person have his say, if only for the sake of discussion." [21]

And Zoshchenko in this book did speak his mind—not only as a satirist but as a writer of great tragic power, in the tradition of Pushkin's *Station Inspector,* Gogol's *Overcoat* and Dostoyevski's *Poor Folk* and *The Double.* All the stories in the collection are about men pinched, hounded and crushed by the revolution, who either could or would not adapt to the new times and conditions.

Akin to *Sentimental Tales* in style and spirit is the long story "M. P. Sinyagin," 1930.[22]

Youth Restored, 1933,[23] stands apart among Zoshchenko's writings. To approach the book as a medical treatise is to find it a tangle of inaccuracies and ineptness, but it is, of course, not a medical treatise despite the solemn pronouncements of various critics of the time; it is a psychological allegory. The critic Anatoli Gorelov, however, was on the right track when he said of *Youth Restored:*

It was not the colors, sounds and smells of life that beckoned to [Zoshchenko's] imagination, but the fixed idea of finding a miraculous formula for restoring youth and youthful feelings. . . .[24]

And Gorelov came very close to the intention of the book in the statement that

over the great murals of history, Zoshchenko hung his pathetic little pictures, not of prophets and revolutionaries, not of great champions and martyrs, but of weary, neurotic people with weak nerves, diseased kidneys, and impaired digestion.[25]

But the critic missed the point that Zoshchenko was comparing the NEP period and the thirties. During the NEP, life did have color, sound and smell. In the thirties, they disappeared, and the new generation did not even know what it is to be young. Their outlook was as dreary and sad as their world, and even the past appeared to them in somber hues. *Youth Restored* contrasts two ways of life. The medical angle is simply a means of evading the restrictions of censorship.

In the equally mystifying *Blue Book* of 1934-1935,[26] Zoshchenko adroitly demonstrated how Communist propaganda distorted history, philosophy, science, and most other things. In both books, there is a tragic note beneath the irony.

The best of Zoshchenko's short stories in his "second period" are collected under the title *Private Life* (1933). The story "A Test of Heroism" is the jewel of the collection.

The narrator, reminiscing about the Civil War, says "I did not meet any special heroes. . . . Though, generally speaking, there were heroes." But one man comes to his mind, an assistant book-keeper in a sovkhoz office.

I had an executive position [at the sovkhoz], instructor in rabbit and poultry breeding. So I have this position, and an awful thing happens to me. Namely, my ducks took to drowning in the pond. . . . And in one month I lost thirty-six ducks in this way—and me the instructor in fowl and rabbit raising.[27]

He disclaims "moral responsibility" for the mishap ("There was famine when we took our exams, so that we had other things to worry about than taking exams") but is nonetheless held responsible:

Well, I'm called to the main office, and the director yells and says all kinds of big and crushing words, such as "You are, of course, a most valuable, experienced and competent man at your job, having even been wounded at the beginning of the Civil War, but hell, if you can't keep ducks from drowning, that is economic counterrevolution and espionage on behalf of British capitalism."[28]

In consideration of the minor nature of the loss, the hero is transferred to office work, pending further clarification of his political loyalty.

The commissar at this office was a Black Sea sailor, name of Shamshurin, a desperate character and a twice-wounded hero of the Civil War.

This Commissar Shamshurin was very strict. He wouldn't stand for anybody being late, he swore something awful on the slightest provocation and suspected all the office workers of lack of devotion to the Communist cause. . . . "I know you," he used to say, "give you a chance and you'll all turn your snouts away from it."

He bawled people out in the worst expressions and kept worrying and asking everybody about their thoughts and whether they were more in sympathy with the Communist movement headed by the Third International or maybe with the aristocratic classes.[29]

Finally Shamshurin devises a scheme for testing the loyalty of his subordinate with the aid of one of his "ideological comrades."

[Commissar Shamshurin] dressed him up as well as he could, in a beige tunic and high leather boots, and made him hold a riding whip with a silver knob, and put on his head the finest cap he could find. Early in the morning he put him in his own office, dressed up like this, as if he were a representative of a new aristocratic government.

Meanwhile he himself hid in a closet, climbed onto a chair and watched with his own eyes through the transom.

The workers were in a state of nerves and panic anyway, expecting the fall of Bolshevism from day to day, so they did not notice anything peculiar. . . .

Out of ten employees, only six were questioned. Three of them talked in an indefinite sort of way, batted their eyelashes and acted scared. One swine started whispering to the new boss about various past events and feelings. Another began to prevaricate that though he himself wasn't exactly of the gentry, but having long been in sympathy with that class and even visited in their houses in the past on many occasions, he had always been highly satisfied with their society and their sumptuous hospitality in the form of canapés, preserves and marinated mushrooms.[30]

Only one of the six, the assistant bookkeeper Nikolai Antonovich, unexpectedly displays independence and high principles:

"I will probably have to work for you," he said, "seeing that I have a family, but I am not particularly in sympathy with you. . . . Without being a Communist . . . I have always stood on the platform of the Soviet regime. . . ."

And suddenly there's a terrific clatter in the closet—from Commissar Shamshurin falling off his chair with surprise.

He falls off the chair and rushes into the room, crying, "Where is he? Let me embrace him!" [31]

Shamshurin's methods of testing loyalty do not meet with the approval of the higher authorities, nor did the original ending of Zoshchenko's yarn (in the first edition):

On the day following this event Commissar Shamshurin received a stern reprimand for rightist deviation with leftist convictions. So you see it is hard to guess what is the right thing to do.[32]

In the second edition the implications were toned down, and the ending reads: "On the day following this event Commissar Shamshurin was called to account for carrying his efforts too far."[33]

Zoshchenko's moods and techniques often bear the mark of his enjoyment of the performances of the well-known circus clown Vasili Gushchinski, his personal friend. Another influence is that of Charlie Chaplin's films.

The lonely misfit of Zoshchenko's stories is a typical Soviet citizen. The Bolshevik regime has made man into a grotesque reflection of himself in a distorting mirror, inwardly and outwardly a caricature of a human being. Zoshchenko's heroes are either such distorted creatures or extremely stupid, primitive, animal-like characters. The best illustrations to his stories were done by the cartoonists Malyutin, Malakhovski and Radlov in an overstated "primitivist manner"; the people in their drawings look like animated blocks of wood.

Zoshchenko's later stories often have a moral tacked on at the end, and the moral often reveals a revulsion for the primitivism imposed on life, as in the last lines of the story "Very Simple":

Goodness, how simple everything is in life.
I wish I hadn't found that out. Maybe that's the reason why I find life so boring now.[34]

There are also jabs at the lack of human dignity in Soviet life, as in the brief story "The Sorrows of Young Werther":

Again I feel like saying something nice, or shouting: "Comrades, we are building a new life, we are victorious, we have overcome tremendous difficulties—what the hell, let us start respecting one another." [35]

Zoshchenko differs from other Soviet satirists, in particular from Mayakovski, in that his stories center not on an ideological premise but on the common man, the plain, unremarkable character who takes no interest in politics but is trapped in politics against his will.

During the thirties Zoshchenko, under duress, tried new media, including several hollowly sententious pieces such as *A Life-History* (1934),[36] "The Black Prince"[37] and "Retribution" (1937),[38] in which the former Zoshchenko spoke, if at all, in Aesopian language.

But eventually he returned to the humorous anecdote. One of his few postwar stories, "The Adventure of a Monkey," 1946,[39] incensed Zhdanov and led to Zoshchenko's virtual expulsion from the Soviet press. His most recent published pieces, three brief stories in *Neva* in 1956,[40] are very feeble.

IL'F AND PETROV

Il'ya Il'f (pseudonym of I. A. Fainzil'berg, 1897-1937) and Yevgeni Petrov were among the last satirists tolerated by the Soviet regime before it finally squashed satire altogether after the NEP period.

Petrov (1903-1942), whose real name was Katayev, was a younger brother of the novelist Valentin Katayev, and it was the latter who prompted them to write the enormously successful novel *Twelve Chairs*, 1928,[41] and thus started them off on a long collaboration ending only with the death of Il'f. (Valentin Katayev himself, although the very epitome of NEP literature, produced his own best work later and is not to be considered here.)

Il'f and Petrov are known primarily for *Twelve Chairs* and its companion piece, *The Golden Calf*, 1931.[42] Both books stem from Gogol's *Dead Souls*, but reflect also the authors' admiration of Mark Twain, O. Henry, and American movies—Harold Lloyd's and Monty Banks' rapid tempo and the touching quality of Chaplin's films.

"Into our two novels we have crammed enough observations, thoughts and imagination . . . to suffice for ten books," commented the authors. "That's how uneconomical we are."[43]

The hero of both novels is the business genius Ostap Bender.

Prose During the Uneasy Truce

Lacking a legal outlet for his talents he becomes a crook—pitting his wits against the crooked Soviet system and displaying astonishing ingenuity. What develops is, as it were, a competition between a lone pirate and the organized pirating of the state. Unlike Gogol's Chichikov, Bender does not inspire real hostility in the reader. The other characters he encounters are mostly Soviet "has-beens"—a poverty-stricken priest, a former marshal of nobility, bankrupt NEP-men, criminals, a hapless owner of an automobile that gives endless trouble. Incredible adventures take place all over Russia, and the impression is conveyed that everywhere in the vast land the common people lived in unspoken fear and misery.

Twelve Chairs came out while literature was not yet strictly controlled, but with *The Golden Calf* the authors ran into considerable difficulties, and the novel was published only because of Gorki's personal intervention.

Many of Il'f and Petrov's sketches which were first published in newspapers and magazines are collected in the books *The Writing of "Robinson"* (1933),[44] *The Serene Blockhead* (1935),[45] and *Tonya* (1937). Their hero is the common man crushed by impossible living conditions and overwork and bemazed by the official directives regulating even his private life and his thoughts. Trifling real-life events are embroidered upon to the point of absurdity, and their implications well driven home. One of the authors' targets is the stupidity of state control over literature. In the story "The Writing of 'Robinson,'" a novelist is commissioned to write a Russian version of *Robinson Crusoe*. When the book is finished, the censor finds that it lacks ideological and social significance, and directs the author to put in a few Party members, also washed ashore. Otherwise, who will watch Robinson's ideology and collect dues from him?

Il'f and Petrov recorded their impressions of a trip to the United States in the book *One-Storied America*, 1936,[46] published in English as *Little Golden America*, a piece of biased journalism rather than literature.

In collaboration with Valentin Katayev, they wrote two comedies, "A Rich Marriage" (1936)[47] and *Under the Circus Dome*.[48] The first is a kolkhoz play showing the unwholesome effect of attempting to live life according to propaganda slogans. The second dramatizes the happiness found in the Soviet Union by an American girl circus performer who had suffered from racial discrimination in the United States. It was one of their rare concessions to propaganda requirements. A film based on the play and entitled *The Circus* was produced in 1936.

In February 1949 *The Literary Gazette* upbraided the publishing house which had recently issued a new one-volume edition of *Twelve Chairs* and *The Golden Calf,* and called both novels "ideologically pernicious."[49]

VLADIMIR VETOV (1893- ?)

Vladimir Vetov (pseudonym of Prince Vladimir Trubetskoi), in his mild and kindly way one of the best humorists of the NEP period, treated the problems of the "superfluous man" in comic vein in his book of short stories *The Extraordinary Adventures of Bochonkin and Khvoshch,* 1928.[50] Their provincial life upset by the imminent industrialization and collectivization, the characters look for relief from boredom, for ways of adding some color to existence, and find a temporary escape from Communism in hunting and fishing.

Vetov's career was interrupted by arrest, in 1931, and deportation to Karaganda.

SEMYON POD"YACHEV (1866-1934)

Before the revolution Pod"yachev had written assiduously of the oppression and sufferings of the Russian muzhik. Many of his early stories concern peasants who went to the city to work and, after endless vicissitudes, ended as half tramp, half "holy fool" *(yurodivyi),* no longer peasants nor yet factory workers.

After the revolution Pod"yachev matured astonishingly as a writer. One marvels at his new sureness of touch. Obviously, the enthusiasm engendered by the democratic, "peasant" revolution greatly stimulated the imagination of the rural intelligentsia.

The Bolsheviks were not very well disposed toward peasant intellectuals and preferred to promote to positions of leadership the least honest, indeed even vicious, elements among the peasantry. The result was a tense struggle between the peasant elite and the lower-echelon Party administrators in the villages. As a writer Pod"yachev fed on this struggle. To deal with it he developed a talent for humor and satire not glimpsed in his prerevolutionary writing. A Party member himself (from 1918 on) and known as an "exponent of the aspirations of the poorer middle-peasant class," he maliciously satirized the lower-level administration in his sketches "The Critic," 1928,[51] and "The Old Party Member," 1927.[52]

His two-volume autobiographical novel *My Life*, published in 1930-1931, is a piece of conscientious craftsmanship and makes interesting reading. There is something satisfying about it that reminds one of a freshly baked rye bread. Curiously enough, the Communist Pod"yachev, instead of hating the past, seems to have been in love with it, in a warmhearted, lyrical way which is not idealization but plainly infatuation.

MIKHAIL VOLKOV (1886- ?)

In his many short stories of the NEP period—notably in the volumes *A Heavenly Life*, 1923,[53] and *Antrop's Tales*, 1926[54]—Volkov, another peasant writer, combined romanticism with satire.

His favorite targets were stupidity and superstitions. In one story peasant women petition the Committee for the Poor to issue rations to the *domovoi* (house spirit), who might cause much mischief if he is not pacified by food offerings.

However, there was genuine love of mankind in Volkov's satire, and he recognized the goodness and compassion inherent in the Orthodox faith despite all the superstitions that cluttered up the peasants' religious beliefs.

He often satirized the Soviet bureaucratic machine, with its endless red tape, as in this description:

> The Manager's Office.
> Disheveled walls. On the walls—
> Karl Marx' picture, and notices:
> "Handshaking Discontinued"
> "Do Not Enter Unannounced";

Recessed in the walls:
Friedrich Engels' bronze bust
And windows ashamed of their broken panes
　　and fluttering cobwebs.
The doors proudly sport inscriptions:
　"Presidium"
　"Do Not Enter Unannounced"
　"Finish Your Business and Go."
Next to the door
A secretary hooks visitors with her eyes:
"What's your business?
No interviews today."
"The Chairman is in conference.
Come back next week." [55]

The tale "Communal Dwelling No. 1331," a candid picture of the housing shortage in the Soviet Union, is perhaps Volkov's best. He takes us inside a large crowded apartment house in Moscow, where we see the occupants' daily routine, all the little incidents and discomforts and tragicomic situations which, added up, turn their life into hell. The secretary of the tenants' association, a former tsarist civil service employee, who is the narrator of the story, looks askance at one of the tenants, the poet Otrubnoi, whose poems are being rejected by publishers. The old man feels that, if the poems are not accepted, they cannot be worth much and that Otrubnoi himself must be either a fool or a loafer. The poet tries to explain that he is a disciple of Dostoyevski and that the authorities detest Dostoyevski, but he fails to convince Koloskov.

The old man has given shelter to a girl, Sonya, who has come to Moscow from the country to attend a technicum but has been refused living quarters though she had passed the entrance examinations. She strikes up a friendship with Otrubnoi, and the old man is out of his mind with worry. All poets, he believes, are clever liars, seducers and drunkards. He spies on the young people and finds that Otrubnoi recites poems and raves about Dostoyevski while Sonya listens starry-eyed from the other end of the room, that he does not take advantage of the girl but even helps her with her studies without any compensation.

Volkov never tired of pointing out that people were better than

Prose During the Uneasy Truce

they were usually thought to be, and deserved trust and respect.

When Otrubnoi falls ill and is taken to a hospital, the board of tenants decide to consider his room "vacated due to death." But he upsets their plans by recovering and demanding his room back, to the extreme annoyance of the chairman of the tenants' association: "What are we supposed to do if all the dead in the cemetery revive and claim their rooms?"[56]

Volkov's humor is often macabre and bitter. As a satirist, he has been underrated. Volkov ceased to publish at the beginning of the 1930's. It has been reported that, as a Bukharin follower, he was expelled from the Party and exiled.

Postscript

Since this book was written, there have been many changes on the Soviet literary scene which affect the repute of writers discussed.

Some who, one must assume, died in concentration camps—for instance, Isaak Babel', Artyom Vesyolyi, Sergei Budantsev, Ivan Katayev, and Boris Pil'nyak—have been posthumously rehabilitated, and the admission has been made in the Soviet press that they were subjected to arbitrary and unjust treatment.

Others whom the Bolshevik cultural policy had condemned to silence, such as Vasili Kazin, Pavel Radimov, Pavel Druzhinin, Anna Akhmatova, Mikhail Zoshchenko, and Yuri Olesha, have again appeared in print. But most of these "revenants" are no longer the writers they once were, to judge by their newly published works. Forced silence has impaired their talent.

Yuri Olesha is a brilliant exception. His contribution to the anthology *Literary Moscow*, which appeared in 1956, gives evidence that he has lost none of his powers under the terrors and alarms of the "unlyrical era."

The literary "thaw" which permitted writers of the 1920's to raise their heads again has even afforded a glimpse of young, able beginners at work. Barring another freeze on the heels of the thaw, there may yet be Russian writers to replace the casualties. But the Soviet winter is long and hard, and the ice does not break up under a little melting at the surface.

Notes

Notes to Chapter 1 (pages 5-41):

1. Blok, "The Twelve" [*Dvenadtsat'*], tr. by Babette Deutsch, in Yarmolinsky, Avrahm, ed., *A Treasury of Russian Verse*, N. Y., Macmillan, 1949, p. 158. The same translation has been used for all the following quotations from the poem.
2. *Zapisnye knizhki Aleksandra Bloka* [Aleksandr Bloks's Notebooks], Leningrad, Priboi, 1930, p. 63.
3. Oral folk rhymes, usually of four verses in trochaic meter, topical or lyrical, sung to popular tunes.
4. Blok, "Zapiska o 'Dvenadtsati' " [Note on "The Twelve"], *Sobraniye sochinenii* [Collected Works], Leningrad, Sovetskii pisatel', 1936, Vol. VIII, p. 239.
5. *Zapisnye knizhki*, p. 92.
6. "Bezvremen'ye" [Bad Times], *Sochineniya v odnom tome* [Works in One Volume], Moscow, GIKhL, 1946, p. 412.
7. "Vozmezdiye" [Retaliation], *ibid.*, p. 243.
8. "Ni sny, ni yav'," *Sobraniye sochinenii*, Vol. IX, p. 213. The story was first published in *Zapiski mechtatelei* [Dreamers' Journal], Petrograd, No. 4, 1921.
9. "Ni sny ni yav'," *Sobraniye sochinenii*, p. 213.
10. *Zapisnye knizhki*, p. 70.
11. Bunin, I. A., "Tretii Tolstoi" [The Third Tolstoi], *Vospominaniya* [Reminiscences], Paris, Vozrozhdeniye, 1950, p. 163.
12. Quoted in Blok, *Zapisnye knizhki*, p. 199.
13. *Dnevnik Aleksandra Bloka* [The Diary of Aleksandr Blok], Leningrad, Izdatel'stvo pisatelei, 1928, Vol. II, p. 67.
14. *Ibid.*, p. 107.
15. "Intelligentsiya i revolyutsiya," *Sobraniye sochinenii*, Vol. VIII, p. 48.
16. *Ibid.*, p. 55.
17. *Dnevnik*, Vol. II, p. 68.
18. Berdyayev, N. A., *Russkaya ideya* [The Russian Idea], Paris, Y.M.C.A. Press, 1946, p. 9.
19. See Blok's untitled poem written August 29, 1914 (from the cycle "Rodina" [Native Land]), in *Yezhemesyachnyi zhurnal*, St. Petersburg, No. 10, 1914.
20. Krestovski, "Parizh, Iyul' 1848 g.," *Sobraniye sochineniya* [Collected Works], St. Petersburg, "Obshchestvennaya pol'za," Vol. IV, 1899, p. 186.

21. *Dnevnik*, Vol. II, p. 112.
22. Entry dated February 17, 1918, in *Zapisnye knizhki*, p. 199.
23. *Ibid.*, p. 187.
24. "Pesnya sud'by," *Sochineniya v odnom tome*, p. 359.
25. "Pushkinskomu domu" [To the Pushkin House], written February 11, 1921, *ibid.*, p. 299.
26. This stanza and those following are cited from Miss Deutsch's translation of "Skify" [The Scythians] in Yarmolinsky, ed., *A Treasury of Russian Verse*, pp. 167-169.
27. See Lundberg, Ye. G., *Ot vechnovo k prekhodyashchemu* [From the Eternal to the Transitory], Berlin, Petropolis, 1923.
28. Miss Deutsch's translation, *loc. cit.*
29. Berdyayev, *Dusha Rossii*, Moscow, Sytin, 1915 (in the series "Voina i revolyutsiya" [War and Revolution]).
30. See Spektorski, Ye., "Aleksandr L'vovich Blok," *Varshavskiye Universitetskiye Izvestiya* [Warsaw University Bulletin], Warsaw, No. 3, 1912, pp. 1-40, and No. 4, pp. 41-80.
31. Quoted in Mochul'ski, K. S., *Aleksandr Blok*, Paris, Y.M.C.A. Press, 1948, p. 13.
32. Blok, *Dnevnik*, Vol. II, pp. 96-97.
33. *Sobraniye sochinenii* [Collected Works], Berlin, Epokha, 1923, Vol. IX, p. 254.
34. In *Sochineniya v odnom tome*, p. 569.
35. "Florentsiya" [Florence], 1909, *ibid.*, p. 191.
36. "Ispoved' yazychnika" [Confession of a Pagan], *ibid.*, p. 459.
37. *Dnevnik*, Vol. II, p. 112.
38. "Ispoved' yazychnika," *Sochineniya v odnom tome*, p. 459.
39. "O naznachenii poeta" [The Calling of Poet], *ibid.*, p. 495. The speech was first published in *Vestnik literatury* [Literary Herald], Petrograd, No. 3, 1921.
40. "V Al'bom 'Pushkinskovo doma'" [In the Album of the Pushkin House], *Sochineniya v odnom tome*, p. 299.
41. "Voloshin, Maksimilian Aleksandrovich," *Literaturnaya entsiklopediya* [Literary Encyclopedia], Moscow, Vol. II, 1929, col. 283.
42. "Arkhaizm v russkoi zhivopisi," *Apollon* [Apollo], St. Petersburg, No. 1, October 1909, p. 43.
43. *Ibid.*, p. 45.
44. "Polden'," in "Literaturnyi al'manakh" [Literary Almanac], *ibid.*, p. 9.
45. "Sozvezdiya," *ibid.*, p. 10.
46. "Emil' Verkharn i Valerii Bryusov" [Emile Verhaeren and Valeri Bryusov], *Vesy* [The Scales], Moscow, No. 2, 1907, p. 75.
47. *Verkharn. Sud'ba, Tvorchestvo, Perevody* [Verhaeren: Fate, Writings and Translations], Moscow, 1919.
48. The "Savage Plain" (*dikoye pole*), sometimes translated "the wild grounds," was the southern strip of Muscovy in the sixteenth and seventeenth centuries, where Cossack "hosts" served as border guards.
49. "Dikoye pole," in *Nashi dni* [Our Days], Moscow, Gosizdat, No. 1, 1922, p. 115.

50. *Ibid.,* p. 113.
51. "Vystavka M. V. Nesterova" [M. V. Nesterov's Exhibition], *Vesy,* No. 3, 1907, p. 107.
52. "Dmetrius Imperator, 1591-1613," in *Demony glukhonemye* [Demons Deaf and Dumb], 2d ed., Berlin, Knigoizdatel'stvo pisatelei, 1923, pp. 43-44. The first edition of the volume was published in Kharkov in 1919.
53. "Protopop Avvakum," *Demony glukhonemye,* 1923, p. 54.
54. *Ibid.,* p. 66.
55. "Sten'kin sud," *ibid.,* p. 45.
56. "Sten'kin sud," p. 47.
57. "Severovostok" [The Northeast], *Stikhi o terrore* [Poems of the Terror], Berlin, Knigoizdatel'stvo pisatelei, 1923, p. 8.
58. *Ibid.,* p. 9.
59. "Terror," *ibid.,* p. 17.
60. "Boinya," *ibid.,* p. 16.
61. "Krasnaya vesna," *ibid.,* pp. 13-14.
62. "Grazhdanskaya voina," *ibid.,* p. 11.
63. "Severovostok," *ibid.,* p. 9.
64. "Gotovnost'" [Readiness], *ibid.,* p. 19.
65. "Kosmos" [Cosmos], *Volya Rossii* [Russia's Freedom], Prague, No. 1-2, January 1924, p. 36.
66. Belyi, *Pervoye svidaniye,* Petrograd, Alkonost, 1921.
67. Berdyayev, N. A., *Krizis iskusstva,* Moscow, Leman and Sakharov, 1918, p. 4.
68. *Ibid.,* pp. 17-18.
69. Malevich, *Bog ne skinut. Iskusstvo, tserkov', fabrika* [God Is Not Deposed: Art, the Church and the Factory], Vitebsk, 1922, p. 4.
70. *Ibid.,* p. 27.
71. *Ibid.,* p. 4.
72. Belyi, *Moskva pod udarom* [Moscow in Jeopardy], Moscow, Krug, 1926, p. 197 (Part 2 of the novel *Moskva* [Moscow].
73. Alekseyev-Askol'dov, "Tvorchestvo Andreya Belovo" [Andrei Belyi's Writing], *Literaturnaya mysl'* [Literary Thought], Petrograd, No. 1, 1922, pp. 75-76.
74. *Ibid.,* p. 78.
75. Belyi, *Moskva pod udarom,* p. 244.
76. "Dnevnik pisatelya" [Diary of a Writer], *Zapiski mechtatelei* [Dreamers' Journal], Petrograd, No. 2-3, 1921, pp. 119-120.
77. *Ibid.,* p. 114.
78. Voronski, "Belyi, Andrei," *Literaturnaya entsiklopediya,* Vol. I, 1929, col. 424.
79. Parts of *Kotik Letayev* were published in the almanacs *Skify* [The Scythians], Petrograd, No. 1, 1917, and No. 2, 1918; and in *Zapiski mechtatelei* for 1921.
80. "Prestupleniye Nikolaya Letayeva" [The Crime of Nikolai Letayev] in *Sovremennye zapiski* [Contemporary Notes], Paris, 1922; *Kreshchonyi kitayets* [The Baptized Chinese], Moscow, Nikitinskiye subbotniki, 1927.
81. *Kotik Letayev,* Petrograd, Epokha, 1922, p. 34.
82. *Ibid.,* p. 41.
83. *Ibid.,* p. 292.

84. *Moskovskii chudak* [A Moscow Crank], Moscow, Krug, 1926, p. 214 (Part 1 of *Moskva*). The two novels *Moskovskii chudak* and *Moskva pod udarom* [Moscow in Jeopardy], respectively Part 1 and 2 of *Moskva*, together constitute Vol. I of the uncompleted epic.

85. *Moskva pod udarom*, p. 215.

86. See, for instance, Ivanov's article "Kruchki" [Cliffs], *Zapiski mechatelei*, No. 1, 1919.

87. *Zimniye sonety*, republished in Ehrenburg, I., *Poeziya revolyutsionnoi Moskvy* [Poetry of Revolutionary Moscow], Berlin, Mysl', 1922.

88. *Perepiska iz dvukh uglov*, Petrograd, 1921.

89. In Zorgenfrei, "Nad Nevoi," in *Strastnaya subbota* [Holy Saturday], Petrograd, "Vremya," 1922, p. 49.

90. Remizov, "Slovo o pogibeli zemli Russkoi" in *Skify*, No. 2, 1918; incorporated in his *Ognennaya Rossiya* [Russia in Flames], Revel, Bibliofil, 1921.

91. In addition to *Ognennaya Rossiya*, see *Shumy goroda* [Noises of the City], Revel, Bibliofil, 1921, which contains writings of 1917-1920.

92. Rozanov, V., "La Divina Comedia," *Apokalipsis nashevo vremeni*, Sergiyev Posad, No. 8-9, 1918, p. 109.

93. "Yezhednevnost' " [Everydayness], *ibid.*, No. 3, 1918, p. 44.

94. "Perezhivaniye" [Life's Trials], *ibid.*, No. 6-7, p. 75.

95. "K chitatelyu" [To the Reader], *ibid.*, p. 2.

96. "Razyskannoye tsarstvo," *ibid.*, p. 5.

97. "Kak my umirayem" [How We Die], *ibid.*, p. 9.

98. *Ibid.*, p. 13.

Notes to Chapter 2 (pages 41-61):

1. Gumilyov, "Naslediye simvolizma i akmeizm" [Acmeism and the Legacy of Symbolism], *Apollon* [Apollo], St. Petersburg, No. 1, 1913, p. 43.

2. Gorodetski, S., "Nekotoriye techeniya v sovremennoi russkoi poezii" [Certain Trends in Contemporary Russian Poetry], *ibid.*, p. 48.

3. Ivanov, Georgi, "Vstupleniye" [Introduction], in Gumilyov, *Chuzhoye nebo* [Alien Sky], Berlin, Petropolis, 1936, pp. 5-6.

4. Gumilyov, "Nastupleniye" [Attack], *Kolchan* [The Quiver], Berlin, Petropolis, 1923, p. 60. The volume *Kolchan* was first published in Petrograd in 1916.

5. "Voina" [War], *Kolchan*, 1923, p. 10.

6. "Smert' " [Death], *ibid.*, p. 62.

7. "Voina," p. 11.

8. "Voin Agamemnona" [Agamemnon's Warrior], *Zhemchuga* [Pearls], St. Petersburg, "Prometei," 1918, p. 32. The volume *Zhemchuga* was first published in Moscow in 1910.

9. *Gondla* (a verse play), Berlin, Petropolis, 1936, p. 74 (first published in 1917).

10. "Zabludivshiisya tramvai" [Stray Trolley], *Ognennyi stolp* [Pillar of Fire], 2d ed., Petrograd and Berlin, Petropolis, 1922, p. 37. The first edition was published in Petrograd in 1921.

11. "Rabochii," *Kostyor* [The Bonfire], 2d ed., Berlin, Petrograd and Moscow, Grzhebin, 1922, pp. 25-26. The first edition was published in Petrograd in 1918.
12. Akhmatova, Anna, "Pamyati Innokentiya Annenskovo" [To the Memory of Innokenti Annenski], *Izbrannye stikhotvoreniya* [Selected Poems], New York, Chekhov Publishing House, 1952, p. 5.
13. Quoted in Ivanov, Georgi, *Peterburgskiye zimy* [Petersburg Winters], Paris, La Source, 1928, p. 67.
14. From *Chotki* [The Rosary], 9th ed., enlarged, Petrograd, Petropolis and Alkonost, 1923, p. 22.
15. Untitled poem in *Anno Domini MCMXXI*, 2d ed., Petrograd, Petropolis and Alkonost, 1923, p. 38.
16. Untitled lines in *Podorozhnik* [Plantain], Petrograd, 1921, p. 44.
17. "Iyul' 1914," *Belaya staya* [White Birds Flying], 4th ed., enlarged, Petrograd, Petropolis and Alkonost, 1923, p. 60.
18. From *Podorozhnik*, p. 36.
19. See Chukovski, Kornei, "Akhmatova i Mayakovskii" [Akhmatova and Mayakovski], *Dom iskusstv* [House of the Arts], Petrograd, No. 1, 1920, pp. 23-42.
20. Akhmatova, "Mayakovskii v 1913 godu" [Mayakovski in 1913], *Iz shesti knig* [From Six Books], Leningrad, Sovetskii pisatel', 1940, p. 43. The poem is dated 1940 and is part of the cycle "Iva" [Willow Tree].
21. See "Muzhestvo," in Akhmatova, *Izbrannye stikhotvoreniya*, p. 1. The translation used here is that of Miss Babette Deutsch in Yarmolinsky, Avrahm, ed., *A Treasury of Russian Verse*, New York, Macmillan, 1949, p. 194.
22. "Iz Tashkentskoi tetradi, 1942" [From a Tashkent Notebook, 1942], *Znamya* [Banner], Moscow, No. 4, 1945, p. 50.
23. *O zhurnalakh "Zvezda" i "Leningrad." Iz postanovleniya TsK VKP(b) ot 14 avgusta 1946 g.* [Concerning the Journals *Star* and *Leningrad*: From the Resolution of the Central Committee of the All-Union Communist Party of August 14, 1946], Moscow, Gospolitizdat, 1952, p. 4.
24. "Iz tsikla 'Slava miru'" [From the "Hail Peace!" Cycle], *Ogonyok* [Flamelet], No. 14, April 2, 1950, p. 20.
25. Mandel'shtam, "Utro akmeizma" [The Morning of Acmeism], *Sirena* [Siren], Voronezh, January 1, 1919.
26. Sovsun, V., "Akmeizm" [Acmeism], *Literaturnaya entsiklopediya* [Literary Encyclopedia], Moscow, Vol. I, 1929, col. 73.
27. Mandel'shtam, "Batyushkov," *Novyi mir* [New World], Moscow, No. 6, 1932, p. 107.
28. "Rakovina," *Stikhotvoreniya* [Poems], Moscow and Leningrad, Gosizdat, 1928, p. 28.
29. Ivanov, *Peterburgskiye zimy*, p. 115.
30. Mandel'shtam, "Nevyrazimaya pechal'" [Inexpressible Sorrow], *Stikhotvoreniya*, p. 12.
31. "Skudnyi luch" [Meager Ray], *Kamen'*, 2d ed., Moscow and Petrograd, Gosizdat, 1923, p. 19.
32. "Agiya Sofiya" [St. Sophia], *Stikhotvoreniya*, p. 40.
33. "Notre Dame," *ibid.*, p. 42.
34. "Lyuteranin," *ibid.*, p. 39.
35. "Vek" [The Age], 1923, *ibid.*, p. 166.

36. "Sumerki svobody," *Tristia,* Petrograd and Berlin, Petropolis, 1922, p. 67.
37. Untitled lines of 1918, *ibid.,* p. 34.
38. No title, *ibid.,* p. 55.
39. Untitled lines of 1919, *ibid.,* p. 40.
40. Untitled lines dated 1918, *ibid.,* p. 36.
41. "Vek," *Stikhotvoreniya,* p. 167.
42. "Nashedshii podkovu" [He Who Finds a Horseshoe], 1923, *ibid.,* p. 172.
43. Untitled lines, *Novyi mir,* No. 6, 1932, p. 107.
44. "Slovo i kul'tura" [The Word and Culture], *O poezii* [On Poetry], Leningrad, Academia, 1928, p. 5.
45. "Barmy zakona" [Royal Mantle of the Law], *Shum vremeni* [The Sound of the Time], Leningrad, Vremya, 1925, pp. 96-97.
46. "Yegipetskaya marka" [The Egyptian Stamp], *Zvezda* [Star], Leningrad, No. 5, 1928, p. 74. The volume *Yegipetskaya marka* was also published in 1928, by Priboi, Leningrad.
47. "Yegipetskaya marka," *Zvezda,* p. 64.
48. *Ibid.,* p. 70.
49. Gorodetski, from the cycle "Druz'ya ushedshiye" [Friends Departed], *Styk* [Junction], Moscow, No. 1, 1925, pp. 63-64.
50. Kuzmin, "Strannichii vecher," *Ekho* [Echo], Petrograd, 1921, p. 9.
51. *Ibid.,* p. 10.
52. Narbut, "Oktyabr'," *Sovetskaya zemlya* [The Soviet Land], Kharkov, 1921, p. 3.
53. See, for instance, *Novyi mir,* No. 6, 1933, p. 43; and *Krasnaya nov'* [Red Virgin Soil], Moscow, No. 10, 1935, p. 96.
54. Untitled poem in Zenkevich, *Izbrannye stikhotvoreniya* [Selected Poems], Moscow, Sovetskii pisatel', 1933, p. 92.
55. *Pashnya tankov,* Saratov, 1921.
56. "Chapayevskiye pominki," *Styk,* No. 1, 1925, p. 77.
57. "Byk na boine," *Nabor vysoty,* Moscow, GIKhL, 1937, p. 40.
58. "Rassvet na Myasnitskaya," *Izbrannye stikhotvoreniya,* p. 93.
59. Rozhdestvenski, "Feodosiya," *Izbrannye stikhi* [Selected Poems], Leningrad, GIKhL, 1936, p. 116.

Notes to Chapter 3 (pages 61-67):

1. Gorki, M., untitled article dated April 27, 1917, in *Revolyutsiya i kul'tura* [Revolution and Culture], Berlin, Ladyzhnikov, 1923, p. 15. The article quoted, like most of Gorki's political writings immediately after the November Revolution, was first published in the Petrograd newspaper *Novaya zhizn'* [New Life], and was reprinted several times in Russia before publication in the Berlin edition cited. Gorki expressed his misgivings also in *Nesvoyevremennye mysli* [Inopportune Thoughts], Petrograd, "Kul'tura i svoboda," 1918.
2. Untitled article of 1917, in *Revolyutsiya i kul'tura,* p. 76.
3. *Ibid.,* p. 57.
4. *Ibid.,* p. 12.

5. The four volumes of *Zhizn' Klima Samgina* [The Life of Klim Samgina] have been translated under four separate titles: (Vol. I) *Bystander*, trans. by B. G. Guerney, New York, Cape and Smith, 1930; (Vol. II) *The Magnet*, trans. by A. Bakshy, New York, Cape and Smith, 1931; (Vol. III) *Other Fires*, trans. by A. Bakshy, New York, Appleton, 1933; and (Vol. IV) *The Specter*, trans. by A. Bakshy, New York, Appleton-Century, 1938.

6. Quoted in Piksanov, N. N., *Gor'kii—poet* [Gorki As Poet], Leningrad, Goslitizdat, 1940, p. 115.

7. Gorki, "Yegor Bulychov and Others," in *Seven Plays of Maxim Gorki*, trans. by Alexander Bakshy in collaboration with Paul S. Nathan, New Haven, Yale University Press, 1946, p. 388. For the first publication, see "Yegor Bulychov i drugiye," in the almanac *God XVII* [Seventeenth Year], Moscow, No. 3, 1933, pp. 5-58.

8. *Vospominaniya o L've Tolstom*, Petrograd, 1919; published in an enlarged second edition in Berlin, 1922.

9. See Gorki's introduction in Il'in, Yakov, ed., *Lyudi Stalingradskovo traktornovo* [People of the Stalingrad Tractor Plant], Moscow, OGIZ, 1933 (in the series *Istoriya fabrik i zavodov* [History of Factories and Plants]).

10. Gorki, L. Averbakh and S. G. Firin, eds., *Belomorskoi-baltiiskii kanal imeni Stalina* [The Stalin Belomor-Baltic Canal], Moscow, Gosizdat, 1934; published in the English language under the title *Belomor*, trans. by Amabel Williams-Ellis, New York, Smith and Haas, 1935.

11. *Bolshevtsy. Ocherki po istorii Bolshevskoi imeni Yagody trudokommuny N.K.V.D.* [Those from Bolshevo: Sketches on the Story of the Yagoda Labor Commune of the NKVD], Moscow, OGIZ, 1936 (in the series *Istoriya fabrik i zavodov*).

12. Voronski, A. K., "Nasha literatura" [Our Literature], in the collective volume *Oktyabr' v iskusstve* [October in Art], Leningrad, "Krasnaya gazeta," 1927, p. 28.

13. Veresayev, *V tupike*, Moscow, 1924; first published in *Krasnaya nov'* [Red Virgin Soil], Moscow, No. 5, 1922; published in English translation under the title *The Deadlock*, New York, Century, 1928.

14. *Syostry*, Moscow, GIKhL, 1933 (*The Sisters*, trans. by Juliet Soskice, London, Hutchinson, 1936).

15. "Isanka," *Novyi mir* [New World], Moscow, No. 3, 1928, p. 14.

16. *Ibid.*, p. 23.

17. *Ibid.*, p. 27.

18. See his *Yunye gody* [Years of Youth], Moscow, "Nedro," 1927.

19. "Nevydumannye rasskazy o proshlom," *Novyi mir*, No. 6, 1940.

20. *Dikiye* [The Dikii Family], Berlin, Ladyzhnikov, 1923, p. 129.

Notes to Chapter 4 (pages 68-90):

1. Tynyanov, "O Khlebnikove" [Concerning Khlebnikov], in Khlebnikov, *Sobraniye proizvedenii* [Collected Works], Leningrad, Izdatel'stvo pisatelei [1930?], Vol. I, p. 20.

2. Khlebnikov, Velemir (name adopted by Khlebnikov in preference to "Viktor"), "Nasha osnova" [Our Principle], *ibid.*, Vol. V, p. 233. The article was first published in 1920.

3. Yakobson (Jakobson), R., "Viktor Khlebnikov," *Noveishaya russkaya poeziya* [Modern Russian Poetry], Prague, "Politika," 1921, p. 30.

4. Quoted in Stepanov, N., "Tvorchestvo Velemira Khlebnikova" [The Writing of Velemir Khlebnikov], in Khlebnikov, *Sobraniye proizvedenii*, Vol. I, p. 33, note.

5. Yakobson, p. 68.

6. Yakobson, "O pokolenii rastrativshem svoikh poetov," *Smert' Vladimira Mayakovskovo* [The Death of Vladimir Mayakovski], Berlin, Petropolis, 1931, p. 9.

7. Khlebnikov, *Noch' v okope*, Moscow, Imazhinisty, 1921.

8. "Otkaz," *Stikhi* [Poems], Moscow [1923], p. 13. In another edition which the author remembers but which is not now available the last word of the poem was "Commissar."

9. "Nochnoi obysk," *Sobraniye proizvedenii*, Vol. I, pp. 252-256, *passim*.

10. *Ibid.*, p. 227.

11. From *Zangezi*, Moscow, 1922, p. 5.

12. "Ladomir," *Sobraniye proizvedenii*, Vol. I, p. 195.

13. *Ibid.*, p. 193.

14. "Azy iz uzy" [A's of Propolis], *ibid.*, Vol. V, p. 29.

15. "Siniye kovy" [Blue Fetters], *ibid.*, Vol. I, p. 285.

16. *Ibid.*, p. 299.

17. *Ibid.*, p. 293.

18. *Zangezi*, p. 29.

19. Untitled sketch "Nikto ne budet otritsat' . . ." [Nobody Will Deny . . .], *Sobraniye proizvedenii*, Vol. IV, p. 116.

20. "Malinovaya shashka," *ibid.*, p. 123.

21. *Ibid.*, p. 122.

22. *Ibid.*, p. 124.

23. *Ibid.*, p. 127.

24. Mayakovski, "Fleita-pozvonochnik" [Spine Flute], *Sobraniye sochinenii* [Collected Works], Moscow and Leningrad, Gosizdat, Vol. I, 1928, p. 227.

25. Chukovski, Kornei, "Vladimir Mayakovskii," *Futuristy* [The Futurists], Petrograd, Polyarnaya zvezda, 1922, p. 61.

26. Kogan, P. S., *Literatura etikh let* [Literature of These Years], 2d ed., Ivanovo-Vosnesensk, Osnova, 1924, p. 144.

27. Mayakovski, "Poyasneniya" [Explanations], *Izbrannye sochineniya* [Selections], Moscow, GIKhL, 1949, p. 486.

28. "Vo ves' golos," *ibid.*, p. 422.

29. "Vladimir Il'ich Lenin," *ibid.*, p. 366.

30. *Ibid.*, p. 376.

31. "Misteriya-Buff" (second variant) in Mayakovski, *Sobraniye sochinenii v odnom tome* [Collected Works in One Volume], Leningrad, GIKhL, 1940, p. 366.

32. Quoted in Katanyan, V., *Mayakovskii. Literaturnaya khronika* [Mayakovski: Literary Chronicle], 2d ed., Moscow, Sovetskii pisatel', 1948, p. 321.

33. *Ibid.*, p. 319.

34. "Khorosho!" *Izbrannye sochineniya*, pp. 414-415.

Notes

35. "Sergeyu Yeseninu," *ibid.*, pp. 173-174.
36. "Razgovor s fininspektorom o poezii," *ibid.*, p. 172.
37. "Poslaniye proletarskim poetam," *ibid.*, p. 176.
38. "O dryani" [About Filth], *ibid.*, pp. 46-47.
39. "Pro eto," *ibid.*, p. 365.
40. *Ibid.*, p. 366.
41. *Ibid.*, p. 356.
42. Berdyayev, Nikolai, *O naznachenii cheloveka* [Man's Destiny], Paris, Sovremennye zapiski, 1931, pp. 279-280.
43. See Yakobson (Jakobson), "O pokolenii rastrativshem svoikh poetov," in *Smert' Vladimira Mayakovskovo*.
44. Berdyayev, p. 279.
45. Quoted in Shklovski, Viktor, *O Mayakovskom* [On Mayakovski], Moscow, Sovetskii pisatel', 1940, p. 214. The lines were first published in *Novyi LEF* [New LEF], Moscow, No. 6, 1928, p. 19.
46. Kruchonykh, "Vstupleniye" [Introduction], *Sdvigologiya russkovo stikha. Traktat obizhal'nyi i pouchal'nyi*, Vol. CXXI, No. 2, Moscow, MAF, 1922, p. 3.
47. "Zima" [Winter], in Kruchonykh, A., G. Petnikov and V. Khlebnikov, *Zaumniki* [Trans-Sensists], [Baku], 1922, p. 7.
48. Petnikov, "Outro," *ibid.*, p. 8.
49. Untitled lines, *ibid.*, p. 10.
50. Bogorodski, *Dayosh. Kak budto stikhi*, Petrograd, 1922.
51. See Kruchonykh, *Sdvigologiya*, pp. 13, 23-25.
52. See Vaginov, "Koslinaya pesnya," *Zvezda*, No. 10, 1927, pp. 53-97.
53. Bobrov, Sergei, *Vosstaniye misantropov* [The Revolt of the Misanthropes], Moscow, Tsentrifuga, 1922, pp. 43-44.
54. *Ibid.*, p. 41.
55. *Ibid.*, pp. 52-53.
56. *Ibid.*, p. 53.
57. *Ibid.*, p. 85.
58. *Ibid.*, p. 117.

Notes to Chapter 5 (pages 90-133):

1. Quoted in Beskin, O., "Kulatskaya literatura" [Kulak Literature], *Literaturnaya entsiklopediya* [Literary Encyclopedia], Moscow, Vol. V, 1931, col. 713.
2. *Ibid.*, col. 712.
3. Klyuyev, "Dolina yedinoroga" [Valley of the Unicorn], *Pesnoslov* [Songbook], Petrograd, Literaturno-izdatel'skii otdel Narkomprosa, 1919, Vol. II, p. 66.
4. *Mednyi kit* [Copper Whale], Petrograd, Izdatel'stvo Soveta rabochikh i krasnoarmeiskikh deputatov, 1919, p. 5.
5. Vol. I contains five poem cycles, four of them bearing the titles of his earlier books and the fifth consisting of poems originally included in the third

and fourth cycles: "Sosen perezvon" [Carillon of Pines], "Bratskiye pesni" [Songs of Fellowship], "Lesnye byli" [Tales of the Forest], "Mirskiye dumy" [Temporal Thoughts], and "Pesni iz zaonezh'ya" [Songs from Beyond the Onega]. Vol. II has three divisions: "Serdtse yedinoroga" [Heart of the Unicorn], which includes the cycle "Izbyanye pesni" [Peasant-Hut Songs]; "Dolina yedinoroga" [Valley of the Unicorn]; and "Krasnyi ryk" [Red Roar], including the long poem "Mednyi kit" [Copper Whale].

6. *L'vinyi khleb*, Moscow, "Nash put'," 1922.
7. *Chetvyortyi Rim*, Petrograd, "Epokha," 1922.
8. *Mat'-Subbota*, Petrograd, "Polyarnaya zvezda," 1922.
9. *Izba i pole. Izbrannye stikhotvoreniya* [Cabin and Field: Selected Poems], Leningrad, "Priboi," 1928.
10. "Plach o Sergeye Yesenine," in Klyuyev, Nikolai, and P. N. Medvedev, *Sergei Yesenin*, Leningrad, "Priboi," 1927.
11. "Zaozer'ye" was published in a Leningrad almanac, *Petrogradskiye poety* [Petrograd Poets], about 1924. No copy of the almanac is now available. The poem, however, is included in an edition of Klyuyev's works published in New York in 1954; see note 13 below.
12. "Derevnya," *Zvezda* [Star], Leningrad, No. 1, 1927.
13. See Klyuyev, "Pogorel'shchina," *Polnoye sobraniye sochinenii* [Complete Works], ed. by Boris Filippov, 2 vols., New York, Chekhov Publishing House, 1954. The word *pogorel'shchina* means, literally, the site of a fire after the fire, the people's plight, and the destruction wrought.
14. "Poetu Sergeyu Yeseninu" [To the Poet Sergei Yesenin], *Pesnoslov*, Vol. II, pp. 66-67.
15. Untitled lines from "Lesnye byli," *Pesnoslov*, Vol. I, p. 202.
16. From "Dolina yedinoroga," p. 49.
17. From *Izbyanye pesni*, Berlin, "Skify," 1920, p. 22.
18. "Zaveshchaniye" [Testament], *Sosen perezvon*, Moscow, Znamenski, 1912, p. 71.
19. *Mednyi kit*, p. 24. The translation used is from Patrick, George Z., *Popular Poetry in Soviet Russia*, Berkeley, University of California Press, 1929, p. 15.
20. *Lenin*, Moscow and Leningrad, Gosizdat, 1924, p. 24.
21. *Mednyi kit*, p. 53. The translation is from Patrick, p. 24.
22. "Krasnaya pesnya" [Red Song], *Izbyanye pesni*, pp. 5-6. The translation is from Patrick, p. 223.
23. *Lenin*, p. 5.
24. *Ibid.*, pp. 5-6.
25. "Zaozer'ye," *Polnoye sobraniye sochinenii*, Vol. II, p. 100.
26. Untitled poem (of 1918 or 1919) in *Lenin*, p. 38.
27. Untitled poem, in *Pesnoslov*, Vol. II, p. 228.
28. Untitled poem, in *Mednyi kit*, p. 65.
29. Untitled poem, *ibid.*, p. 57.
30. "Respublika" [Republic], *Pesnoslov*, Vol. II, p. 216.
31. "Derevnya," p. 126.
32. *Ibid.*, p. 128.
33. An extremely interesting account of the last years of Klyuyev's life is given in Filippov, Boris, "Nikolai Klyuyev. Materialy k biografii" [Nikolai

Klyuyev: Materials for a Biography], in Klyuyev, *Polnoye sobraniye sochinenii*, Vol. I; see especially pp. 88-110.
34. "Pogorel'shchina," *ibid.*, Vol. II, p. 134.
35. *Ibid.*, p. 136.
36. See Ivanov-Razumnik, *Pisatel'skiye sud'by* [The Fate of Writers], New York, "Literaturnyi Fond," 1951, p. 37.
37. Quoted in Mashbits-Verov, N., "Sergei Klychkov," *Na literaturnom postu* [On Literary Guard], Moscow, No. 8, 1927, pp. 31-32. The novel was published in 1925 (*Sakharnyi nemets*, Moscow, Sovremennye problemy).
38. Klychkov, *Seryi barin*, Kharkov, Proletarii [1926], p. 17.
39. *Gost' chudesnyi*, Gosizdat, 1923. This book contains poems previously published in the collections *Kol'tso Lady* [Lada's Ring], *Dubravna*, *Potayonnyi sad* [The Secret Garden], and *Bova*.
40. Untitled verses, in *Gost' chudesnyi*, p. 67.
41. "Predchuvstviye" [Premonition], *ibid.*, p. 70.
42. "Dedova pakhota" [Forefathers' Ploughing], *ibid.*, p. 13.
43. *Talisman*, Leningrad, Gosizdat, 1927.
44. *V gostyakh u zhuravlei*, Moscow, Federatsiya, 1930.
45. *Ibid.*, p. 65.
46. *Ibid.*, pp. 30-31.
47. Quoted in Mashbits-Verov, p. 31.
48. *Chertukhinskii balakir'*, Moscow and Leningrad, Gosizdat, 1926, p. 109.
49. *Ibid.*, p. 32.
50. *Ibid.*, p. 44.
51. *Ibid.*, p. 102.
52. *Ibid.*, p. 103.
53. *Ibid.*, p. 158.
54. From *Poslednii Lel'* [The Last Lel'], quoted in Beskin, O., "Klychkov," *Literaturnaya entsiklopediya*, Vol. V, 1931, col. 322.
55. *Ibid.*, col. 323.
56. *Chertukhinskii balakir'*, p. 33.
57. *Poslednii Lel'*, Kharkov, Proletarii, 1927.
58. *Chertukhinskii balakir'*, p. 22.
59. *Ibid.*, p. 212.
60. *Ibid.*, p. 271.
61. *Knyaz' mira*, Moscow, Krug, 1929.
62. *Ibid.*, pp. 85-86.
63. Oreshin, "Alyi khram" [Crimson Temple], in the collection *Alyi khram*, Moscow, Gosizdat, 1922, pp. 5-6. The translation is from Patrick, pp. 242-243.
64. "Kvasok" [Kvass], *Rzhanoye solntse* [Rye Sun], Moscow, GIZ, 1923, p. 8. The translation is from Patrick, p. 244.
65. "Noch'" [Night], *Alyi khram*, p. 18.
66. "Garmonist," *Rzhanoye solntse*, p. 135.
67. "Komissarka," *ibid.*, p. 146.
68. "Poyekhali" [We're Off], in *Rodnik* [The Spring], Moscow, Gosizdat, 1927, p. 189.

69. "Moskva-reka" [Moscow River], *ibid.*, pp. 56-57.
70. "Zhuravlinaya" [Crane's (Song)], *Solomennaya plakha* [Straw Block], Moscow, Gosizdat, 1924, p. 184.
71. "Zemlya rodnaya" [Native Land], *Rodnik*, p. 161.
72. "Uyezdnoye" [The District], *Solomennaya plakha*, pp. 93-95, *passim*.
73. "Sel'kor Tsyganok," *Rodnik*, p. 279.
74. *Ibid.*, p. 280.
75. *Ibid.*, p. 281.
76. *Ibid.*, p. 282.
77. "Militsioner Lyuksha," *ibid.*, p. 311.
78. *Ibid.*, p. 315.
79. *Ibid.*
80. *Na golodnoi zemle*, Moscow, Krasnaya nov', 1922, p. 5.
81. *Ibid.*, p. 13.
82. "Skvoznyachok," in the almanac *Nashi dni* [Our Days], Moscow, No. 1, 1922, pp. 261-278.
83. *Lyudishki*, Moscow, GIZ, 1927.
84. See Ivanov-Razumnik, "Poety i revolyutsiya" [Poets and the Revolution], in the anthology *Skify* [The Scythians], Petrograd, No. 2, 1918, p. 2.
85. Mayakovski, V. V., "Upadochnoye nastroyeniye sredi molodyozhi" [Low Spirits Among Young People] (from a speech of 1927), in his *Sobraniye sochinenii* [Collected Works], Moscow and Leningrad, Gosizdat, Vol. X, 1933, pp. 317-329.
86. Yesenin, "O sebe" [About Myself], *Sobraniye stikhotvorenii* [Collected Poems], Moscow and Leningrad, Gosizdat, 1926, Vol. I, p. xxxix.
87. Polonski, *O sovremennoi literature* [On Contemporary Literature], Moscow, Gosizdat, 1928, pp. 14-15.
88. Yesenin, *Klyuchi Marii*, Moscow, Izdatel'stvo Moskovskoi trudovoi arteli khudozhnikov slova, 1920, p. 13.
89. *Ibid.*, pp. 14-15.
90. *Ibid.*, p. 15.
91. *Ibid.*, p. 26.
92. "O sebe," *Sobraniye stikhotvorenii*, Vol. I, pp. xxxvii-xxxix, *passim*.
93. "Iordanskaya golubitsa" [The Jordan Dove], *ibid.*, Vol. II, p. 60. The translation is that of Miss Babette Deutsch, in Yarmolinsky, Avrahm, ed., *A Treasury of Russian Verse*, New York, Macmillan, 1949, p. 246.
94. "Iordanskaya golubitsa," *Sobrianiye stikhotvorenii*, Vol. II, p. 61.
95. "Inoniya," *ibid.*, p. 65.
96. *Ibid.*, p. 66.
97. *Ibid.*, p. 73.
98. "Otchar'," *ibid.*, p. 36.
99. "Vozvrashcheniye na rodinu" [Returning Home], *ibid.*, p. 99.
100. "Prishestviye," *ibid.*, p. 47.
101. "Tovarishch" [The Comrade], *ibid.*, p. 32.
102. "Kobyl'i korabli," *ibid.*, p. 82.

103. *Ibid.*, p. 83.
104. *Ibid.*, p. 85.
105. "Sorokoust," *ibid.*, p. 89.
106. *Ibid.*, p. 88.
107. *Ibid.*, p. 90.
108. No title, *ibid.*, Vol. IV (*Stikhi i proza* [Verses and Prose]), p. 130. The translation is that of Babette Deutsch, under the title "A Moony Thin Desolation," in Yarmolinsky, *A Treasury of Russian Verse*, p. 248.
109. Untitled poem in *Sobraniye stikhotvorenii*, Vol. I, pp. 198-199.
110. *Moskva kabatskaya*, Leningrad, 1924.
111. Untitled lines in *Sobraniye stikhotvorenii*, Vol. I, p. 210 (first published in the Imaginist journal *Gostinitsa dlya puteshestvuyushchikh v prekrasnom* [Inn for Wayfarers in the Beautiful] in 1924 under the title "Moskva kabatskaya" [Tavern Moscow], but not included in the cycle published separately under the same name.
112. "Chornyi chelovek," *Sobraniye stikhotvorenii*, Vol. III, p. 224; first published in *Novyi mir* [New World], Moscow, No. 1, 1926, pp. 5-9.
113. From "Moskva kabatskaya," *Sobraniye stikhotvorenii*, Vol. I, p. 191. The translation is that of George Reavey in Reavey and Marc Slonim, ed. and trans., *Soviet Literature: An Anthology*, New York, Covici Friede, 1934, p. 357.
114. Nikitina, "Sergei Yesenin," in *Yesenin. Zhizn', lichnost', tvorchestvo* [Yesenin: Life, Personality and Writings], ed. by Nikitina, Moscow, Izdatel'stvo Rabotnikov Prosveshcheniya, 1926, p. 12.
115. "Pamyati Sergeya Yesenina" [In Memory of Sergei Yesenin], *ibid.*, p. 94.
116. See Bukharin, N., *Partiya i oppozitsionnyi blok* [The Party and the Opposition Bloc], Leningrad, Priboi [1926?]; and *Partiya i oppozitsiya na poroge XV parts"yezda* [The Party and the Opposition on the Threshold of the XV Party Congress], Moscow and Leningrad, Gosizdat, 1927.
117. See, for instance, Rozenfel'd, B., "Yesenin," *Literaturnaya entsiklopediya*, Vol. IV, 1930, col. 86.
118. Kogan, P. S., *Literatura etikh let, 1917-1923* [Literature of These Years, 1917-1923], 2d ed., Ivanovo-Vosnesensk, Osnova, 1924, p. 123.
119. Yesenin, "Pugachov," *Sobraniye stikhotvorenii*, Vol. III, p. 46.
120. "Strana negodyayev," *ibid.*, pp. 175-176.
121. *Ibid.*, p. 176.
122. *Ibid.*, p. 199.
123. Ivanov, in Yesenin, *Stikhotvoreniya 1910-1925* [Poems of 1910-1925], Paris, Vozrozhdeniye, n.d., pp. 31-32.
124. Shiryayevets, "Skladen'" [Icon Stand], *Volzhskiye pesni* [Volga Songs], Moscow, "Krug," 1928, p. 107.
125. From the cycle "Golodnaya Rus'" [Starving Rus'], *ibid.*, p. 151.
126. Radimov, "Perekrestok" [Crossroads], *Derevnya* [The Village], Revel and Berlin, Bibliofil [1923], p. 19. The collection was first published in Kazan' in 1922.
127. "Pokhorony" [Burial], *Krasnaya nov'* [Red Virgin Soil], Moscow, No. 1, January-February 1923, p. 94.
128. Druzhinin, "Rossiiskoye," *Krasnaya nov'*, No. 12, 1926, pp. 140-141.
129. Pribludnyi, *Topolna kamne*, Moscow, "Nikitinskiye Subbotniki," 1926.

Notes to Chapter 6 (pages 133-138):

1. Shershenevich, *2 × 2 = 5* [*Dvazhdy dva pyat'*], Moscow, 1920.
2. L'vov-Rogachevski, *Imazhinizm i yevo obrazonostsy* [Imagism and Its Image-Bearers], n.p., "Ordans," 1921.
3. Quoted in Rozenfel'd, B., "Imazhinizm" [Imaginism], *Literaturnaya entsiklopediya* [Literary Encyclopedia], Moscow, Vol. IV, 1930, col. 461.
4. *Ibid.*
5. Ivnev, Ryurik, *Chetyre vystrela v Yesenina, Kusikova, Mariyengofa, Shershenevicha* [Four Shots at Yesenin, Kusikov, Marienhof, and Shershenevich], Moscow, Imazhinisty, 1921, pp. 26-27.
6. Shershenevich, "Estradnaya arkhitektonika" [Music Hall Architectonics], *Loshad', kak loshad'* [The Horse As Horse], Moscow, Pleyad, 1920.
7. L'vov-Rogachevski, p. 35.
8. Quoted *ibid.*, pp. 34-35.
9. Quoted *ibid.*, p. 38.
10. Mariyengof (Marienhof), A., *Buyan-ostrov*, Moscow, Imazhinisty, 1920, pp. 7-8.
11. *Brityi chelovek*, Berlin, Petropolis, n.d.
12. *Roman bez vran'ya*, Leningrad, Priboi, 1927.
13. "Yekaterina," *Literaturnyi sovremennik* [Literary Contemporary], Leningrad, No. 9, 1936, pp. 57-83; No. 10, pp. 86-107.
14. Ivnev, untitled poem dated May 3, 1919, in *Solntse vo grobe* [Sun in a Coffin], Moscow, Imazhinisty, 1921, pages unnumbered.
15. *Lyubov' bez lyubvi*, Moscow, Sovremennye problemy, 1925.
16. *Otkrytyi dom*, Leningrad, Mysl', 1927.
17. *Geroi romana*, Leningrad, 1928.
18. Kusikov, untitled lines in *V nikuda* [Into the Nowhere], Moscow, Imazhinisty, 1920, p. 25.

Notes to Chapter 7 (pages 138-140):

1. Bednyi, *Sobraniye sochinenii 1909-1922* [Collected Works of 1909-1922], Moscow, Krokodil, 1923.
2. "Nabat," quoted in Tseitlin, A. G., "Bednyi, Dem'yan," *Literaturnaya entsiklopediya* [Literary Encyclopedia], Moscow, Vol. I, 1929, col. 384.
3. "Do etovo mesta" [To This Point], *Sobraniye sochinenii*, p. 77.
4. Quoted in Kogan, P. S. *Literatura etikh let* [Literature of These Years], 2d ed., Ivanovo-Voznesensk, "Osnova," 1924, p. 27.
5. See Georgi Ivanov's introduction to Yesenin, *Stikhotvoreniya* [Poems], Paris, Vozrozhdeniye, 1952.

Notes to Chapter 8 (pages 141-145):

1. Quoted in Lelevich, G., "Bessal'ko, Pavel Karpovich," *Literaturnaya entsiklopediya* [Literary Encyclopedia], Moscow, Vol. I, 1929, col. 471.

2. Bogdanov, *Inzhener Menni*, 5th ed., Moscow, Moskovskii rabochii, 1923, p.129.
3. *Ibid.*, p. 141.
4. "O khudozhestvennom nasledstve" [Concerning the Art Heritage], *Iskusstvo i rabochii klass* [Art and the Worker Class], Moscow, Proletarskaya kul'tura, 1918, p. 44.

Notes to Chapter 9 (pages 145-156):

1. Quoted in *Kniga dlya chteniya* [Reader], comp. by L'vov-Rogachevski, Leningrad, Priboi, 1926, Vol. I, p. 364.
2. Quoted in *Novyi chtets-deklamator* [New Reader-Declaimer], Moscow, "Kniga," 1923, p. 125.
3. Gastev, *Poeziya rabochevo udara*, Petrograd, Proletkul't, 1918.
4. *Pachka orderov*, Riga, 1921. These poems were included in the fourth, fifth, and sixth editions of *Poeziya rabochevo udara*, Moscow, 1923-25.
5. Quoted in Pertsov, V., "Sovremenniki" [Contemporaries], *Novyi LEF* [The New LEF], Moscow, No. 8-9, 1927, p. 78.
6. From *Pachka orderov*; quoted in Arvatov, B., in *Novyi LEF*, No. 1, March 1923, p. 244.
7. See, for instance, Gastev, *Snaryazheniye sovremennoi kul'tury* [The Accouterments of Contemporary Culture], 1923; and *Vosstaniye kul'tury* [Revolt in Culture], Kharkov, 1923. A fuller exposition of Gastev's views, with copious quotations, may be found in Kaun, Alexander, *Soviet Poets and Poetry*, Berkeley and Los Angeles, University of California Press, 1943, pp. 135-140.
8. Zelinski, K., "Gastev," *Malaya sovetskaya entsiklopediya* [Small Soviet Encyclopedia], Moscow, 2d ed., Vol. III, 1935, col. 16.
9. Bogdanov, "O khudozhestvennom nasledstve" [Concerning the Art Heritage], *Iskusstvo i rabochii klass* [Art and the Worker Class], Moscow, Proletarskaya kul'tura, 1918, p. 31.
10. See "Raketa" [Rocket], *Bol'shaya sovetskaya entsiklopediya* [Large Soviet Encyclopedia], 2d ed., Moscow, Vol. XXXV, 1955, p. 665; and "Reaktivnyi dvigatel'" [Jet Propulsion Engine], *ibid.*, Vol. XXXVI, 1955, p. 149.
11. Quoted in Belyayev, A. R., "K. E. Tsiolkovskii," *Vsemirnyi sledopyt* [World Pathfinder], Moscow, No. 11-12, 1930.
12. Tsiolkovski, *Gryozy o zemle i nebe i effekty vsemirnovo tyagoteniya* [Fancies of the Earth and Sky and the Effects of Universal Gravitation], 1895; see Perel'man, Ya. I., *Tsiolkovskii. Zhizn' i tekhnicheskiye idei* [Tsiolkovski: Life and Technical Ideas], Moscow and Leningrad, ONTI, 1937, p. 52.
13. Dubovskoi, V., *O proletarskoi literature* [On Proletarian Literature], Moscow, Novaya Moskva, 1924, p. 23.
14. See Chernyshev, N. G., *Problemy mezhplanetnykh soobshchenii v rabotakh K. E. Tsiolkovskovo i drugikh otechestvennykh uchyonykh* [Problems of Interplanetary Communication in the Work of K. E. Tsiolkovski and Other Native Scientists], Moscow, Znaniye, 1953, p. 21.
15. Kirillov, "Razgovor so zvyozdami," *Stikhotvoreniya 1913-1923* [Poems of 1913-1923], Moscow, Mospoligraf, 1924, p. 123.
16. "Kholmy polei" [Knolls on the Fields], *ibid.*, p. 112.

17. Trotski, Lev, *Literatura i revolyutsiya,* 2d enlarged ed., Moscow, Goszidat, 1924, p. 160.
18. Kirillov, untitled verse in *Stikhotvoreniya 1913-1923,* p. 63.
19. "25 oktyabrya," *ibid.,* p. 106.
20. Untitled lines from the cycle "Semnadtsatyi god" [The Year 1917], *ibid.,* p. 103.
21. Untitled lines, *Izbrannye stikhotvoreniya 1917-1932* [Selected Poems of 1917-1932], Moscow, Sovetskaya literatura, 1933, p. 45.
22. "Zvyozdnyi reis" [Star Voyage], *Stikhotvoreniya 1913-1923,* p. 137.
23. "Pered sudom" [On Trial], *ibid.,* p. 148.
24. Polonski, *Ocherki literaturnovo dvizheniya revolyutsionnoi epokhi (1917-1927)* [Sketches of the Literary Movement of the Revolutionary Period (1917-1927)], 2d ed., Moscow, Gosizdat, 1929, p. 52.
25. Kirillov, "Poety" [Poets], *Izbrannye stikhotvoreniya 1917-1932,* p. 49.
26. Lelevich, G., "Kirillov, Vladimir Timofeyevich," *Literaturnaya entsiklopediya,* Vol. V, 1931, col. 219.
27. Kirillov, untitled lines in *Izbrannye stikhotvoreniya 1917-1932,* p. 48.
28. "V ssylke" [In Exile], *ibid.,* p. 115.
29. Lunacharski, A. V., *Vvedeniye v istoriyu religii,* Moscow and Leningrad, Gosizdat, 1923.
30. Gerasimov, "My" [We], *Kuznitsa* [Smithy], Moscow, No. 2, 1920, p. 24.
31. Blok, Aleksandr, *Stikhotvoreniya,* Leningrad, Izdatel'stvo pisatelei, 1932, Vol. I, p. 194.
32. Gerasimov, *Severnaya vesna* [Northern Spring], Moscow, Gosizdat, 1924, p. 14.
33. Untitled lines beginning "Vot osen' . . ." in *Kuznitsa,* No. 1, 1920, p. 24.
34. Grigor'yev, S., "Novaya fabrika" [The New Factory], *Gorn* [Furnace], Moscow, No. 1, 1922, p. 115.
35. Quoted in Kogan, P. S., *Literatura etikh let* [Literature of These Years], 2d ed., Ivanovo-Vosnesensk, Osnova, 1924, p. 65.
36. Gerasimov, "Pcholka" [Bee], *Novyi mir* [New World], Moscow, No. 5, 1925, pp. 38-39.

Notes to Chapter 10 (pages 157-172):

1. Aleksandrovski, "Dve Rossii" [The Two Russias], in *Antologiya revolyutsionnoi poezii* [An Anthology of Poetry of the Revolution], Moscow, Izvestiya, 1924, p. 93.
2. In *Shagi* [Steps], Moscow, Moskovskii rabochii, 1924; quoted in B-skovo, N., *Novyi mir* [New World], Moscow, No. 3, 1925, p. 155.
3. "Derevnya" [Village], in *Kostyor. Stikhi 1918-1928* [Bonfire: Verses of 1918-1928], Moscow, Federatsiya, 1929, p. 142.
4. In *Kuznitsa* [Smithy], Moscow, No. 7, December 1920-March 1921, p. 5.
5. Untitled lines in *Kostyor,* p. 17.
6. "Sever" [The North], in *Gorn* [Furnace], Moscow, No. 4, 1919, p. 6.
7. Untitled lines, *ibid.,* No. 8, 1923, p. 161.

Notes

8. "Dve Rossii," in *Kuznitsa*, No. 7, December 1920-March 1921, p. 4.
9. Kazin, "Son" [A Dream], *Rabochii mai* [Workers' May], 3d ed., Moscow, Gosizdat, 1927, p. 46.
10. "Moi otets" [My Father], *Izbrannye stikhi* [Selected Verses], Moscow, GIKhL, 1934, p. 5.
11. Untitled lines, *ibid.*, p. 44.
12. Untitled lines in *Priznaniya* [Confessions], Moscow and Leningrad, Gosizdat, 1928, p. 19.
13. See, for instance, Beskin, O., "Kazin," *Literaturnaya entsiklopediya* [Literary Encyclopedia], Moscow, Vol. V, 1931, cols. 27-29.
14. "Vesenneye" [Springtime], *Stikhotvoreniya. Lirika, Epigramy, Poemy* [Poems: Lyrics, Epigrams and Narrative Poems], Moscow, GIKhL, 1937, p. 20.
15. Untitled lines in *Priznaniya*, p. 36.
16. "Lis'ya shuba i lyubov'," *Krasnaya nov'* [Red Virgin Soil], Moscow, No. 5, 1925, pp. 9-10; also published as a separate book, Moscow, Sovremennye problemy, 1926.
17 "Lis'ya shuba i lyubov'," *Krasnaya nov'*, p. 10.
18. *Ibid.*, p. 13.
19. *Ibid.*, p. 14.
20. *Ibid.*, p. 15.
21. *Ibid.*, p. 5.
22. *Ibid.*, p. 6.
23. Untitled lines in *Priznaniya*, p. 52.
24. "Garmonist" [Accordion Player], *Stikhotvoreniya*, pp. 39-40.
25. "Ostanovka" [The Stop], *ibid.*, p. 107.
26. "Epokha" [The Times], *Priznaniya*, p. 11.
27. "Veshneye vdokhnoven'ye" [Breath of Spring], *Stikhotvoreniya*, p. 18.
28. Untitled poem in *Priznaniya*, p. 9.
29. *Ibid.*, p. 10.
30. "Posledneye pis'mo," *Stikhotvoreniya*, p. 108.
31. *Ibid.*, p. 111.
32. *Ibid.*, p. 112.
33. "Gazeta," *ibid.*, pp. 91-92.
34. *Ibid.*, pp. 92-93.
35. "Bandit," *ibid.*, p. 160.
36. *Ibid.*, p. 190.
37. *Ibid.*, p. 195.
38. *Ibid.*, p. 192.
39. "S parakhoda—'Radishchev,'" in *Sbornik stikhov* [Anthology of Verse], Moscow, GIKhL, 1943, p. 280.

Notes to Chapter 11 (pages 172-178):

1. Sivachov, "Zholtyi d'yavol," quoted in Yakubovski, Georgi, *Pisateli-Kuznitsy* [Smithy Writers], Moscow, Federatsiya, 1929, pp. 147-148.

2. Lyashko, *Domennaya pech'*, 3d ed., Moscow and Leningrad, ZIF, 1929, p. 23.

3. "Stremena," in the almanac *Nashi dni* [Our Days], Moscow, No. 4, 1923, pp. 227-263.

4. *V razlome*, later included in his *Izbrannoye* [Selections], Moscow, GIKhL, 1933.

5. "Zvyozdnyi serp," *ibid.*

6. *Sladkaya katorga* republished, Moscow, Sovetskii pisatel', 1950.

7. *Russkiye nochi, 1941-1944*, Moscow, Sovetskii pisatel', 1945.

8. Nizovoi, *Mityakino*, Moscow, Novaya Moskva, 1925, pp. 217-218; first published in *Rabochii zhurnal* [Workers' Review], No. 2, 1924.

9. See Yakubovski, G., *Literaturnye portrety* [Literary Portraits], Moscow and Leningrad, GIZ, 1926, pp. 91-94. Yakubovski had read "My Spiritual Journey" [*Puti dukha moyevo*] in manuscript.

10. Nizovoi, "Yazychniki," *Molodaya gvardiya* [Young Guard], Moscow, No. 3, 1922, p. 14; published in book form, Moscow, Zhizn' i znaniye, 1923.

11. "Chernozem'ye," *Molodaya gvardiya*, No. 3, 1923, p. 18; published in book form Moscow, Krug, 1923.

Notes to Chapter 12 (pages 179-202):

1. Quoted in Aleksandrova, V., "Yevgeni Zamyatin," in Zamyatin, *My* [We], New York, Chekhov Publishing House, 1952, p. iv.

2. Zamyatin, "Peshchera," *Ostrovityane* [The Islanders], Petrograd and Berlin, Grzhebin, 1923, pp. 172-173. The story was first published in *Zapiski Mechtatelei* [Dreamers' Journal], Petrograd, No. 5, 1922. An English translation by D. S. Mirsky was published in the *Slavonic Review*, London, No. 4, 1923.

3. "Avtobiografiya" [Autobiography] in Vol. I (*Uyezdnoye*) of his *Sobraniye sochinenii* [Collected Works], Moscow, Federatsiya, 1929.

4. See Voronskii, A., *Na styke. Literaturnye siluety* [At the Meeting Point: Literary Silhouettes], Moscow and Petrograd, Gosizdat, 1923, p. 61.

5. Zamyatin, "Ya boyus'," *Dom iskusstv* [House of the Arts], Petrograd, No. 1, 1921, p. 43.

6. *Ibid.*

7. *Ibid.*, p. 45.

8. "O sevodnyashnem i o sovremennom" [That of the Day and That of the Age], *Russkii sovremennik* [Russian Contemporary], Leningrad, No. 2, 1924, pp. 263-264.

9. *Ibid.*, p. 263.

10. *My*, New York, Chekhov Publishing House, 1952; in English translation, *We*, tr. by G. Zilboorg, New York, Dutton, 1924.

11. *My*, p. 5.

12. *Ibid.*, p. 149.

13. Voronski, pp. 69-70.

14. Sakulin, *Iz istorii russkovo idealizma* [From the History of Russian Idealism], Moscow, Sabashnikov, 1913, Vol. I, p. 188.

15. Zamyatin, *Gerbert Uel's* [Herbert Wells], Petrograd, 1922, p. 7.

16. *Ibid.,* p. 12.
17. *Ibid.,* p. 18.
18. Quoted *ibid.,* p. 39.
19. Quoted *ibid.*
20. Zamyatin, "Ostrovityane," in the almanac *Skify* [The Scythians], Petrograd, No. 2, 1918. The story was later included in the collection of stories under the same name.
21. "Lovets chelovekov," *Ostrovityane,* pp. 72-95.
22. "Mamai," *Dom iskusstv,* No. 1, 1921, p. 7.
23. "Rasskaz o samom glavnom," *Nechestivye rasskazy* [Impious Stories], Moscow, Krug, 1927, p. 49. The story was first published in *Russkii sovremennik,* No. 1, 1924.
24. "Drakon," *Ostrovityane,* p. 159.
25. *Navodneniye,* Leningrad, Izdatel'stvo pisatelei, 1930; first published in *Zemlya i fabrika* [Land and Factory], Moscow, No. 4, 1929.
26. "O tom, kak istselen byl inok Erazm" [How the Novice Erazm Was Healed], *Russkii sovremennik,* No. 4, 1924, pp. 43-55.
27. *Ogni Svyatovo Dominika,* Petrograd, Mysl', 1923.
28. *Blokha,* Leningrad, Mysl', 1925.
29. *Obshchestvo pochotnykh zvonarei,* Leningrad, Mysl', 1926.
30. See the foreword to "Attila," *Novyi Zhurnal* [New Journal], New York, No. 24, 1950, p. 7.
31. *Bich bozhii,* Paris, Dom knigi, n.d.
32. See Zamyatin, "Pis'mo Stalinu," *Litsa,* New York, Chekhov Publishing House, 1955, pp. 277-282.
33. Shklovski, "Peterburg v blokade," *Khod konya* [Knight's Move], Moscow and Berlin, Gelikon, 1923, p. 29.
34. *Gamburgskii schot,* Leningrad, Izdatel'stvo pisatelei, 1928.
35. "Svyortok," *Khod konya,* p. 17.
36. "Samovarom po gvozdyam," *ibid.,* p. 45.
37. "Drama i massovye predstavleniya" [The Drama and Mass Productions], *ibid.,* p. 61.
38. "O razlukakh i poteryakh," *Znamya* [Banner], Moscow, No. 7-8, 1943, p. 175.
39. *Ibid.,* p. 165.
40. Babel', "Pis'mo" [The Letter], *Konarmiya* [Cavalry Corps], Moscow and Leningrad, Gosizdat, 1926, p. 14. A translation of the volume was published under the title *Red Cavalry,* tr. by N. Helstein, New York, Knopf, 1929. "The Letter," tr. by Jacob J. Robbins, is also included in Kunitz, Joshua, ed., *Russian Literature Since the Revolution,* New York, Boni and Gaer, 1948, pp. 58-61.
41. "Chesniki," *Konarmiya,* pp. 153-154.
42. "Gedali," *ibid.,* pp. 36-37.
43. "Rabbi," *ibid.,* p. 43.
44. "Put' v Brody," *ibid.,* p. 45.
45. "Argamak," *Novyi mir* [New World], Moscow, No. 3, 1932, p. 127.
46. "Perekhod cherez Zbruch" [Crossing the Zbruch], *Konarmiya,* p. 3.
47. Budyonnyi, "Babizm Babelya iz 'Krasnoi novi' " [The Babism of the Babel' of *Krasnaya nov'*], *Oktyabr'* [October], Moscow, No. 3, 1924.

48. Polonski, *O sovremennoi literature* [Contemporary Literature], Moscow and Leningrad, Gosizdat, 1928, p. 9.

49. Babel', *Rasskazy*, Moscow, GIZ, 1925.

50. *Istoriya moyei golubyatni* [Story of My Dovecote], Moscow, Zif, 1926.

51. *Odesskiye rasskazy*, Moscow, Krug, 1926; 2d ed., Moscow and Leningrad, GIKhL, 1931.

52. *Benya Krik. Kino-povest'* [Benya Krik: A Movie Story], Moscow, Krug, 1926, p. 62.

53. *Ibid.*, p. 79.

54. "Gapa Guzhva," *Novyi mir*, No. 10, 1931, p. 20.

55. "Mariya," *Teatr i dramaturgiya* [The Theater and Playwriting], Moscow, No. 3, 1935, pp. 45-59.

56. *Zakat*, Moscow, Krug, 1928.

57. "Ob oshibkakh sovremennoi dramaturgii" [Mistakes of Contemporary Playwriting], *Klassovaya bor'ba v literature* [The Class Struggle in Literature], Moscow, GIKhL, 1938, p. 90.

58. "Komissiya po literaturnomu nasledstvu I. Babelya" [Commission on the Literary Legacy of I. Babel'], *Literaturnaya gazeta* [Literary Gazette], Moscow, April 28, 1956.

59. See Ninov, "Literatura i istoriya" [Literature and History], *ibid.*, June 23, 1956.

60. "Nachalo" [The Beginning], in the almanac *God dvadtsat' pervyi* [The Twenty-first Year], Moscow, No. 13, 1938, p. 79.

61. See Isakov, K. S., *Filonov*, Leningrad, 1929.

62. Voronski, *Na styke*, p. 115.

63. Pil'nyak, "Golyi god" [The Naked Year], *Sobraniye sochinenii* [Collected Works], Moscow and Leningrad, Gosizdat, 1929, Vol. I, p. 126. The book *Golyi god* was first published in Berlin in 1922. There is an English translation, *The Naked Years*, tr. by Alec Brown, New York, 1928.

64. "Golyi god," *Sobraniye sochinenii*, pp. 156-157.

65. *Ibid.*, p. 141.

66. *Ibid.*, p. 128.

67. *Ibid.*, p. 115.

68. "Mashiny i volki," *ibid.*, Vol. II, p. 143.

69. *Ibid.*, p. 91.

70. Quoted in Kovarski, N. A., "Svidetel'skoye pokazaniye" [Testimony], in the collective volume *Boris Pil'nyak. Mastera sovremennoi literatury* [Boris Pil'nyak: Masters of Contemporary Literature], Leningrad, Academia, 1928, p. 80.

71. "Mashiny i volki," p. 249.

72. *Ibid.*, p. 250.

73. "Ivan Moskva," *Sobraniye sochinenii*, Vol. III, pp. 165-232; first published in *Krasnaya nov'* [Red Virgin Soil], Moscow, No. 4, 1927; published in English under the title *Ivan Moscow*, tr. by A. Schwartzman, Boston, Christopher, 1935.

74. "Povest' nepogashonnoi luny," *Novyi mir*, No. 5, 1926.

75. Voronski, A., "Pis'mo v redaktsiyu" [Letter to the Editors], *ibid.*, No. 6, 1926.

Notes

76. See the foreword to Pil'nyak, *Povest' nepogashonnoi luny*, Sofia, Rus', 1926; and Glinka, Gleb, *Na Perevale*, New York, Chekhov Publishing House, 1954, p. 370.
77. See Glinka, *loc. cit.*
78. See note 76 above.
79. *Krasnoye derevo*, Berlin, Petropolis, 1929.
80. *Volga vpadayet v Kaspiiskoye more*, Moscow, Nedra, 1930; in English translation, *The Volga Falls to the Caspian Sea*, tr. by L. Malamuth, New York, Cosmopolitan, 1931.
81. "O'kei," *Novyi mir*, Nos. 3-6, 1932; also in book form, Moscow, Federatsiya, 1933.
82. *Korni yaponskovo solntsa*, Leningrad, Priboi, 1927.
83. *Kamni i korni*, Moscow, Sovetskaya literatura, 1934.
84. "Sozrevaniye plodov," *Novyi mir*, No. 10, 1935, p. 28.
85. *Ibid.*, p. 21.
86. Platonov and Pil'nyak, "Che-Che-O," *Novyi mir*, No. 12, 1928.
87. Pil'nyak and S. M. Belyayev, "Myaso," *Novyi mir*, Nos. 2-4, 1936.
88. Pil'nyak and L. Farid, "Vesna v Khorezme," *Novyi mir*, Nos. 1-3, 1934.

Notes to Chapter 13 (pages 202-211):

1. Polonski, "Pamyati Furmanova" [In Memory of Furmanov], *Novyi mir* [New World], Moscow, No. 4, 1926, p. 152.
2. Furmanov, "Predisloviye" [Foreword], *Chapayev*, 2d ed., Moscow, Gosizdat, 1924. p. 5. The first edition was published in 1923.
3. Furmanov, *Chapayev*, 8th ed., Moscow, Gosizdat, 1930, p. xv (Vol. I of his *Sobraniye sochinenii* [Collected Works]).
4. *Ibid.*, p. 51.
5. See Kosarev, V., in *Pravda*, January, 4, 1920.
6. Furmanov, *Sobraniye sochinenii*, Vol. I, p. 116.
7. *Myatezh*, Moscow and Leningrad, Gosizdat, 1925.
8. Furmanov and S. Polivanov, "Myatezh," in Furmanov, *Sobraniye sochinenii*, Vol. III, 1928, p. 356 (Appendix).
9. *Ibid.*, p. 385.
10. Budantsev, "Myatezh," in the almanac *Krug*, Moscow, No. 2, 1923; published in book form in 1925 under the same title, and in 1927 under the title *Komandarm* [Army Commander].
11. "Sarancha," *Krasnaya nov'* [Red Virgin Soil], Moscow, No. 9, 1927, p. 47.
12. "Kollektsiya mednykh monet," in *Lyubov' k zhizni* [Love for Life], Moscow, GIKhL, 1935, p. 217.
13. Arosev, A. Ya., *Kak eto proizoshlo*, Moscow, Krasnaya nov', 1923.
14. "Nedavnye dni," *Krasnaya nov'*, No. 2, 1922. The tale was also published in Arosev's book *Dve povesti* [Two Short Novels], Moscow, Krug, 1923 and as a separate volume in two editions, 1926 and 1927.

15. "Zapiski Terentiya Zabytovo" *Dve povesti*; also published as a separate book in Berlin, Russkoye tvorchestvo, 1922.
16. *Korni*, Moscow, GIKhL, 1933.
17. Yarov, *Devyatnadtsatyi god*, Moscow, Proletarii, 1926, p. 94.
18. Pavlov, M., in *Krasnaya nov'*, No. 12, 1927, p. 222.

Notes to Chapter 14 (pages 211-215):

1. See the photostat of this letter dated May 21, 1920, in the book *A. S. Serafimovich*, Moscow and Leningrad, Izdatel'stvo Akademii Nauk, 1950, facing p. 184.
2. *Zheleznyi potok* [Iron Flood], 5th ed., Moscow, GIZ, 1930, p. 224 (Vol. VIII of Serafimovich, *Polnoye sobraniye sochinenii* [Complete Works]; first published in the almanac *Nedra*, No. 4, 1924.
3. Quoted in *A. S. Serafimovich*, p. 123.
4. Kovtyukh, Yepifan, *Tamanskii pokhod* [The Taman' Campaign], a pamphlet, Smolensk, 1932, p. 12.
5. Furmanov, Dmitri, "Yepifan Kovtyukh" in "Rasskazy," *Molodaya gvardiya* [Young Guard], Moscow, No. 12, 1926; also in Furmanov, *Sobraniye sochinenii* [Collected Works], Moscow and Leningrad, Gosizdat, Vol. III, 1928.
6. Reisner, *Front*, Moscow, Krasnaya nov', 1924, p. 5.
7. *Ibid.*
8. See Rozhdestvenski, "Larisa Reisner," *Izbrannye stikhi* [Selected Verse], Moscow, GIKhL, 1938, pp. 163-164.
9. See Pasternak, "Pamyati Reisner" [To the Memory of Reisner], *Stikhotvoreniya v odnom tome* [Poems in One Volume], Leningrad, 1933, pp. 289-290.

Notes to Chapter 15 (pages 215-223):

1. Tarasov-Rodionov, "Shokolad," *Molodaya gvardiya* [Young Guard], Moscow, No. 6, 1922, p. 80. There is an English translation *Chocolate*, tr. by C. Malamuth, New York, Doubleday, Doran, 1932.
2. Averbakh, "O 'Shokolade' A. Tarasova-Rodionova" [A. Tarasov-Rodionov's "Chocolate"], *Molodaya gvardiya*, No. 10, 1925, pp. 208, 210.
3. Quoted in Gul', Roman, *Dzerzhinskii*, Paris, 1936, p. 100.
4. *Linyov*, Leningrad, Molodaya gvardiya, 1924; 2d ed., under title *Trava i krov'* [Grass and Blood], Moscow, Gosizdat, 1926.
5. *Fevral'*, Moscow, Gosizdat, 1928, p. 5 (Vol. I of *Tyazholye shagi* [Heavy Tread]; the second volume *Iyul'* [July], was published in Moscow, Moskovskoye tovarishchestvo pisatelei, 1933). *Fevral'* has been published in English translation under the title *February 1917*, tr. by W. A. Drake, New York, Covici-Friede, 1931.
6. Yakovlev, *Pobeditel'*, Moscow, Nedra, 1927, p. 83.
7. *Oktyabr'*, 3d ed., Moscow, Nikitinskiye subbotniki, 1925, p. 10; the first edition was published in 1923 by ZIF, Moscow.

8. *Oktyabr'*, 3d ed., pp. 20-21.
9. *Ibid.*, p. 5.
10. *Ibid.*, p. 9.
11. *Ibid.*, p. 3.
12. *Ibid.*, p. 6.
13. *Ibid.*, p. 7.
14. "Povol'niki," in the almanac *Nashi dni*, Moscow, No. 2, 1922; published in a collection of Yakovlev's stories under the same title, Moscow, Krug, 1923.
15. "Zhgel'," *Novyi mir* [New World], Moscow, No. 2, 1925; issued in book form, Moscow, Gosizdat, 1927.
16. "Chelovek i pustynya," in the almanac *Svitok* [Scroll], Moscow, No. 4, 1926, pp. 79-241.
17. *Pobeditel'*, p. 98.
18. *Ibid.*, p. 183.
19. *Ibid.*, p. 208.
20. *Bol'shaya Volga*, Moscow, Molodaya gvardiya, 1933.
21. *Ogni v pole*, Moscow, Sovetskaya literatura, 1934.
22. *Pioner Pavel Morozov*, Moscow, Detgiz, 1936.
23. *Stupeni*, Leningrad, Sovetskii pisatel', 1946.
24. Neverov, *Tashkent-gorod khlebnyi*, Moscow, Zif, 1923.
25. "Gusi-lebedi," *Molodaya gvardiya*, Nos. 2-5, 1923; published in book form Moscow, Zif, 1924.
26. "Andron Neputyovyi," *Nedra* [The Depths], Moscow, No. 2, 1923, pp. 173-208; published in book form, Moscow, Nedra, 1925.
27. *Smekh i gore*, Moscow, Krasnaya nov', 1922.

Notes to Chapter 16 (pages 224-229):

1. Excerpts from this article are given in Edgerton, William, "The Serapion Brothers: An Early Soviet Controversy," *The American Slavic and East European Review*, Vol. VIII, No. 1, February 1949; and in Reavey, George, and Marc Slonim, *Soviet Literature: An Anthology*, New York, Covici Friede, 1934. For a fuller treatment of the Serapion Brothers as a group, see also Struve, Gleb, *Soviet Russian Literature, 1917-50*, Norman, University of Okhaloma Press, 1951, pp. 45 ff.
2. Gorki, Maxim, "Pamyati L. Luntsa" [To the Memory of L. Lunts], *Beseda* [Colloquy], Berlin, No. 5, 1924, p. 62.
3. Lunts, "Na Zapad!" [To the West!], *Beseda*, No. 3, 1923, p. 261.
4. Editorial note, *ibid.*, p. 259.
5. Gorki, pp. 61-62.
6. Lunts, "Gorod pravdy," *Beseda*, No. 5, 1924, p. 67.
7. *Ibid.*, p. 68.
8. *Ibid.*, p. 76.
9. *Ibid.*, p. 77.

10. *Ibid.*, p. 82.

11. *Ibid.*, p. 96.

12. *Ibid.*, p. 100.

13. Polonski, *O sovremennoi literature* [Contemporary Literature], 2d ed., Moscow and Leningrad, Gosizdat, 1929, p. 7.

14. Ivanov, *Bronepoyezd No. 14-69*, Moscow, Gosizdat, 1922.

15. "Bronepoyezd 14-69" (play), *Sobraniye sochinenii* [Collected Works], Moscow and Leningrad, Vol. VI, 1931, p. 12; published in English, *Armoured Train 14-69*, tr. by Gibson-Cowan and A. T. K. Grant, New York, International Publishers, 1933.

16. "Golubye peski," *Sobraniye sochinenii*, Vol. V, 1929, p. 296.

17. *Ibid.*, p. 186.

18. *Ibid.*, p. 169.

19. *Ibid.*, p. 129.

20. "Gibel' zheleznoi," *ibid.*, p. 84; first published in *Krasnaya nov'* [Red Virgin Soil], Moscow, No. 1, 1928, pp. 3-57.

21. "Begstvuyushchii ostrov," *Tainoye tainykh*, Moscow, Gosizdat, 1927, p. 149.

22. Polonski, p. 36.

23. "Khabu," *Krasnaya nov'*, No. 2, 1925, pp. 9-49. *Khabu* is the Tungus name for the black-red fox.

24. *Pokhozhdeniya fakira*, Moscow, GIKhL, 1934.

25. "Dvenadtsat' molodtsov iz tabakerki," *Novyi mir* [New World], Moscow, No. 1, 1936, pp. 48-112.

Notes to Chapter 17 (pages 229-233):

1. Aseyev, "Okean" [The Ocean], *Sobraniye stikhotvorenii* [Collected Poems], Moscow and Leningrad, Gosizdat, 1928, Vol. I, p. 113. The book *Okeania* [Oceania], in which the poem first appeared, was published in Moscow in 1916.

2. *Budyonnyi. Poema groznykh let* [Budyonnyi: A Tale of the Terrible Years], Moscow, Krug, 1922; republished under the title "Skaz o Budyonnom" [Tale of Budyonnyi], *Sobraniye stikhotvorenii*, Vol. III, pp. 159-176.

3. "Liricheskoye otstupleniye" [Lyrical Digression], *LEF*, Moscow, No. 2, 1924, p. 13.

4. *Mayakovskii nachinayetsya*, Moscow, Sovetskii pisatel', 1940, p. 5.

5. *Ibid.*, p. 7.

6. Tret'yakov, "Okop" [Trench], *Novyi LEF* [New LEF], Moscow, No. 2, 1927, p. 22.

7. "Rychi Kitai," *LEF*, No. 1, 1924, pp. 23-33; published in book form, Moscow, Ogonyok, 1926.

8. "Protivogazy," *LEF*, No. 4, 1924, pp. 89-108.

9. "Khochu rebyonka," *Novyi LEF*, No. 3, 1927, pp. 3-11.

10. *Tvoya poema*, Moscow, Pravda, 1938.

11. *Zolushka*, Moscow, GIKhL, 1935.

Notes to Chapter 18 (pages 233-240):

1. "Editorial Manifesto of the On Guard Group," quoted in Reavey, George, and Marc Slonim, *Soviet Literature: An Anthology*, New York, Covici Friede, 1934, pp. 403-406, *passim*.
2. For a full account of the development of RAPP from the nucleus of the earliest group of Soviet proletarian writers, see Brown, Edward J., *The Proletarian Episode in Russian Literature 1928-1932*, New York, Columbia University Press, 1953.
3. Trotsky, L. D., *Literatura i revolyutsiya*, Moscow, Gosizdat, 1924, p. 141.
4. Lenin, V. I., "Partiinaya organizatsiya i partiinaya literatura," *Sobraniye sochinenii* [Collected Works], 2d ed., Moscow, Vol. VIII, 1929, p. 388.
5. Lenin, "Luchshe men'she, da luchshe," *Izbrannye proizvedeniya v dvukh tomakh* [Selected Works in Two Volumes], Moscow, Gospolitizdat, 1946, Vol. II, p. 831.
6. Voronski, A., "O proletarskom iskusstve i khudozhestvennoi politike nashei partii," *Krasnaya nov'* [Red Virgin Soil], Moscow, No. 7, 1923, p. 264.
7. *Ibid.*, p. 265.
8. Quoted in Brown, p. 14.
9. See "Doklad G. Sannikov na vechere-otkrytii 'Kuznitsa' 17-vo oktyabrya 1924 g." [Speech of G. Sannikov at the Open Meeting of the "Smithy" on October 17, 1924], *Rabochii zhurnal* [Workers' Review], Moscow, No. 3-4, 1924, p. 235.
10. Libedinski, "Nedelya," *Nashi dni* [Our Days], Moscow, No. 2, 1922, pp. 63-144; published in book form Moscow, Molodaya gvardiya, 1923; English translation *A Week*, New York, Huebsch, 1923.
11. See Libedinski, "Kak ya rabotal nad 'Nedelei' (Beseda s molodymi pisatelyami v zhurnale 'Rezets')" [How I Worked on *A Week* (Talk with Young Writers at the Journal *Rezets*)], in the collective volume of essays *General'nye zadachi proletarskoi literatury* [General Problems of Proletarian Literature], Moscow and Leningrad, LAPP, 1931, p. 131.
12. *Ibid.*, p. 134.
13. "Zavtra," in *Molodaya gvardiya* [Young Guard], Moscow, Nos. 1, 7-8, 1923; published in book form, Leningrad, Molodaya gvardiya, 1924.
14. *Chistka Leningradskoi partorganizatsii* [Purge of the Leningrad Party Organization], Leningrad, Krasnaya gazeta, 1933, p. 16.
15. *Komissary*, published in sections by various periodicals in 1925, and in book form, Leningrad, Priboi, 1926.
16. "Vysoty," *Zvezda*, No. 4, 1929, pp. 46-103; in book form, Leningrad, Priboi, 1930.
17. *Rozhdeniye geroya*, Leningrad, Priboi, 1930.
18. For a full discussion of Libedinski's *Birth of a Hero* and the controversy over it, see Brown, *The Proletarian Episode in Russian Literature*.
19. *Rasskazy tovarishchei* [Comrades' Stories], Moscow, 1933.
20. See "Gvardeitsy" [Men of the Guard], *Znamya* [Banner], Moscow, No. 1-2, 1942, and No. 2-3, 1943; and "Opolchentsy" [Home Guards], *ibid.*, No. 1, 1946.
21. *Gory i kamni*, Moscow, Sovetskii pisatel', 1947.
22. *Zarevo*, Moscow, 1952.
23. Bezymenski, "Prelyude" [Prelude], *Order na mir* [Order for the World], Moscow, Molodaya gvardiya, 1926, p. 83.

24. "Prolog k poeme 'Guta'" [Prologue to the Poem "Glassworks"], *Inoye solntse* [Another Sun], Moscow, Novaya Moskva, 1924.

25. Utkin, *Povest' o ryzhem Motele, gospodine inspektore, rabbine Issaiye i Komissare Blokh,* Moscow, 1926.

26. See Likharev, "Srednyaya Aziya," *Literaturnyi sovremennik* [Literary Contemporary], Moscow, Nos. 8 and 10, 1936.

Notes to Chapter 19 (pages 240-260) :

1. Voronski, "Na perevale" [Over the Crest], *Krasnaya nov'* [Red Virgin Soil], Moscow, No. 6, 1923, pp. 312-322.

2. "Iskusstvo, kak pozhaniye zhizni i sovremennost'," *ibid.,* No. 5, 1923.

3. *Literaturnye zapiski,* Moscow, Krug, 1926.

4. *Za zhivoi i myortvoi vodoi,* Moscow, Vol. I, Krug, 1927; Vol. II, Federatsiya, 1929 (translated under the title *Waters of Life and Death,* tr. by L. Zarine, London, Allen and Unwin, 1936).

5. Quoted in Voronski, *Glaz uragana* [Eye of the Hurricane], Moscow, Nedra, 1931, p. 1.

6. *Rasskazy i povesti* [Stories and Tales], Moscow, Sovetskaya literatura, 1933.

7. "Tri povesti" [Three Tales], *Novyi mir* [New World], Moscow, No. 9, September 1934.

8. See Glinka, Gleb, "A. K. Voronskii," *Na Perevale* [Over the Crest], New York, Chekhov Publishing House, 1954, p. 48. The introductory article to this collection of writings by Pereval members is a very interesting account of the organization and of the part played in it by Voronski. See also McLean, Hugh, "Voronskij and VAPP," in *American Slavic and East European Review,* Vol. VIII, No. 3, October 1949, pp. 185-200.

9. Glinka, "Na Perevale," *Na Perevale,* p. 16.

10. Vesyolyi, "Reki ognennye," in *Piruyushchaya vesna* [Festive Spring], Kharkov, Proletarii, 1929, p. 31. Portions of the novel were published in various periodicals during 1923-1924; it was issued in book form in Leningrad, Molodaya gvardiya, 1924.

11. "Reki ognennye," *Piruyushchaya vesna,* p. 7.

12. All republished in *Piruyushchaya vesna.* The last, *Dikoye serdtse,* was issued in book form Moscow, Zif, 1926.

13. "Gordost," *Piruyushchaya vesna,* p. 517.

14. "Sud skoryi," *ibid.,* pp. 519-526.

15. Charnyi, *Pevets partizanskoi stikhii. Tvorchestvo Artyoma Vesyolovo* [The Bard of the Guerrillas: The Writing of Artyom Vesyolyi], Moscow, Sovetskaya literatura, 1933, p. 17.

16. "Strana rodnaya," *Piruyushchaya vesna,* p. 316. The novel was published in book form, Moscow, Novaya Moskva, 1926, after the appearance of parts in various periodicals during 1925-26.

17. "Strana rodnaya," *Piruyushchaya vesna,* p. 317.

18. *Ibid.,* p. 223.

19. *Rossiya krov'yu umytaya,* Moscow, Federatsiya, 1932. A preliminary sketch under this same title had previously been published in *Piruyushchaya vesna,* 1929.

20. *Gulyai Volga*, Moscow, Moskovskoye tovarishchestvo pisatelei, 1933.
21. Platonov and Boris Pil'nyak, "Che-Che-O," *Novyi mir*, No. 12, 1928, p. 256. "Che-Che-O" represents the pronunciation in a local dialect of the initials of the term *Tsentral'naya chernozyomnaya oblast'* (Central black-earth oblast).
22. Platonov, "Bessmertiye" [Immortality], *Reka Potudan'* [The River Potudan'], Moscow, Sovetskii pisatel', 1937, p. 64.
23. Platnov, *Proiskhozhdeniye mastera* [The Making of a Master], Moscow, Federatsiya, 1930.
24. Platnov, "Priklyucheniye" [An Adventure], *Novyi mir*, No. 6, June 1928.
25. *Gorod Gradov*, Moscow, Federatsiya, 1929.
26. "Usomnivshiisya Makar" [Doubting Makar], *Oktyabr'* [October], Moscow, No. 9, September 1929, p. 28.
27. "Pervyi Ivan," *ibid.*, No. 2, 1930.
28. Platonov, "Vprok," *Krasnaya nov'*, No. 3, March 1931, pp. 3-39.
29. See Averbakh, L., "O tselostnykh masshtabakh i chastnykh Makarakh" [Global Production and Individual Makars], in *Na literaturnom postu*, Moscow, No. 21-22, November 1929, pp. 10-17; and also in *Oktyabr'*, No. 2, 1929.
30. Fadeyev, "Ob odnoi kulatskoi khronike," *Izvestiya*, Moscow, July 3, 1931.
31. Same title, in *Krasnaya nov'*, No. 5-6, May-June 1931, pp. 206-209.
32. Berezov, P. I., "Pod maskoi," *Proletarskii avangard*, Moscow, No. 2, 1932.
33. Platonov, "Pushkin—nash tovarishch," *Literaturnyi kritik* [Literary Critic], Moscow, No. 1, 1937, p. 60; see also his "Pushkin i Gor'kii" [Pushkin and Gorki], *ibid.*, No. 6, 1937.
34. "Yepifanskiye shlyuzy," *Molodaya gvardiya* [Young Guard], Moscow, No. 6, June 1927, pp. 55-77.
35. Gurvich, A. M., *V poiskakh geroya* [In Search of a Hero], Moscow and Leningrad, GIKhL, 1938, p. 57.
36. Platnov, "Takyr," *Reka Potudan'*, p. 152.
37. "Bessmertiye" [Immortality], *ibid.*, pp. 50-51.
38. Gurvich, p. 71.
39. *Rasskazy o rodine*, Moscow, GIKhL, 1943.
40. *V storonu zakata solnsta*, Moscow, Sovetskii pisatel', 1945.
41. "Sem'ya Ivanova," *Novyi mir*, No. 11-12, 1946, pp. 97-108. After the war Platonov also published *Soldatskoye serdtse* [A Soldier's Heart], Moscow, Detgiz, 1946.
42. *Volshebnoye kol'tso*, Moscow, 1954.
43. Vetrov, "Kedrovyi dukh," *Pereval*, Moscow and Leningrad, No. 1, 1924, pp. 5-56.
44. Guber, "Sharashkina kontora," *ibid.*, No. 3, 1925, pp. 3-49.
45. "Oskolki," *ibid.*, No. 6, 1928.
46. "Izvestnaya Shurka Shapkina," in the volume of short stories of the same name, Moscow and Leningrad, 1928.
47. "Upravdel," *Novyi mir*, No. 7, 1928.
48. *Nespyashchiye* [Those Who Do Not Sleep], Moscow, Federatsiya, 1931.
49. "Bab'ye leto," *Krasnaya nov'*, No. 5, 1934, pp. 40-97.
50. Katayev, "Serdtse," *Pereval*, No. 6, 1928, pp. 81-166.
51. See *Povesti* [Short Novels], Moscow, Federatsiya, 1928. The volume contains

"Serdtse" [The Heart], "Poet," and "Zhena" [The Wife].
52. "Moloko," published in the seventh *Pereval* almanac, the name of which had been changed to *Rovesniki* [Contemporaries], Moscow, 1930.
53. *Chelovek na gore*, Moscow, Moskovskii tovarishchestvo pisatelei, 1934.
54. "Vstrecha," *Krasnaya nov'*, No. 1, 1934, pp. 18-58.
55. "Khamovniki," *ibid.*, No. 6, 1934, pp. 83-90.
56. Zarudin, *Sneg vishennyi*, Smolensk, 1923.
57. *Polem-yunost'yu*, Moscow, Krug, 1928.
58. "Drevnost'," *Rovesniki*, No. 7, 1930.
59. "Tridtsat' nochei na vinogradnike," *Rovesniki*, No. 8, 1932, pp. 3-224.
60. "V narodnom lesu," *Novyi mir*, No. 1, 1936, pp. 5-43; No. 2, pp. 129-170.
61. See Glinka, pp. 405-409.
62. Vikhryov, *Palekh*, Moscow, Nedra, 1930, p. 12.
63. *Ibid.*, p. 15.
64. *Ibid.*, p. 73.
65. *Ibid.*, p. 18.
66. *Ibid.*, p. 91.
67. Yevdokimov, *Kolokola*, Moscow, Zif, 1926; 3d ed., 1927.
68. *Siverko*, Moscow, GIZ, 1925.
69. *Chistiye prudy* [Clear Pools], Kharkov, Proletarii, 1927.
70. *Zaozer'ye*, Moscow, 1928, 2 vols.
71. *Zelyonye gory*, Moscow, 1928.
72. *Boris Musatov*, Moscow, Iskusstvo, 1924.
73. *Isaak Levitan*, Moscow, Iskusstvo, 1941.
74. *Poslednyaya babushka iz Semigor'ya*, Moscow, GIKhL, 1934.
75. "Zhar-ptitsa," *Novyi mir*, Nos. 2-4, 1936.
76. Akul'shin, *O chom shepchet derevnya*, Moscow, Moskovskii rabochii, 1925, p. 7.
77. Zavadovski, *Polova*, Moscow, Novaya Moskva, 1926.
78. Zavadovski, "Vrazhda," in the volume of the same name, Moscow, Novaya Moskva, 1926.
79. "Na belom ozere," *Krasnaya nov'*, No. 9, 1925, p. 7.
80. *Ibid.*, p. 4.
81. Malyshkin, "Padeniye Daira," *Al'manakh arteli pisatelei "Krug"* [Almanac of the *Krug* (Circle) Cooperative of Writers], Moscow, No. 1, 1923; published in book form Moscow, Krug, 1926.
82. "Sebastopol'," *Novyi mir*, Nos. 1-3, 1929; several later printings in book form.
83. "Lyudi iz zakholust'ya," *Novyi mir*, Nos. 10-11, 1937, and No. 1, 1938.

Notes to Chapter 20 (pages 260-268):

1. Sel'vinski, "Nasha biografiya," *Lirika* [Lyrics], Moscow, GIKhL, 1934, p. 10.
2. *Ulyalayevshchina*, Moscow, Krug, 1927, p. 33.
3. *Ibid.*, p. 92.

Notes

4. *Ibid.*, pp. 68-69.
5. *Ibid.*, p. 60.
6. *Ibid.*, p. 145.
7. *Ibid.*, p. 147.
8. "Kazn' Stetsyury," *Gosplan literatury* [A State Plan for Literature], Moscow and Leningrad, Krug [1925], p. 55.
9. "Komandarm 2," *Molodaya gvardiya* [Young Guard], Moscow, Nos. 7-10, 1929; published in book form Moscow, Gosizdat, 1930.
10. Quoted in Timofeyev, L., "Konstruktivizm," *Literaturnaya entsiklopediya* [Literary Encyclopedia], Moscow, Vol. V, 1931, col. 455.
11. See Zelinski, "Gosplan literatury," in *Gosplan literatury*, p. 26.
12. Sel'vinskii, *Elektrozavodskaya gazeta*, Moscow, Ogonyok, 1931, pp. 22-23.
13. *Pushtorg*, 2d ed., Moscow and Leningrad, GIKhL, 1930, p. 100.
14. *Ibid.*, p. 107.
15. "Chelyuskiniana," *Novyi mir* [New World], Moscow, No. 1, 1937, p. 114. The third part of the poem was published *ibid.*, No. 5, 1938, pp. 142-176.
16. *Umka-belyi medved'*, Moscow, GIKhL, 1935.
17. "Ot Poltavy do Ganguta," *Tragediya* [Tragedies], Moscow, Sovetskii pisatel', 1952, p. 357.
18. "Rytsar' Ioann," *Izbrannye proizvedeniya* [Selected Writings], Moscow, GIKhL, 1953, pp. 208-209.
19. Inber, untitled lines in *Tsel' i put'* [The Goal and the Way], Moscow, Gosizdat, 1925, p. 11.
20. "Vas'ka Svist v pereplyote," *Krasnaya nov'* [Red Virgin Soil], Moscow, No. 9, 1926, pp. 109-113.
21. Quoted in Zelinski, Korneli, "Yevropeyanka" [A Woman of European Spirit], *Na literaturnom postu* [On Literary Guard], Moscow, No. 11-12, 1928, p. 74.
22. Inber, "Na linii vody" [At the Water Line], *Izbrannaya proza* [Selected Prose], Moscow, GIKhL, 1952, p. 395.
23. *Pulkovskii meridian*, Moscow, Pravda, 1946, p. 3.
24. *Pochti tri goda. Leningradskii dnevnik* [Almost Three Years: Leningrad Diary], Leningrad, Goslitizdat, 1947.

Notes to Chapter 21 (pages 269-298):

1. Gorelov, "O tvorchestve Mikhaila Slonimskovo" [On the Writing of Mikhail Slonimski], *Put' sovremennika* [The Way of the Contemporary], Leningrad, Izdatel'stvo pisatelei, 1933, p. 10.
2. Slonimski, *Shestoi strelkovyi*, Petrograd, Vremya, 1922.
3. "Mashina Emeri," *Sochineniya* [Works], Moscow and Leningrad, 1928, Vol. I, p. 204; first published in a volume of stories under the same title, Leningrad, Atenei, 1924.
4. Gorelov, p. 31.
5. Romanov, *Sobstvennost'*, Moscow, GIKhL, 1933, pp. 4-5.
6. *Ibid.*, p. 6.
7. *Ibid.*, p. 7.

8. The first part, fourth edition, was published as Vols. X-XII of Romanov, *Polnoye sobraniye sochinenii* [Complete Works], Moscow, Nedra, 1928. After Romanov's death the critic V. Yermilov stated that two volumes of the second part had also been completed by the author and that there were further sections in draft form.

9. Quoted in L'vov-Rogachevski, *Panteleimon Romanov. Kriticheskiye stat'i* [Panteleimon Romanov: Critical Articles], Moscow, Nikitinskiye subbotniki, 1928, p. 8.

10. *Ibid.*, p. 26.

11. *Ibid.*, p. 12.

12. "Rybolovy," *Polnoye sobraniye sochinenii*, Vol. III, p. 30.

13. "Glas naroda," *ibid.*, Vol. II, pp. 125-131.

14. "Stikhiinoye bedstviye," *ibid.*, Vol. IV, pp. 26-31.

15. "Khoroshiye mesta," *ibid.*, Vol. III, pp. 5-9.

16. "Vesna," *ibid.*, Vol. V, p. 247.

17. *Ibid.*, p. 254.

18. "Taina," *ibid.*, p. 114.

19. "Sud nad pionerom," *Molodaya gvardiya* [Young Guard], Moscow, No. 1, 1927, pp. 86-91.

20. "Bez cheryomukhi," *Polnoye sobraniye sochinenii*, Vol. VI, p. 15. This story and its companion piece, "The Big Family," are both included in *Without Cherry Blossom*, tr. by L. Zarine, New York, Scribners, 1932.

21. "Bez cheryomukhi," p. 9.

22. *Ibid.*, p. 5.

23. *Ibid.*, pp. 7-8.

24. "Pravo na zhizn', ili problema bespartiinosti" [The Right to Live, or the Problem of Being Outside the Party], *ibid.*, Vol. IX, p. 5.

25. *Ibid.*, p. 6.

26. *Ibid.*, pp. 24-25.

27. *Ibid.*, pp. 59-60.

28. *Novaya skrizhal'*, 2d ed., Moscow, Nedra, 1928, p. 31 (Vol. VIII of *Sobraniye sochinenii*); translated under the title *The New Commandment*, tr. by Valentine Snow, New York, Scribners, 1933.

29. *Novaya skrizhal'*, p. 22.

30. *Ibid.*, p. 203.

31. *Ibid.*, p. 253.

32. *Ibid.*, p. 254.

33. *Tovarishch Kislyakov (Tri pary sholkovykh chulok)*, Berlin, Kniga i stsena, 1931, pp. 61-62; published in English translation under the title *Three Pairs of Silk Stockings*, tr. by Leonide Zarine, New York, Scribners, 1931.

34. *Tovarishch Kislyakov*, p. 68.

35. *Ibid.*, p. 78.

36. *Svetlana*, Riga, Didkovski, 1934.

37. See Lebedev-Polyanski, "Pis'mo pervoye" [First Letter], *Na literaturnom postu* [On Literary Guard], Moscow, No. 7, 1927; quoted in *Panteleimon Romanov*, Moscow, Nikitinskiye subbotniki, 1928, p. 138.

38. "Novye lyudi" [New People], *Novyi mir*, No. 3, 1936, pp. 157-163.

39. Seifulina, "Virineya," *Krasnaya nov'* [Red Virgin Soil], No. 4, 1924; in book form, Simferopol', Krymizdat, 1925, and many later editions.
40. "Kain kabak," *Sobraniye sochinenii* [Collected Works], Moscow and Leningrad, GIZ, 1928, Vol. V, p. 128; first published in *Novyi mir*, Nos. 4 and 6, 1926.
41. *Pravonarushiteli*, Novonikolayevsk, Sibgosizdat, 1921.
42. *Chetyre glavy*, Barnaul, Altaiskii gubgosizdat, 1921.
43. "Noyev kovcheg" and "Peregnoi" in the volume *Peregnoi*, Novonikolayevsk, Sibirskiye ogni, 1923.
44. "Loskutki myslei o literature" [Bits and Pieces of Thoughts on Literature], *Sobraniye sochinenii*, Vol. I, p. 281.
45. Sobol', "Salon-vagon," *Salon-vagon. Bred. Povesti* ["Lounge Car" and "Delirium": Short Novels], Moscow, Svernye dni, 1922, p. 100.
46. *Ibid.*, p. 183.
47. "Knyazhna," *Sobraniye sochinenii* [Collected Works], Moscow and Leningrad, Zif, 1926, Vol. IV, p. 60.
48. *Ibid.*, p. 64.
49. "Chelovek i yevo pasport," *ibid.*, p. 68.
50. *Ibid.*, p. 65.
51. *Ibid.*, pp. 70-71.
52. "Memuary vesnushchatovo cheloveka," *ibid.*, p. 109; also published in book form in 1926.
53. "Memuary," *Sobraniye sochinenii*, p. 111.
54. "Kogda tsvetyot vishnya," *ibid.*, p. 94.
55. "Kitaiskiye teni," *ibid.*, pp. 5-6.
56. *Ibid.*, p. 12.
57. *Ibid.*, p. 11.
58. *Ibid.*, p. 13.
59. Quoted in Pleskov, V., "Na trudnom puti" [On a Hard Road], *Katorga i ssylka* [Penal Servitude and Exile], Moscow, No. 2, 1926, p. 235.
60. Slyozkin, "Drugimi glazami (Korob pisem)," *Sobraniye sochinenii* [Collected Works], Moscow, 1928, Vol. V, p. 161; first published in book form, Moscow, Sovremennyi problemy, 1926.
61. "Drugimi glazami," *Sobraniye sochinenii*, pp. 205-206.
62. "Kozyol v ogorode," *ibid.*, Vol. IV, p. 225.
63. *Ibid.*, p. 246.
64. *Predgroz'ye, Leto 1914 g.*, Moscow, Zif, 1928.
65. *Brusilov*, Moscow, Sovetskii pisatel', 1947.
66. Gladkov, *Tsement*, Moscow, Zif, 1926 (Vol. II of *Sobraniye sochinenii* [Collected Works]); in English translation, *Cement*, tr. by A. S. Arthur and C. Ashleigh, New York, International Publishers, 1929.
67. See Lebedev-Polyanski, "Fyodor Gladkov," in *Kriticheskiye stat'i*, Moscow, Nikitinskiye subbotniki, 1928, p. 7.
68. Gladkov, "Burelom," *Sobraniye sochinenii*, Vol. I, 1926, p. 223; first published Novorossiisk, 1921.
69. *Energiya*, serialized in *Novyi mir* in 1932 and 1937-1938, was first published in its entirety in book form in Moscow, Gosizdat, 1939; there have been at least two later editions, in 1947 and 1950.
70. *Energiya*, Moscow, GIKhL, 1950, p. 221.

71. "P'yanoye solntse," *Sobraniye sochinenii*, Vol. III, 1928, p. 189.
72. Nekrasov, N. A. "Moroz Krasnyi-nos" [Rednose Frost], *Polnoye sobraniye sochinenii* [Complete Works], 10th ed., 1909, Vol. I, p. 300.
73. Gladkov, *Tragediya Lyubashi*, Moscow, GIKhL, 1935, p. 16.
74. *Ibid.*, p. 158.
75. "Krov'yu serdtse," *Sobraniye sochinenii*, Vol. III, p. 341.
76. *Ibid.*, pp. 346-351, *passim*.
77. "Vdokhnovennyi gus'," *Malen'kaya trilogiya*, Moscow, Goslitizdat, 1936, p. 177.
78. *Povest' o detstve*, Moscow, Sovetskii pisatel', 1949.
79. *Vol'nitsa*, Moscow, Sovetskii pisatel', 1951.

Notes to Chapter 22 (pages 298-317):

1. Olesha, "Vishnyovaya kostochka" [The Cherry Stone], in the volume of the same name, 2d ed., Moscow, Sovetskaya literatura, 1933, p. 95; the story was first published in *Oktyabr'* [October], Moscow, No. 8, August 1929. An English translation is contained in Reavey, George, and Mark Slonim, *Soviet Literature*, New York, Covici Friede, 1934.
2. "Ya smotryu v proshloye," *Vishnyovaya kostochka*, p. 82.
3. *Zavist'*, Moscow and Leningrad, Zif, 1928, p. 24; first published in *Krasnaya nov'* [Red Virgin Soil], Moscow, Nos. 7-8, 1927. The novel has been published in English translation: *Envy*, tr. by P. Ross, London, Westhouse, 1947.
4. *Zavist'*, 1928, p. 31.
5. *Ibid.*, p. 51.
6. *Ibid.*, p. 147.
7. Gurvich, A. M., *V poiskakh geroya* [In Search of a Hero], Moscow and Leningrad, Iskusstvo, 1938, p. 141.
8. *Zavist'*, 1928, p. 11.
9. *Ibid.*, p. 37.
10. Gurvich, p. 143.
11. *Zavist'*, 1928, p. 107.
12. "Lyubov'," *Vishnyovaya kostochka*, pp. 5-6; published earlier in the book *Lyubov'*, Moscow, Zif, 1928.
13. "Vishnyovaya kostochka," *Vishnyovaya kostochka*, p. 94.
14. *Zapiski pisatelei*, Moscow, Ogonyok, 1932.
15. "Koye-chto iz sekretnykh zapisei poputchika Zanda," *30 dnei* [Thirty Days], Moscow, No. 1, 1932.
16. *Tri tolstyaka* (novel), Moscow, Zif, 1928; the play of the same name was published in Moscow, Federatsiya, 1929.
17. Gurvich, p. 138.
18. Olesha, *Spisok blagodeyanii*, Moscow, Federatsiya, 1931, p. 4.
19. *Ibid.*, p. 5.
20. *Ibid.*, pp. 24-26, *passim*.
21. *Ibid.*, pp. 9-10.

22. "Strogii yunosha," *Novyi mir* [New World], Moscow, No. 8, 1934, p. 73.
23. *Ibid.*, p. 83.
24. See Babitsky, Paul, and John Rimberg, *The Soviet Film Industry*, New York, Research Program on the U.S.S.R., 1955, pp. 154-155.
25. See, for instance, "Zerkal'tse" [Little Mirror], *Ogonyok* [The Flamelet], Moscow, No. 1, 1946, p. 9.
26. Leonov, *Derevyannaya koroleva. Bubnovyi valet. Valina kukla*, Petrograd, Izd. Sabashnikovykh, 1923.
27. *Tuatamur*, Moscow, Izd. Sabashnikovykh, 1924; published in English under the same title, tr. by I. Montagu and S. Nolbandov, London, Colletts, 1935.
28. "Sluchai s Yakovom Pichunkom," *Literaturnaya mysl'* [Literary Thought], Petrograd, No. 2, 1923.
29. "Gibel' Yegorushki," in the almanac *Krug* [Circle], Moscow, No. 3, 1924, pp. 85-118.
30. "Buryga," in the almanac *Shipovnik* [Sweetbrier], Moscow, No. 1, 1922, pp. 39-56.
31. *Petushikhinskii prolom*, Moscow, Izd. Sabashnikovykh, 1923.
32. *Konets melkovo cheloveka*, Moscow, Izd. Sabashnikovykh, 1924.
33. "Zapiski Kovyakina," *Russkii sovremennik* [Russian Contemporary], Petrograd, Nos. 1-2, 1924; published in book form, Moscow, Gosizdat, 1927.
34. "Barsuki," *Krasnaya nov'*, Nos. 6-8, 1924; in book form, Leningrad, Gosizdat, 1925; English translation *The Badgers*, London, Hutchinson, 1946.
35. Quoted in Kovalyov, V. A., *Romany Leonida Leonova* [The Novels of Leonid Leonov], Moscow and Leningrad, Akademiya Nauk S.S.S.R., 1954, p. 28.
36. Leonov, *Vor*, Moscow, 1928, p. 253. The novel was serialized in *Krasnaya nov'*, Nos. 1-7, 1927. An English translation was published in 1931: *The Thief*, tr. by H. Butler, New York, Dial Press.
37. "Sot'," *Novyi mir*, Nos. 1-5, 1930, and in book form Moscow, GIKhL, 1931; in English translation under the title *Soviet River*, tr. by Ivor Montagu and Sergei Nolbandov, New York, Dial Press, 1932.
38. *Saranchuki*, Moscow, GIZ, 1931.
39. *Skutarevski*, serialized in *Novyi mir*, Nos. 5-9, 1932, and published in book form, Moscow, Sovetskaya literatura, 1934; in English, *Skutarevsky*, tr. by Alec Brown, New York, Harcourt Brace, 1936.
40. *Doroga na okean*, first serialized in *Novyi mir*, Nos. 9-12, 1935, and published in book form, Moscow, Goslitizdat, 1936; in English, *Road to the Ocean*, tr. by N. Guterman, New York, Fischer, 1944.
41. Quoted in Kovalyov, pp. 219-220.
42. "Russkii les," *Znamya* [Banner], Moscow, Nos. 10-12, 1953; in book form, Moscow, Molodaya gvardiya, 1954.
43. "Polovchanskiye sady," *Novyi mir*, No. 3, 1938; in English translation "The Orchards of Polovchansk," tr. by J. J. Robbins, in *Seven Soviet Plays*, New York, Macmillan, 1946.
44. "Volk," *Novyi mir*, No. 5, 1939.
45. *Nashestviye*, Moscow, Iskusstvo, 1942; translated "Invasion," in *Four Soviet War Plays*, London, Hutchinson, 1943.
46. "Lyonushka," *Novyi mir*, No. 1, 1943.
47. *Obyknovennyi chelovek*, Moscow, Iskusstvo, 1944.

48. "Zolotaya kareta," *Oktyabr'* [October], Moscow, No. 4, 1955.
49. Quoted in Shteinman, Zelik, *Navstrechu zhizni. O tvorchestve Boris Lavrenyova* [Welcome to Life: The Writing of Boris Lavrenyov], Leningrad, Izd. pisatelei, 1934, p. 10.
50. Lavrenyov, "Veter," *Veter,* Kharkov, Proletarii, 1928, p. 21 (Vol. III of Lavrenyov, *Sobraniye sochinenii* [Collected Writings]). The story was first published in *Literaturno-khudozhestvennyi al'manakh dlya vsekh* [Everybody's Literary Almanac], Leningrad, No. 1, 1924, pp. 3-70.
51. "Veter," *Veter,* p. 8.
52. "Sorok pervyi," *Sobraniye sochinenii,* Vol. II, 1928, p. 54; first published in *Zvezda* [Star], Leningrad, No. 6, 1924.
53. "Rasskaz o prostoi veshchi," *Sobraniye sochinenii,* Vol. IV, 1929, p. 66; first published in the almanac *Kovsh* [Harbor], No. 2, 1925.
54. "Sedmoi sputnik," *Sobraniye sochinenii,* Vol. I, 1928, p. 111. An abridged version appeared in *Zvezda,* No. 6, 1927.
55. "Sedmoi sputnik," *Sobraniye sochinenii,* p. 114.
56. *Razlom,* Leningrad, LTI, 1927.
57. "Vragi," *Zvezda,* No. 1, 1929.
58. "Mir v steklyshke," *Sobraniye sochinenii,* Vol. I, p. 305; first published in *Proletarii* [The Proletarian], Kharkov, No. 2, 1927.
59. "Gravyura na dereve," *Sobraniye sochinenii,* Vol. V, 1929, p. 155; first in *Zvezda,* Nos. 8-9, 1928.
60. *Za tekh, kto v more,* Moscow, Gosizdat, 1947.
61. Grin, "Korabli v Lisse" [Ships in Liss], *Fantasticheskiye novelly* [Fantastic Tales], Moscow, Sovetskii pisatel', 1934, p. 495.
62. Paustovski, K., "Aleksandr Grin," in the almanac *God XXII* [The Twenty-second Year], Moscow, GIKhL, 1939, p. 411.
63. "Krysolov" *Fantasticheskiye novelly,* p. 284; first published in *Rossiya* [Russia], Moscow, No. 3, 1924, pp. 47-79.
64. "Krysolov," *Fantasticheskiye novelly,* p. 277.
65. *Ibid.,* p. 286.
66. *Ibid.,* p. 288.
67. *Ibid.,* p. 290.
68. *Ibid.,* p. 338.
69. "Povest' okonchennaya blagodarya pule," *Ogon' i voda* [Fire and Water], Moscow, Federatsiya, 1930, p. 193.
70. "Vragi," *ibid.,* pp. 72-73.
71. Paustovski, p. 412.
72. *Ibid.,* p. 413.
73. Grin, *Doroga v nikuda* [The Road to Nowhere], Moscow, Federatsiya, 1930, p. 119.

Notes to Chapter 23 (pages 318-329):

1. Gumilevski, "Strana Giperboreyev," *Vsemirnyi sledopyt* [Universal Pathfinder], Moscow, No. 11, 1929.

2. Tarasenkov, An., "Gumilevski, Lev Ivanovich," *Literaturnaya entsiklopediya*, Moscow, Vol. III, 1930, col. 87.
3. Gumilevski, *Sobachii pereulok*, 2d ed., Moscow, Nikitinskiye subbotniki, 1928, p. 18 (Vol. III of Gumilevski, *Sobraniye sochinenii* [Collected Writings]).
4. *Ibid.*, p. 84.
5. *Ibid.*, pp. 85-86.
6. *Ibid.*, pp. 32-33.
7. Malashkin, "Luna s pravoi storony, ili neobyknovennaya lyukov," *Molodaya gvardiya* [Young Guard], Moscow, No. 9, 1926; published in a volume of stories under the same name, Moscow, Molodaya gvardiya, 1927.
8. "Malashkin," *Literaturnaya entsiklopediya*, Vol. VI, 1932, col. 735.
9. Malashkin, "Bol'noi chelovek," in *Luna s pravoi storony*, 2d ed., Moscow, Molodaya gvardiya, 1927; and as a separate book in 1928.
10. *Pokhod kolonn*, Moscow, GIZ, 1931.
11. "Sasha Rozhkov," *Ogonyok* [The Flamelet], Moscow, No. 13, 1941.
12. Kozakov, *Meshchanin Adameiko*, Leningrad, Priboi, 1927.
13. "Partiinoye delo," in his *Popugayevo schast'ye* [Parrot's Luck], Leningrad, Priboi, 1924.
14. *Devyat' tochek*, Vol. I, Leningrad, Priboi, 1930; Vol. II, Moscow, Sovetskii pisatel', 1935; Vol. III, Moscow, Sovetskii pisatel', 1939.
15. Grabar', *Sel'vinity*, Moscow and Leningrad, GIKhL, 1933, pp. 36-37.
16. "Na kirpichakh," *Lyudi-cheloveki*, Leningrad, Priboi [1927], p. 156.
17. *Ibid.*, p. 158.
18. *Ibid.*, p. 159.
19. *Ibid.*, p. 160.
20. *Ibid.*, p. 165.
21. *Ibid.*, p. 139.
22. "Zapiski primazavshevosya," *Molodaya gvardiya*, No. 7, 1927, p. 8.
23. *Ibid.*, p. 32.
24. "Lakhudrin pereulok" [Lakhudrin Alley], in the volume *Zhuravli i kartech'* [Cranes and Buckshot], Moscow, Gosizdat, 1928, p. 155.
25. *Bol'shoi pokker*, Leningrad, Izd. pisatelei, 1933.
26. Nikiforov, "Ivan Brynda," *Krasnaya nov'* [Red Virgin Soil], Moscow, No. 1, 1925.
27. *Ili—ili*, Leningrad, Priboi, 1926.
28. *U fonarya*, 18th ed., Moscow, GIKhL, 1936, p. 249; first edition Moscow Zif, 1928.
29. *Ibid.*, 18th ed., p. 249.
30. *Ibid.*
31. "Vorobei," *Zemlya i fabrika* [Land and Factory], Moscow, No. 2, 1928, p. 156.
32. *Ibid.*, p. 269.
33. "Zhenshchina," *ibid.*, No. 6, 1929; in book form, 2d ed., Moscow, Zif, 1930.
34. *Vstrechnyi veter*, Moscow, Moskovskii rabochii, 1930.
35. "Yedinstvo," *Novyi mir* [New World], Moscow, Nos. 1-4, 1933.
36. *Sedye dni*, Moscow, GIZ, 1925.

37. *Tridtsat' tri okazii*, Moscow, Zif, 1927.
38. "Zapozdalaya vesna," *Povesti* [Short Novels], Moscow, Zif, 1927.
39. *Mastera*, Moscow, GIKhL, 1936, p. 37; first published in *Novyi mir*, Nos. 6-9, 1935.

Notes to Chapter 24 (pages 329-347):

1. Bulgakov, *Dni Turbinykh (Belaya Gvardiya)* [Days of the Turbins (The White Guard)], Paris, Konkord, Part I, 1927, pp. 45-46. The novel was first published under the title "Belaya gvardiya" in the periodical *Rossiya* [Russia], Moscow. Nos. 4-6, 1924; it was issued in book form under the same title, Moscow, Nedra, 1926 (see Lidin, V., *Pisateli* [Writers], Moscow, Sovremennye problemy, 1926, p. 56), but was quickly withdrawn.
2. *Dni Turbinykh*, Paris, Part I, p. 69.
3. "Rokovye yaitsa," *Nedra* [The Depths], Moscow, No. 6, 1925, pp. 79-148; reprinted in Bulgakov's volume of stories entitled *D'yavoliada* [Devilry], Moscow, Nedra, 1925. "Rokovye yaitsa," "D'yavoliada" and two other of Bulgakov's stories are contained in Bulgakov, *Sbornik rasskazov* [Collected Stories], New York, Chekhov Publishing House, 1952.
4. "D'yavoliada," *Nedra*, No. 4, 1924, pp. 221-260; also in the volume *D'yavoliada*.
5. Bulgakov mentioned that the Berlin organization Nakanuniye had bought his "Zapiski na manzhetakh" but had not brought it out (see his autobiographical notes in Lidin, V., *Pisateli*, p. 56); and one of the former editors of Nakanuniye has stated that the book was printed but destroyed without publication and that only a few proof copies survived.
6. See Ivanov-Razumnik, *Pisatel'skiye sud'by* [The Fate of Writers], New York, Literaturnyi fond, 1951, p. 28.
7. Bulgakov, "Days of the Turbins," tr. by Eugene Lyons, in *Six Soviet Plays*, ed. by Lyons, Boston, Houghton Mifflin, 1934.
8. *Zoikina kvartira*, Moscow, MTI, 1927.
9. For further details on "Crimson Island" [*Bagrovyi ostrov*], see Novitski, Pavel, in *Repertuarnyi byulleten' Glaviskusstva R.S.F.S.R.* [Repertory Bulletin of R.S.F.S.R. Glaviskusstvo], Moscow, No. 12, 1928, pp. 9-10.
10. See Ivanov-Razumnik, p. 28.
11. The comedy *Mandat* is available in a mimeographed copy at the New York Public Library, No. 461,508A, n. p., n. d.
12. Meierhold, *Rekonstruktsiya teatra*, Moscow, GIKhL, 1931.
13. Erdman himself referred to the writing of this play in a talk to students of the State Theatrical Institute in 1930, and the title is mentioned in Gorski, Igor', *Luch sveta udaryayet v tyuremnoye okno* [A Ray of Light Strikes the Prison Window], Riga, Kul'tura, 1943, p. 14.
14. For a more detailed account of the film *Vesyolye rebyata* (shown abroad under the title *Jazz Comedy*) see Babitsky, Paul and John Rimberg, *The Soviet Film Industry*, New York, Praeger, 1955, pp. 163-164.
15. See "Sportivnaya chest'" [A Sportsman's Honor], *Iskusstvo kino* [Film Art], Moscow, No. 6, 1951, pp. 1-2.

16. See Vinogradov, V. V., "Yazyk Zoshchenko" [Zoshchenko's Language], *Mikhail Zoshchenko. Mastera sovremennoi literatury* [Mikhail Zoshchenko: Masters of Contemporary Literature], Leningrad, Academia, 1928.

17. Zoshchenko, "Vesyoloye priklyucheniye," *Sentimental'nye povesti* [Sentimental Tales], 3d ed., Moscow and Leningrad, Priboi, 1930, pp. 187-188 (Vol. IV of *Sobraniye sochinenii* [Collected Writings]). The first edition was published under the title *O chom pel solovei. Sentimental'nye povesti* [What the Nightingale Sang About: Sentimental Tales], Moscow and Leningrad, GIZ, 1927.

18. "Ot avtora" [From the Author], *Sentimental'nye povesti*, 3d ed., pp. 3-4.

19. "O chom pel solovei," *ibid.*, p. 158.

20. *Ibid.*, pp. 160-161.

21. *Ibid.*, p. 162.

22. "M. P. Sinyagin," *Novyi mir* [New World], Moscow, No. 12, 1930, pp. 112-140.

23. *Vozvrashchonnaya molodost'*, Moscow, GIKhL, 1933.

24. Gorelov, *Ispytaniye vremenem* [Trial by Time], Leningrad, GIKhL, 1935, p. 91.

25. *Ibid.*, p. 93.

26. Zoshchenko, *Golubaya kniga*, Moscow, Sovetskii pisatel', 1935; first serialized in *Krasnaya nov'* [Red Virgin Soil], Moscow, Nos. 3 and 10, 1934, and Nos. 6, 7 and 12, 1935.

27. "Ispytaniye geroyev," *Lichnaya zhizn'*, 2d ed., Leningrad, GIKhL, 1934, pp. 22-23.

28. *Ibid.*, p. 24.

29. *Ibid.*, pp. 24-25.

30. *Ibid.*, pp. 25-26.

31. *Ibid.*, p. 27.

32. *Ibid.*, 1st ed., Leningrad, Lenogiz, 1933, p. 26.

33. *Ibid.*, 2d ed., p. 28.

34. "Ochen' prosto," *ibid.*, p. 150.

35. "Stradaniya molodovo Vertera," *ibid.*, p. 11.

36. *Istoriya odnoi zhizni*, Leningrad, Izd. Pisatelei, 1934.

37. "Chornyi prints," *Literaturnyi sovremennik* [Literary Contemporary], Leningrad, No. 3, 1937.

38. "Vozmezdiye," *Novyi mir*, No. 10, 1937.

39. "Priklyucheniya obez'yany," *Zvezda* [Star], Leningrad, No. 5-6, 1946.

40. See *Neva*, Moscow and Leningrad, No. 6, 1956, pp. 83-91.

41. Il'f and Petrov, *Dvenadtsat' stul'yev*, Moscow, Zif, 1928; English translation under the title *Diamonds to Sit On*, tr. by Elizabeth Hill and Doris Mudie, London, Methuen, 1930.

42. *Zolotoi telyonok*, Moscow, Zif, 1931; published in English translation under the title *The Little Golden Calf*, tr. by Charles Malamuth, New York, Farrar and Rinehart, 1932.

43. Quoted in Ardov, V., "Il'f i Petrov" [Il'f and Petrov], *Znamya* [Banner], Moscow, No. 7, 1945, p. 121.

44. *Kak sozdavalsya Robinzon*, Moscow, Sovetskaya literatura, 1933.

45. *Bezmyatezhnaya tumba*, Moscow, Ogonyok, 1935.

46. *Odnoetazhnaya Amerika,* Moscow, GIKhL, 1936; published in English under the title *Little Golden America,* New York, Farrar and Rinehart, 1937.
47. "Bogataya nevesta," *Teatr i dramaturgiya* [Theater and Playwriting], Moscow, No. 1, 1936.
48. *Pod kupolom tsirka,* Moscow, Iskusstvo, 1935.
49. "Seryoznye oshibki izdatel'stva Sovetskii pisatel'" [Serious Mistakes of the Publishing House "The Soviet Writer"], *Literaturnaya gazeta,* Moscow, February 9, 1949.
50. Vetov, *Neobyknovennye pokhozhdeniya Bochonkina i Khvoshcha,* Moscow, Zif, 1928.
51. Pod"yachev, "Kritik," *Prozhektor* [Searchlight], Moscow, No. 40, 1928.
52. "Staryi parteinyi," *Lapot'* [Bast Shoe], Moscow, No. 18, 1927.
53. Volkov, *Raiskoye zhit'yo,* Moscow, Zif, 1926.
54. The first edition was published under the title *Baiki Antropa iz Lis'ikh Gor* [Tales of Antrop from Lis'i Gory], Leningrad, Priboi, 1926; 2d ed. under the title *Baiki Antropa,* Moscow, Moskovskoye tovarishchestvo pisatelei, 1927.
55. "O dugakh" [On the Subject of Shaftbows] in the volume of stories entitled *T. T.,* Moscow, Moskovskoye tovarishchestvo pisatelei, 1928, p. 201.
56. "Zhiltovarishchestvo No. 1331," *ibid.,* p. 96.

Index

Abramov, A. V.; *see* Shiryayevets, Aleksandr
Abyssinia, 44
Adamovich, Georgi, 61
Africa, 42, 43, 44
Agadzhanova, Natal'ya, 218, 233
Agapov, Boris, 263
Aimard, Gustave, 312
Akhmatova, Anna, 41, 46-50, 51, 348
Akul'shin, Rodion, 258
Aleksandrov, Grigori, 334
Aleksandrovski, Vasili, 157-161
Alekseyev-Askol'dov, S. A., 32-33
Amfiteatrov, Aleksandr, 195
Andersen, Hans Christian, 305
Andreyev, Leonid, 63, 292
Annenski, Innokenti, 23, 46
Anthès, d', 21, 87
Antonov, Gerasim, 128
Apollinaire, Guillaume, 75
Aristophanes, 82
Arosev, Aleksandr, 208-212
Artsybachev, Mikhail, 66, 67, 137, 138, 195, 222, 291, 292, 294, 322
Arvatov, Boris, 229
Aseyev, Nikolai, 88, 229-233
Asmolov, 138
Assanov, 149
Astrakhan, 28, 174
Averbakh, Leopold, 63, 216, 233, 247, 248
Avvakum, Archpriest, 26, 27, 96, 130

Babel, Isaak, 189-194, 348
Bagayev, Aleksandr, 172
Bakhmet'yev, Vladimir, 177
Baku, 174
Bakunin, Mikhail A., 76
Banks, Monty, 342
Batyushkov, 50
Beatrice, 300
Bednyi, Dem'yan, 138-140, 211
Belyayev, Father, 39
Belyayev, Sergei, 202
Belyi, Andrei, 30-38, 75, 144-145, 150, 166, 195, 291
Benar, Nataliya, 88
Berdyayev, N. A., 14, 18, 30, 31, 33, 85
Berezov, Pavel, 248
Berezovski, Feoktist, 177
Bergavinov, 265
Bergson, Henri, 240
Beriya, Lavrenti, 293
Berlin, 28, 30, 136, 332
Bessal'ko, Pavel, 172-173, 236
Bezymenski, Aleksandr, 233, 238-239
Bibik, Aleksei, 174
Bim and Bom, 82
Blok, A. L. (father), 18,19
Blok, Aleksandr, 1, 5-22, 28, 34, 37, 38, 46, 47, 56, 70, 72, 92, 93, 118, 120, 124, 150, 154, 158, 198, 205, 225, 239, 253, 282
Blok, Mme. Aleksandr, 14
Bobrov, Sergei, 89-90

Bogdanov, A., 141-145, 147-148, 150, 154, 157, 175, 235
Bogorodski, Fyodor, 88, 309
Bolotnikov, Ivan, 266
Bom; see Bim
Bonaparte; see Napoleon
Boratynski, 50
Bova, Prince, 101
Brik Boris, 233
Brik, Osip, 76, 230, 293
Britain, Great, 44
Bruno, Giordano, 149
Brusilov, 288
Bryansk, 173
Bryusov, Valeri, 37-38, 42, 144, 150
Budantsev, Sergei F., 206-208, 212, 348
Buddha, 74
Budyonnyi, Semyon, 189, 190, 192, 231
Bugayev, Boris Nikolayevich; see Belyi, Andrei
Bukharin, N. I., 3,, 127-128, 129, 204, 281, 347
Bulgakov, Mikhail A., 329-333
Bunin, Ivan, 9, 12, 63, 93, 195, 273, 282, 287, 312
Burlyuk, David, 68, 75
Buslayev, 119, 133

Capri 142
Catherine the Great, 47, 137
Caucasus, 138, 212
Chagall, Marc, 302
Chapayev, 2, 59, 202, 203, 204-206, 210
Chaplin, Charlie, 82, 299, 332, 341, 342
Chapygin, 245
Charnyi, M., 243
Chekhov, Anton P., 42, 273
Chekrygin, Vasili, 84, 85
Chicherin, A. N., 263
China, 200, 333
Chirikov, Yevgeni, 63
Chukovski, Kornei, 48, 75, 118, 158
Churlyanis, 30, 33, 34, 166
Chuzhak, N., 230
Coleridge, Samuel Taylor, 46
Cooper, James Fenimore, 312

Crimea, 286
Czechoslovakia, 214

Dante, 300
Deborin, 238
De Mille, Cecil B., 265
Dmitri the Pretender, 26
Dneprostroi, 293
Dorogoichenko, Aleksei, 172
Dorokhov, Pavel N., 174
Doroshevich, Vlas, 195
Dostoyevski, Fyodor, 1, 18, 25, 39, 68, 76, 137, 185, 199, 210, 240-241, 248, 253, 320, 321, 332, 338, 346
Doyle, Arthur Conan, 312
Dreiser, Theodore, 218, 222
Drozhzhin, Spiridon, 130
Druzhinin, Pavel, 132, 348
Dubovskoi, V., 149
Dubravna, 101
Dubrovskaya, 100
Duncan, Isadora, 127-128
Durov, Anatoli, 82
Durov, Vladimir, 82
Dzugashvili, Svetlana, 49

Ehrenburg, Il'ya, 307
Eisenstein, Sergei, 218, 232
Engels, Friedrich, 123, 346
Epstein N. S.; see Golodnyi, Mikhail
Erdman, Nikolai, 136, 333-335
Estonia, 88
Euripides, 23
Ewers, Hans, 199

Fadeyev, Aleksandr, 247
Fainzil'berg, I. A.; see Il'f, Il'ya
Farid, L., 202
Fedin, Konstantin, 224, 270
Filipchenko, Ivan, 171-172
Filonov, 195, 302
Finland, 63
Firin, 63
Flaubert, Gustave, 191
Fofanov, Konstantin, 89, 308

Index

Fonvizin, 82
Freud, Sigmund, 240, 272, 290, 298
Frunze, 200, 203
Furmanov, Dmitri, 2, 202-206, 212, 213
Fyodorov, Fyodor, 132
Fyodorov, Nikolai, 25, 83, 85, 86

Gabrilovich, Yevgeni, 263
Galileo, 149, 158
Garshin, 177
Gastev, Aleksei, 146-147
Gautier, Théophile, 42
Gerasimov, Mikhail, 147, 153-158, 160, 161, 176, 296
Germany, 197
Gershenzon, 34, 38
Giovagnoli, Raffaello, 176
Gippius, Zinaida, 38
Gladkov, Fyodor, 3, 178, 288-298
Glinka, Gleb, 254
Godunov, Boris, 26
Gogol, Nikolai, 10, 31, 37, 65, 103-104, 245, 259, 282, 284, 287, 332, 333, 338, 342, 343
Golodnyi, Mikhail, 239, 240
Goncharov, 273
Gorbachov, Georgi, 117, 191
Gorbov, Dmitri, 242, 254
Gorbunov, K., 63
Gorelik, Z. A., 242
Gorelov, Anatoli, 270, 271, 338
Gorenko, Anna Andreyevna; see Akhmatova, Anna
Gorki, Maxim, 4, 20, 46, 61, 62, 63, 75, 104, 142, 174, 194, 212, 224-225, 255, 281, 305, 313, 343
Gorodetski, Sergei Mitrofanovich, 41, 56
Grabar', Leonid, 321-324
Grigor'yev, Apollon, 31, 119, 131, 142, 241
Grin, Aleksandr, 1, 46, 60, 100, 104, 298, 311-317
Grinevski, A. S.; see Grin, Aleksandr
Gruzdev, Il'ya, 224
Guber, Boris, 252, 254
Gumilevski, Lev, 318-319

Gumilyov, Nikolai, 41-46, 51, 56, 57, 70, 179, 240, 308
Gurvich, A. M., 195, 206, 250, 251, 300, 301, 303
Gushchinski Vasili, 341
Gusev-Orenburgski, Sergei, 63

Haggard, Rider, 42, 312
Hamsun, Knut, 312
Heine, Heinrich, 20
Henry, O., 342
Heraclitus, 149, 195
Hesiod, 65
Hoffmann, E. T. A., 224, 305
Homer, 65
Hugo, Victor, 176, 199, 290
Huxley, Aldous, 185

Il'f, Il'ya, 288, 342-344
Il'inski, Igor', 82, 299
Inber, Vera, 263, 266-268
Ionov, Il'ya, 145
Isakowski, 117
Ivan, Tsar, 99
Ivanov, Georgi, 42, 52, 61, 121, 130, 140
Ivanov, Vsevolod, 224-225, 227-229
Ivanov, Vyacheslav, 34, 38, 47, 139
Ivanov-Razumnik, 18, 117, 332
Ivanovo-Voznesensk, 203
Ivnev, Ryurik, 121, 137-138

Jakobson, Roman, 69, 70, 85
Japan, 201, 227
Jesus Christ, 8, 14, 15, 17, 21, 25, 26, 28, 29, 74, 77, 96, 104, 112, 124, 140, 153, 154, 205
Joyce, James, 33

Kalinin, F., 144
Kaluga, 148, 149
Kamenev, L. B., 12
Kameneva, O.., 12
Kamenski, Vasili, 68, 86-88
Karaganda, 344

Karavayeva, Anna, 240
Karpov, Pimen, 130, 132
Katayev, Ivan, 240, 252-254, 348
Katayev, Valentin, 342, 343-344
Katayev, Yevgeni; *see* Petrov, Yevgeni
Kaverin, Veniamin, 224, 307
Kazin, Vasili, 157, 161-171, 348
Kellerman, Bernard, 176
Kerensky, Aleksandr, 225, 260
Kerzhentsev, P., 144
Khabias, N., 88
Khlebnikov, Viktor, 68-74, 86, 87, 88, 230
Khodasevich, Vladislav, 122-123, 144
Kiev, 25, 91, 93, 329, 330
Kipling, Rudyard, 43
Kirillov, Vladimir, 147, 149-153, 155, 158, 160, 161, 176, 296
Kiriyenko-Voloshin; *see* Voloshin, Maksimilian
Kirsanov, Semyon, 88, 230, 233
Klychkov, Sergei, 100-109, 112, 117, 120, 130, 305
Klyuyev, Nikolai, 91-100, 102, 103, 109, 110, 112, 117, 120, 121, 130
Kochkuro, Nikolai; *see* Vesyolyi, Artyom
Koestler, Arthur, 215, 241
Kogan, P. S., 76, 128, 289
Koktebel, 22
Kolchak, 174
Koleno, 111
Kol'tsov, 101
Konstantinovo, 120
Koonen, Alisa, 49
Korenev, Gennadi, 132
Kornilov, Boris, 169
Korolenko, 177, 282
Kostroma, 203
Kovalevski, Vyacheslav, 137
Kovalyov, Mikhail Aleksandrovich; *see* Ivnev, Ryurik
Kovtyukh, Yepifan, 212-213
Kozakov, Milhail, 321
Kozhukh, 212
Krasnov, General, 215
Krestovski, Vsevolod, 14
Kruchonykh, Aleksei, 68, 87, 88

Kryuchkov, 138
Kuban', 203, 292
Kulikovo, 16
Kuprin, Aleksandr, 63, 312
Kushner, Boris, 230
Kusikov, Aleksandr, 138
Kustodiyev, B. M., 161
Kuzmin, Mikhail, 46, 57
Kuznetsov, Nikolai, 240

Lassalle, Ferdinand, 149
Lavrenyov, Boris, 308-311
Lavrov, P. L., 272
Lazarenko, Vitali, 82
Lebedev, P. I., 144
Lebedev-Polyanski, 281, 289
Lel', 101, 108
Lelevich, G., 123, 152, 233
Lenin, Nikolai, 12, 13, 61, 78, 92, 95, 96, 97, 114, 123, 142, 150, 175, 212, 217, 220, 235, 237, 256, 260, 267, 282, 308
Leningrad, 92, 130, 136, 170, 187, 267, 284
Leonardo, 154
Leonov, Leonid, 305-307
Lermontov, 44, 110, 113, 312
Leshonkov, Sergei Antonovich; *see* Klychkov, Sergei
Leskov, 104, 185, 187, 245, 287, 335
Levidov, Mikhail, 230
Levitan, Isaak, 257
Lezhnyov, Abram, 191, 242, 254
Libedinski, Yuri, 211, 215, 233, 236-238, 289
Liège, 208
Likharov, Boris, 240
Lloyd, Harold, 342
Lo Gatto, Professor Ettore, 92
London, Jack, 83, 174, 184, 312
Lotaryov, I. V.; *see* Severyanin, Igor'
Lunacharski, Anatoli Vasil'yevich, 37, 76, 79, 141, 142, 144, 153, 154, 273
Lundberg, 18
Lunts Lev, 224-227
Luzgin, S., 63
L'vov-Rogachevski, 133, 135, 274

Index

Lyashchenko, Nikolai; *see* Lyashko, Nikolai
Lyashko, Nikolai, 175-177, 289

Makarov, Aleksandr, 172
Makhno, 193, 260
Malakhovski, 341
Malashkin, Sergei, 319-321
Malenkov, Georgi, 333
Malevich, K. S., 31, 32, 75, 166
Malinovski, Aleksandr Aleksandrovich; *see* Bogdanov, A.
Malyshkin, Aleksandr, 211, 215, 259-260
Malyutin, 341
Mamontov, 205
Manasses, Constantine, 23
Mandel'shtam, Osip, 41, 50, 51, 52, 53, 54, 55, 56, 69
Marienhof, Anatoli, 135-137, 227
Marinetti, 68, 146
Mariyenof; *see* Marienhof, Anatoli
Marx, Karl, 14, 36, 40, 76, 77, 78, 96, 98, 122, 123, 127, 129, 142, 184, 192, 197, 209, 212, 236, 238, 240, 241, 256, 263, 285, 290, 298, 316, 328, 345
Mashirov A. I.; *see* Samobytnik, A. I.
Maupassant, Guy de, 191
Mayakovski, Vladimir, 1, 20, 48, 49, 68, 70, 75-86, 88, 118, 131, 132, 172, 229, 230, 231, 233, 238-239, 334, 341
Medvedev, P. N., 92
Meierhold, 82, 232, 239, 334
Mendeleyev, 98
Merezhkovski, Dmitri, 38
Minsk, 189
Mitin, 238
Mochul'ski, K. S., 21
Mohammed, 74
Moscow, 16, 28, 30, 34, 36, 37, 39, 54, 58, 74, 93, 100, 120, 127, 132, 140, 157, 163, 170, 178, 184, 203, 208, 221, 227, 242, 248, 253, 254, 257, 262, 273, 284, 285, 286, 321, 333, 346
Musatov, Boris, 257

Nachayev, Yegor, (Georgii), 145
Napoleon, 200, 202, 207
Narbut, Vladimir, 58
Nasedkin, Vasili, 132
Naumov, 131
Nekrasov, 93, 101, 110, 295
Nesterov, 25
Neverov, Aleksandr, 223
New York, 182
Nicholas I, 22
Nikiforov, Georgi, 3, 178, 324-329
Nikitin, Ivan, 110
Nikitin, Nikolai, 224, 225, 307
Nikitina, Ye. F., 127
Nikon, Patriarch, 26, 27, 97
Nizovoi, Pavel, 177-178
Notre Dame, 52
Novikov, Andrei, 240

Obradovich, Sergei, 157, 172
Odessa, 193, 312
Odoyevski, V. F., 183
Oksyonov, Innokenti, 263
Olesha, Yuri, 298-304, 348
Olimpov, 89
Ol'minski, 216
Olonets, Lake, 91, 94
Oreshin, Pyotr, 102, 109-117, 120, 132
Orwell, George, 185
Otsup, Nikolai, 61

Palekh, 201, 254, 255, 256, 257
Panfyorov, Fyodor, 4
Papanin, 265
Paris, 14, 22, 130
Pasternak, Boris, 1, 56, 89, 214, 299
Paul I, 229
Paustovski, Konstantin, 313, 317
Pavlenko, Pyotr, 240
Payan, 181
Pertsov, V., 230
Peshkov, Aleksei M.; *see* **Gorki, Maxim**
Peter the Great, 27, 91, 173, 248, 249
Petlyura, Simon, 329, 330
Petnikov Grigory, 87, 88

Petrograd, 8, 9, 12, 15, 30, 34, 38, 39, 42, 45, 52, 74, 118, 120, 145, 153, 158, 172, 179, 180, 185, 188, 208, 313, 314
Petrov Yevgeni, 288, 342-344
Petrovski, Dmitri, 230
Picasso, Pablo, 31, 33
Pil'nyak, Boris, 195-202, 236, 246, 348
Platonov, Andrei, 1, 140, 202, 242, 245-251
Plekhanov, Georgi, 241
Pod"yachev, Semyon, 344-345
Poe, Edgar Allan, 42, 312
Poland, 189, 191
Poletayev, Nikolai, 171, 172
Polivanov, S., 206
Polonskaya, Yelizaveta, 224
Polonski, Yyacheslav, 90-91, 118, 152, 192, 203, 227, 229, 276
Polyanski, V.; see Lebedev, P. I.
Popov, A. S.; see Serafimovich, Aleksandr
Potebnya, 119, 133
Pozner, Vladimir, 224
Prague, 187
Pribludnyi, Ivan, 132-133
Pridvorov, Yefim A.; see Bednyi, Dem'yan
Pugachov, Yemel'yan, 13, 27, 74, 87, 128, 131, 193, 198, 202, 204, 205, 206, 211, 220, 242, 261
Pushkin, Aleksandr, 17, 18, 21, 22, 41, 47, 49, 65, 68, 76, 87, 110, 113, 126, 130, 139, 166, 248, 273, 329, 333, 338

Radimov, Pavel, 130, 131, 348
Radlov, 341
Raskolnikov, 25
Rasputin, Grigori, 113
Razin, Sten'ka, 13, 27, 78, 86, 87, 131, 161, 193, 198, 202, 204, 206, 220, 242, 261, 293
Reclus, Elisée, 241
Reid, Mayne, 312
Reisner, Larisa,, 211, 214, 216
Remizov, Aleksei, 34, 39, 104, 185, 195, 222, 245, 281, 282, 324, 329
Riga, 146
Rodov, Semyon, 123, 158, 172, 233
Roerich, Nikolai, 24
Romanov, Panteleimon, 272-281, 288
Romanovs, the, 10
Rovinski, 119
Rozanov, Vasili, 39, 40-41
Rozhdestvenski, Vsevolod, 60, 214
Rubens, Peter Paul, 49
Runyon, Damon, 336
Ryazan', 120
Rybinsk, 194
Rzheshevski, Aleksandr, 233

Sadof'yev, Il'yev, 145
Saint Nicholas, 24, 121, 131
Saint Petersburg; see Petrograd
Saint Sophia, 52
Saksonskaya, N., 88
Sakulin, P. N., 183
Saltykov-Shchedrin, 297, 320, 332, 333
Samobytnik, A. I., 144-145
Sannikov, Grigori, 157, 172
Seifulina, Lidiya, 281-282
Sel'vinski, Il'ya, 260-265, 267
Selyaninovich, Mikula, 107
Semirech'ye, 203
Serafimovich, Aleksandr, 63, 203, 211-214, 218, 289
Serapion brothers, 179, 188, 224-225, 227, 229, 234, 270, 272, 307, 335
Sereda, 203
Serge, Victor, 215
Sergiyev-Posad, 39
Severyanin, Igor', 86, 88, 230, 308
Shchedrin; see Saltykov-Shchedrin
Shershenevich, Vadim, 133-136, 227
Shiryayevets, Aleksandr, 130-131
Shiryayevo, 130
Shishkov, Vyacheslav, 132
Shklovski, Viktor, 187-189, 230
Shkulyov, Filipp, 130
Shmelyov, Ivan, 63
Shmidt, Otto, 265
Sholokhov, Mikhail, 1, 66, 189, 245, 270, 329

Index

Shteinman, 309
Siberia, 100, 172, 217, 281, 282, 291, 312
Sivachov, Mikhail, 3, 173-174
Skachko, A. L., 174-175
Skobelev, A. S.; *see* Neverov, Aleksandr
Skoropadski, Hetman, 329-330
Skryabin, Aleksandr, 30, 33
Slonimski, Mikhail, 224, 270-272
Slyotov, Pyotr, 254
Slyozkin, Yuri, 286-290
Smidovich, Vikenti V.; *see* Veresayev, V. V.
Smirenski, 89
Sobol', Andrei, 282-286
Sofia, 200
Sologub, Fyodor, 38
Solov'yov, Vladimir, 18
Spain, 187
Spasski, Sergei, 89
Stalin, Joseph V., 49, 81, 82, 86, 114, 140, 187, 210, 238, 248, 267, 298, 328, 333
Stanislavski, 16
Stenich, V., 33
Svetlov, Mikhail, 239-240

Taman', 212
Tambov, 128
Tarasenkov, 318
Tarasov-Rodionov, Aleksandr, 215-217, 241, 282
Tashkent, 223, 250
Tchaikovsky, Modest Il'ich, 100-101
Theodosia, 313
Tikhonov, Nikolai, 46, 224
Titian, 154
Tolstoi, Aleksei, 270, 307
Tolstoi, Lev, 1, 62, 68, 76, 170, 240, 241, 243, 329
Tret'yakov, Sergei, 88, 230, 232, 239
Trotsky, 61, 127, 129, 140, 150, 183, 232, 234, 237, 240, 242
Trubetskoi, Prince Vladimir; *see* Vetov, Vladimir
Tsiolkovski, Konstantin, 148-150
Tufanov, 89

Tukhachevski, 213
Tumannyi, Dir, 263
Tupikov, P. G.; *see* Nizovoi, **Pavel**
Turgenev, Ivan, 95, 113, 201
Turkestan, 203, 207, 286
Tvardovski, 117
Tver', 100-101, 104
Twain, Mark, 342
Tychina, Pavlo, 230
Tynyanov, Yuri, 49, 69, 126
Tyulyapin, Konstantin, 133
Tyutchev, 162, 163

Ukraine, the, 58, 213, 288, 330
United States, 128, 201, 258, **343, 344**
Urals, the, 204, 260
Uralsk, 204
Ushakov, Nikolai, 240
Ust'-Medveditskaya, 212
Utkin, Iosif, 239

Vaginov, Konstantin, 89
Vasil'yev, Pavel, 120, 169
Vasilisa the Beautiful, 101
Veresayev, V. V., 63-65, 156, 222, **228**, 277
Verhaeren, Emile, 23, 24, 75, **146**
Veselovski, Aleksandr, 149
Vesyolyi, Artyom, 1, 240, 242-245, 252, 281, 330, 348
Vetov, Vladimir, 187, 344
Vetrov, Vladimir, 252
Vikhryov, Yefim, 201, 254-257
Vinogradov, Professor, 335
Vishnevski, Vsevolod, 49
Vogau, B. A.; *see* Pil'nyak, Boris
Volga, 109, 113, 116, 131, 200, 203
Volkov, A., 43
Volkov, Mikhail, 178, 345-347
Voloshin, Maksimilian, 22-29, 53-54
Vol'pin, M., 334
Voronski, Aleksandr K., 35, 63, 117, 130, 183, 196, 200, 211, 234-235, 240-242, 254
Voroshilov, Klimenti, 190

Voynich, Ethel, 176
Vyatka, 312

Wagner, Richard, 154
Wells, H. G., 183, 184, 298, 331
White Sea, the, 91, 94
Whitman, Walt, 146
Wilde, Oscar, 136
Wrangel, General, 79-80, 82

Yakolev, Aleksandr, 3, 212, 217-223, 260, 281
Yakubovski, Georgi, 157
Yarov, N., 211
Yasni, Aleksandr, 240
Yermak, 245
Yesenin, Sergei, 70, 80, 85-86, 92, 99, 102, 117-130, 132, 134, 136, 140, 158, 239, 253
Yevdokimov, Ivan, 257-258

Yezhov, 245, 293
Yudenich, 188
Yudin, 238

Zabolotski, Nikolai, 169
Zaitsev, Boris, 253, 273
Zamyatin, Yevgeni, 34, 89, 179-187, 224, 226, 228, 282, 287, 335
Zarudin, Nikolai, 253-254
Zavadovski, Leonid, 258-259
Zelinski, Korneli, 147, 263, 264
Zenkevich, Mikhail, 58-60
Zharov, Aleksandr, 239
Zhdanov, 342
Zhukovski, N. Ye., 50, 319
"Zhutkins," the, 239
Zinoviev, 324
Zola, Emile, 218, 222, 329
Zorgenfrei, V. A., 38, 39
Zoshchenko, Mikhail, 39, 187, 224-225, 335-339, 341-342, 348

ST. MARY'S COLLEGE OF MARYLAND LIBRARY
ST. MARY'S CITY, MARYLAND
37206